D1468646

THE UNITED STATES AND LATIN AMERICA: THE NEW AGENDA

The United States and Latin America: The New Agenda

Edited by
Victor Bulmer-Thomas and James Dunkerley

Published by
Institute of Latin American Studies, University of London
and
David Rockefeller Center for Latin American Studies,
Harvard University

Distributed by
Harvard University Press
Cambridge, Massachusetts
London, England

First published in Great Britain by the Institute of Latin American Studies, University of London, with the David Rockefeller Center for Latin American Studies, Harvard University.

Institute of Latin American Studies
31 Tavistock Square, London WC1H 9HA, UK

David Rockefeller Center for Latin Americas Studies
Harvard University, 61 Kirkland St., Cambridge, Mass., USA

A catalogue record for this book is available from the Library of Congress in Washington D.C.: Catalog Card No. 99-72075

ISBN 0 674 92595 5 (hardcover)
ISBN 0 674 92596 3 (paperback)

Printed and bound in Great Britain by
Short Run Press Ltd, Exeter, EX2 7LW, UK

CONTENTS

PART III: DRUGS AND MIGRATION

PART IV: CUBA

****

ACKNOWLEDGEMENTS

This book arose out of a Study Group convened by Victor Bulmer-Thomas and James Dunkerley at the Institute of Latin American Studies, University of London, over the Spring of 1998. The original stimulus to review US relations with Latin America came from the passage of the Helms-Burton Act, which seemed to be a Cold War initiative out of both place and time. Equally, the attention paid to European initiatives in the hemisphere, renewed moves towards regional integration, the mercurial state of international relations in a 'post-Communist era', and the accentuation of such issues as migration, drugs and conditionality in aid all suggested the agenda deserved scrutiny to assess how much it had, in reality, altered.

Revised drafts of the papers commissioned from US, Latin American and European scholars and discussed in the Study Group were presented at a conference organised by John Coatsworth at the David Rockefeller Center for Latin American Studies, Harvard University, in October 1998. The Study Group was made possible by financial support from the European Commission; the conference was sponsored by the William and Flora Hewlett Foundation. The editors wish to thank both bodies for their generosity and flexibility. They are also grateful to all the participants of the Study Group for their comments and suggestions throughout a particularly prolonged process.

LIST OF CONTRIBUTORS

Victor Bulmer-Thomas is Professor Emeritus of Economics at the University of London and Senior Research Fellow at its Institute of Latin American Studies, where he was Director from 1992 to 1998. From 1986 to 1997 he was joint-editor of the *Journal of Latin American Studies*. His more recent publications include *The Economic History of Latin America since Independence* (1994), (as editor) *The New Economic Model in Latin America and its Impact on Income Distribution and Poverty* (1996) and *Reflexiones sobre la integración centroamericana* (1997).

Rodolfo Cerdas Cruz is the founder of CIAPA, a social science research centre in Costa Rica. Fomerly Director of the School of Political Sciences at the University of Costa Rica, he is the author of the chapter on modern Costa Rica in the *Cambridge History of Latin America* and many articles and books, including *The Communist International in Central America, 1920–1936* (1993).

John H. Coatsworth is Monroe Gutman Professor of Latin American Affairs at Harvard University, where he also serves as Director of the David Rockefeller Center for Latin American Studies. He was elected President of the American Historical Association in 1995. His recent books include *The United States and Central America: The Clients and the Colossus* (1994), and *Latin America and the World Economy since 1800* (edited with Alan M. Taylor, 1998).

Jorge I. Domínguez is Clarence Dillon Professor of International Affairs and Director of the Weatherfield Center at Harvard University. Among his recent books are *Democratic Politics in Latin America and the Caribbean* (1998); as editor, *International Security and Democracy: Latin America and the Caribbean in the Post-Cold War Era* (1998); and, with James McCann, *Democratizing Mexico: Public Opinion and Electoral Choices* (1996).

James Dunkerley is Director of the Institute of Latin American Studies, University of London, where he also holds a chair in politics at Queen Mary and Westfield College. He has been joint-editor of the *Journal of Latin American Studies* since 1998. His books include *Power in the Isthmus. A Political History of Modern Central America* (1988), and *Political Suicide in Latin America* (1992).

E.V.K. FitzGerald is Director of the Centre for International Finance at Queen Elizabeth House, Oxford, and a Fellow of St Antony's College, Oxford. The author of books on the economy of Peru, he has written articles on NAFTA, international capital markets and income distribution. Most recently he has published (with R. Cubero and A. Lemann) *The Development Implications of the Multilateral Agreement on Investment* (1998).

Eduardo Gamarra, an associate professor of political science, is currently Director of the Latin American and Caribbean Center at Florida International University. He is the author, co-author and editor of several books, including *Revolution and Reaction: Bolivia, 1964–85* (1988); *Democracy, Markets and Structural Reform in Latin America* (1995); and *Entre la Droga y la Democracia* (1994).

Elizabeth Joyce is Senior Research Associate at the Institute for European-Latin American Relations (IRELA) in Madrid. In 1997 she served as a Fulbright Senior Research Fellow at the Government Department, Georgetown University, where she conducted research on US foreign drug policy. Apart from several articles, she is the editor, with Carlos Malamud, of *Latin America and the Multinational Drug Trade* (1997).

Maxine Molyneux is Senior Lecturer in Sociology at the Institute of Latin American Studies, University of London. In addition to books on Africa and the Middle East, she has published on Cuba, Nicaragua and Argentina. Her specialist expertise is in gender. An edited volume (with Elizabeth Dore), *The Hidden Histories of Gender and the State in Latin America*, will appear in 1999 and a collection of essays in 2000.

Sheila Page is Senior Research Fellow in Economics at the Overseas Development Institute, London. She is the editor of *Development Policy Review* and the author of work on global trade governance and on the structure and impact of tourism industries in developing countries. Her recent publications include *World Trade Reform: Do Developing Countries Gain or Lose* (1994) and *The Gatt Uruguay Round: Effects on Developing Countries* (1991).

Jorge F. Pérez-López is an international economist who was born in Santa Clara, Cuba, and came to the United States in 1962. Formerly an editor of *Cuban Studies*, he has published *The Cuban Second Economy: From Behind the Scene to Center Stage* (1995) and *The Economics of Cuban Sugar* (1991) in addition to several edited works.

Marcelo M. Suárez-Orozco is a professor in the areas of human development and psychology and learning and teaching at Harvard University Graduate School of Education. He is co-director of the Harvard Immigration Project. Amongst several edited works the most recent is *Crossings: Mexican Immigration in Interdisciplinary Perspectives*, the inaugural volume in the series published by the David Rockefeller Center and distributed by Harvard University Press.

Roberto Steiner is Research Associate at Fedesarrollo in Colombia. He was previously Senior Economist and Director of the Research Department of the Central Bank of Colombia as well as acting as consultant in the Office of the Chief

Economist for Latin America at the World Bank. The author of *Los Dólares del Narcotráfico*, he is the editor of six books, including (with J.A. Ocampo) *Foreign Capital in Latin America* (1995).

Juan Triana Cordovi is a Director of the Centro de Estudios de la Economía Cubana, with publications including *La economía cubana en 1996: Resultados, problemas y perspectivas* and *Cuba: Consolidación de la reanimación económica*. He was a Visiting Research Fellow at the Institute of Latin American Studies, London, in 1998.

Laurence Whitehead is Official Fellow in Politics at Nuffield College, Oxford. His research focuses on democratisation, economic policy-making and social revolutions throughout Latin America and the Caribbean as well as the European Union. The author of many articles and edited books, he has been joint-editor of the *Journal of Latin American Studies* for over a decade.

LIST OF TABLES

LIST OF FIGURES

PART I

OVERVIEW

CHAPTER 1

THE UNITED STATES AND LATIN AMERICA
IN THE LONG RUN (1800-1945)

James Dunkerley

'The principal object of your mission is to cultivate the most friendly relations with Bolivia. The enemies of free Government throughout the world point with satisfaction to the perpetual revolutions in the South American Republics. They hence argue that man is not fit for Self Government; and it is greatly to be deplored that the instability of those Republics and in many instances their disregard for private rights have afforded a pretext for such an unfortunate assumption. Liberty cannot be preserved without order; and this can only spring from a sacred observance of the law. So long as it shall be in the power of successive military chieftains to subvert the Governments of the Republics by the sword, their people cannot expect to enjoy the blessings of liberty. Anarchy, confusion, and civil war must be the result. In your intercourse with the Bolivian authorities you will omit no opportunity of pressing these truths upon them, and of presenting to them the example of our own country, where all controversies are decided at the ballot box... Instead of weakening themselves by domestic dissensions, the Spanish race in these Republics have every motive for union and harmony. They nearly all have an enemy within their own bosoms burning for vengeance on account of the supposed wrongs of centuries, and ever ready, when a favourable opportunity may offer, to expel or exterminate the descendants of their conquerors.'

James Buchanan, Secretary of State, 1848[1]

'We must have Cuba. We can't do without Cuba, and above all we must not suffer its transfer to Great Britain. We shall acquire it by a *coup d'état* at some propitious moment, which from the present state of Europe may not be far distant. How delighted, then, am I to feel that you have selected a diplomatist and fit for the work – one who, possessing no vanity himself and knowing when to speak and when to be silent, is so well calculated to flatter the pride of the Dons – who by the gentle arts of insinuation and persuasion can gradually prepare the queen mother, the ministers and courtiers for the great surrender – and who above all is a perfect master both of the language of Louis le Grand and of the knight of rueful countenance. Cuba is already ours. I can feel it in my finger ends.'

James Buchanan, 1849[2]

Consideration of relations between the USA and Latin America over the long range must necessarily be a broad and speculative undertaking, but it does offer a number of interpretative opportunities. Perhaps the most important of these is simply to review the current, brief post-Cold War scenario in an extended pre-Cold War context, which might modulate some of the claims of conclusive 'newness' that have understandably proliferated within a generation of academics and policy-makers mostly born and entirely educated after 1945. Equally, there is merit in taking stock not only of developments within the USA over the long-run, but also in relations between the hemisphere and Europe – if only to test the standard view of a constantly burgeoning and unchallenged inequality within the Americas.

In a recent, polemical textbook Peter Smith (1996) has emphatically restated what might be characterised as the 'imperialist thesis', at the end of which he presents a very suggestive table of 'strategic options' (see Table 1.1).

Smith's depiction here registers the different levels of interaction, policy and response as well as respecting the external dimensions of a relationship that is frequently assumed to be hermetically hemispheric and univocal. Although it is evident more in the table than in the main body of the book, this variegated picture suggests that Latin America has not always followed in craven fashion the kind of advice offered to Sheridan senior by Swift in 1725 about the importance of openly supplicant form:

Take the Oaths heartily to the powers that be, and remember that Party was not made for depending Puppies... take care of going regularly through all the forms of Oaths and Inductions, for the least wrong step will put you to the trouble of repassing your patent, or voiding your Living.

That is what Ronald Reagan called 'saying uncle', and it is what, from an opposite point of view, Rodolfo Cerdas Cruz exhorted the Sandinistas to do in order to avoid a rhetorically-accelerated conflict in the 1980s (Cerdas Cruz, 1986). Yet even in 1945 communications were far less developed than today, a more general and distended pattern of decision-making, formulation and implementation of policy giving the vocal aspect of inter-American relations less immediately acute consequences – if not always a less urgent *timbre* – than has been the case in recent, televisual decades. Whereas it is possible to measure – albeit imperfectly – industrial production, trade flows and the concentration of weaponry, this more cultural aspect of foreign relations is quite elusive and vulnerable to anachronistic interpretation. In fact, it is probably the feature most misunderstood if viewed exclusively with the sensibilities of the 'historical present' of the late 20th century.

Table 1.1:
Peter Smith's 'Strategic Options' for Latin America

Strategy	Imperial Era 1790-1930s	Cold War 1940s-80s	1990s-
Collective unity (political integration)	attempted (economic integration)	attempted	unlikely
Extra-hemispheric protection	attempted (Europe)	attempted (USSR)	—
Subregional hegemony	attempted (Brazil / Argentina)	—	possible (Brazil)
International law/organisation	success	attempted	—
Non-socialist revolution	Mexico	Bolivia	—
Socialist revolution	—	Cuba/Nicaragua	—
Third world solidarity	—	attempted (NAM/G77)[3]	—
Alignment with USA	attempted (Brazil / Client States)	success (authoritarians)	attempted (Mexico + ?)

Source: Smith (1996), p. 331.

The eras or epochs identified in Table 1.1 are not, of course, determined by the bilateral relations of the USA with the rest of the American colonies/republics. In those terms, and from the perspective of the USA, one could propose a sub-periodisation of the 'Imperial Era':

1780-1820 Acquisition and consolidation of continental US territory from Europe (Louisiana purchase; war of 1812; Florida purchase)

1823-1860 Doctrinal rejection of Europe from political intervention; consolidation of continental US territory from Mexico; operational parity with Britain achieved in Caribbean (Monroe Doctrine; war of 1846-8; Clayton-Bulwer treaty)

1860-1880 Vacuum of power; temporary loss of ideological confidence; momentary European resurgence (Civil War; French occupation of Mexico)

1880-1898 Hemispheric ambitions openly expressed (Pan Americanism)

1898-1930 Hemispheric ambitions aggressively pursued (Roosevelt Corollary; dollar diplomacy)

1933-1940 Diplomatic relations modulated; economic reconsolidation (Good Neighbor Policy)

1941-1945 Wartime acceleration of continental integration and political fault-lines; full emergence of Pacific theatre; full ideologisation of external powers and rearticulation of international politics.

A chronology seen from the Latin American perspective would not be radically different although there are, of course, quite distinct crises and ruptures for each country (Paraguay, for instance, was at war in the 1860s and 1930s, when US influence in the region was at a relatively low level). The key challenge, though, is to discern a balance between the long-run processes and the discrete events/ruptures which lie behind any set of dates like these. Of course, some, such as Richard Morse or Claudio Véliz, would reject this chronology as being a distraction from the deeper, historiocultural differentiation between the Anglo and Iberian societies transplanted across the Atlantic.[4] Others, such as Samuel Flagg Bemis, find a more compelling matrix of distinction in physical conditions, particularly the climate, which opens and dominates Bemis's 1943 study of US Latin American policy:

> It is a scientific fact of political, economic and social geography, that the areas of best and of second best climatic energy coincide geographically with the more impressive evidence of human civilization, such as maximum wheat production, maximum of professional occupations, maximum of industrial production, greatest numbers of schools, of colleges, of automobiles... favourable climate is a necessary basis of modern civilization.[5]

When measured against such maxims – written in the midst of a world war fought between states with eminently 'temperate' climates – the observations made in 1787 by Thomas Jefferson strike one as almost post-modern in their fluid, pluralist approach to the latitudes:

> The glimmerings which reach us from South America enable us only to see that its inhabitants are held under the accumulated pressure of slavery, superstition and ignorance. Whereas they shall be able to rise under this weight, and to shew themselves to the rest of the world, they will probably shew they are like the rest of the world...(those) going from a country in the old world remarkably dry in its soil and climate fancied there [to be] more lakes and fogs in South America than in Europe. An inhabitant of Ireland, Sweden, or Finland, would have formed the contrary opinion.[6]

Jefferson's (controversial and risky if not, at \$15 million, inordinately expensive) decision to press ahead with the Louisiana purchase in 1803 both gained control of the Mississippi and effectively committed the states – I use the term deliberately in the plural – to a westward, continental and federal expansion. Even at the start this had sharp implications for Mexico (which some, such as Vice-President Aaron Burr, wanted to annex from Spain into a separate slave-holding confederacy) and Cuba (where the whites of Saint-Domingue abandoned by Bonaparte fled in greater numbers than to New Orleans). In the short-term the purchase enabled the USA to exploit Spain's weakness by raiding and then annexing-through-purchase Florida in 1819, at the height of the independence wars in the south. In the medium-term it led – through the creation of the republic of Texas – to the Mexican war of 1846-8, the treaty of Guadalupe Hidalgo and the payment of another $15 million for all the remaining territory up to the Pacific between present-day Canada and Baja California (the Oregon limits had previously been settled with Britain). The traditional longer-term projection is of a vocational expansionism supported throughout by the ideology of 'manifest destiny' (a term first used in 1845) and revived by the needs of corporate capitalism from the reconstruction era into the 20th century. This lineage stretches, then, directly from Jefferson's pragmatism in exploiting European conflicts through Monroe's opposition to new European intervention in the hemisphere in defence of its new republics, and through Polk's clumsy appropriation of that doctrine to justify the violent acquisition of American lands, to Roosevelt's corollary, fashioned for the correction of domestic affairs of other continental states regardless of the European factor. It is, however, a problematic and challenged inheritance which can too readily be rendered 'natural' and uncontradictory. I shall here give some emphasis to these problems and moments of indeterminacy because the literature on the left from Thoreau to Chomsky has glossed over them whereas that on the right merely dismisses them as operational infelicities or products of a naïve idealism.

Cuba

The exception to my qualification-through-complication approach is Cuba. The island has evidently been problematic to the USA from the first years of the republic in a relationship that is only partially comprehensible through the lens of international political economy. Buchanan's opening declaration is illustrative of a sentiment towards Cuba within the US political class that alternates between attraction and frustration, for which any adequate explanation must rely in part on psychology. Jefferson was privileged in that during his presidency the issue was so little developed. Yet even he declared that he would place at the southern tip of the island a notice – *nec plus ultra* (nothing beyond here) – exhibiting a confidence expressed rather more explicitly by John Quincy Adams, secretary of state to Monroe, as Spain was losing the military struggle to retain its mainland colonies:

> It may be taken for granted that the dominion of Spain upon the American continent, north and south, is irrevocably gone. But the islands of Cuba and Puerto Rico still remain nominally, and so far really, dependent upon her... Cuba, almost in sight of our shores, from a multitude of considerations has become an object of transcendent importance to the commercial and political interests of our Union... there are laws of political as well as physical gravitation; and if an apple severed by the tempest from its native tree cannot choose but to fall to the ground, Cuba, forcibly disjoined from its own unnatural connection with Spain, and incapable of self-support, can gravitate only towards the North American Union.[7]

Nearly thirty years later Buchanan, himself on the cusp of the presidency, was no less confident. After the Civil War Grant prepared a serious financial offer, and was only one of four presidents so to do. Theodore Roosevelt felt that he had participated in the act fulfilled – an island penetrated is as metaphorically available as an apple, fallen by grace of gravity or proffered by the hands of Eve – and today Messrs Helms and Burton chafe so because their law forbidding Europe (or anyone else) to have intercourse with Cuba is not fully upheld. As much as one resists recourse to the analysis of Lacan (because of its frenzied germination and dullard propagation) the energy that charges between the real, the symbolic and the imaginary orders in this respect is compelling.[8] Jefferson was fond of quoting the phrase with which Cato the Elder ended all his speeches to the Roman senate – '*Delenda est Cartago*' (Carthage must be destroyed) – and he habitually dubbed Britain as Carthage for its lack of republican asceticism. He would surely despond if he knew that this ritualistic incantation has since 1959 remained an integral part of US public rhetoric as applied to the Caribbean island administered by Fidel Castro. Prospero watches amazed as he is called Caliban by Caliban himself.[9] The temptation to pathologise is exceptionally strong.

What Jefferson anticipated and most of his successors insisted upon in the case of Cuba was the 'non-transferability' thesis, derived from the Monroe doctrine and initially intended to preserve as American and independent all Europe's ex-colonies in the hemisphere. For Buchanan, as for Edward Everett, who was secretary of state seven years after him, the objective of this policy was to retain Cuba as either a formal colony of Spain or a US protectorate or direct possession but decidedly nothing else. This aim was upheld from 1823 to 1960 by quite widely differing measures and under very distinct circumstances: the replacement of the Platt Amendment by sugar quotas in 1934, for example, is certainly a far from inconsequential matter and relates – as do the events of 1895-1902 – to the emphatic agency of the Cuban people. Equally, the period after 1960 is not homogeneous. Up to the collapse of the USSR this loss was overwhelmingly approached as a modern, ideological issue. After 1990 it becomes possible to reinterpret US policy towards Cuba in terms of 'non-transferability', albeit still within the rhetorical guise of democratic anti-communism, which was too familiar and reassuring to ditch.

Monroe

The Monroe Doctrine has been widely viewed as a charter for expansionism and intervention, but it is best seen as a declaration of containment. Although in 1823 those identified as its targets were the European states ruled by monarchies and possessed of colonies, the Doctrine was always available for self-application at the service of isolationism – a current that has its domestic roots far closer to those of 'manifest destiny'/expansionism than is normally recognised:

> We have here no concern with South America; we have no sympathy, we can have no well founded sympathy with them. We

are sprung from different stocks, we speak different languages, we have been brought up in different social and moral schools, we have been governed by different codes of law, we profess radically different forms of religion... How can our mild and merciful peoples, who went through their revolution without shedding a drop of civil blood, sympathise with a people that are hanging and shooting each other in their streets, with every fluctuation of their ill-organised and exasperated fractions? ...We are told it to be a maxim clearly established in the history of the world that none but the temperate climates, and the climates which produce and retain the European complexion of skin in its various shades, admit of the highest degrees of national civilization.[10]

This attitude would endure through quite different political conditions, but on the brink of Latin American independence Monroe had no need to make open recourse to it because the principle of non-intervention could be stated directly and plausibly in terms of the balance of international power:

It is impossible that the allied powers should extend their political system to any portion of either continent without endangering our peace and happiness; nor can anyone believe that our southern brethren, if left to themselves, would adopt it of their own accord. It is equally impossible, therefore, that we should behold such interposition, in any form, with indifference. If we look to the comparative strength and resources of Spain and those new governments, and their distance from each other, it must be obvious that she can never subdue them. It is still the true policy of the United States to leave the parties to themselves, in the hope that other powers will pursue the same course.[11]

I stress this element of containment because, of course, Spain did contrive to retain Cuba and Puerto Rico until the very end of the 19th century, much of the Caribbean remains under direct colonial rule from Europe beyond 1945 – some is still part of France – and there was little domestic consensus within the USA over how to respond to major extra-hemispheric powers. Furthermore, in his diary Secretary of State Adams gives an account of the cabinet debate over the presidential message that was to contain the Doctrine that underscores the possibility of self-application, as both a mark of virtue and a prophylactic against tempting alliances and adventures:

After much discussion, I said I thought we should bring the whole answer to Mr Canning's proposal to a test of right and wrong. Considering the South Americans as independent nations, they themselves, and no other nation, had the *right* to dispose of their condition. *We* have no right to dispose of them, either alone or in

conjunction with other nations. Neither have any other nations the
right of disposing of them without their consent...[12]

It is worth recalling that this statement was written three years before Canning
made his celebrated boast: 'Contemplating Spain such as our ancestors had known
her, I resolved that if France had Spain, it should not be Spain with the Indies. I
called the New World into existence to redress the balance of the Old.'

On the other hand, the argument that the Monroe Doctrine effectively 'called
the Old World into existence to redress the balance in the New' has always been
fortified by the examples of Polk in the Mexican war and Roosevelt in the
occupation of Cuba, where high-minded rhetoric was deployed in support of
military aggression. By explicitly extending the exclusionist component of the
Doctrine to the USA itself, and by asserting the rights of 'other peoples' to join the
Union, Polk simultaneously warned London against interference in the case of
Texas in 1845 and provided himself with a formal – if flimsy – *casus belli* against
Mexico the next year (Merk, 1966). Some fifty years later Roosevelt, by explicitly
introducing as new considerations for the application of the Doctrine the internal
condition and political behaviour of the states of the hemisphere, made the truly
qualitative jump from the avowal of principle to the assertion of conditionality:

> All that we desire is to see all neighboring countries stable, orderly
> and prosperous. Any country whose people conduct themselves well
> can count upon our hearty friendliness. If a nation shows that it
> knows how to act with decency in industrial and political matters, if
> it keeps order and pays its obligations, then it need fear no
> interference from the United States. Brutal wrongdoing, or an
> impotence which results in the general loosening of the ties of
> civilized society, may finally require intervention by some civilized
> nation, and in the Western Hemisphere the United States cannot
> ignore this duty; but it remains true that our interests, and those of
> our southern neighbours, are in reality identical.'[13]

If the Monroe Doctrine has widely been understood in the light of these
sentiments – so readily applicable to the 1990s – this is because Roosevelt is seen
to have made public and plain those attributes of 'manifest destiny' that were ever
present and yet seldom enunciated so bluntly. But, as already suggested, it is one
thing to assert superiority and quite another to engage in political expansionism,
especially that requiring military intervention. Although Polk's war completed the
process begun by Jefferson in 1803 and transformed the USA into a truly
continental power in the space of a few months through the actions of a mixed
regular and volunteer army, the president – never a popular figure – did not face
opposition simply from figures on the 'left', such as Emerson, Greeley and
Thoreau.[14] The position of Calhoun was characteristically blunt:

I know... that we have never dreamt of incorporating into our Union any but the Caucasian race – the free, white race... I protest against such a union as that [with Mexico]. Ours, sir, is the Government of a white race [with which the Mexicans are not fit to be connected].[15]

Calhoun had been secretary of state in the previous administration, and he might be thought here to be maximising his pro-slavery position in opposition to the government, but even a Democrat expansionist like Lewis Cass was clear about the social restrictions on annexation: 'We do not want the people of Mexico either as citizens or subjects. All we want is a portion of territory which they nominally hold, uninhabited, or, where inhabited at all sparsely so, and with a population which would soon recede, or identify itself with ours.'[16] These are, of course, elite views, but the evidence suggests that they conformed to an important body of popular opinion within the white male constituency of Jacksonian America. This was a population, the humorists had it, for whom, 'Thet Mexicans worn't human beans – an orange outing nation. A sort o'folks a chap could kill an never dream on't arter...'[17] At this level the distinction between conquest, annexation and dismemberment could readily be confused or lost. Of the 73,000 volunteers enlisted in the USA for the war with Mexico, 25,000 came from the free North Eastern states, but many of these, like Thomas Tennery arriving in Matamoros from Illinois, held convictions that were comparable to those of Calhoun in their origin, if not in their virulent application:

Everything appears dull, the houses, the inhabitants little above savages and without energy or business of any importance going on. This appears to be caused by the want of commerce, with the indolence of the inhabitants and perhaps the want of a settled government that will secure some property. But to bring about this change the country must be inhabited by a different race of people. The Spaniards and the Indians do not make a race of people with patriotism and candor enough to support a republic, much less to form, sustain and establish one out of the present deranged fabric called the Republic of Mexico.[18]

A racially-based pessimism of this type was shared by many in the Latin American elite, but for such an ardent advocate of European immigration as Juan Bautista Alberdi the whole thrust of the Monroe Doctrine was to re-impose isolation from a vital source of civilisation, both north and south of the Rio Grande (where the US border with Mexico had been newly fixed). Furthermore, Alberdi saw the defence of the political form of republicanism – which could uphold the institution of slavery as well as any other – as spurious in the extreme:

We do not dissent from the republic in itself, in the abstract and ideal, but from the republic deformed and monstrous, which we see in practice; from the republic with tyranny and misery, with disorders, with revolutions; we dissent in a word from the governments of Bolivia, Peru, New Granada, La Plata, which only by sarcasm can be called republics... to isolate oneself from Civilized Europe is to recolonise oneself.[19]

By the time Teddy Roosevelt was making a similar contrast between form and content (or procedure and substance), the USA was strenuously exercising its claims to represent an alternative source of civilisation. However, until the 1890s there existed a palpable gap between US claims and capacities – a gap made all the more obvious by the extravagance of the claims. Few Latin American presidents could ever plausibly strike the tone adopted by Polk in his address to Congress in December 1847:

> No country has been so much favoured, or should acknowledge with deeper reverence the manifestations of Divine protection. An all-wise Creator directed and guarded us in an infant struggle for freedom, and has constantly watched over our surprising progress, until we have become one of the great nations of the earth.[20]

At the time of the Mexican War most heads of state in Central and South America could point to some recovery from the wars of independence and growing commercial ties with Britain, but usually in the context of political behaviour that Alberdi so scorned and which President Carlos Soublette, regaling the Venezuelan Congress, listed as part of a litany with equally providential or natural qualities as that presented by Polk:

> Unfortunately, evils of every description have occurred during the last year, and all kinds of misfortunes have assailed us: floods, failures of the harvest, disease and contagious epidemics, discontent and disquietude in the public mind, mobs and tumultuous assemblies, and sometimes even the necessity of employing force to suppress seditious practices; all of which, together with their consequences so fatal to commercial and industrial transactions, have contributed to increase the losses and difficulties which have been experienced...[21]

This is a familiar image, and nowhere is it more acutely drawn than in the comparison between the USA and Mexico in 1848. It is, however, worth noting that the campaign ended by the treaty of Guadalupe Hidalgo was conducted with ordnance still dominated by muskets and muzzle-loading weaponry, that on its eve the total enlistment of the US army numbered less than 9,000, and that after the termination of hostilities this returned to only 11,000. The eventual logistical undertaking was indeed formidable, and it relied critically upon a capacity to raise troops and taxes in a manner quite beyond the divided and disoriented authorities in Mexico. Yet the USA fought the war in terms comparable to Mexico, sometimes needing more than a natural incidence of good luck – Taylor's 'victory' at Buena Vista, for instance. Their troops were still raised with the promise of land grants, and most volunteers lacked uniforms; Polk's law partner Gideon Pillow had himself appointed major-general, and at the end of the war the navy of what Polk was describing as a great world power possessed just 21 ships of all types built after 1840.[22]

The activity and influence of the Department of State is usefully reconsidered in this same light. In 1833 it employed in diplomatic posts a total of 152 personnel, served by six clerks in Washington. By 1856 the total establishment in Washington had risen to 57, including a single librarian and a solitary translator (of Spanish and French); there were ten full embassies abroad (by contrast, at the end of World War II, the Department itself employed 3,767 personnel and the Foreign Service 7,000 with a budget of $50 million).[23]

Economics and Ambition

For the broader development of the economies of north and south Table 1.2 suggests that it would be mistaken to identify any clear US supremacy before the 1890s. Even in 1912, had the Latin American states followed the advice offered them today by Peter Smith and dealt with the USA as a united bloc, they would have possessed appreciable bargaining power. Of course, by that stage the USA had experienced qualitatively greater development of its industrial production and infrastructure, and before World War I she was far less dependent upon overseas trade – 13 per cent of GDP in 1850; 12 per cent in 1910 – than were the European powers to which Latin America was still largely oriented at the start of the 20th century: Great Britain 51 per cent; France 33 per cent; and Germany 36 per cent (all in 1910) (Mann, 1993, p. 283). As can be seen from Table 1.3, the levels of US-Latin American trade are decidedly modest throughout the 19th century, and, indeed, only Cuba and Brazil are partners of any consequence for the decades after the Civil War (when they retained the slavery abolished in the USA).

Table 1.2:
USA and Latin America: Population and Exports, 1985-1912

Year	Exports ($000)	Population (000)	Exports *per capita* (US$)
Latin America			
1850	159,484	30,381	5.2
1870	344,123	38,628	8.9
1890	602,147	51,662	11.7
1912	1,580,534	77,456	20.4
USA			
1850	162,000	23,192	7.0
1870	400,000	39,818	10.0
1890	859,607	62,948	13.7
1912	2,307,000	94,569	24.4

Derived from Bulmer-Thomas (1994), pp. 38, 69, 432-3.

From a Latin American viewpoint the explicit or implicit maintenance of the Monroe Doctrine up to World War I had to be assessed in the light of the military and commercial capacity of *both* the USA *and* the European powers. In this regard the Civil War (1861-65) represented a short but very severe interruption of the developing balance of power. For Thomas Schoonover the war not only offered France, Spain (and Great Britain) a rich opportunity to pursue their interests by force in Mexico and elsewhere – as the hapless Secretary of State William Seward, an expansionist if ever there was one, looked the other way – but it also stymied the political possibility of an unprecedented ideological convergence between Washington and Mexico based on liberalism and republicanism that he finds incarnated in the meeting between Lincoln and Romero in January 1860. It is, though, difficult to see the ideological issue as greater than that of the international balance of power when, in July 1862 – nearly sixty years after the Louisiana purchase and following the withdrawal of British and Spanish forces from Mexico – Napoleon III declared:

> The prosperity of America is not a matter of indifference to Europe, for it is that country which feeds our manufactories and gives an impulse to our commerce. We have an interest in the republic of the United States being powerful and prosperous but not that she should take possession of the whole of the Gulf of Mexico, thence command the Antilles as well as South America, and be the only dispenser of products of the New World.[24]

Table 1.3:
US Trade, 1830-1990 ($ million)

	1830	1840	1850	1860	1870	1880	1890	1900
Total								
Exports	72	124	144	334	471	836	858	1,394
Imports	63	98	174	354	436	668	789	850
Canada								
Exports	3	6	10	23	25	29	40	106
Imports	—	1	5	24	36	33	39	39
Cuba								
Exports	5	6	5	12	14	11	13	26
Imports	5	9	10	32	54	65	54	31
Mexico								
Exports	5	3	2	5	6	8	13	36
Imports	1	1	1	2	3	7	23	29
Brazil								
Exports	2	2	3	6	6	9	12	12
Imports	2	5	9	21	25	55	59	58

Source: US Dept. Commerce (1975), pp. 904-6.

Porous though it proved, Lincoln's naval blockade relieved Latin American governments of any severe choice over recognition between the belligerent parties in North America, but, particularly in Central America, the recourse of the Confederacy to privateers as well as the fear of slavery recently reawakened by William Walker and other filibusters required discretion in statements and activity (there was also the reasonable analogy with the break-up of the isthmian union 25 years earlier that had not been reversed by force and that had important international consequences for the concept of sovereignty.)[25] Clearly, the fact that the USA was plunged into an internecine slaughter without parallel elsewhere in the continent did more than interrupt trade and reduce prior claims of unity and internal stability to competitive sectional ideology. Beyond the conflict itself, reconstruction and the attendant caution in foreign affairs slackened the immediate pressure on Cuba (itself at war from 1868) and, arguably, offered Latin America a unique window of opportunity at a time of expanding trans-Atlantic commerce.

On the other hand, Walter LaFeber has long argued that it is precisely at this stage (1860-98) that the United States came to pose a profound threat to the rest of the region by transforming itself into a 'new empire':

> Two important features distinguished it from the old. First, with the completion of the continental conquest Americans moved with increasing authority into such extracontinental areas as Hawaii, Latin America, Asia and Africa. Second, the form of expansion changed. Instead of searching for farming, mineral or grazing lands, Americans sought markets for agricultural staples or industrial goods.[26]

For LaFeber, Seward is the man of vision who when, in May 1864, he is urged to face down Napoleon in Mexico, responds, 'Five years, ten years, twenty years hence, Mexico will be opening herself as cheerfully to American immigration as Montana and Idaho are now'.[27] This was after Gettysburg, with immigration to the USA exceeding 250,000 a year for the previous 15 years, contributing to an unparalleled acceleration of what would a century later be termed the 'military-industrial complex' (it is only in 1865 that the US currency was standardised). It might be thought justified confidence. Seward, though, saw still longer cycles at play, claiming that his vision derived from

> a political law – and when I say political law, I mean a higher law, a law of Providence – that empire has, for the last three thousand years... made its way constantly westward, and that it must continue to move on westward until the tides of the renewed and of the decaying civilizations of the world meet on the shores of the Pacific Ocean.[28]

Such assurance about underlying movements could, of course, encourage resistance to intervention, as in the case of Calhoun, for whom 'manifest destiny' had twenty years earlier needed little or no executive encouragement: '*Time* is acting for us; and if we have the wisdom to trust its operation, it will assert and maintain our rights with restless force, without costing a cent of money or a drop of blood...'[29]

LaFeber argues that the myth of the frontier was widely believed, and that mass apprehension at its imminent 'closure' in the 1880s had critical consequences for economic planning, international strategy and the popular imagination. His first book might certainly be deemed a child of its teleological times in that he identified a Rostow-like 'take-off' period in 1843-57 and assumes patterns of causation that are rather unsophisticated by today's standards.[30] Yet the last third of the 19th century is evidently a watershed of critical importance, not least, of course, because Seward was able to buy Alaska from the Tsar at a price of $7.2 million ($5 billion in today's prices) within two years of the end of the Civil War, thereby reducing European-administered territory on the American continental mainland to British Honduras and the Guyanas (Canada gained self-government in the same year). Moreover, Seward was far from extraordinary in his emphasis upon the burgeoning Pacific dimension and the emergence of a tri-continental theatre, with its considerable consequences for naval strategy and inter-oceanic communication. The 1882 Exclusion Act, which banned all immigrant labour from China for a period of ten years, was just as important a point of closure – of free inter-continental migration – as was the previous year's proposal by Washington of a Pan-American Congress to secure intracontinental cooperation in the context of a fully global theatre.[31]

The 1881 Pan-American Congress failed to take place because Secretary of State Blaine was removed from office (as a result of the assassination of President Garfield), and replaced by Freylinghuysen, who agreed with him on the essential issues but was not convinced of the value of a summit – a quite rare initiative for that epoch. The fact that one was only eventually held in 1889-90 is a reminder of the importance to US foreign policy of domestic political actions and individual initiative. The original objective had been to seek a means of averting regional conflicts in the wake of the prolonged Paraguayan War (1865-70) and the War of the Pacific (1879-83). The congress finally held in Washington followed this through with a proposal for compulsory arbitration that was fiercely resisted by Chile, which had annexed large and rich portions of Peruvian and Bolivian territory. However, the agenda in 1890 also included extradition and citizenship, monetary and exchange controls, uniform customs and commercial regulations, health and sanitation issues and, perhaps most important of all, a draft convention for the settlement of financial claims. From Washington's perspective this last issue was not restricted to the growing interests of US companies and investors. Between the French intervention in Mexico and the 1890 congress the failure to repay debts had led to the threat or use of force by eight European countries (Denmark; France; Germany; Great Britain; Italy; Russia; Spain) against five Latin American states (Colombia; Haiti; Nicaragua; Santo Domingo [now Dominican Republic]; Venezuela). The next year Washington and London found themselves supporting different sides in the Chilean civil war, and, in the wake of the economic crisis of 1893, they clashed over British claims to the Orinoco for which Venezuela sought international arbitration.

In short, at the start of the last decade of the 19th century the Monroe Doctrine seemed both to have been fully revived and to have been given an expression that was at least tolerable to many Latin American governments. In 1902 this would take the form of the Drago Doctrine, designed to prohibit the use of European force to collect debts – an initiative that itself inspired the Roosevelt Corollary. That, in turn, did not elicit universal repudiation. In 1906 the veteran Brazilian statesman Rio Branco embraced both Monroe and Roosevelt with a racial stereotyping typical of its day but deployed with unusual emphasis at the service of a strategy of 'cohabitation' between Brazil and the USA. This was a strategy that 75 years earlier Bolívar had come to fear as a serious threat to Latin American union, just as it is one that Peter Smith today sees as a potential option for the 'age of uncertainty':

> Latin America has nothing to fear from Anglo-Saxon America. The United States is a nation of English origin and principles and therefore beneficial for the civilization of other peoples because the sentiment of individualism is so much part of their race that English or North American imperialism, if it should manifest itself, would never be of the same type as German or Latin imperialism, which seek to destroy or annihilate everything, contorting everything in order to create from the incompatibilities and irreconcilables the same kind of country in all regions of the world. Nothing, absolutely nothing, in the policies of the United States would be able to cause uneasiness to the national sensitivity of the other American countries. Just the opposite, these nations find in the preponderance of the first nation of the continent support for their causes and aspirations.[32]

It is, though, not the case that prior to the renewed use of military intervention by the USA itself in 1898, Pan-Americanism was viewed in a universally favourable and instrumental manner in the south. Over previous decades relations with the USA had taken on increasing importance as an issue within the domestic political life of the Latin American states, generating a degree of division and controversy. This was particularly true in the Caribbean Basin, and within it especially true of Cuba. Further afield, as in Argentina, with relatively weak economic and cultural ties with the USA, matters could appear less urgent. Hence, on the eve of the First Pan-American Congress José Martí, a Cuban émigré based in New York, wrote his dispatch for *La Nación* of Buenos Aires with an energy that impresses almost as much as does the continued relevance of his theme:

> The customs union proposal that would permit free entrance of the products of every nation to all countries of the union should be no cause for alarm; merely announcing it would make the proposal collapse... Taking United States products duty free – because its

cosmopolitan factories produce all that is known or can be suggested by the entire world – would be like tossing the principal customs revenues into the sea... Why go as allies, at the height of youth, into the battle the United States is able to launch upon the rest of the world? Why must it fight its battles with Europe in the American republics, and rehearse its system of colonization on the territory of the free nations?   ...Why in the halls of this Congress arrange projects of reciprocity with all the American nations when one such project, that of Mexico, has for years been waiting in vain for congressional sanction, because the special interests affected by that project, to the detriment of the national interests, oppose it?[33]

World Power in Local Context

Six years later, when Martí was killed in the Cuban independence struggle, Great Britain had backed down over Venezuela, accepted the US-sponsored dismantling of the Moskito 'kingdom' in Nicaragua, and was visibly withdrawing her longstanding support for Spain over Cuba (scarcely, though, on a point of anti-colonial principle – what San Juan del Norte in Nicaragua had ceased to promise now needed resolute defence in Mafeking in South Africa). Nonetheless, as can be seen from Table 1.4, the US military apparatus could not yet match that of Great Britain, even if generous allowance is made for the skills of the veterans of the Indian wars or the widespread deployment of British troops. Moreover, from a Latin American perspective, the maintenance of British naval bases at Halifax, Bermuda, Jamaica, St Lucia, the Falklands and Ascension Island was, prior to the construction of the Panama canal, a consideration of greater gravity than it might appear today, when the canal itself has lost much of its direct strategic importance and we have become accustomed to aviation-directed military operations.

Table 1.4:
Military Personnel and Warship Tonnage, 1880-1914

		1880	1900	1914
USA	Troops	34,000	96,000	164,000
	Tonnage	169,000	333,000	985,000
Britain	Troops	367,000	624,000	582,000
	Tonnage	650,000	1,065,000	2,714,000
Germany	Troops	426,000	524,000	891,000
	Tonnage	88,000	285,000	1,305,000
Russia	Troops	791,000	1,162,000	1,352,000
	Tonnage	200,000	383,000	679,000

Source: Kennedy (1989), p. 261.

Table 1.5:
USA and Latin America, 1898-1932

Year	Non-Recognition	Loan Manipulation	Supervision Elections	Support Rebels	Troops Deployed
1898					Cuba / Puerto Rico
1899					
1900			Cuba		
1901					
1902					
1903				Panama	Dominican Republic / Panama / Honduras
1904					
1905					
1906					Cuba / Nicaragua
1907		Honduras / Dominican Republic		Honduras	Honduras
1908			Cuba		
1909				Nicaragua	
1910	Nicaragua				
1911		Nicaragua			
1912	Central America / Mexico				Cuba / Nicaragua
1913	Peru	Dominican Republic			
1914			Dominican Republic	Mexico	Mexico
1915	Haiti		Haiti		Haiti
1916	Dominican Republic / Central America	Nicaragua	Nicaragua		Dominican Republic
1917	Costa Rica	Costa Rica	Haiti		
1918			Panama / Haiti		
1919					
1920	Mexico / Bolivia		Cuba		
1921					
1922					
1923	Honduras	Honduras			
1924			Dominican Republic		Honduras
1925	Ecuador / Nicaragua	Ecuador			
1926					Nicaragua
1927					
1928			Nicaragua		
1929					
1930	Guatemala / Bolivia / Peru / Argentina / Brazil				
1931	El Salvador / Peru				
1932	Chile	Chile	Nicaragua		

Derived and expanded from Drake (1991), p. 4.

So familiar are the interventionist images conjured up by Table 1.5 that it is worth reminding ourselves that the Liberal dictator of Nicaragua, José Santos Zelaya, sought a European alliance to play off the USA a full decade after the invasion of Cuba, and that another decade later the Tinoco brothers thought that they could manage without Washington's *imprimatur* in Costa Rica. There are, nevertheless, slim pickings for revisionists in this area after 1898, and the main interest lies in the different temporal and spatial distribution of US authority in both its own terms and in those of European decline.

In this regard, let us revert briefly to the global context before picking up the hemispheric story. As can be see from Table 1.6, by the time war had erupted in Europe, the US economy had overtaken those of its principal competitors.

Table 1.6:
Comparative Economic Strength, 1914

	Population (million)	National Income ($ billion)	Per Capita Income ($)
USA	98	37	337
UK	45	11	244
Germany	65	12	184

Source: Kennedy (1989), p. 314.

However, over the next 25 years the performance of US industry was markedly superior, creating the kind of parallax in the inter-war era (Table 1.7) depicted by Ian Clark:

> The incipient global system at the turn of the century seemed [between 1918 and 1940] to have reverted to an earlier European one in which Britain and France appeared as centres of world politics. Much of this was, of course, illusory, contingent upon the introversions of the United States and the Soviet Union and the mirage of a Europe fully restored.[34]

Table 1.7:
Indices of Manufacturing Production, 1913-38

	1913	1920	1925	1930	1938	(% share) 1938
World	100	93.2	120.7	137.5	182.7	100.0
USA	100	122.2	148.0	148.0	143.0	28.7
UK	100	92.6	86.3	91.3	117.6	9.2
Germany	100	59.0	94.9	101.6	149.3	13.2
Japan	100	176.0	221.8	294.9	552.0	3.8
USSR	100	12.8	70.2	235.5	857.3	17.6

Source: Kennedy (1989), pp. 386; 426.

This, it should be recalled, is the productive back-drop of an international scenario wherein the USA refuses to join the League of Nations, the USSR is born and remains a pariah, and Japan becomes mired in an imperialist war in Manchuria.

To what degree were US-Latin American commercial ties affected by the activity signalled in Table 1.5 – known popularly as 'the big stick' and 'dollar diplomacy' – and the impact of World War I?

Table 1.8:
Latin American Trade with the USA, 1913-29 (%)

	1913		1918		1929	
	Exports	**Imports**	**Exports**	**Imports**	**Exports**	**Imports**
Latin America	29.7	24.5	45.4	41.8	34.0	38.6
Mexico / Central America / Panama	67.2	53.5	83.5	78.1	57.4	65.7
Cuba / Dominican Republic / Haiti	73.9	55.2	66.1	76.8	68.9	59.6
South America	16.7	16.9	34.9	25.9	25.1	31.4
Argentina	4.9	14.7	29.3	21.6	8.3	23.2
Brazil	32.3	15.7	34.0	22.7	45.5	26.7
Chile	21.3	16.7	56.8	41.5	33.1	30.8
Peru	33.2	28.2	39.1	46.8	28.8	41.4
Uruguay	4.0	12.7	25.9	13.2	10.7	30.2
Venezuela	28.3	32.8	60.0	46.7	26.5	57.5

Source: Bulmer-Thomas (1994), p. 159.

Table 1.8 suggests that during the war, which the USA entered in April 1917, the US share of Latin American commerce rose from around a quarter to just under a half, falling back to a third on the eve of the 1929 depression. But within the region the pattern varied, the already very high levels of trade with the Caribbean Basin proving less flexible whilst the shift in South America is more towards buying from the USA than selling to it. Table 1.9 shows this development in the cases of Brazil and Argentina, the two largest economies in the south, in terms of US and UK market share – the key variable, after all, in LaFeber's thesis – the swing during the war years being more marked in terms of imports than exports. Table 1.10 follows the pattern through the period covering both world wars and the depression because it is the sequential and compound impact of these global crises that really accounts for the state of play in 1945. Seen from this perspective, the picture bears out Clark's observation about the inter-war period upholding merely an illusion of European resurgence. At the Armistice in 1918 the USA had captured almost half of the hemispheric trade. By 1929 this had fallen back appreciably, being further but more modestly eroded through the depression. Over the critical 25-year period of 1913-38 the UK, which was at the start the main competitor of the USA in the region, saw its share of the Latin American market halved, falling well behind Nazi Germany in 1938. This, it should be recalled, is a year before Europe goes to war, but three more years were to elapse before the USA entered a conflict in which the collapse of trans-Atlantic trade was only the most severe of a number of disruptive factors (the figures for 1948 indicate the weak demand for Latin American goods from all the conquered states – Allied and Axis alike).

Table 1.9:
Argentina and Brazil: Trade with UK and USA, 1913-19 (%)

		1913	1915	1917	1919
Brazil					
Exports	- USA	32.7	41.8	46.1	41.4
	- UK	13.3	12.1	12.6	7.2
Imports	- USA	15.7	32.2	47.1	48.0
	- UK	24.5	21.9	18.0	16.2
Argentina					
Exports	- USA	4.7	13.0	29.3	18.3
	- UK	24.9	24.4	29.2	28.5
Imports	- USA	14.7	19.2	36.3	35.5
	- UK	31.1	35.6	21.8	23.5

Source: Albert (1988), pp. 76-94.

Table 1.10:
Latin American Trade Partners, 1913-48 (%)

			1913	1938	1941	1945	1948
USA	-	Exports	29.7	31.5	54.0	49.2	32.8
	-	Imports	25.5	35.8	62.4	58.5	52.0
UK	-	Exports	20.7	15.9	13.1	11.8	13.3
	-	Imports	24.8	12.2	7.8	3.6	8.1
Germany	-	Exports	12.4	10.3	0.3	-	2.1
	-	Imports	16.5	17.1	0.5	-	0.7
France	-	Exports	8.0	4.0	0.1	-	2.3
	-	Imports	8.3	4.0	0.1	-	1.9
Japan	-	Exports	-	1.3	2.7	-	0.9
	-	Imports	-	2.7	2.6	-	0.1

Source: Bulmer-Thomas (1994), pp. 74; 76; 240.

It was, however, investment and loans rather than trade shares that agitated the public profile of US-Latin American relations in the years up to the Good Neighbor policy depicted in Table 1.5. In this respect the pattern shifts in a manner that might help explain the lessened pretension and lower overall incidence of US military intervention – Nicaragua excepted – in the 1920s compared with the previous two decades. Investment both moves south from the Caribbean Basin into less directly 'manageable' South America and it diversifies, arguably away from more labour-intensive and so more politically sensitive sectors. Table 1.11 aggregates direct and portfolio investment, and while direct investment more than doubles to account for two-thirds of the total, portfolio investment increases more than fourfold over this period – something that might be thought consistent with expansion out of 'enclave' agricultural and mining operations.

Table 1.11:
US Direct and Portfolio Investment in Latin America, 1914 and 1929

	1914	1929
Latin America ($ million)	1,614.0	5,369.0
By Region (%)		
Mexico / Central America / Panama	57.7	23.5
Cuba / Dominican Republic / Haiti	20.0	20.4
South America	22.3	56.1
By Sector (%)		
Agriculture	18.7	24.1
Mining / Smelting	43.3	22.0
Oil	10.2	20.1
Railways	13.8	6.3
Public Utilities	7.7	15.8
Manufacturing	2.9	6.3
Trade	2.6	3.3
Other	0.8	2.2

Source: Bulmer-Thomas (1994), p. 161.

In this sphere Rio Branco was surely mistaken in his analysis of US ambitions, which increasingly required precisely a uniform approach to property and particularly to capital. This could be no mere issue of disposition. If Theodore Roosevelt had been educated at Harvard, his ranching days in North Dakota provided the basis for macho 'rough-riderdom', redolent of the frontier. Yet he was no more emphatic upon this matter than was Woodrow Wilson, political scientist, progressive president of Princeton, and ardent advocate of social justice, who gave vent to the characteristic 'Anglo' complaint to an audience at Mobile in October 1913:

> There is one peculiarity about the history of the Latin American states which I am sure they are keenly aware of. You hear of "concessions" to foreign capitalists in Latin America. You do not hear of concessions to foreign capitalists in the United States. They are not granted concessions. They are invited to make investments. The work is ours, though they are welcome to invest in it. We do not ask them to supply the capital and do the work. It is an invitation, not a privilege.[35]

This cultural gap was one that, a dozen years later, José Carlos Mariátegui identified as the distinction between Pan-Americanism, 'based upon economic interest and business', and Ibero-Americanism, 'founded upon sentiment and tradition'. For Mariátegui these were both ideals and irreconcilable. And yet – as so often in his writing – the analysis captures with a sedulous logic an image that transcends these common lines, proposing new contradictions:

> The economy is... more powerful than space... Ibero-America appears for all practical purposes to be at odds, divided and balkanized. However, her unity is no utopia; it is not an abstraction. The men who make history in Ibero-America are not so different from one another... The Argentine is more optimistic, more assured than the Peruvian, but the two are equally irreligious and sensual... Is it the fault of the USA if we the Ibero-Americans know more of the thought of Theodore Roosevelt than that of Henry Thoreau?... The country which has produced the greatest captains of industry has at the same time produced the most powerful masters of idealism.[36]

This was written in the wake of the presidency of Warren Harding, whose name is these days only dimly remembered, who made knowledge of Spanish obligatory for US diplomats posted to the region, and who, according to Kenneth Grieb, had a 'low-key, practical' approach to hemispheric relations. Harding withdrew troops from the Dominican Republic and eastern Cuba, wanted to do the same in Nicaragua, mediated the Tacna-Arica dispute, and refused to countenance military options in seeking to overcome the challenge posed by article 27 of the Mexican constitution (Grieb, 1977). Yet, like all his successors down to Bill Clinton, he had perforce to confront the problem of public property in Mexico, which in the early 1920s was still enmeshed with the question of political disorder. Following the Bolshevik revolution this had been transformed from an issue of cultural recalcitrance into an ideological perversion of the law of nations:

> Intercourse, from the standpoint of business, consists in the making of contracts and the acquisition of property rights... and the most important principle to be maintained at this time with respect to international relations is that no State is entitled to a place within the family of nations if it destroys the foundations of honorable intercourse by resort to confiscation and repudiation.[37]

Whatever the tactical preference of the White House, and no matter how propitious the conjuncture, it seemed that the USA was now so 'integrated' with Latin America, and particularly with Mexico, that Washington could no longer conduct foreign policy towards these states without automatically interfering in their domestic affairs. And yet the anti-colonial political culture of the USA would no more countenance deviation from the norms of separate sovereignties than could its logistical resources keep even small and local protectorates, such as

Nicaragua, Haiti and Cuba, peacefully compliant. Moreover, as both the Mexican Revolution and the peculiar insurgency brewing in Nicaragua indicated, direct intervention was far from cheap, created diplomatic embarrassment elsewhere, and seemed to compound bad relations in the region itself. Most importantly, of course, it could not be guaranteed to achieve even short-term objectives.

There were few more lucid expressions of the resentment caused in Latin America by this experience than that voiced by Honorio Pueyrredón, the Argentine delegate at the Sixth Pan-American Conference early in 1928. Although David Sheinin dissents from the common interpretation that this broadside was representative of an Argentine tradition of critical independence of the USA – a tradition that might be argued to have endured down to Menem – it was keenly remembered by Cordell Hull as he set about designing an alternative policy in 1933:

> I retained a vivid, uncomfortable memory from reading the pyrotechnic clash between our Government and Argentina at the Pan-American Conference at Havana in 1928. The United States Delegation, headed by former Secretary of State Hughes, sustained repeated attacks from the Argentine Delegation, largely over our intervention... A powder magazine was built at Havana which could easily explode into numerous discordant factions among the 21 American nations.[38]

Hull was, of course, defending his own political record as well as that of F.D. Roosevelt when, in retirement, he wrote,

> Over a long period until almost 1933 the United States had pursued policies towards Latin America of so arbitrary – and what some of those countries considered so overbearing – a nature that prejudice and feeling throughout Central and South America against our country was sharp indeed.[39]

But he had at least registered that the diplomatic response to this lay in the realm of temper, form and recognition of difference – while Frank Kellogg, his predecessor in the Coolidge administration, saw these as simply exasperating problems to be overcome:

> If I had the time, I could justify every act we have performed; in fact, we have been patient beyond any degree to which we would ordinarily be with a more responsible government [than Mexico]. The same is true as to Central America countries. The United States has no desire to dominate them, as you know, but it is hard to make these countries realise that we are not imperialistic and ambitious.[40]

The Limits of Neighbourliness

If the outward features of the Good Neighbor Policy may be traced to the diminishing returns to be had from close invigilation of Latin American political life, its foundations may be found behind Hull's tantalising 'almost'. Not, perhaps, in 1929 itself, but in the chaos stemming from the 1929 crash and the need for a radical review of economic policy in the context of fierce isolationist sentiment in the USA and what appeared to be the spread of the 'Mexican scenario' to the rest of the sub-continent as governments identified with the pursuit of economic liberalism and obeisance to its political forms were swept away.

Equally, during the depression political conflict had quickened markedly in Europe, further reducing the competition faced by the USA in Latin America. Neither a trans-Atlantic nor a hemispheric audience needed the 'demonstration effect' of an interventionism that was increasingly controversial at home and – especially after the Japanese invasion of Manchuria – at open odds with US policy elsewhere in the world. On the commercial front, Roosevelt and Hull possessed a strong card in the ability to bargain reductions in the 1930 Smoot-Hawley tariff in order to restore some of the 70 per cent fall in imports from Latin America between 1929 and 1932 (against which the duty had not been primarily aimed). As with the Morill tariff of 1861, once a protectionist measure had served its initial purpose, it was overtaken by eulogies to freer – even free – trade, a practice in which the British had diligently instructed the USA after the abolition of the corn laws.[41] Nevertheless, the economies of the south so badly needed restoration of the US market that it must have been an enticement as well as a balm to hear Roosevelt announce his new policy to the Pan-American Union just five weeks after taking office:

> The essential qualities of a true Pan-Americanism must be the same as those which constitute a good neighbour, namely, mutual understanding, and through such understanding, a sympathetic appreciation of the other's view... We all of us have peculiar problems, and, to speak frankly, the interest of our citizens must, in each instance, come first. But it is equally true that it is of vital importance to every nation of this continent that the American governments, individually, take, without delay, such action as may be possible to abolish all unnecessary and artificial barriers and restrictions which now hamper the healthy flow of trade...[42]

Within weeks the overthrow of the Machado regime in Cuba put these worthy sentiments to the test, the mediation of Sumner Welles replacing the despatch of troops, and the abrogation of the Platt Amendment by the US Congress in May 1934 being underpinned – as already suggested – by the introduction of sugar quotas. Early in 1936 Welles reminded an audience in Baltimore that Roosevelt had formally declared, 'that armed intervention by the United States in any other American republic was a thing of the past', and he presented the removal of Platt, the new quotas, negotiations with Panama over the canal and mediation in the Chaco War as just as much a replacement of 'dollar diplomacy' as was the evacuation of troops from Haiti and Nicaragua. Yet Walter LaFeber argues that,

> Between 1933 and 1939, Franklin D. Roosevelt's Good Neighbor policy did not change the Central American policy it inherited, but built on it. The Good Neighbor carried on interventionism in Central America and tightened the system far beyond anything Theodore Roosevelt or Woodrow Wilson probably imagined.[43]

LaFeber may here be overstating an important point precisely because of the success of the proponents of the Good Neighbor in presenting their policy as a radical shift in both the form and the content of US-Latin American relations (a success often reflected in subsequent academic literature critical of Cold War inflexibilities and in search of some prior virtue). It is also a moot point whether recognition of dictatorships, a replacement of private by public US loans, and the negotiation of trade agreements constituted something beyond the imagination of Theodore Roosevelt and Wilson (it is certainly difficult to conceive of Washington's response to the nationalisation of oil companies in Bolivia and Mexico in the late 1930s without the wider parameters of the Good Neighbor Policy.) What LaFeber misses as he strains simultaneously to recognise and deny change is that the new policy was not primarily about the domestic political condition of the Latin American states – this part of the Roosevelt Corollary had been relegated beneath economic considerations – and that it was far more concerned than previously about the internal US and extra-hemispheric impact of the use of military force. Indeed, if we survey the Latin America of March 1933, when Franklin Roosevelt came to office – a month after the 44 year-old Adolf Hitler became Chancellor of Germany – there are exceptionally few elected governments upholding the full rule of law; arguably, only Colombia. (In the light of their political reputations, it is worth recalling that in 1932 the US ambassador to San José had to arbitrate forcefully to stave off crisis following the re-election of Cleto Jiménez in Costa Rica, whilst in Uruguay, the new Terra regime was the country's first dictatorship since 1904.) Had the institution and maintenance of a liberal democratic regime in Latin America been a priority for the Roosevelt administration, it would have been engaged in intervention to a far greater degree than its predecessors – even in Central America, where the Good Neighbor Policy was under sharpest scrutiny because of the small and vulnerable nature of the isthmian states.

The key shift in this respect comes not early in 1933 but late in 1941, with the US entry into the war and the full embracing of the anti-dictatorial ideology that was at the heart of the Allied cause and propaganda. This naturally made more acute the contradictions inherent in support for (or even recognition of) figures such as Somoza and Trujillo, but those difficulties were still deemed subordinate to the need for Latin American governments – of every type – to toe the US line on foreign policy. Sufficient compliance on that front would make it easier to explain away the anomalies of authoritarian regimes supporting a democratic cause through reference to war-time exigencies.

In World War I the late entry of the USA had meant that the issue of diplomatic recognition and declarations of neutrality or war never became a critical issue in hemispheric relations (and Washington's lead was fully followed only by Brazil and the smaller states of the Caribbean Basin).[44] The fact that the second global war drew political ideology so much more tightly into the weave of international relations meant that those governments that did not follow Washington's example needed strong arguments of expediency – such as Chile's fear of a coastal attack from the Pacific – to avoid being tarnished as worse than a fair-weather Pan-American, from which it was but a small step to being a crypto-fascist. Yet the pattern was again far from one of uniform acquiescence.[45]

This story has been exhaustively explored and debated – in good part because it forms an essential preamble to the Cold War cycle in hemispheric relations – particularly in terms of the hostile relations between the USA and the Argentine military dictatorship that would mutate into the Peronist government less than a year after the war. It is, though, worth recalling the concern expressed by Washington at the state of play prevailing in June 1942, that is, under the civilian Ortiz government, before the presidency of the much more pro-Axis Castillo, and a full 18 months before the military coup that brought Perón to power. Again, one must make allowance for the fact that Cordell Hull was writing in self-vindication as well as at a time when relations between Buenos Aires and Washington remained very tense, but in a sense it is precisely the image – rather than the more prosaic reality – that counted, both at the time and in the late 1940s (Hull refers to US protest at Argentina's agreement to accept a new ambassador from Japan):

> Our note recited numerous instances of Argentine territory being used as a base for Axis operations. The Argentine Government had failed to prevent group or individual activities detrimental to the security and welfare of the American republics. Axis agents were openly engaged in espionage and other work to defeat our war effort. Other agents of the Axis were working to undermine democratic institutions. Newspapers, radio stations, and publishing houses were disseminating totalitarian propaganda. Argentina had become a communications center for the Axis nations. Each message and even each word we said, that the Argentine Government permitted to be transmitted to the Axis nations, either directly or indirectly, might mean the loss of valuable material needed for the prosecution of the war, and, what was more, the loss of precious lives of citizens of the American republics now engaged in defending the hemisphere.[46]

Here the issue of communication is certainly prominent, and it is presented in a tone of accusatory anxiety fully resonant with that of the post-war years, when US policy was designed and directed by men who had become accustomed to the culture and logic of war. Henceforth, the existence of a nuclear arsenal as well as the IMF qualitatively altered the context and repertoire of 'intervention' and 'deterrence'. This did not, however, immediately affect Latin America, which – Argentina included – signed up to the unambiguous celebration of democratic liberty and economic cooperation in the Act of Chapultepec of 6 April 1945 – three weeks before the death of Hitler – in understandable expectation of hemispheric as well as global renewal.

Notes

1. Buchanan, Washington, to John Appleton, 1 June 1848, in Buchanan (1911), pp. 75-6.
2. Buchanan, Washington, to Secretary of State Clayton, 17 April 1849, in Buchanan (1911), pp. 360-1.
3. NAM/G77 is the 'non-aligned' movement that was created in the 1950s.
4. For Morse the years 1760-1920 in Latin America are 'colonial'. See Morse (1973), p.12. For Véliz the years 1850-1930 constitute a 'liberal pause' in a general centralist, corporatist history. See Véliz (1980).
5. Bemis (1943), p. 6.
6. Jefferson (1954), pp. 267-7.
7. Adams (1913), pp. 372-3.
8. For a suggestive approach in these terms, see David Slater (1997).
9. Richard (1994), pp. 163-4; Rodó (1900).
10. *North American Review*, vol. XXXI, 1821. This article is anonymous, but my strong suspicion is that the author is either Edward Everett, president of Harvard in the 1840s and secretary of state in the early 1850s, or his brother Alexander, who was appointed ambassador to Spain by Adams.
11. Quoted in Dexter Perkins (1927), pp. 84-5. For a discussion of the background, see Gleijeses (1992).
12. Quoted in May (1975), p. 204.
13. Roosevelt to Elihu Root, Washington 20 May 1904. Roosevelt (1967), p. 73.
14. Although Thoreau opens his *Resistance to Civil Government* with the claim that, 'the people would not have consented to [the Mexican war]', he goes on to state that, 'the opponents to... reform in Massachusetts are not a hundred thousand politicians at the South, but a hundred thousand merchants and farmers here, who are more interested in commerce and agriculture than they are in humanity, and are not prepared to do justice to the slaves and to Mexico, *cost what it may*'. Thoreau (1996), pp. 1; 5.
15. Quoted in Merk (1963), p. 59. Calhoun saw any major annexation as positively dangerous: 'Can we incorporate a people so dissimilar to us in every respect – so little qualified for free and popular government – without certain destruction to our political institutions?' Quoted in Weinberg (1968), p. 361. At the other end of the political spectrum Emerson opined, 'The United States will conquer Mexico, but it will be as a man swallows the arsenic, which brings him down in turn. Mexico will poison us' (1969, p. 206). Emerson's

primary fear here was not the incorporation of 'alien' populations but the expansion and acceleration of the US conflict over slavery.

16. Quoted in Deconde (1992), p. 34.
17. James Russell Lowell, quoted in Deconde (1992), p. 55.
18. Tennery (1970), pp. 37-8. The enlistment figures are given in Ellsworth (1940), p. 318. According to my Rand McNally US road atlas, seven of the twelve towns in the country called Polk are in former slave states. (The president himself was from Tennessee.) This is what the most advanced scholarship might call a 'correlative imaginary', which generates and sustains, 'an ideational horizontal integration with a shared space, through a form of interpellation which correlates with social spaces'. Radcliffe and Westwood (1996), p. 28.
19. *Del Gobierno en Sud América*, quoted in Pierson (1920), pp. 366; 371.
20. Message of 7 December 1847, reprinted in *British and Foreign State Papers, 1846-47*, XXXV, p. 170.
21. Message of 31 January 1845, reprinted in *British and Foreign State Papers, 1845-46*, XXXIV, p. 1251.
22. Weigley (1984), p. 597; Ganoe (1964), p. 208; Report of Navy Secretary John P. Kennedy to the President, 26 August 1852, in *British and Foreign State Papers, 1851-52*, XL, pp. 114-5.
23. Johnson (1971), p. 50; Stuart (1949), pp. 110; 414. In 1850, the year in which the trans-Atlantic slave trade was effectively suppressed, the Slave Trade Department of the British Foreign Office comprised one superintendent and four clerks. In 1853 the total establishment of the Foreign Office based in London was 53, including chambers keepers, porters and doorkeepers. R. Anstey (1980), p. 33.
24. Quoted in Schoonover (1978), p. 141. It should not be forgotten that Chile, Peru and Ecuador were menaced by the Spanish fleet in the 1860s.
25. For Ephraim Squier, ex-ambassador to Nicaragua for the USA and now a railroad promotor in Honduras, 'The southern troubles are directing the attention of northern capital and enterprising men to Central America and the West Indies as a source whence to draw future tropical staples. Secession will be good for sugar and cotton production'. Quoted in Schoonover (1991), p. 17.
26. LaFeber (1963), p. 1.
27. Quoted in LaFeber (1993a), p. 9.
28. Quoted in LaFeber (1963), pp. 25-6.
29. Quoted in Smith (1996), p. 45.
30. Rostow had British 'take-off' in 1783-1802; that of the USA, France and Germany in 1830-50; Sweden, Japan, Russia/USSR, Italy, Canada and Australia in 1870-1901; and Argentina, Brazil and Mexico, Turkey, Iran, India, China and South Korea from 1933 onwards. Rostow (1960), p. xviii. For a recent radical reconsideration of LaFeber, see Bergquist (1996).
31. Ian Clark argues for the *primacy* of the Pacific/Asiatic theatre for the USA in 1895-1905, with the non-partition of China and the rapidly growing Russian

interest there and in Japan: 'It offered a stage for the United States to convert its growing economic and technical muscle into a degree of diplomatic leverage: its stake in the Philippines in 1898, the Hay "Open Door" note in relation to China, and the hosting of the Portsmouth peace settlement between Russia and Japan all bear witness to America's coming of international age.' Clark (1989), p. 5.

32. Quoted in Smith (1996), p. 100.
33. 'The Washington Pan-American Congress', *La Nación*, 19-20 December 1889, reprinted in Martí (1975), pp. 356-7.
34. Clark (1989), pp. 96-7.
35. Quoted in Gautenbein (1950), p. 97.
36. 'La Unidad de la América Indo-Española', *Variedades*, Lima, 6 December 1924, in Mariátegui (1988), pp. 16; 28.
37. Secretary of State Hughes, 18 May 1922, quoted in Smith (1972), pp. 190-1.
38. Hull (1948), p. 308; Sheinin (1991).
39. Hull (1948), p. 308.
40. Kellogg to Bliss, 7 November 1927, quoted in Sheinin (1991), p. 6.
41. Writing from London in 1852, the US Whig leader Thurlow Weed commented wryly, 'There is a fable, I believe, of a fox who, having lost his own tail, persuaded his friends that tails were quite useless. England has got to the end of protection, and is now endeavouring to persuade America, a nation that possesses, like England, all the elements required for manufacturing independence, that as she can manufacture for us, we should abandon the protective policy. She does not tell us, however, that when, deluded by the popular theory of Free Trade, we shall have withdrawn the pressure of American competition, John Bull, generous as he is, will consult his own rather than our interests, in his prices.' Weed (1884), p. 202.
42. Speech of 12 April 1933, quoted in Gautenbein (1950), pp. 160-1.
43. LaFeber (1993b), p. 83.
44. Latin American countries had taken one of three positions with respect to the Central Powers by 1918: declaration of war (Brazil, Cuba, Costa Rica, Guatemala, Haiti, Honduras, Nicaragua, Panama); breaking of diplomatic relations (Bolivia, Dominican Republic, Ecuador, Peru, Uruguay); declaration of neutrality (Argentina, Chile, Colombia, Mexico, Paraguay, El Salvador, Venezuela).
45. Only some states declared war on all the Axis powers: Cuba, Haiti, Dominican Republic, Panama, Costa Rica, Honduras, Nicaragua, El Salvador, and Guatemala (all in December 1941); Mexico (May 1942); and Bolivia (April 1943). Some declared war on Germany alone: Brazil (August 1942) and Colombia (November 1943). Ecuador declared war on Japan only (February 1945) and a significant group of countries remained neutral until 1945: Chile, Venezuela, Uruguay (February), and Argentina and Paraguay (March).
46. Hull (1948), p. 1380.

CHAPTER 2

US-LATIN AMERICAN RELATIONS DURING THE COLD WAR AND ITS AFTERMATH

Jorge I. Domínguez

Did the Cold War matter for US-Latin American relations? In many respects, the answer is no. The United States had faced military, political, and economic competition for influence in the Americas from extracontinental powers before the Cold War, just as it did during the Cold War. The United States had pursued ideological objectives in its policy towards Latin America before, during, and after the Cold War. And the pattern of US defence of its economic interests in Latin America was not appreciably different during the Cold War than at previous times. From these singular perspectives, it is difficult to assert that the Cold War was a significantly distinctive period of US-Latin American relations; it looked like 'more of the same'.

Nonetheless, the Cold War emerges as significantly distinctive in US relations with Latin America because ideological considerations acquired a primacy over US policy in the region that they had lacked at earlier moments. From the late 1940s until about 1960, ideology was just one of the important factors in the design of US policy towards Latin America. The victory and consolidation of the Cuban revolutionary government changed that. In its subsequent conduct of the key aspects of its policy towards Latin America, the US government often behaved as if it were under the spell of ideological demons.

Moreover, from the mid-1960s to the end of the Cold War in Europe, this ideologically-driven US policy often exhibited non-logical characteristics. I will argue that US policy was illogical when at least one of two closely related criteria were met: 1) the instruments chosen to implement US policy were extremely costly and certainly disproportionate to the goals that were sought; or 2) the instruments chosen to implement US policy were markedly inappropriate to reach the goals that were sought. These two criteria were often associated with stunning failures of accurate diagnosis of the nature of a problem.[1] (To say that a policy is instrumentally rational need not require that it be applauded, of course; such rationality establishes common grounds for civil disagreement over policy.)[2]

To focus on the most important cases, this chapter concentrates on those instances when the United States promoted or orchestrated an attempt to overthrow a Latin American government or when the United States used military force to seek to achieve its aims. Force is the most potent instrument any state can employ, and the overthrow of other governments is the most intrusive policy one state can pursue against another short of annexation. The President of the United States adopted these decisions to use force; thus at these times the US government was more likely to behave as a 'unified actor'.

I will argue that the United States deployed military force or otherwise sought to overthrow a Latin American government whenever it felt ideologically threatened by the prospects of communism in a Latin American country, and only then. In contrast, the United States did not engage in such actions, even when other Latin American governments acted in ways seriously adverse to US interests, if there was no ideological threat of communism. That is, the active engagement of the Soviet Union in particular cases, or the expropriation of the property of US citizens and firms, did not by themselves trigger a US use of force if the Latin American government that was acting contrary to US preferences signalled credibly that it harboured no hint of association with communism.

The primacy of ideology as the shaping factor in US relations with Latin America vastly increased the likelihood of US military intervention in Latin America even though US goals could have been achieved by other means at much lower cost. Ideological politics led often, consequently, to illogical US actions. This is what made the Cold War distinctive in the Americas.

Explaining the Cold War in the Americas: I

Superpower Competition?
US-Soviet competition was the central feature of the Cold War. The United States and the Soviet Union were the only major powers capable of exerting influence everywhere throughout the world as each sought to 'balance' the other. The predominant scholarly approach for the analysis of competition between major powers has been 'neorealism'. Three fundamental neorealist assumptions have been: 1) that the most important actors in world politics are territorially organised entities called states; 2) that the behaviour of states is substantively and instrumentally rational; and 3) that states seek power, and calculate their interests in terms of power, relative to the nature of the international system that they face, which is marked by the absence of effective centralised international authority, i.e. inter-state anarchy.[3]   Neorealists understand the Cold War everywhere, and certainly in the Americas, as a function of US-Soviet competition.

The most rigorous effort to apply neorealism to US-Latin American relations has been developed by Michael Desch, although he found it necessary to modify several neorealist propositions. Desch argues that the United States had a strategic interest in Latin America only in order to 'prevent an adversary from presenting a wartime, military threat to its ability to defend itself or defend intrinsically valuable areas of the world' (Desch, 1993, p. 137). Under those circumstances, Latin America had considerable 'extrinsic' value to the United States, to employ Desch's terminology; otherwise, Latin America mattered little to the United States.

That analysis implies that the Cold War was not an analytically significant departure in US-Latin American relations. US strategic interests and concerns were not significantly different when the United States faced the Soviet Union, imperial Germany, or Nazi Germany. Indeed, Desch analyses detailed case studies of each of these instances. Secondly, neorealists understand US strategic interests as focused on Mexico and the Caribbean islands: the physically bordering countries and the sea-lanes. Neorealism cannot explain either US preoccupation with Argentina's domestic policies under Juan Perón at and after the end of World War II nor the US anti-communist crusade in Central America and the Caribbean in the 1980s: 'These expansive policies', seeking to influence the internal political structures of these small countries, 'turned out to be not only impractical but also counterproductive' (Desch, 1993, p. 140).

Neorealist scholarship leaves us with several insights. International competition between the United States and a major extra-hemispheric power precedes the Cold War. US concern with the territory of its neighbours and near-neighbours – and the US use of military force – can be understood as an attempt to keep such major powers from exercising power in the Americas. That was as true of the Roosevelt Corollary at the beginning of the 20th century as of the US intervention in Grenada in 1983. As a pre-eminent US scholar of US interventions in the first fifth of the 20th century, Dana Munro, put it: 'What the United States was trying to do [through its military interventions] ...was to put an end to conditions that... [posed] a potential danger to the security of the United States' (Munro, 1964, p. 531). The Cold War as such adds no analytically significant explanation to this form of US behaviour. Neorealism sheds light also on another point: for the most part, the United States did not deploy its military force in South America. Neorealism is a parsimonious and effective guide, therefore, both to the areas of long-standing US concern and to the relative US abstention from the use of force in South America.

And yet, neorealism leaves us with a puzzle. There is too much unexplained US behaviour. It does not suffice to note that US policies towards Perón in the mid-1940s or towards Central America in the 1980s may have been misguided and counterproductive. They did occur and, consequently, neorealism is an insufficient scholarly guide to US relations with the region.

Moreover, both standard neorealism and Desch's partially modified version leave us with a strong prediction: the end of US competition with an extra-hemispheric power is likely to lead to a significant decline in US attention to Latin America, presumably including a decline in the practice of US military intervention (Desch, 1993, p. 149; Desch, 1998). But as the Cold War was barely ending in Europe, the United States invaded Panama militarily to overthrow its government. In 1994, the United States invaded Haiti militarily towards a similar end. And after the Cold War ended in Europe, the United States signed on to the North American Free Trade Agreement (NAFTA) and promoted a hemispheric free trade agreement – a form of economic behaviour neorealists might understand more readily while the US faced an adversarial superpower than when it did not.

In short, neorealism explains well important aspects of continuity in US foreign policy but it leaves unexplained – for the distant past, the present, and the Cold War periods – what it must consider cases of anomalous US behaviour.

Ideological Contest?

The Cold War was also an ideological struggle, not just a contest between superpower 'billiard balls'. US presidents were committed to combat communism, not just the Soviet Union. To that end, some were prepared to 'pay any price, bear any burden'. Others were convinced that the United States faced nothing less than an 'evil empire'. During the Cold War, most US elites and much of the public believed profoundly in the righteousness of their cause and deeply feared and loathed what they understood as communism. This ideology explains US military intervention, direct and indirect, and other belligerent US actions during the Cold War.

And yet, the Cold War did not give birth to the significance of ideological themes either in US foreign policy generally or in US relations with Latin America specifically. The US Declaration of Independence bristles with ideology, and US policy has embodied explicit ideological themes since the proclamation of the Monroe Doctrine. This doctrine is often presented as a statement in the tradition of *Realpolitik* – the first comprehensive statement by a US president consistent with neorealist expectations: the Monroe Doctrine sought to deter European reconquest in the Americas (European powers could retain the colonies they still held). And yet, that reading is a half-truth. The key sentence of President James Monroe's Message to Congress (2 December 1823) features an ideological policy:

> We owe it, therefore, to candour and to the amicable relations existing between the United States and those powers to declare that we should consider any attempt on their part to extend their system to any portion of this hemisphere as dangerous to our peace and safety.[4]

It was not just their power but also their *system*, which was 'essentially different', that Monroe sought to keep away. Monroe's ideological intent was instantly understood by Austrian chancellor von Metternich. The United States, he wrote to his Russian counterpart, had 'distinctly and clearly announced their intention to set not only power against power, but, to express it more exactly, altar against altar'.[5]

The main impediment to the US pursuit of ideological objectives in the 19th century was its relative military weakness. The United States could defeat Mexico, but it could not project its power much beyond. By the late 19th century, the United States was ready to fight European powers for the first time since 1812. On 11 April 1898, President William McKinley explained his justification for declaring war on Spain and for intervening in Cuba:

> First. In the cause of humanity and to put an end to the barbarities, bloodshed, starvation, and horrible miseries now existing there, and which the parties to the conflict are either unable or unwilling to stop or mitigate. It is no answer to say this is all in another country... and

is therefore none of our business. It is especially our duty, for it is right at our door...[6]

Of course, McKinley had other reasons for the declaration of war, but this first reason was no mere fig leaf. Many US citizens joined him in the belief that the United States had this humanitarian *duty*. (This first clause is also an eerie forecast about a possible future in US-Cuban relations.) From the outset, US imperialism was clothed as a moral crusade. The ideological concerns of US foreign policy reached a climax during Woodrow Wilson's presidency. Sustained and systematic intervention in the internal affairs of Mexico, Central American, and Caribbean states marked this epoch of US-Latin American relations.

Thus, it was noteworthy when President Bill Clinton's National Security Adviser, Anthony Lake, proclaimed that the Clinton administration considered itself an example of pragmatic Wilsonianism committed to a policy of 'enlargement' of the areas of democracy worldwide (White House, 1995). These ideological motivations explain, in part, the US military intervention in Haiti in 1994 and some aspects of US policy towards Cuba in the 1990s; recall the names of the key legislation: the 'Cuban Democracy Act' of 1993 and the 'Cuban Liberty and Democratic Solidarity Act' of 1996.

Ideology explains the neorealists' anomalies, namely, US intervention in cases where no competing superpower credibly threatened it. For nearly two centuries the US government has claimed a right to exclude certain 'systems' from the Americas, and during the 20th century it has claimed to know which system ought to prevail throughout the hemisphere. The Cold War was thus not very different from periods that preceded it. Before, during, and after the Cold War, ideological considerations have been front and centre in US policy towards Latin America, even if other considerations have mattered as well. (Franklin Roosevelt's Good Neighbor Policy stands as a brief interlude in an otherwise sustained US commitment to intervene in the domestic affairs of its neighbours.) Neorealist and ideological perspectives agree on one point: the Cold War was but one episode in a long and continuous US policy towards Latin America.

A difficulty with an ideological explanation, however, is that its very timelessness makes it difficult to understand why the US ideological demons are activated and mobilised at particular times. What renders them salient at some times more than at others? US policy towards Latin America, in practice, was not particularly ideological before 1898 and, until the Cold War, ideology was the predominant factor in US policy towards the region only during Woodrow Wilson's first term. We shall return to these issues.

The Defence of Capitalist Rules?
The first successful US overthrow of a Latin American government during the Cold War occurred in Guatemala in 1954. The US Central Intelligence Agency (CIA) orchestrated the process that brought down the constitutional government of President Jacobo Arbenz. One reason for intervention was the perceived need to protect the United Fruit Co. from expropriation. The next US attempt to overthrow

a Latin American government occurred in Cuba; although this one did not succeed, nonetheless US policy was once again motivated, in part, by the commitment to protect the interests of many US citizens and firms from wholesale expropriation.

Tempting though it may seem to understand US policy during the Cold War as an effort to make the Americas safe for capitalism, the historical record does not support it. US military interventions in the Dominican Republic in 1965 and in Grenada in 1983 cannot be understood with reference to the protection of US economic interests. Nor did the United States seek to overthrow every government that expropriated US firms. For example, a military government seized power in Peru in 1968. Over the next several years, it would expropriate many US firms. Instead of overthrowing this government – a government that also purchased a military arsenal from the Soviet Union – the United States patiently negotiated a mutually satisfactory settlement.

Nor does this record with regard to the defence of capitalist interests distinguish well the Cold War years from those that preceded it or those that followed it. True enough, many US interventions in the domestic affairs of its neighbours and near-neighbours in the early 20th century resemble the Guatemala 1954 case; US economic interests were threatened, and the US intervened, among other reasons, to protect them. But the United States dealt with Mexico's expropriation of foreign-owned petroleum firms in 1938 in ways that foreshadowed its dealings thirty years later with the Peruvian military government: after some delay and much diplomatic conflict, a mutually satisfactory settlement was reached. Since the end of the Cold War in Europe, moreover, the US military interventions in Panama in 1989 and in Haiti in 1994 seem unrelated to the defence of economic interests.

A perspective focused on the US defence of the interests of private US firms concurs with the neorealist and ideological analyses on one point: US policy towards Latin America during the Cold War is not markedly different from US policy towards the region before or after the Cold War. On the other hand, whereas both the neorealist and the ideological approaches shed some light on important aspects of US policy towards Latin America, the relationship between US policies to overthrow Latin American governments, on the one hand, and the motivation to protect economic interests, on the other, is weak.

Explaining the Cold War in the Americas: II

The Cold War was a distinctive period in the history of US relations with Latin America for two general and somewhat contradictory reasons. First, the Cold War was the one period in the history of US policy towards Latin America when ideology was repeatedly more important than balance-of-power or economic considerations; at no other moment in that history did ideological considerations so dominate US policy across many presidents from different political parties. Ideology was so overpowering that US policy towards Latin America exhibited marked nonlogical characteristics.

Second, the Cold War was the only moment in the history of US relations with Latin America when a country in this region became a military and political ally of the chief adversary of the United States. Cuba and its foreign policy shaped (and mis-shaped) much of US policy towards the region. Because Cuba was a real adversary, the US government had rational reasons to seek to counter Cuban (and Soviet) influence. Thus, there is a tension between these two distinctive features of the Cold War in the Americas. The illogic of US policy would become evident only when the US response to the 'Cuban threat' went well beyond a reasonable cost-benefit calculation concerning means and ends or when inappropriate means were employed systematically.

The 'Normal' Logic of US Policies towards Latin America

During the first half of the 20th century the key US policies towards Latin America can be understood as rational responses to the opportunities and dangers present in an anarchic international system. The United States acted 1) to gain territory and influence; 2) to exclude rival powers; and 3) to protect and advance the material economic interests of its citizens and firms.

The United States went to war against Spain in 1898 to seize territory; although the humanitarian intervention to stop the carnage during the Cuban war of independence was no doubt an important consideration, it was not the US government's principal concern. The United States seized Panama from Colombia in order to build the canal. Imperialism was, above all, about dominion.

US interventions, military and otherwise, throughout much of the Caribbean and Central America in the early years of the 20th century can be logically understood. At long last capable of enforcing the Monroe Doctrine, the United States sought to keep European powers out of the Americas. The United States intervened to pre-empt rivals from doing so. The background to the Roosevelt Corollary to the Monroe Doctrine was a genuine fear of the prospects of European military deployments in the 'American Mediterranean'. In 1902-3, British, German, and Italian gunboats were deployed off the coasts of Venezuela. They sank three Venezuelan gunboats, blockaded the mouth of the Orinoco river, and bombarded Puerto Cabello. During World War I, Germany systematically though unsuccessfully sought to establish a naval base in the Caribbean, and an alliance with Mexico that culminated in German Foreign Minister Arthur Zimmermann's formal offer to Mexico of a military alliance to reconquer the lost northern territories. Once European military threats eased after World War I, US interventions in Mexico, the Caribbean and Central America were gradually liquidated, paving the way for the Good Neighbor Policy.

These US interventions, and especially the years characterised by what is known as 'dollar diplomacy', were also motivated in part by a desire to promote and defend US economic interests. In many cases, the US government took the lead in luring US firms to invest in Latin American countries. The Good Neighbor Policy also sought to foster US economic interests in the region while, at the political level, it constructed a hemispheric alliance against the Axis powers during World War II.

The only instance when ideology overwhelmed other factors was President Woodrow Wilson's decision in 1914 to authorise a military intervention in Mexico at the port of Veracruz. Neither balance-of-power nor economic considerations explain that outcome. Wilson's policies helped to bring down the government of General Victoriano Huerta, the Mexican leader most favourably disposed towards US investors during the decade of the revolution. The decision to use military force to help shape Mexico's domestic circumstances reveals nonlogical features: those means could not have reached the hoped-for goal, while the US military action was wholly disproportionate to Mexican provocations (Quirk 1962). Even Woodrow Wilson came to terms with the Mexican revolutionary government as the United States prepared to enter World War I; ideology and the pursuit of Pancho Villa were sacrificed in 1917 in order not to drive Mexico into a war alliance with imperial Germany.

During the Cold War, US actions against Fidel Castro's government in Cuba were motivated by the Cuban-Soviet alliance and by Cuba's expropriation of US economic interests. Arguably, some US policies in 1959 and 1960 made a difficult situation worse, but the Cuban revolutionary government's decisions in international and domestic affairs stemmed from its own volition.[7] Fidel Castro was not pushed into the arms of the Soviet Union; he took the lead.[8] US policies to prevent or reverse Soviet military deployments to Cuba, Cuban military deployments to other countries, Cuban military and financial support of revolutionary movements elsewhere, and Cuban actions against the property of US citizens and firms can be readily justified rationally even if one may differ with specific policies. Most US policies towards Cuba were not disproportionate; US coercive measures were also appropriate given the nature of Cuban government actions. In time, the US government also behaved rationally when it curtailed its trade embargo policies (in 1975) so as not to impinge on third countries and when it reached bilateral agreements with Cuba over migration and air piracy, among others. (US government-sponsored terrorism against Cuba in the 1960s was counterproductive and, in my view, both illogical and immoral, however.)

In response to Cuban support for insurgencies in various Latin American countries, other aspects of US policy were also rational and cost-effective: there was a plausible relationship between the means used and the ends pursued. For example, the United States supported Venezuela's demand for collective inter-American sanctions on Cuba in retaliation for Cuban support for insurgent forces in Venezuela and the landing of Cuban military personnel in Venezuela. Such actions enlisted Latin American support for what was already US policy towards Cuba. Similarly, US counterinsurgency training, finance and equipment for the Bolivian army to defeat Ernesto (Che) Guevara's expedition to Bolivia was also cost-effective; with modest US effort and expenditure, this policy contributed significantly to the failure of Cuba's policy to support revolutions in South America.

In short, most US policies towards Latin America related to the use of force before the Cold War and some such US policies during the Cold War were quite logical. They reflect the rational behaviour of a major power in an anarchic international system seeking territory, influence, the exclusion of its rivals from its zones of influence, and the protection of the economic interests of its citizens.

The Persistent Illogic of US Policy towards Latin America

Cuba's alliance with the Soviet Union, and its capacity to survive a no-holds-barred US effort to bring down Fidel Castro's government, traumatised US policy towards Latin America, however.   The United States came to exaggerate systematically the nature of the threat to its interests and began to incur costs well beyond what rational calculations of the relationship between ends and means would suggest.

In some cases, just an ideological whiff of communism triggered US actions that were premature, excessive, or very costly. In many instances of US over-reaction, the Soviet Union was either wholly uninvolved or only marginally so. Also in many instances there was either no threat to US economic interests and no means of advancing them, or there were clearly less costly ways to protect US economic interests well short of military intervention or other efforts to bring down a Latin American government.

During the Cold War and before the Cuban revolution, there was already one case of the dominance of ideology in US policy: the overthrow of President Jacobo Arbenz's government in Guatemala.   US actions to overthrow the Arbenz government were motivated principally by the interest in preventing any government in the Americas from developing an *entente* with the Soviet Union and by concern for United Fruit's interests. The means chosen to overthrow Arbenz were cost-effective: no US troops were employed and little CIA money was spent. On the other hand, Guatemalan relations with the Soviet Union and Eastern European communist countries were incipient at best, and in part understood as Guatemala's defensive response to US hostility. The Guatemalan communist party was weak. The United States greatly exaggerated the import of Soviet-Guatemalan relations though it did not exaggerate the threat to United Fruit; on the other hand, the United States made no serious attempt to pursue negotiations as an alternative to the use of force. Anti-communist ideological concerns no doubt were the key motivating factor. US means were disproportionate and inappropriate for the goals at stake.

The significance of the ideological factor in the Guatemalan case is clearer through a comparison to nearly coterminous events in Bolivia. The 1952 Bolivian revolution expropriated the tin companies, the largest of which was incorporated in the United States and had important US investors. The US government accepted a negotiated settlement to compensate for the expropriation of the tin mines; over the course of a decade, the companies received approximately one-third of what they claimed was their due (Krasner, 1978, pp. 282-5).

The United States had no fear of communism in the Bolivian case and was, therefore, capable of advancing its interests quite rationally.   The principal difference to the very same Eisenhower administration between the Guatemalan and Bolivian cases was the ideological 'threat of communism' in Guatemala and its absence in Bolivia.   Without such ideological fear, the United States and

Guatemala might have reached a comparable property settlement.

On 28 April 1965, the United States intervened militarily in the Dominican Republic, eventually deploying 23,000 US soldiers ashore. They were the first combat-ready US forces to enter a Latin American country in almost forty years. As Abraham Lowenthal (1972, p. 153) well put it: 'The US government's preoccupation with avoiding a "second Cuba" had structured the way American officials looked at the Dominican Republic throughout the early 1960s.' Although accidents and other motivations were an important part of this story, President Lyndon Johnson and his closest advisers believed above all that a 'second Cuba' was simply unacceptable. It turned out that there was no 'second Cuba' in the making. The Soviet Union was wholly uninvolved and Cuba was involved only trivially. There was no threat to US economic interests which, in any event, were not sizeable. The US response was illogical: the United States deployed massive force to ward off a threat that did not exist.

On 4 September 1970, Salvador Allende won a plurality of the votes in Chile's presidential elections. His Popular Unity coalition was led by the socialist and communist parties. Eleven days later President Richard Nixon instructed CIA Director Richard Helms to 'leave no stone unturned... to block Allende's confirmation' as President.[9] The CIA instigated a coup to block the constitutional process. Thus, the United States attempted to subvert Chilean democracy out of the ideological fear that an Allende government might become a second Cuba, too.

During the nearly three years of Allende's presidency, the United States deployed a broad panoply of overt and covert policies against it.[10] It was reasonable for the United States to oppose the uncompensated Chilean expropriation of US firms, but these expropriations did not require Allende's overthrow. Rather, a settlement could have been reached through negotiations, as a settlement would be reached in the nearly coterminous case of Peru (see below). Allende's foreign policy had strong pragmatic elements.[11] It was reasonable to expect that Allende's government would settle the two most contentious expropriation cases (copper and telephone) in part because it already had been negotiating many more compensation cases than the Peruvian government had at the same time (Blasier, 1985, pp. 258-70).

Nor did the United States have reason for fearing Soviet-Chilean relations. The Soviet Union dealt with Allende's Chile within the same broad framework for its relations with other Latin American governments that did *not* become the object of such US policies (Blasier, 1987, pp. 38-41). The Soviet Union did not subsidise Chilean imports or exports, did not provide free military equipment, did not absorb huge bilateral trade deficits, and did not become an important factor in Chilean international economic relations – all in contrast to Soviet policies towards Cuba. The nature of the Soviet-Chilean relationship could hardly justify US policies towards Allende's Chile. The intense US opposition to Allende's election and government derived principally from ideological fears; the means chosen to address those fears were disproportionate and inappropriate.

As with the comparison between Guatemala and Bolivia in the early 1950s, so too the ideological character of US policy towards Chile can be better understood by examining a parallel case where a Latin American government gave comparable provocation to the US government but the very same Nixon administration chose the path of negotiation, not overthrow. The Peruvian government of General Juan Velasco Alvarado had much more extensive military relations with the Soviet Union than Allende's Chile ever did. In 1972, Peru purchased 250 T-55 tanks from the Soviet Union and, in the years that followed, it would go on to purchase supersonic fighter bombers, helicopters and more tanks. Hundreds of Soviet military trainers were deployed to Peru. In the mid-1970s, Peru accounted for one-fifth of Latin America's total arms imports; about half of Peru's military imports came from the USSR (Berríos, 1989). Peru also expropriated a large number of US firms during the first half of the 1970s; Peru's hard-line stance against compensation for the International Petroleum Company was as tough as the Allende government's position with regard to the copper and telephone sectors. As noted above, by the time of Allende's overthrow in 1973, Peru had negotiated fewer compensation agreements than had Chile (in part because the Peruvian government had expropriated fewer US firms than Chile had). On the objective merits of these cases, Peru posed a greater threat to US interests. And yet the Peruvian military government, albeit radical in a number of its social and economic policies, never 'smelled' communist. The US government did not fear the Peruvian government ideologically and it was, therefore, quite ready to bargain with it. In 1974, the United States and Peru reached a satisfactory comprehensive settlement of the expropriation disputes, while the United States chose to tolerate the Soviet-Peruvian military relationship. If it had not been for the ideological demons, US policy toward Chile might have been the same.

Ronald Reagan's policy towards Nicaragua in the 1980s underscored again the centrality of ideology for US policy towards the region. President Reagan's closest advisers were willing to break the law to supply weapons to the Nicaraguan Resistance (better known as the contras) despite the explicit prohibition of such actions by the US Congress (Tower Commission, 1987). In putting the president at risk of impeachment, they revealed how important they thought Central America was for US policy.

Reagan himself devoted perhaps more time and gave more speeches on Nicaragua than on any other single issue of foreign policy during his second term. The President escalated his rhetorical commitment to the cause of overthrowing Nicaragua's Sandinista government. In April 1983, Reagan addressed a special joint session of Congress to defend his Central American policy: 'If Central America were to fall, what would be the consequences for our position in Asia, Europe, and for alliances such as NATO? If the United States cannot respond to a threat near our own borders, why should Europeans or Asians believe that we are seriously concerned about threats to them?' In Lars Schoultz's apt phrase, this rhetoric was the 'ultimate simplification' – the results of transforming an ideological faith into the test of credibility for the United States worldwide.[12] And in his 1985 State of the Union address, President Reagan argued that support for 'freedom fighters', such as the contras, was 'self-defence' required to enable Nicaraguans to 'defy Soviet-supported aggression and secure rights which have been ours from birth'. Days later, Reagan defined his policy more briefly. His support for the contras would stop when the Sandinistas 'say uncle'.[13]

Nicaragua's Sandinista government expropriated property belonging to the Somoza family and its associates, and also some property belonging to wealthy Nicaraguans. There was, however, relatively little US direct foreign investment in Nicaragua and most of it remained unaffected by expropriation policies. The US government had two reasons for concern about Sandinista policies. The first was Nicaragua's relations with the Soviet Union. The second was Nicaragua's support for revolutionaries in El Salvador.

The Soviet Union and other Eastern European governments delivered significant military assistance to the Sandinista government, including tanks, armed transport vehicles, rocket launchers and armed helicopters. (On the other hand, the Soviet Union did not offer security guarantees or a military alliance to Nicaragua; it did not supply weapons that could have been readily used for offensive purposes beyond Nicaragua's borders, such as MiG fighter aircraft; many of the tanks supplied were quite heavy, useful to intimidate opponents but not readily manoeuvrable in Central America's rugged tropical terrain.) The Soviets and the East Europeans also supplied significant financing for Nicaraguan international economic transactions.

Nicaragua and Cuba helped the Salvadorean revolutionaries. They provided save havens where those revolutionaries could rest, recover from wounds, and train. They permitted the revolutionaries to store large caches of weapons. Certainly in 1980-81, both Nicaragua and Cuba supplied significant military assistance to the Salvadorean revolutionaries (Blasier, 1987, pp. 144-53). Cuba would continue to supply material assistance to the Salvadorean insurgency until 1991 (*Granma,* 18 June 1991, p. 8).

It was rational for the United States, therefore, to support the government of El Salvador politically, economically, and militarily to defend itself. It was rational for the United States to act coercively towards Nicaragua to prevent its international aggression and to increase the cost to the Soviet Union of continuing with its military assistance.[14] But it would have been much more cost-effective for the United States to have pursued simultaneously a strategy of serious negotiation to achieve those same ends. Such a strategy was readily available. It would have addressed all major US concerns, but it would have left the Sandinista government in power in Nicaragua – an outcome that the Reagan administration was simply unprepared to accept ideologically.

Instead, the Reagan administration systematically opposed and undercut the various attempts at negotiations, either under the auspices of the so-called Contadora Initiative (organised by Colombia, Mexico, Panama and Venezuela) or under the later Arias Plan or Esquipulas Plan (inspired by Costa Rican President Oscar Arias and organised by the Central American presidents). The Reagan administration also opposed negotiations within El Salvador to settle the internal war (Carothers, 1991, pp. 86-92). The ideologically driven US policies prolonged the wars in Central America and increased their cost to the people of the region and to the United States. US policy was illogical.

Peace came to Nicaragua and El Salvador only with the end of the Cold War in Europe. The Bush administration, ably led by Assistant Secretary of State for Inter-American Affairs Bernard Aronson, negotiated directly with the Nicaraguan government in 1989 (paving the way for the 1990 elections that the Sandinistas lost) and subsequently played a decisive role in facilitating the internal negotiations within El Salvador. The Bush administration was prepared to accept a Sandinista government in Nicaragua or a government of the left in El Salvador if they were to win the elections – the outcome the Reagan administration always rejected ideologically. But this highly rational and successful outcome belongs to the post-Cold War period.

The 1983 US intervention in Grenada exemplifies US ideologically driven policies as well. The New Jewel Movement (in power between 1979 and 1983) did not threaten US economic interests. On the contrary, Grenada's economic growth depended on promoting tourism from the United States. To that end, Grenada had contracted with Cuba for the construction of an airport. The Reagan administration portrayed that airport as a serious strategic menace even though its configuration was what would be expected from its ostensible purposes (after the US invasion, the United States completed the airport).

The New Jewel Movement was, indeed, a communist party. It sought close relations with the Soviet Union and Cuba. It received military and financial support from both, although that support was modest. Grenada lacked naval or air forces to project military power. It had not intervened in the domestic politics of neighbouring countries; it had correct state-to-state relations with its neighbours. After the US invasion of Grenada in October 1983, US troops captured important Grenadan documents that demonstrated the extremely limited support that the Soviets were giving to Grenada. At the time of the US invasion, there were 784 Cubans working in Grenada; of these, 636 were construction workers (Domínguez, 1989, pp. 162-71).

The US intervention in Grenada was, therefore, a costly, massive deployment of US force to kill a threat that existed only in ideological terms. The US government saw red in Grenada, and it charged ahead.

Implications for the Post-Cold War Period

There are at least three legacies from the Cold War years for the period since the end of the Cold War in Europe. They are the tendency of US policy to rely on force and coercion; the transformation (but not disappearance) of ideological policies; and the policy towards Cuba.

From the mid-1920s to the mid-1960s, US combat troops did not enter a Latin American country to occupy its territory or overthrow its government. As part of its ideological crusade against communism in the Americas, however, the United States deployed its own troops to the Dominican Republic and Grenada and waged a sustained war on Sandinista Nicaragua. US forces were deployed throughout the region in counter-insurgency operations. Each of these operations was a military success. And at the end of each episode of the use of military force, the Latin American government was friendlier towards the United States. This was true in counter-insurgency operations in the 1960s, in the invasions of Grenada and the Dominican Republic, and in the electoral defeat of the Sandinistas. More expansively, the invasions of the Dominican Republic and Grenada would be credited with establishing the bases for enduring democratic rule in each country. (In fact, the Dominican Republic's democratic experience owes much more to events well after, and apart from, the US invasion; the US invasion restored power to those closer to the country's authoritarian past. The argument that the US invasion contributed to democracy in Grenada is stronger because the invasion destroyed the New Jewel Movement's military power. In neither case, however, was the establishment of democracy a reason for the invasion.) As a result, US officials acquired the habit of thinking that military force was an appropriate instrument for frequent use in the region.

Since the end of the Cold War in Europe, the United States militarised those aspects of its policy towards drug-trafficking that dealt with drug interception in source countries. The main resistance to such militarisation came from US military officials. US government civilians, however, embraced the use of military instruments much more readily (Council on Foreign Relations, 1997).

In December 1989, President Bush ordered a military invasion of Panama to overthrow its government, accused of participating in drug trafficking. The restoration of democracy to Panama was also cited as a goal of the US invasion. In the years that followed, not much progress was made towards ending Panama's role in international drug money-laundering – the main role Panama had long had in this international trade. However, the US destruction of the Panamanian military did make a direct and powerful contribution to setting a sounder basis for democracy in Panama.

In September 1994 President Clinton ordered the US military to occupy Haiti and overthrow its government. The US government sought to create more manageable circumstances to cope with the flow of undocumented Haitians to the United States; having established a constitutional government in Haiti, the United States could then refuse to accept refugees or asylum-seekers from Haiti. Nonetheless, the establishment of constitutional government in Haiti was itself an important goal of the US military action.

In each of these two cases, a plausible counter-factual case can be made that more cost-effective means might have been employed. In the case of Panama, the United States lost patience with multilateral efforts and with bilateral negotiations that had a reasonable chance of success in inducing General Manuel Noriega's departure from power. In the case of Haiti, the Clinton administration in 1993 had achieved a negotiated solution to the crisis; only the White House's own ineptitude sabotaged the settlement and required, in the end, the massive military deployment one year later.

These counter-factuals are somewhat less persuasive, however, than those mentioned earlier for the Cold War years. A negotiated solution in Panama in 1989 or in the early 1990s would not have destroyed the Panamanian Defense

Force. And yet the destruction of this military force is almost certainly an essential basis for constructing democracy in Panama in the 1990s and beyond. Similarly, a negotiated solution in Haiti in 1993 would not have weakened the military power structure as much as did the 1994 invasion; the extended international police and military presence in Haiti following the 1994 invasion were necessary to give constitutional government a chance. Thus, troubling as the tendency to use force may be, a stronger case can be made for the period since the end of the Cold War in Europe than for the years of the Cold War: in the 1990s, at long last, the use of military force turned out to be *appropriate* in important respects to the achievement of the ideological goal of fostering democracy – a goal that was part of the explicit rationale for the invasion – even if the use of such considerable military force could probably have been avoided to reach other reasonable US objectives.

These reflections suggest, in turn, both the persistence and the transformation of US ideological objectives in its relations with Latin America. The United States has come to value the defence and promotion of democracy as a significant foreign policy objective. This transformation began already during the Cold War in the US Congress and during the Carter presidency. It acquired broad bipartisan support only when the Reagan administration endorsed the promotion of democracy as a key objective during its second term (Carothers, 1991).

Beyond the invasions of Panama and Haiti, the United States has invested considerable effort and substantial diplomatic resources to defend democratic institutions in Peru, Guatemala, and Paraguay either to mitigate the effects of a coup (the Peruvian case) or to prevent the coup altogether in the two other instances. In each of these cases the United States has chosen to act in concert with other Latin American governments, often – though not exclusively – through the Organisation of American States. The Clinton administration also sought the UN Security Council's prior authorisation for its military occupation of Haiti – the first time ever that a US government had requested prior multilateral endorsement for its use of military force in the Americas (Vaky and Muñoz, 1993; Valenzuela, 1997).

If these trends persist, then the Monroe Doctrine would be transformed into a multilateral instrument though, interestingly, not repealed. The key difference is that, as the 20th century ends, nearly all the countries of the Americas believe in their collective right to intervene in the domestic affairs of any American state where democracy is threatened.

The third legacy of the Cold War is the persisting conflict between Cuba and the United States – the reason why this chapter has insisted that the phrase 'end of the Cold War' always be modified by 'in Europe'. The objectives of a rational US policy towards Cuba have been reached, and the United States could declare victory. The Soviet-Cuban alliance has ended and the new Russian Federation has withdrawn its troops from Cuba and suspended all subsidies to Cuba. Cuba has repatriated all its troops from Angola, Ethiopia and Nicaragua, and smaller missions from other countries. Cuba has terminated its military assistance to revolutionary movements. And its government has changed policy to welcome direct foreign investment.

Instead, the US government in the 1990s – unthreatened by any other power or by the Cuban government itself – embarked on a crusade to overthrow the Cuban government. It did so through legislation (the Cuban Democracy Act, most closely associated with then US Representative Robert Torricelli, and the Cuban Liberty and Democratic Solidarity Act, better known as the Helms-Burton Act) to impose US policies on its main allies and trading partners, flouting international trade practices and its own past opposition to secondary trade boycotts. The new policies assisted the much-weakened Castro government to rally nationalist support. These new US policies were costly to US foreign policy generally and counterproductive for the new US goals of democratising Cuba. In the last act of the Cold War, the United States at long last adopted illogical policies towards Cuba.

Conclusions

US relations with Latin America during the Cold War exhibited important continuities with preceding US policies. The Cold War years proved distinctive, however, because anti-communist ideological objectives overwhelmed other US foreign policy goals towards Latin America in each and every case when the United States chose to deploy its military forces or chose to overthrow a Latin American government through some other means. (The only exception was the assassination of the Dominican Republic dictator Rafael Trujillo in 1961.)

The most likely reason for this behaviour is found in the politics of decision making. From the perspective of a policy-maker, the price for failing to stop a defeat is much higher than the price for over-reacting and incurring higher costs.[15] The price for failing to stop a defeat is paid by the policy-maker; the price for incurring higher costs is paid 'only' by taxpayers and soldiers. Thus, arguments about proportionate means and costs apply principally to the foreign policy of the United States as a state, but much less so to the actions of individual foreign policy-makers.

When the ideological fear of communism was absent, the United States did not deploy its military forces nor seek to overthrow Latin American governments that expropriated a great many US firms (as had revolutionary Bolivia, and Peru under General Velasco). The difference between Bolivia and Guatemala and Peru and Chile was not expropriation, but the whiff of communism in Guatemala and Chile; otherwise the offending behaviour was quite similar. Since there was no ideological fear of communism, the United States did not seek to topple General Velasco's government in Peru even though it developed the closest military relationship with the Soviet Union that any Latin American government other than Cuba had attempted to that date. The United States had greater reason to be alarmed by Velasco's Peru than by Allende's Chile, but the latter, and only the latter, raised the ideological fear of communism. Since the fear of communism was present in this case, the United States invaded the Dominican Republic even though there was no threat to US economic interests and no Soviet or Cuban involvement, and it sought to overthrow Chile's constitutional order even before Salvador Allende had a chance to do anything.

A spectre haunted the United States. It was the spectre of communism anywhere in the Americas. Every US president during the Cold War fervently believed in that opening boast from *The Communist Manifesto* as if Marx and Engels had had the Guatemalan highlands and the Chilean lake region in mind when they wrote it. That ideological fever was more dangerous than the behaviour of the rival superpower, more frightening than property expropriation. Peru's many expropriations and its relations with the Soviet Union, and Bolivia's expropriation of the tin mines, could be tolerated so long as their governments knew, as Metternich had forewarned, before which altar they should kneel.

So powerful was the Cold War that its legacies of militarisation and ideology endure, even if the latter is being transformed in the 1990s in constructive ways. The Cold War's ideological demons are making their own last stand in the new US government zealotry towards Cuba. Could the following text be used to justify US military intervention in Cuba in the years ahead?

> The present condition of affairs in Cuba is a constant menace to our peace and entails upon this Government an enormous expense...
> [Given] the expeditions of filibustering that we are powerless to prevent altogether, and the irritating questions and entanglements thus arising – all these and others that I need not mention, with the resulting strained relations, are a constant menace to our peace and compel us to keep on a semi war footing with a nation with which we are at peace.
>
> President William McKinley
> 11 April 1898[16]

Notes

1. These ideas first occurred to me years ago upon reading Krasner (1978).
2. My approach does not question the rationality or worth of the 'grand' values or goals of US policy over time. Were one to question such values and goals, then the case for the illogicality of much of US policy becomes stronger.
3. The preeminent neorealist scholar has been Kenneth Waltz (1979). For discussion, see also Grieco (1995, p. 27), and Keohane (1983, p. 507).
4. Quoted in Perkins (1963, pp. 56-57).
5. Quoted in Perkins (1963, p. 392).
6. Text in Richardson (1898, pp. 10:139 and ff.).
7. For a thoughtful examination of alternative hypotheses, see Welch (1985).
8. See the memoirs of the first Soviet envoy to Cuba, Alexeev (1984).

9. See the analysis and memoirs by Nathaniel Davis (1985), US Ambassador to Chile (1971-73). Quotation from page 7. Confirmation was required by the Chilean Congress because Allende did not win a majority of votes cast.
10. For a discussion of the magnitude and nature of US actions, see US House of Representatives (1975) and Davis (1985, chap. 12).
11. See, for example, Fortín (1975). Fortín was the last Ambassador-designate from Chile to the United States in the Allende government.
12. Both quoted passages from Schoultz (1987, pp. 269-70).
13. Quoted in Pastor (1987, p. 250).
14. The most intelligent scholarly defence of Reagan administration policy towards Central America was Ronfeldt's (1983).
15. I am grateful to Laurence Whitehead for bringing this point to my attention.
16. Text in Richardson (1898, pp. 10;139 and ff.).

CHAPTER 3

THE EUROPEAN UNION AND THE AMERICAS

Laurence Whitehead

The Post-Cold War Context

Many old illusions were dispelled a decade ago, when the Berlin Wall came down. The way was cleared for new projects to emerge, and perhaps for new illusions as well (Ruggie, 1996.) The universal and irreversible triumph of liberal pluralism and market economics was no doubt the most euphoric of these anticipations. Some Anglo-Saxon elites were especially attracted to this message, but it was not necessary to swallow the complete vision in order to be energised by its enthusiasm. In fact, if we now look back on what has been achieved since 1989, adopting the perspective of a decision-maker, in say New York or Los Angeles, it would be difficult not to experience a sense of vindication, and a degree of confidence that history can be moved in a desired direction. Of course, the record of accomplishments is still patchy, and no doubt the cautious will still guard against over-confident extrapolations. But, by and large, for the United States and its closest friends around the world, international liberalism does indeed seem to have occupied much of the social space hitherto pre-empted by the gridlock of the Cold War. Even though the eventual outcome may be no final end of history, even if new threats and alternative dangers are all too likely to surface, the 1990s have been a good decade for Washington; for the USA; for international investment; for liberal democracy; and for a US-led, originally western, but now global alliance. The gains made since 1989 will not lightly be surrendered. Both the geostrategic/geoeconomic benefits, and the more subjective psychological (they used to be called ideological) advances of this period seem likely to prove cumulative. As yet, at least, no equivalent backlash or counter-current has emerged that seems capable of turning back these successes from without. If the current USA-led liberalising impulse does eventually stall or reverse, it will most probably be due more to inner contradictions than to outer resistance. For example, the financial crisis in East Asia that began in 1997 seems to owe more to the former than to the latter.

In the case of the European Community (EC) the dismantling of the Berlin Wall in 1989 breathed new life into a fairly old project. At a stroke it enlarged the Europe of the Twelve, by reunifying Germany. Further enlargement necessarily followed. Austria, Finland, and Sweden turned the twelve into fifteen,[1] and in July 1997 the European Commission recommended opening accession negotiations with a further six candidates for membership (Cyprus, the Czech Republic, Estonia, Hungary, Poland and Slovenia). A second tier of potential members was also identified for later consideration (Bulgaria, Latvia, Lithuania, Romania and Slovakia). Thus, forty years after the original six founding members signed the Treaty of Rome in 1957, the European Union has expanded throughout western Europe (incorporating former anti-communist dictatorships of southern Europe), and seems well on the way to adding large slices of ex-communist central and eastern Europe as well.

This 'widening' was just one facet of a broader regional integration project, which also involved both economic and political convergence, and which would necessarily alter the profile of European influence in the global arena (Redmond and Rosenthal, 1997). This recent so-called 'deepening' of European integration can be traced back long before 1989, but there is no doubt that both its timing and its content were significantly shaped by the new opportunities arising from the ending of the Cold War (Laurent and Maresceau, 1998). On the economic front, the twelve[2] had already committed themselves to create a 'single European market' by the end of 1992 (understood to mean the free movement of goods, services, people and capital throughout the Union).[3] The Maastricht Treaty, ratified in 1992, added a further economic objective – economic and monetary union – and by May 1998 it had been agreed that eleven of the fifteen would create a single currency, regulated by a European Central Bank.[4] The new currency, the euro, was launched on 1 January 1999, and mid-2002 is the point at which the separate national currencies must cease to exist.

Inevitably these steps towards economic union will require closer co-ordination of a wide range of policy areas that had hitherto been regarded as purely national prerogatives. In fact, Maastricht has turned the 'Community' into a 'Union' (albeit still of national states) with consequences that are profoundly political as well as economic. Thus at the same time as they prepare for eastern enlargement and for the enthronement of the euro the fifteen have also felt obliged to negotiate over a new treaty of closer political union. With a wider and more heterogeneous membership and an accumulation of policy commitments, the European Union (EU) will inevitably have to streamline its decision-making processes. As the Amsterdam summit of June 1997 underlined, huge dilemmas lie immediately ahead. The vision of an 'ever-closer' political union has yet to be converted into a detailed and workable project that will command the allegiance of all the different constituencies and peoples whose interests are supposed to be represented and harmonised by the EU. This is not the place to dwell on the many divisive internal choices to be made (e.g. concerning the Common Agricultural Policy, the cohesion funds, the democratic deficit, the locus of executive power, the powers of the European court). It must suffice to note that until all these unresolved issues of widening, deepening, and converging have been clarified, the rest of the world cannot very reliably assess what kind of European Union they will be dealing with in the 21st century (Piening, 1997). Nor can the Europeans be expected to focus their energies on how to project their influence to the world as a whole, before they have settled their own still uncertain issues of identity and internal organisation (Rhodes, 1998).

Thus, whereas the ending of the Cold War inaugurated a period of enhanced self-confidence and forward momentum in the United States, the consequences for Europe were more contradictory and multi-dimensional. The continent's pre-existing liberal integration project was certainly reinvigorated, and the EU's basic alignment with the USA was reaffirmed. However, for Europe the issue was not simply to proceed as before, but with renewed optimism. Instead it was to reconfigure for a radically changed environment, to embark upon a huge new venture with no assurance as to the outcome, and to reinvent a Europe far different from anything yet known to the peoples of the Old World. Viewed from Washington, the collapse of the Soviet bloc was vindication and an opportunity to move ahead on a largely preordained path. Viewed from Europe it was more of a shock to the system, and opened the way for a somewhat unpredictable *fuite en avant*.

In the case of Latin America, the strongest impulse transmitted from Berlin in 1989 was undoubtedly the boost it gave to Washington's power, prestige and ideological leadership in the Americas. However, whereas for the USA this boost was an unqualified advantage, in Latin America the reception was inevitably a little more mixed. Obviously Castro in Cuba and the Sandinistas in Nicaragua suffered a devastating setback. But conservative military establishments were also disconcerted, as were various strands of nationalist opinion, and significant components of the sub-continent's cultural elites. For the most part such undercurrents were fairly subdued, not least because – after a decade of debt crisis – many illusions of regional autonomy had been shed. If the USA had won the Cold War, then at least the victor was a prosperous and liberal neighbour, and most Latin Americans with any influence in their respective societies were at least willing to express goodwill provided any contortions required were not too undignified. Many (especially the latest cohort of recent graduates from US schools and universities) were much more positive than that. A post-Cold War Latin America might be post-ideological, open for business, and ready to reward those in tune with the North American way to conjugate democracy and markets. From this viewpoint the Brady Plan,[5] NAFTA (see Chapter 5), and the Free Trade Area of the Americas (see Chapter 4) all look very reassuring. They suggest that an empowered USA might be positively beneficial for all those in Latin America who know how to adapt to a more liberal international environment. However, the 1995 decertification of Colombia (see Chapter 10), the 1996 Helms-Burton Act (see Chapter 11), and the 1997 denial of 'fast-track' trade negotiating authority to the Clinton administration have had a sobering effect. They have served as reminders of the constraints that are liable to accompany such an asymmetrical partnership.

Balancing all these considerations, the dominant Latin American view has clearly been that there is more to gain than to lose from co-operating with Washington in these post-Cold War conditions, and that moreover one might as well make the best of it, given the absence of any realistic alternatives. This broadly liberal internationalist external orientation has been underpinned by a succession of developments *within* the region that point in the same direction. For example, big business has been restructured in an outward-looking direction, thanks to liberalisation, privatisation and the inflow of foreign investment. The civilian political class has benefited from region-wide democratisation, as have most professional occupations and the main cultural elites. When given the choice to turn away from liberalisation, the electorate has typically preferred to endorse policies of cautious reformism. From within the region have emerged a variety of intergovernmental initiatives (such as the Rio Group, and MERCOSUR[6]) that broadly complement US-led liberalisation plans. To some extent they may also even compete with them, generating a more local sense of ownership of these processes.

Thus, whereas the ending of the Cold War enhanced US self-confidence, and precipitated Europe into a *fuite en avant*, the impact on Latin America was neither so uplifting as in the first case, nor so disturbing as in the second. For those who are broadly accustomed to living within Washington's proximate sphere of regional influence, a confident and expansive USA is no doubt preferable to living with a paranoid or defensive hegemon. Nevertheless there is a long Latin American tradition of seeking some external counterweight to the overwhelming presence of their northern neighbour. For good or for ill, during the Cold War it was the Soviet bloc that provided the most radical and durable international alternative. Since 1989 a big question for the sub-continent has been whether the eclipse of this alternative has left Washington in sole possession of the stage, or whether some other at least partial and intermittent counterweights might become available. The most obvious candidate for this role, of course, is the emerging and enlarging European Union. The accession of Spain and Portugal in 1986 strengthened Europe's role as a supporter of democratisation in Latin America (O'Donnell, Schmitter and Whitehead, 1986); and European integration also provided encouragement for Latin America's latest efforts in the same direction (Smith, 1993). On such topics as extra-territoriality, the social character of democracy, and the need to guard against the excesses of Anglo-Saxon market capitalism, Latin America and Europe may find some common ground. But whereas the Soviet alternative to the US was far too drastic, European social democracy could well prove too tame.

This chapter investigates such topics. It surveys the development of EU-Latin American relations in the 1990s and makes a provisional attempt to assess the medium term potential of this option in a liberalised post-Cold War setting. Prospective surveys of this kind are always risky, since they may easily be overtaken by unforeseeable events, and in any case it is difficult to achieve a balanced perspective on issues of immediate controversy. In this case these risks are exacerbated by two specific considerations. The European integration process is gathering momentum and thus generating internal tensions that make its external profile particularly hard to define (Tsoukalis, 1993). At the same time both Europe and Latin America continue to attach the highest priority to their relations with the USA, so that all assessments of the EU-Latin American relationship need to be situated in a triangular, rather than just a bilateral, perspective (Kaufman Purcell, 1995). To handle these difficulties this chapter adopts two successive approaches. The main empirical part (next section) describes a series of specific issues and initiatives that have occupied the energies of European and Latin American policy-makers in the mid- and late-1990s (Leiva, 1997). Although in most cases a relatively clear-cut outcome is beginning to emerge, at the time of writing (late-1998) none of these dossiers have reached final closure. This section therefore provides something of a 'snapshot' of EU-Latin American relations at a particular moment, without necessarily identifying all the underlying dynamics. The third section of this chapter attempts to compensate for this by focusing on the European side of the relationship, and by stepping back from the immediate empirical concerns of section two, to adopt both a more comparative and a more theoretical perspective. The final section outlines some provisional conclusions about the medium-term prospects for EU-Latin American relations.

EU-Latin American Relations from the San José Process to the Rio Summit

The San José Process and Central America
The European Union began life as a regional customs union, and its external relations were initially focused on preferential arrangements for trade with Europe's recent ex-colonies (the Lomé Convention).[7] It was not until the mid-1970s that the European Commission began negotiating co-operation agreements with other 'developing' countries (e.g. with Mexico in 1975), and these early exploratory moves were essentially confined to matters of trade and technical co-operation. The San José Process, which began in the early 1980s, was a major new departure in that it involved high level political mediation, it was long-term and contractual in character, and it committed the community as a collectivity to the promotion of peace and reconstruction in Central America as a sub-region (Roy, 1992). It was explicitly non-discriminatory in character (in contrast to its treatment by the Reagan administration, the legally recognised government of Nicaragua was treated by the EC as a negotiating partner, on the same footing as the other governments of the region), and relied on co-operation and incentives, to the exclusion of coercion, within the confines set by international laws.

This unusual and highly political initiative was undertaken by a joint agreement between all members of the European Community. It was launched at the height of the final phase of Cold War polarisation, and it was targeted on Central America because, after the Sandinista Revolution of 1979 in Nicaragua, the isthmus had become one of the prime arenas of open conflict. It involved annual meetings at foreign minister level between all European states and the five governments of the isthmus, and it embraced political reconciliation, economic reconstruction and regional integration (CEPAL/BID, 1998). It would be too much to claim that this sustained initiative by the Europeans played more than a secondary role in shaping the eventual outcome, but it was a remarkable display of solidarity that did help stabilise the region and scale down the conflict. It materially supported the Central American moderates and their Latin American allies, who designed first the Contadora initiative (see note 6) and then the Esquipulas formula for a regional settlement.[8] It was resolutely at variance with the approach promoted by the Reagan administration, but did not lead to direct conflict with the USA because Washington was quite divided on the issue and Europe was in accord with a substantial body of opinion in the US Congress (Smith, 1995).

Turning to the post-Cold War period, the European Union became the major provider of aid for reconstruction after the peace processes were signed. Central America in the 1990s has received a higher level of European aid *per capita* than any other region of the world. In addition, the high level dialogue institutionalised through the San José Process has continued into the post-conflict period. However, what used to be annual meetings have now become biennial, and the EU has sought to involve a wide array of Non-Governmental Organisations (NGOs) and elements from 'civil society', in order to scale back the emphasis on government-to-government agreements. The EU proceeds by inter-governmental accord and by formal bi-regional agreement, so once it has entered into a commitment it is likely to continue. Nevertheless, as something approaching normality has returned to the isthmus, European priorities have shifted to other trouble spots, and – insofar as they are Latin America focused – to more weighty regions within the sub-continent. As a result, there is surprisingly little recognition, either in Europe or even in Central America, of the extent to which the San José Process has proved one of the EU's most durable and unalloyed successes.

Europe's Banana Regime and the World Trade Organisation (WTO)
The essential background to this convoluted issue is that, just as the USA obtains its bananas from a limited number of small republics (mostly in Central America, but notably including Ecuador), so those European states with possessions or former colonies in the Caribbean have also become locked into long-term supply relationships with small, and highly dependent, Caribbean islands. The nature of the banana trade is important here: the fruit is highly perishable, and must be distributed in bulk to distant northern markets within days of packing. This is a big volume, specialist, enclave industry, which typically links plantation regions with few productive alternatives to high income markets that require a steady and predictable delivery of the fruit.

The EU, in contrast to the USA, receives much of its supplies from relatively high cost sources, and – again unlike the USA – several European consuming nations are also supplied by highly subsidised outlying regions of their own territory (e.g. the Canary Islands, Crete, Guadeloupe, Madeira).[9] If these Caribbean and Mediterranean island suppliers are required to compete on cost and quality with the larger plantations of the Latin American mainland, many of them will face severe contraction or even go out of business altogether. Islands with large numbers of banana workers may not be able to offer alternative forms of employment, and so may have to shed population. Thus, one major concern of EU policy-makers must be to shelter these dependent suppliers from disruptive competition. Another, of course, should be to promote the interests of European banana consumers. The EU is divided between these two objectives, since a majority of the fifteen members have no colonial ties with the Caribbean, and no southern European island suppliers. With the extension of Europe to the post-communist east, a large new population of banana consumers is arising, which will also expect the best quality fruit from the cheapest sources of supply.

Since trade harmonisation was at the heart of the integration process from the beginning, the EU has long taken the lead in designing Europe's banana import regime. The resulting tangle contains many of the vices of the Common Agricultural Policy. Disparate systems of colonial preference were amalgamated into a rigid, bureaucratic, and non-transparent set of arrangements that distort economic incentives and invite clientelism and corruption. By 1993 not only were the European ex-colonies grouped in the Lomé convention (71 African, Caribbean, and Pacific (ACP) nations) benefiting from preferential tariffs and pre-assigned quotas, but in addition importers from the least efficient producers (mostly small islands in the Caribbean) were also obtaining licenses to import bananas at reduced tariffs which could be sold on to more productive competitors. Yet two-thirds of the bananas consumed in Europe come from 'dollar' sources (i.e. Latin American producers) which were of course penalised by this combination of tariffs, quotas and cross subsidies.

With the creation of the Single European Market in 1992[10] and the completion of the Uruguay Round in 1993,[11] conflict over this discrimination against Ecuadorean and Central American suppliers came to a head. Since the European banana market was on the way to becoming the largest in the world, it was critical to Latin America producers whether such discriminatory practices would expand or be curbed. And the creation of the World Trade Organisation gave them a process of appeal and a dispute settlement mechanism that might serve as a lever against a hitherto impervious bureaucracy in Brussels. Thus, the Latin Americans had adequate reasons of their own to go to the WTO, although the impetus came more particularly from Washington. Although the USA grows no bananas, it hosts some very powerful banana producing and trading corporations. Either as a response to their lobbying (and perhaps campaign contributions) or because dismantling European agricultural protectionism is a broader goal of US trade policy, Washington has consistently stiffened the will of the main Latin American producers to challenge the EU through the WTO in Geneva.

In September 1997 a WTO-appointed court ruled against the existing European banana regime. The ruling outlawed tradable licenses, and the EU was forced to accept the need to provide a ten year programme of direct subsidies to the twelve high cost Caribbean island producers who stand to lose most from their abolition. But a dispute remains over the issue of quotas. The court accepted that the EU could maintain a tariff on dollar bananas (thereby upholding the legally enshrined rights of the ACP countries under the Lomé Convention to preserve acquired benefits). But in June 1998 (against the wishes of the Dutch) European farm ministers decided to preserve two separate import quotas (one for ACP, the other for Latin America) in addition to this tariff. The majority of European governments evidently feel that they can go no further towards allowing the forces of competition to do their work, without putting socio-political stability in the eastern Caribbean at risk.[12] They are prepared to risk further challenge at the WTO, perhaps recognising that they would be likely to lose again (since WTO policy is to convert quotas into tariffs), but hoping that in this case the Latin Americans will accept compensation, rather than insist on still further reform. Washington is preparing for a trade war unless Brussels backs down, and it has targeted British and French products for potential retaliation. Whether escalation reaches this extreme, and if it does, whether the United States can keep the Latin American plaintiffs on its side, remains to be seen.

The banana story may seem so specialised and obscure that only specialists need take an interest. Yet its ramifications are extensive. For a substantial number of small countries it concerns a vital national interest. It defines the real content and significance of European policies towards Latin America in a way that contrasts strikingly with much summit-level rhetoric. It highlights the cumbersome processes of European policy-making, and the sub-optimal nature of some of the results. And it confirms that EU-Latin American relations are almost always a triangular affair, with the USA deeply involved here as elsewhere.

The Lomé Convention

Bananas are important, but they are far from being all that matters in the Americas about the Lomé Convention. The present trade and aid pact (Lomé IV) expires in February 2000, but negotiations are already underway to design a successor convention. There is a strong possibility that the existing single agreement linking 15 European countries with 71 ACP nations will eventually be replaced by a series of regional free trade areas. As far as the Caribbean is concerned, although small British, Dutch, and French ex-colonial possessions formed the original heart of the agreement, the economic and demographic balance has now changed. Following the accession of Spain to the EC in 1986, and the flight of the Duvalier clan from Haiti to France, the Dominican Republic and Haiti were added to the list of Lomé members.[13] In the current negotiations, Cuba has also been invited to attend as an observer.

It is at least possible that after 2000 (or more plausibly after 2005) all the main islands of the Caribbean (except Puerto Rico) may be grouped in a new regional association linking them with the EU, conferring some trade and investment benefits, and channelling a political dialogue backed by some co-operation funds. But at present this may seem quite unrealistic, given the fragmentation of European interests in this area, the low priority it generally attracts, and the overwhelming influence exerted on most of the Caribbean by the USA. In addition, many in the Caribbean have expressed strong reservations about the consequences of a divorce from Europe's other, higher profile and perhaps needier, ex-colonies in Africa and the Pacific. There is also serious concern that the EU may lay down highly constraining and inflexible standards of social and political conduct, and then withhold benefits whenever it judges that the region has fallen short of its contractual commitments.

Since the formal negotiations only opened on 30 September 1998, it is not possible to say more at this stage, except to note that in the long run a central issue for the whole region will be the course of developments in Cuba. Although Havana has been conceded observer status at the negotiations, the EU foreign ministers meeting in Luxembourg on 29 June 1998 emphasised that the island's prospects of future membership of Lomé would depend on achieving 'substantial progress' on human rights, good governance and political freedom. Tentative indications are that the existing 71 nation ACP agreement may be extended for one last five-year cycle (to 2005) after which regional free trade agreements will begin to take over, being phased in gradually by perhaps 2015. There might be some enhanced version of the Generalised System of Preferences, probably targeted on the poorest of the ex-colonies, but this remains controversial.

The Helms-Burton Law and Cuba

Since the end of the Cold War, Washington has lifted sanctions against communist-ruled Vietnam, and has developed increasingly warm relations with communist-ruled China.[14] Cuba, however, is required to repudiate communism before the USA will lift the unilateral economic sanctions that were first imposed in the immediate aftermath of the 1959 revolution.[15] In fact, both by the Torricelli Law of 1992 and again by the Helms-Burton Act in 1996, these sanctions have been tightened and their economic and political conditionality has been made more explicit. They have been 'codified' (meaning that it requires an act of Congress, and not just a presidential decision, to vary their terms). On the economic front the restitution of property has been made a *sine qua non* of normalisation, and on the political side Helms-Burton has specified a very precise definition of both the required process and timetable of any democratisation in Cuba, and the substantive content of that outcome.

The European Union never followed the US line on economic sanctions against Castro's Cuba, it never took the same view about the need to reverse the confiscations, and it has never endorsed the highly partisan version of democratisation specified by the US Congress. Indeed, in the early 1990s, under the influence of the Socialist government then in power in Spain, the EU experimented with quite the opposite approach. The goal was still to dismantle the economic and political monopolies enshrined in Cuba's constitution, but through gradualistic reform, reintegration into the international market economy and constructive engagement rather than through confrontation and imposition. In short the EU's approach to Cuba resembled Washington's approach to China and Vietnam.

In 1996, however, this cautious effort hit the buffers. It was set back by three inter-related developments. The González government in Spain was replaced by a conservative administration, under premier Aznar, which initially chose to take a more hard-line stance on Cuba. After the Cuban airforce shot down two small unarmed planes from Miami in February 1996, Clinton signed away much of his discretion over US-Cuba policy by accepting the Helms-Burton legislation. In the wake of these twin gestures of external hostility, the Castro regime battened down the hatches, clearly signalling both to the EU and to domestic dissidents that the 1976 Constitution would not be abandoned while Castro remained in power. Instead of bargaining with Havana over the terms for controlled liberalisation in Cuba, the EU found itself entangled in a battle with Washington over the extraterritorial pretensions of the USA's new sanctions law.

Helms-Burton creates two main instruments through which citizens and corporations outside US jurisdiction may be coerced into conforming with US policy. Title III opens the way to legal action through the US courts against non-US citizens who may be held to have 'trafficked' in confiscated property in Cuba (note that the alleged offence will not have occurred on US soil, and need not involve anyone who was a US citizen at the time of the 'confiscation'). Title IV involves the denial of entry visas to officers (and their families) of foreign corporations which, in the opinion of the State Department, may be guilty of 'trafficking'. These are extraordinary provisions even within the US legal tradition, and they are clearly at variance with US obligations under such international agreements as the Uruguay Round and NAFTA. However, in response to an EU complaint to the World Trade Organisation, Washington has made it clear that it regards Cuba as a 'national security' issue and would therefore refuse to abide by an adverse ruling from the WTO courts.[16]

The EU's initial response was to co-ordinate a series of legal measures intended as antidotes to the extra-territorial pretensions of Helms-Burton. European courts are supposed to offer protection and redress to business coerced by this law. The WTO procedure was also invoked. But in the course of 1997 Trade Commissioner Leon Brittan entered into negotiations with President Clinton's representative Stuart Eizenstat, in search of a compromise solution. Every six months since 1996 the Clinton administration has waived Title III of the law, and in response in September 1997 the EU suspended its WTO complaint. Further negotiations gave rise to a settlement announced on 18 May 1998. This includes assurances that Title IV would also no longer be deployed against European firms. Clinton also undertook to request a modification of Title III, from the US Congress. In return the Commission dropped its complaint in the WTO, sought common ground with the USA on the issue of 'democracy promotion' in Cuba, and accepted certain rather unspecific 'disciplines' intended to discourage future European investments in expropriated properties in Cuba (existing European investments would not be retroactively affected). However, it is still not entirely clear whether the US Congress will co-operate with this settlement. Italy's foreign minister has publicly asserted in Havana that the agreement neutralises the threat of Helms-Burton for European investors, whereas Eizenstat has argued in Washington that it effectively multilateralises the core principles of the law. There is also some uncertainty about the extent to which the Council of Ministers will feel bound by the terms of the compromise proposed by the Commission. If Washington fails to deliver on its side of the bargain, or if any European enterprises are sanctioned for 'trafficking', the deal could unravel, perhaps with acrimony.

Viewed more dispassionately, it is difficult to present the record of EU policy towards Cuba since the end of the Cold War as much of a success. Neither Washington nor Havana have been particularly inclined to heed remonstrances from Brussels. Caught in the cross fire (lacking room for manoeuvre because of US divisions over Central America in the 1980s), the EU seems mostly to have bent under US pressure. Perhaps, on a longer term view, it will become apparent that the principles defended by the Europeans offer a better way forward for dealing with the Cuban issue than those endorsed by the US Congress. But even if that proves the case, it is probably Washington, rather than Brussels, that will have to take up the baton and that will gain most of the rewards.

Relations with the Andean Community, Chile and Mexico

Thus far, the discussion has focused on very specific EU negotiations concerning a relatively narrow geographical subset of countries. The last two sub-headings of this section are much broader, both in geographical scope and in the range of issues for consideration. Optimists about EU-Latin American relations will argue that there is far more scope for positive developments on this larger canvas. This sub-heading deals with three discrete and complex relationships, each of which might well deserve separate consideration. They receive joint attention here, since the focus is on the immediate negotiating agenda. The EU strategy is to leave out no sub-region, and to manage each specific relationship with an eye on the 1999 summit (see below), which will deal with the sub-continent as a whole. In consequence, although the strongest EU interest is in MERCOSUR (see below) the other countries of South America cannot be left too far behind, and it is also necessary to 'balance the ticket' by cultivating relations with Mexico.

The Andean Pact was founded by the Andean states in 1969 (Venezuela joined in 1973), but lost Chile in 1976.[17] Thereafter European relations with Venezuela and the west coast of South America were heavily influenced by Cold War considerations. In the 1980s democratic Colombia and Venezuela were viewed as like-minded partners in the effort to damp down the Central American conflict, whereas Peru was immersed in its own guerrilla war, and Pinochet's Chile remained on the sidelines as the only remaining military dictatorship of the six (Bolivia and Ecuador were the other countries). Support from the EC may have helped keep the Andean Pact formally in existence, but it was in fact moribund and unsuited to the new requirements of economic liberalisation.

At the end of the Cold War the European Community began to inject some new life into the Andean Pact by negotiating a regionally specific variant of the Generalised System of Preferences, intended to reward the countries of the sub-region for their collaboration in the 'war on drugs' (Joyce, 1997). A 'third generation' co-operation agreement was reached in 1993,[18] and in 1996 the five member states agreed to modify their treaty, converting the pact into an 'Andean Community' with a more liberal and market-oriented outlook. In principle the EU stands ready to encourage this development, but in practice progress has been slow. Three main reasons can be given: the five remain disunited over economic, political, and even security issues; several countries also face grave internal tensions; and in any case the success and prospective enlargement of MERCOSUR tends to divide the Community, and offer each country an alternative path towards regional integration.[19]

With regard to Chile, the return to democracy in 1990 has facilitated an improvement in relations with a wide range of democratic regimes and regional groupings. This includes trade and co-operation agreements with Bolivia, Canada,

Colombia, Ecuador, Mexico, and Venezuela (with Peru not far behind); an association agreement with MERCOSUR; and a framework co-operation agreement with the EU. These last two were approved in 1996, as it became apparent that the US Congress would not authorise any early enlargement of NAFTA beyond Mexico (Chile had been identified in December 1994 as the next in line for membership). The negotiations leading to the 1996 framework agreement were quite innovative for Europe (Leiva, 1997). This was the first time that the EU had entered into a 'global' agreement (i.e. one covering both trade liberalisation *and* political dialogue) with a single country (as opposed to a regional grouping) beyond the immediate periphery of Europe. Since Chile was neither a full member of MERCOSUR, nor (any longer) a member of the Andean Community, the Commission either had to negotiate with a single country, or leave the most economically successful country of South America out of its portfolio of relationships. Once this precedent had been set, this made it easier to proceed with a similar 'single country' relationship with Mexico (IRELA, 1997a).

In December 1997 the foreign ministers of the EU signed up to an Economic Partnership, Political Co-ordination and Co-operation Agreement with Mexico, thus establishing a framework for trade liberalisation negotiations that began in 1998. This is clearly a crucial component of any strategy to establish a Latin America-wide presence for the EU, which in turn is indispensable if Europe is to project itself as having a global presence. It is noteworthy that whereas in the rest of the hemisphere the EU goes out of its way to promote schemes of regional integration, in this case the ties are directly with Mexico alone, and so involve by-passing NAFTA. Mexico has its own reasons for favouring the same approach. It wishes to demonstrate that, despite the intensification of its always very strong (and asymmetrical) relationship with the USA, and now also with Canada, it remains a major sovereign state with considerable autonomy of action in international affairs. From this standpoint, a comprehensive politico-economic agreement with the EU might serve partially to counterbalance the swamping effects of Mexico's immersion in NAFTA. However, the ongoing negotiations are likely to prove difficult, in part because neither side will be very inclined to undertake burdensome economic commitments to promote a relatively secondary relationship, and in part because it is not clear how well 'political dialogue' with Europe will serve the Mexican aim of asserting its sovereignty and autonomy.[20] The EU includes a standard 'democracy clause' in all agreements of this kind, and that could open the way to critical comments in some European parliaments on such touchy and hitherto 'off limits' topics as human rights in Mexico, especially in the wake of the Chiapas insurgency.

Relations with MERCOSUR, and the Rio Summit of 1999

For both objective and subjective reasons, relations between the EU and MERCOSUR presently outrank all other European links with Latin America and can be expected to define the overall bilateral relationship. Without a robust commitment and a cumulative strengthening of ties between these two common markets,[21] other EU initiatives in the region would lack weight. If the EU can make a success of its strategy towards MERCOSUR, then the other elements of its Latin American agenda should fall into place with relative ease. Trade and investment statistics highlight the particular dynamism and promise of Argentine and Brazilian markets for European business. Brazil's prominent role in MERCOSUR underscores that through dialogue and convergence with MERCOSUR Europe would also be identifying itself with a particular outlook and set of aspirations for the western hemisphere as a whole.

The summit of European Union and Latin American heads of state, in June 1999 in Rio de Janeiro, demonstrates both these opportunities and their associated difficulties (IRELA, 1998). When it comes to specifics, all four MERCOSUR countries have highly competitive agricultural export sectors. So they view not only Europe's Common Agricultural Policy but also the Lomé agreement as major impediments to free trade. Even if eastern enlargement does encourage the EU to relax its agricultural protectionism, MERCOSUR countries have reason to fear that they will remain in the outer circle of the beneficiaries (IRELA, 1997b). There is not much prospect that the EU can counter this objection any time soon. The search for areas of mutual economic benefit has therefore focused on the auto trade, energy, privatised utilities, the financial sector, and on infrastructure projects linked to regional integration (Euro-Latin American Forum, 1995). In general, these initiatives involve commercial expansion both within and between the two regional markets, but they are driven as much by investment as by trade flows. European business interests have found many of these sectors attractive, and therefore create private sector constituencies which lobby for further EU-MERCOSUR co-operation. But in most of these sectors the Europeans face fairly stiff competition from other business enterprises, both Latin American and North American. In the long run, therefore, the success of EU-MERCOSUR economic integration will depend upon the relative efficiency and stamina of the European private sector, rather than on the political will of the various heads of state.

Nevertheless, there is a political dimension to MERCOSUR which creates an elective affinity between the South American and the European integration processes, and differentiates it from NAFTA. There are also cultural ties, perhaps even some shared values, which help to cement an EU-MERCOSUR bond. After all, Argentina and Brazil have received millions of European immigrants, many of whom now occupy positions of influence in their respective societies, and who often continue to cultivate family and linguistic ties with the old world (Coffey and Corrêa de Lage, 1988). From the EU's point of view, it is a matter of no small importance that MERCOSUR is bringing together a series of new (or restored) democracies and is overcoming long-standing national hostilities (especially between Argentina and Brazil) (Foro Euro Latino-Americano, 1998).

On a broader strategic canvas, by supporting MERCOSUR the EU can hope to strengthen its approach to the creation of a South American Free Trade Area, which in turn may prepare the ground for a Free Trade Area of the Americas of a more inclusive and balanced variety than might be achieved through unilateral extensions of NAFTA (SELA, 1998). In addition, the EU is acting with one eye on the possibility that a new 'Millennium Round' of global trade negotiations may get underway, with agriculture and services occupying a prominent role. In that event the Europeans have reason to fear the emergence of a US-led trading bloc in the Americas, and therefore stand to benefit from cultivating good relations with major trading partners in South America, so that any such negotiations remain triangular.

EU-Latin American Relations in a Comparative Perspective

This section deliberately focuses on the EU rather than on Latin America. There are three reasons for this choice: the EU component of the relationship is the more uncertain; the distinctive characteristics of the EU as an emerging partner and international actor are less clearly understood; and in principle the EU has greater margin for manoeuvre than Latin America, which is in any case locked into an asymmetrical involvement with the USA.

In the first section of this chapter European integration in the 1990s was characterised as a *fuite en avant*.   The ministers, diplomats, bureaucrats, parliamentarians and legal advisers who draft EU treaties, legislation and regulations are often well ahead of European public opinion, and work on a vision of the future that is fairly detached from many existing social realities. Admittedly such insulation is not entirely unknown in Latin America.   But European integration involves a larger leap of the imagination, sustained over a wider area and for a longer period, and in the face of more deeply entrenched national traditions of rivalry and conflict. The advances achieved by the EU in the 1990s are quite remarkable, and the creation of the euro and the enlargement to the east more or less ensure that this momentum will be maintained into the new millennium. So from a Latin American perspective any uncertainty concerns the *quality* of future relations with a powerful EU, rather than the *existence* of such an entity.

The efforts required to forge an 'ever closer' union in Europe raise major uncertainties about the attention and resources that this new actor will be able or inclined to devote to the 'outer tier' of its external relationships. For example, there is an ongoing tension between the priorities of the southern European members (led by Spain) for whom a strong EU presence in Latin America is both a national interest and a source of prestige, and the northern European interest in enlargement to the post-communist east. Even if the southern European lobby does win some of its battles, it is not certain that Latin America will be a major beneficiary, given that some wine growing regions near the Mediterranean will be clamouring for cohesion funds, and that the EU's 'Barcelona Process' (focused on North Africa) is a more pressing geopolitical concern for these countries. (As a small illustration it can be noted that France, Greece, Portugal and Spain are the four EU countries which include small banana growing provinces within their respective national jurisdictions, and which are therefore most resistant to the Latin American 'dollar banana' lobby discussed above.)

Turning from 'widening' to 'deepening', one of the most powerful integration initiatives is the establishment of a European Central Bank (ECB) in Frankfurt.[22]

But again there are major uncertainties about what this might portend for Latin America.   The trade impact is likely to be less important than possible repercussions in the financial sector, particularly if the euro is perceived as a strong store of value.   As a possible rival to the dollar the euro might have some attractions, but not necessarily if it became a dominant currency managed without regard to extra-European vulnerabilities.   Washington's institutional arrangements for managing the dollar and defending a US-led world financial system may be too politicised and too interventionist for the comfort of some Latin American finance ministers, but the Frankfurt-based alternative could easily prove too depoliticised and even more unresponsive to financial crises.

The Maastricht Treaty forbids the ECB from any intervention in currency markets that might jeopardise the over-riding goal of European price stability, and there will be no early transfer of bank supervisory responsibilities from national to Europe-wide institutions.   The ECB has no mandate to bail-out banks in trouble, and the euro has no lender of last resort.   How this rule-based system, with no clear focus of political direction, would perform under conditions of international financial crisis remains highly uncertain, but it would not be surprising if some Latin American governments reached the conclusion that for all its faults Washington's way of handling the dollar economy was easier to live with.

These broad-brush observations about the ECB illustrate the more general point that the EU's distinctive institutional and behavioural characteristics are as yet not well understood, even within Europe let alone outside the continent.   As an example, consider the compromise on Qualified Majority Voting (QMV) that was reached in the 1997 Amsterdam Treaty (which modifies the Maastricht Treaty as it applies to the EU's emerging Common Foreign and Security Policy).   If the ever-closer union is to develop a stronger foreign policy dimension, at a time when the membership is likely to rise above twenty, then the principle of unanimity will have to be diluted.   But not a few member states regard foreign and security policy as essential attributes of national sovereignty.   The Amsterdam Treaty temporarily squared this circle by extending QMV to the *implementation* of unanimously-agreed decisions, while also institutionalising the procedure of the veto 'for important and stated reasons of national policy'.   How this decision-making procedure will work in practice, and especially in relation to regions such as Latin America that are not generally at the core of European national foreign policy concerns, can only be discovered through close and sustained observation.   Comparing the USA and the EU as foreign policy actors, not only does the former have a military capability out of all proportion with that of the latter, it also has a capacity for prompt and authoritative decision-making in the face of emergencies.   Hawaii cannot veto a Washington initiative in the Pacific, but Greece can over-ride all other EU members to block a policy in the Balkans.   Of course, there is nothing very surprising in the observation that, however close this union may become, the EU is not and will not become a conventional state.   From a 'realist' perspective it follows logically that real power must lie elsewhere, and that it is a misconception to take EU pretensions at face value or to imagine that we are dealing with a major new international actor.   Yet realism is flawed as a means of interpreting the international significance of the EU.

For all its limitations as an instrument for the purposive projection of power, the emerging union is so large, so prosperous, so highly institutionalised, and so difficult to budge, that over the long haul the other states and regions in the international system will find themselves under sustained and cumulative pressure to adapt to many of its requirements. It is precisely the features that differentiate it from a conventional nation state that can be turned to its advantage as sources of influence and leverage. For example, the fact that Europe's military capabilities and strategic interests in Central America were negligible opened the way for a broad-based strategy of European mediation that was acceptable to the contending parties. The existence of a cumbersome process of internal decision-making meant that the San José Process was slow to develop, but also that once in place it offered a reliable structure of incentives in favour of peaceful reconciliation. On many international issues, including intervention in civil wars, and bail-outs in financial crises, the EU is singularly ill-equipped to take a leading role. But on other issues, such as the even-handed propagation of various norms and standards that are required and observed *within* Europe, the EU may be exceptionally well-placed to exert a consistent external influence.

There is a striking congruence between the interests and outlook of many civil society groupings in Europe and their counterparts in Latin America which support and reinforce official levels of bi-regional co-operation (Freres, 1998). If it abides by WTO rulings, it reinforces that institution and powerfully encourages others to do likewise. Similarly, the introduction of a 'democracy clause' into all its international agreements (which has to be submitted for ratification to all 15 national parliaments as well as to the European Parliament) promotes a higher political and human rights standard than is, for example, written into the NAFTA treaty. As the principal exemplar of the practice of pooling national sovereignty in the cause of open regionalism and a convergence on liberal values, it is well-placed to propagate and reinforce such experiments elsewhere in the world, both by example and by more direct and legally binding forms of commitment. Thus, although the EU fails to conform to the standard realist criteria for deploying international power, it has an important and distinctive role as an actor and an influence in the post-Cold War world. Both its methods of operation and its arenas of influence are specific and distinct from those of the member states of which it is composed.

It is as yet too soon to conclude that the external impact of the EU will prove a clear-cut vindication of either idealist, or legalist, or constructivist alternatives to state-based realism. Latin American partners of the EU, attracted by these alluring features which may appear to differentiate Europe from the USA, need to be alert to the counter-currents. In theory, the highest standards of normative behaviour may be elevated to the status of treaty commitments that are binding Europe-wide, but if so we need to consider how effectively these rhetorical commitments can be monitored if not through the overburdened national machinery of accountability. In the areas of transparency and consistency of policy implementation the Union still has much to prove. There is a possibility that member states might feel licensed to concentrate on the pursuit of short term and sectional self-interest, leaving their broader responsibilities to an isolated bureaucracy. In this event realists could trump their critics by demonstrating that conflicts of state power within the union outweighed the appearance of a higher collective standard achieved at the regional level.

In the immediate aftermath of the Cold War an upsurge of liberal optimism encouraged a variety of regional, inter-regional, and globalising experiments that seemed to downgrade the value and effectiveness of the nation state. State shrinking has undercut some traditional patterns of political behaviour, but it has also spurred democratic politicians to innovate and apply their energies in new arenas, including regional integration schemes. Such experiments have been actively pursued both in Europe and in Latin America in the 1990s, and help to explain the rise of bi-regional encounters and agreements over that period. The Rio summit of 1999 provides a vivid illustration of the hope that convergence between like-minded statesmen may permit collaborative solutions to many problems that are not being effectively managed at the purely national level. However, it remains to be demonstrated that durable benefits will be delivered through such bi-regionalism (IRELA, 1998). Both in Europe and in Latin America much of public opinion and most social actors remain largely attuned to the process of decision-making and mechanisms of resource allocation that still operate at the national level. To the extent that they experience a 'decline of the state' many are more disposed to seek protection in some more local or parochial identity with which they are familiar, rather than to face the uncertainties of international cosmopolitanism. It may be comforting to know that your nation is converging with its neighbours around a set of values and institutions that will reinforce your security, but it is often difficult to dispel the alternative hypothesis that the national protections to which you were accustomed are being dismantled by insensitive elites that no longer share a common destiny with their co-nationals. Both in Europe and in Latin America localist and defensive counter-currents have been stirred up by post-Cold War experiments in regional integration and internationalisation. Even if the realists are proved wrong by the outcome of these experiments, it still remains to be seen whether the alternative to their version of the nation state will turn out to be a form of liberal internationalism. One serious alternative could be a backlash in favour of more defensive and localist identities, a constructivism of the sub-national rather than of the supra-national.

Conclusions

Finally, between the foregoing rather abstract theoretical observations and the highly specific issues treated in section two of this chapter, it is possible to formulate five plausible middle range conclusions about the prospective development of EU-Latin American relations over the medium term.

    1. Whatever the eventual outcome of the realist/liberal internationalist debate, the prospects both in Europe and in Latin America are that a relatively open

form of regionalism will continue to develop over the near term. Enlargement and the euro more or less ensure this in Europe, as does the detailed timetable for the Free Trade Area of the Americas that emerged from the April 1998 Santiago summit for Latin America. Within this framework there is every reason to expect a continuation, and perhaps an intensification of bi-regional collaboration. This is most certain at the heads of state and declaratory level, but it is also fairly probable that practical steps towards further convergence will be taken as well. The EU's existing framework co-operation agreements with Chile, MERCOSUR and Mexico are likely to progress in one form or another, and eventually to acquire treaty form. Nevertheless the balance between rhetoric and substance remains to be determined. Most critical here will be a European judgement about the priority to attach to this region, and the feasibility of making internal adjustments for the sake of this external relationship. Also important will be the perceived progress of economic and political reforms in Latin America. The 'democracy clause' has the potential to create difficulties with Mexico over Chiapas, and there are also risks of European disillusion on human rights questions with major partners in South America (IRELA, 1997a). From the other side, Latin American leaders may regret some aspects of EU performance, but they are almost certain to welcome European interest in their region and to view European rhetoric as an attractive antidote to the discourse of Washington.

2.   Although trade liberalisation will occupy a prominent position in bi-regional communiqués and agreements, it is less certain how much trade dynamism will result. One key area concerns reform of the Common Agricultural Policy in areas where Latin American agriculture enjoys a strong comparative advantage. Acting alone the Latin Americans would not succeed in gaining much advantage here, but eastern enlargement and competing pressures on the EU budget may force a degree of reform for other reasons. In this regard, as in most trade matters, the cause of liberalisation is probably best served by increased reliance on the WTO, but it is possible that bi-regional co-operation can be harnessed to that end. The more the two regions confine themselves to rhetoric and long term promises in the arena of commerce, the more likely it is that trade directed with, and through, the USA will outstrip direct European-Latin American exchange.

3.   Trade in goods, trade in services, and international investment flows are in general closely linked, and this applies to European-Latin American exchanges as well. European banks and utilities have been major investors in some of Latin America's most substantial privatisation programmes (especially in the Southern Cone) and European auto companies have also invested heavily. Clearly much of this has been in competition with US corporations, and overall it is likely that US direct foreign investment (notably in Mexico) has been somewhat more successful than the European variant. But the market has expanded enough to create considerable opportunities for both, and that situation could well continue. For example, European construction companies might be particularly well placed to participate in infrastructure investments geared to promoting integration in MERCOSUR. Overall, however, the North American business community seems confident that if regional integration is market-led rather than state directed most

Latin American businessmen will regard the USA as the first partner of preference. European investors should not expect uncontested markets, except perhaps in a few Caribbean islands where colonial, ACP, or anti-communist barriers block open access.

4.   As a result of NAFTA, US corporations greatly expanded both the absolute level and their relative share of trade with Mexico.   In consequence Europeans found themselves at something of a disadvantage in this market, a situation reinforced by the 1995 peso crisis and its aftermath.   To a lesser extent European investment has also been affected.   Had NAFTA enlargement proceeded according to Washington's plan, the EU had reason to fear that similar tendencies might have been experienced more widely.   Thus, the Clinton administration's failure to secure 'fast track' authority in 1997 was greeted with a certain sense of relief among those most enthusiastic about European-Latin American co-operation. The framework for a Free Trade Area of the Americas (FTAA) agreed in Santiago in April 1998 looks quite reassuring from this standpoint.   Europeans will hope that the eventual FTAA is less discriminatory than might have been the case under the NAFTA enlargement scenario.   This gives them a clear motive to support the development of MERCOSUR, and its possible extension into a South American Free Trade Area (SAFTA) before the final round of the FTAA negotiations, which will probably not take place until about 2003.   It also reinforces EU interest in an enhanced agreement with Mexico (to counteract any suggestion that Europe is willing to relinquish competition in any major world market).   And it underscores the necessity (from a European standpoint) for the FTAA to be WTO-compatible. The logic of the EU position is therefore clear.   What remains to be seen is whether a strategy predicated on the success of MERCOSUR can weather the strains arising from Brazil's financial crisis, and if it can provide a solid basis for the EU to project its ideas and defend its interests in the Americas as a whole.

5.   Latin Americans would be unwise to over-estimate the weight Europe attaches to their concerns, as compared with EU relations with the USA.   In April 1998 Leon Brittan, the Commissioner responsible for trade, not only withdrew the EU's complaint before the WTO concerning extra-territoriality.   He also unveiled controversial proposals (subsequently criticised by Paris) concerning a 'New Transatlantic Marketplace (NTM)'.   The idea was for Brussels and Washington to undertake early negotiations to extend the liberalisation of trade and investment beyond the limits set by the Uruguay Round. These US-European negotiations would be WTO-compatible, and would not require prior 'fast track' authority from the US Congress.   Proposed agenda items included the abolition of customs duties on all industrial products by 2010; progress towards bilateral free trade in services (starting in 2000); mutual recognition agreements in various areas of regulation; a Multilateral Agreement on Investment; and (most controversially it would seem) efforts to diminish bilateral friction in the area of agricultural trade.   Government procurement policies and intellectual property rights would also be placed on the agenda.   If this programme of negotiations between the world's two strongest economic partners had gathered momentum, then EU-Latin American convergence would have been pushed to the sidelines.   Admittedly, Latin Americans could well

benefit from a successful NTM in that whatever concessions the USA exchanged with the EU, both would then be more likely to extend to the rest of the Americas as well. However, this latest initiative from Brussels also highlights the fact that the EU-Latin American relationship is both asymmetrical and of secondary importance to the two sides. Although Latin America might benefit from the NTM, the region would presumably play no direct part in shaping this agreement. On the other hand, if a downturn in world trade were to increase friction between Brussels and Washington, Latin America could easily suffer collateral damage.

These five medium term generalisations are not inconsistent with either the 'snapshot' of current EU-Latin American relations presented in section two, or the more theoretical and long-term reflections presented in the third section. The same relationships have been investigated at three different levels of analysis. The processes under discussion are so recent, and are developing so rapidly, that all three levels of analysis must be highly provisional. The justification for this exercise is that even when it is too soon to reach definite conclusions about a process it may be desirable to clarify the main forces at work, and to outline their broader implications.

Notes

1. It would have been seventeen, but governments in Norway and Switzerland failed to win the support of their electorates in referendums.
2. The original six signatories of the Treaty of Rome (Belgium, France, Germany, Italy, Luxembourg, Netherlands) became nine in 1973 with the addition of Denmark, Ireland and the United Kingdom, ten in 1981 (Greece) and twelve in 1986 (Portugal and Spain).
3. The original European Economic Community (EEC) became the European Community (EC) in 1973 and the European Union (EU) in 1993.
4. Only Demark and the UK (given an opt-out by the Maastricht Treaty) and Sweden and Greece remained outside.
5. The Brady Plan, launched in 1989 and named after the US Treasury Secretary, finally provided Latin American countries with an exit from the debt crisis.
6. The Rio Group in which almost all Latin American countries are now represented, is an outgrowth of the Contadora Group set up in 1984 by Colombia, Mexico, Panama and Venezuela to find a peaceful solution to the Central American crisis. On MERCOSUR, see Chapter 4.
7. The first Lomé Convention, signed in 1975, was preceded by the Yaoundé Convention that had been limited mainly to former French colonies.
8. The Esquipulas formula, often known as the Arias Plan, embraced all the Central American countries in an effort to solve the region's crisis without the use of force. President Arias of Costa Rica was subsequently awarded the Nobel Peace Prize for his contribution.
9. The Canary Islands are part of Spain, Crete is part of Greece, Guadeloupe part

of France and Madeira part of Portugal.

10. The formation of a single market in the EU made it impossible to operate the system of national quotas through which the banana trade had previously been organised.

11. The Uruguay Round, launched in 1986, paved the way for the replacement of GATT by the WTO in 1995.

12. Eastern Caribbean democratic leaders have attempted to promote this message in Washington, but without success. Either the USA does not believe its policies will promote social collapse, takeover by drugs interests etc. or it believes the EU would have to cope with such outcomes alone.

13. Neither country, however, was permitted to benefit from the banana protocol outlined above.

14. This was particularly apparent during the visit of President Clinton to China in July 1998.

15. This is made quite explicit in Title II of the 1996 Helms-Burton Law.

16. With the strengthening of the powers of WTO under the Uruguay Round, 'national security' is now almost the only safeguard countries have against WTO rulings with which they do not agree.

17. Chile's withdrawal was due to its preference for low external tariffs at a time when the Andean Pact was committed to a high common external tariff.

18. The EC signed 'first generation' agreements with Latin American states in the 1970s. Each 'generation' has been more ambitious in scope.

19. Bolivia became an associate member of MERCOSUR in 1996; the remaining countries signed a framework agreement with MERCOSUR in March 1998 that is expected to lead to associate membership.

20. It is also worth remembering that a free trade agreement with South Africa has still not been signed, although Europe launched negotiations in 1995.

21. Strictly speaking, and despite its name, MERCOSUR is a customs union (and an incomplete one as well) rather than a common market, as free movement of labour is not permitted.

22. The ECB was set up in mid-1998 in preparation for the launch of the euro on 1 January 1999. Its autonomy has yet to be fully tested, but it has been given formidable powers in setting interest rates and controlling inflation across the EU.

PART II

TRADE AND DEMOCRACY

CHAPTER 4

TRADE RELATIONS IN THE AMERICAS: MERCOSUR, THE FREE TRADE AREA OF THE AMERICAS AND THE EUROPEAN UNION

Victor Bulmer-Thomas and Sheila Page

Throughout the 20th century, the USA has been the principal market for Latin America's exports and the main source of its imports.[1] Even before the First World War the USA had replaced the United Kingdom (UK) as the leading trade partner for the region[2] and US dominance has never subsequently been challenged. By the mid-1990s, the US share of Latin America's exports exceeded 45 per cent, while its share of imports was above 40 per cent. Although the share of trade accounted for by the USA tends to vary inversely with distance (highest in the Caribbean basin and lowest in the southern cone), there is no doubting its dominant position at the regional level.

That Latin America should be so dependent on US imports, despite their changing composition over the 20th century, is perhaps not surprising; as the most advanced economy in the world, the USA has been well placed to respond to Latin America's need for new capital goods while US multinationals in the region have underpinned the demand for intermediate products. More impressive is the way the dominant position of the USA in Latin America's trade flows has survived the changing composition of the region's exports. As the structure has shifted away from primary products towards manufactured goods and services (including tourism), the USA has been the principal destination for the new exports as well as the traditional ones. This contrasts with the European Union (EU), where imports from Latin America remain dominated by primary products and where non-traditional exports have achieved only limited success.

Viewed from the standpoint of the USA, the trade relationship has been much more modest. Latin America accounts for a small share of US exports and imports[3] and this has only changed in exceptional conditions such as the Second World War. The US share of world trade is nearly three times greater than Latin America's so that even if the USA had 100 per cent of the region's trade, it would still only account for 35 per cent of US exports and imports. Yet Latin America is not a negligible market for the United States, and geography and geopolitics combine to give the region an importance that economics alone cannot explain.

Throughout almost all of this long period of US economic dominance of Latin America's trade, regional integration has not been on the agenda. The USA did not need Preferential Trade Agreements (PTAs) to conquer the Latin American markets and Latin America's exports were not excluded from the USA through the absence of tariff preferences.[4] Gestures in the direction of PTAs, such as the bilateral trade treaties pursued by US Secretary of State Cordell Hull in the 1930s, were the exception rather than the rule. Even when Latin American countries adopted their own PTAs in the 1960s, this did little to erode the dominant US position and the USA never budged from its commitment to global free trade through the General Agreement on Tariffs and Trade (GATT). Furthermore, Latin America had no interest in pressing for economic integration with the United States in view of the uncompetitive nature of its industrial base.[5]

It is at first sight, therefore, somewhat puzzling that US administrations in the 1990s, starting with that of President Bush (1989-93), have been pushing an agenda of hemispheric integration. If the USA was able to maintain its dominant economic position in Latin America throughout the long period of economic nationalism and high levels of protection, why should it favour PTAs at a time when the region's markets are much less restricted and globalisation offers further liberalisation? Similarly, why do many Latin American countries no longer fear the consequences of economic integration with the USA and why, on the contrary, have they become vociferous advocates of a Free Trade Area of the Americas (FTAA)? Finally, how is the revival of regionalism within Latin America related to the US initiatives, and how will it influence responses to them?

This chapter will look first at how regional groups are analysed, as this is relevant both for their internal dynamics and for their relations with other regions. It will then summarise the evolution of US policy and the degree of integration within NAFTA, MERCOSUR and potentially in the FTAA. After a summary of EU policy, it will consider how this complex of relationships will develop. The revival of regionalism within Latin America means that in looking at Latin American countries' trade relations with the USA and Europe, it is now MERCOSUR which is the key negotiator and this is analysed in the context of the FTAA.

How to Explain Regions and their Policies

One view of regional groups is that they are caused and defined by relations with others.[6] On this view, NAFTA or MERCOSUR could be reactions to the global revival of regionalism, and MERCOSUR might be a reaction to NAFTA and to US initiatives for an FTAA in particular. Some regions do seem to have little identity beyond reaction to others, but MERCOSUR at least is more than this. It is not only integrated in trade and investment: the institutional integration of MERCOSUR has gone well beyond the minimum necessary to gain trade liberalisation advantages and includes political and security motives. Its interests in its relations with others are now a combination of those of the individual countries and those of a region in process of formation.

Both the conventional economic classification of PTAs, customs unions and common markets and the regulatory structure for them under the World Trade Organisation (WTO) assume that trade is their basic motive and characteristic and the most important potential source of effects on third parties. Analysis often assumes that there is a continuum from less to more integrated, along a single path. The briefest look at the empirical evidence or at the literature from disciplines other than economics shows that neither of these propositions is true. Further, as tariffs, the simplest economic component of regions, become both low and regulated at multilateral level, the non-tariff elements of regions necessarily become more important. The fact that regions have become more numerous and possibly more significant at a time when tariffs are falling is a strong indication that they are based on other linkages.

The traditional approach is to ask what are the static advantages over the *status quo* of removing the costs of tariffs and other border barriers to production and to competition in international markets. The benefits in terms of reducing costs and competing in larger markets and competing without cost disadvantages from trade barriers, however, all go up with larger areas of free trade. This gives the world as the optimum region, although a greater weight in trade flows for 'nearer' regions may mean that the marginal benefits decrease.

In using this approach to explain the composition of regions, it is necessary to ask whether the economic objectives of the members are efficiency or development; in looking at the scale, it is necessary also to consider two types of decision: whether to form a region in the first place, and then whether to expand it to new members. At the second stage, the question of whose welfare we are considering becomes important, because individual members may have different interests from the region as a whole. Some members may lose from expansion in a region in which some products are not produced in all members, but the non-producers nevertheless have a tariff on imports. Any gains in some industries from access to the new members may be diminished if other producers are also admitted to the region (the gains to producing members from trade diversion are reduced). The gains to the non-producer are of course increased. As scales of production increase, and choice and variety become more important, the benefits of improving access rise, and the potential for a single producer dominating the region may become greater, so a larger region is necessary to avoid monopoly. This suggests increasing advantages for regions, and for larger regions, over time.

But the essence of formal regionalism is policy. MERCOSUR (like the EU) is a new organisation; it is not a simple agreement to liberalise nor is it unilateral liberalisation. NAFTA has much less institutional structure, while the nature of the FTAA remains unclear. It is not only prospective economic advantages that a region seeks, but either protecting these from future policy changes or developing institutions which fit new economic relationships. This raises the important question of whether the demand for regional regulation and institutions comes from the economic actors, who want the same regulatory and administrative institutions which they find useful at national level, or from political authorities, which see their controls over economic actors diminishing and which therefore want to combine with other governments to restore their authority.

Is increased regulation at regional (or country or global) level seen by firms as an unnecessary cost, effectively a tax (the strong market approach), or as a necessary part of the infrastructure, as worth paying for as good communications or water supply? Both assumptions are used, implicitly or explicitly, in much regional analysis. Globalisation of production and sales can be seen as carrying a risk that firms operating at international level want to and can escape national controls on the environment, competition policy, minimum product (or labour) standards, and perhaps also avoid taxation. Alternatively, companies are assumed to want a stable regulatory environment, on trade policy and access, but also regulation of foreign investment, intellectual property, and treatment of profits and remittances. One of the most conventional benefits cited in analysis of the role of the WTO and of the Uruguay Round outcome is the constraints which they impose on unilateral changes in access to markets through tariff and non-tariff measures. Whether it is countries attempting to pursue escaping companies or companies attempting to find national standards abroad and in cross-national dealings, the focus here is on regulating a process which is continuing, not obtaining new access and static efficiency gains. Either would imply that regions, and then larger regions, are more required as economic links deepen and widen.

Why regions rather than a global framework? If the regions are where more than average trade or investment growth has already occurred, then the demand for new regulation, whether from firms or governments, will come sooner or more strongly. In this model, growing and concentrated trade leads to new organisations, rather than only being the result of regions, although clearly there may be causation in both directions. The question for MERCOSUR is whether these links with the USA are now important enough to make new institutions (such as an FTAA) desirable. Examination of trade links (see below) shows that the MERCOSUR countries have a lower interest than other Latin American countries in improving trade access to the USA; they depend less on it. This is not 'independence', of course, but it does increase their freedom both to have conflicts with the USA and to accept agreements with it without fearing dominance. Other explanations of regions are geography, the role of political and cultural similarity, bargaining power and security, but these are poor explanations for *changes* in interest in regionalism.

The analysis of trade creation and trade diversion logically must come second to the analysis of why countries join particular regions. It only deals with the effects once a region and its coverage have been defined. In practice, as well, such analysis follows the decision to join a region, and is never decisive.

Forming alliances for military purposes is not normally considered a form of regionalism, but the two are not entirely separate. If countries believe that regions bring economic gains, at a minimum they will be unwilling to include countries that are potential enemies. Countries with a strong level of fear or distrust are unlikely to have the necessary degree of trust to sign any long-term agreement. The association, however, is closer. The argument that trading binds countries together and therefore increases security dates at least from Adam Smith's view that commerce promotes peace. A complementary argument was that discriminatory trade could create tensions (see Schiff and Winters, 1997, p. 5). This motive also can be used to explain initiatives by an outside country to encourage regions, even when it is not itself a prospective member. A possible corollary (which the EU certainly fits) is that ex-enemies may want a region to prevent conflict.

It is probable that at least some of the regionalisation activities of the last ten years have been the results of pre-1994 efforts to increase Uruguay-Round-inspired bargaining power grouping. Europe's initial impulse to the Single European Market (SEM) exercise was in part explicitly an attempt to increase its economic power, as well as its competitiveness, against the larger industrial countries, the USA and Japan. NAFTA, it has been argued, was in part the response of the USA to the SEM, in part a result of loss of patience with the GATT, and in part a warning to other countries negotiating within the Uruguay Round. The sequence would continue, with MERCOSUR perhaps a counterweight to NAFTA, and the EU forming links with both Mexico and MERCOSUR as balances to NAFTA (see Chapter 3).

For MERCOSUR, it has been argued that a sense of common interests was created, perhaps deliberately, before economic integration was attempted. Hurrell (1996, p. 1) argues that for MERCOSUR the 1970-85 period is when 'the essential political/security foundations for future economic cooperation are prepared'. This is a variant of the security or military argument. The proposition is that while it was security interests which brought the countries together in the first instance (as in Europe), the habit of cooperation then helped to create a common identity.

Integration in the Americas – The Evolution of US Policy

The willingness of 34 countries in the Americas (shown at the presidential summit in Miami in December 1994 and endorsed at the second summit in Santiago in April 1998) to pursue hemispheric integration is in sharp contrast to the almost total lack of interest shown in regional integration ten years earlier. At that time, the debt crisis was the most pressing issue for both debtors (Latin American and Caribbean countries) and creditors (Canada and the USA) and regional integration was seen by many as part of the problem rather than as part of the solution. This conversion from scepticism to enthusiasm needs to be explained, although the path taken has not been the same for all countries. In particular, it is necessary to distinguish the US road to Damascus from that taken by Latin American countries.

Although the USA has both favoured and used protectionism for most of its independent history, it emerged from World War II as a convert to free trade. This conversion was a consequence of its absolute advantage across a very broad range of industrial sectors and services making it almost certain that the USA would gain from a move to multilateral free (or at least freer) trade through GATT. The USA championed the cause of multilateral free trade through the GATT 'rounds' beginning at the end of the 1940s and it is exceedingly unlikely that GATT would have been so successful in freeing trade in manufactured goods if the USA had not thrown its weight behind the organisation.

The conversion to free trade was qualified by the survival of protectionism in a number of activities (e.g. agriculture and shipping), which were therefore kept outside the remit of GATT. Similarly, the USA was as ready as other developed countries to embrace covert protectionism for textiles and clothing in the Multi-Fibre Arrangement (MFA) and its predecessors dating from 1961. Indeed, it would not be difficult to produce other examples of US protectionism in the post-war era. However, there is no doubt that successive US administrations from President Truman onwards were committed to free trade and believed that it would be good for the USA and good for the rest of the world.

Not surprisingly, therefore, proposals for PTAs by other countries were not greeted with enthusiasm by the USA and post-war US administrations made no such proposals themselves. One exception was the European Economic Community (EEC), established by the Treaty of Rome in 1957, but US support was heavily conditioned by its interest in western European security and the perceived need for a strong bulwark against the threat of Soviet expansion. Thus, US support for European integration should not be interpreted as support for PTAs in general.

The movement towards integration in Latin America at the end of the 1950s was greeted with little enthusiasm, although in the end the USA did not oppose it. US multinational enterprises (MNEs) already established in the region stood to benefit and others were quick to exploit the new opportunities for profitable investment created by the widening of the protected regional market. High rates of nominal and effective protection created a risk of trade diversion, from which US exporters would suffer, but a network of incentives and exceptions lowered tariffs on many capital and intermediate products – the products of most interest to US suppliers. As a result, the US share of Latin America's total imports held up well and was not seriously damaged by the growth of intra-regional trade.

While the executive remained firm in its commitment to multilateral free trade, Congress – with its potent mix of domestic interests and pressure groups – was more ambivalent. Indeed, as early as 1948 Congress had failed to ratify the treaty agreed in Havana to create an International Trade Organisation (ITO) with greater scope and powers than GATT despite the administration's support for an ITO.[7] Congressional desire to amend trade treaties already agreed by the executive led to the adoption of 'fast-track' negotiating authority in the 1970s, under which Congress would be given a simple choice to approve or disapprove treaties in those cases where it had given a negotiating mandate to the executive. Through this legislative device, US administrations were able to give credibility to their continued commitment to multilateral free trade.

This commitment started to be shaken for the first time in the second half of the 1980s. The prolonged negotiations of the Uruguay Round from 1986 created two problems for the USA. There was no certainty that the Uruguay Round would be successfully completed, putting GATT and the multilateral trading system at risk; secondly, US trade negotiators were finding it increasingly difficult (with the increased membership of GATT) to win approval for the new trade agenda favoured by the USA including financial services, intellectual property safeguards and investment protection.

The US administration therefore dropped its resistance to PTAs and negotiated the Canada-US Free Trade Agreement (CUFTA) that came into force in 1989.

Although an automobile agreement had been reached between the USA and Canada in the 1960s and a free trade agreement with Israel in the early 1980s, CUFTA was the first significant US venture into a PTA and it included many new features. It extended free trade into areas untouched by GATT without exposing US producers to the dangers of global competition and it embodied part of the new trade agenda favoured by the USA with arbitration panels to resolve any disputes.

Flushed with its success in launching CUFTA in 1989, the new administration of President Bush agreed in 1990 to negotiate a PTA with Mexico. Canada, fearful of being sidelined, asked to make the negotiations trilateral[8] and the North American Free Trade Agreement (NAFTA) was ready for ratification by 1993. Embodying many more features than CUFTA, NAFTA faced predictable opposition from special interests in Congress. However, it passed after Bush's successor, President Clinton (1993-), threw his weight behind the project despite its Republican origins, and NAFTA came into force on 1 January 1994.

Bipartisan support for NAFTA seemed to herald a new approach to PTAs and even the passage of the Uruguay Round in 1993 did nothing to dint the new US enthusiasm. On the contrary, the Clinton administration participated fully in the Asia-Pacific Economic Cooperation (APEC) forum arguing for a commitment to preferential tariffs and in December 1994 the USA promoted the idea of a Free Trade Area of the Americas (FTAA), receiving the endorsement of all other countries present.[9]

The Summit of the Americas in December 1994 represented the high point of US support for PTAs. The Mexican devaluation a few days later took the gloss off NAFTA for many in the USA and President Clinton was unable to win from Congress the fast-track authority needed to extend NAFTA to Chile.[10] Even the administration began to have doubts and questions were raised in Washington about the wisdom of MERCOSUR (see below) and Brazilian plans for a South American Free Trade Area (SAFTA). However, at least in public, the Clinton administration remained committed to the FTAA and the president endorsed MERCOSUR on his visit to Brazil and Argentina in October 1997. This ensured that the FTAA remained firmly on the agenda at the Second Summit of the Americas in April 1998.

The Nature and Evolution of MERCOSUR

MERCOSUR is a customs union among four countries. As a group, it has PTAs with Chile and Bolivia, and is negotiating with others, including the Andean group as a region, but the PTAs (and the FTAA) are seen as very different from the core. This is a different model from the EU, which has expanded by requiring the whole '*acquis*' to be adopted by any new member in its region. When it has signed PTAs, these have been with clearly non-European countries. MERCOSUR appears to be the same as the SACU model, the Southern African Customs Union negotiating to become 1 (or 5) of the members of a Southern African Development Community, but there SACU may be breaking down into a PTA. As MERCOSUR

Table 4.1:
MERCOSUR Trade Patterns
(i) Intra-Regional Trade as Percentage of Total[1]
(ii) Intensity[2]

	Exports							Imports						
	1990	1991	1992	1993	1994	1995	1996	1990	1991	1992	1993	1994	1995	1996
ARGENTINA														
Share of intra-region trade (4)	14.84	16.51	19.02	27.32	30.67	32.33	33.28	21.49	21.00	25.25	25.10	23.91	22.77	24.45
Intensity (4)	16.95	16.84	15.54	18.09	20.95	21.81	20.09	16.05	16.50	19.35	17.63	16.65	16.62	17.44
Share of intra-region trade (6)	19.11	21.55	25.08	33.19	38.28	40.57	41.93	30.03	26.84	30.52	29.92	28.44	25.98	27.42
Intensity (6)	17.02	17.37	16.47	18.04	21.63	22.27	20.70	18.68	17.38	19.28	17.76	16.45	15.24	16.04
BOLIVIA														
Share of intra-region trade (6)	38.01	30.74	25.77	22.94	19.77	16.53	19.61	41.63	33.40	32.02	31.43	32.34	29.21	26.85
Intensity (6)	33.84	24.79	16.92	12.47	11.17	9.07	9.69	25.90	21.62	20.23	18.66	18.70	17.14	15.71
BRAZIL														
Share of intra-region trade (4)	4.20	7.30	11.45	13.98	13.60	13.23	15.30	10.07	10.49	8.68	9.94	12.73	13.70	15.95
Intensity (4)	4.80	7.45	9.35	9.26	9.28	8.93	9.23	7.52	8.24	6.65	6.98	8.87	10.00	11.38
Share of intra-region trade (6)	6.32	10.25	14.96	17.98	16.97	16.97	18.62	12.51	12.88	10.47	11.30	14.44	15.96	17.84
Intensity (6)	5.63	8.27	9.82	9.77	9.59	9.31	9.19	7.78	8.34	6.61	6.71	8.35	9.36	10.44
CHILE														
Share of intra-region trade (6)	8.66	9.87	11.36	13.60	13.14	12.22	12.82	14.91	16.70	17.35	15.95	17.59	16.99	15.99
Intensity (6)	7.71	7.96	7.46	7.39	7.43	6.71	6.33	9.28	10.81	10.96	9.47	10.17	9.96	9.35
PARAGUAY														
Share of intra-region trade (4)	39.52	35.14	37.44	39.59	52.02	55.28	57.49	30.76	31.06	38.40	38.57	41.68	41.83	45.34
Intensity (4)	45.14	35.83	30.59	26.21	35.53	37.29	34.70	22.97	24.39	29.42	27.10	29.02	30.54	32.34
Share of intra-region trade (6)	43.07	41.93	44.90	45.79	56.43	61.37	61.08	32.94	33.88	41.31	41.54	45.37	44.62	47.21
Intensity (6)	38.34	33.81	29.48	24.90	31.88	33.68	30.16	20.49	21.94	26.10	24.66	26.24	26.17	27.62

Table 4.1: (cont.)
MERCOSUR Trade Patterns

	Exports							Imports						
	1990	1991	1992	1993	1994	1995	1996	1990	1991	1992	1993	1994	1995	1996
URUGUAY														
Share of intra-region trade (4)	35.09	34.70	31.94	42.43	46.94	47.25	48.10	40.21	40.07	40.68	48.45	49.21	46.11	44.00
Intensity (4)	40.08	35.39	26.10	28.10	32.06	31.87	29.04	30.03	31.47	31.17	34.04	34.27	33.66	31.38
Share of intra-region trade (6)	36.21	36.26	35.06	45.71	49.19	49.24	49.98	41.70	41.72	42.40	50.26	50.79	47.89	45.71
Intensity (6)	32.24	29.24	23.02	24.85	27.79	27.02	24.68	25.94	27.01	26.79	29.84	29.37	28.09	26.74
MERCOSUR TOTAL														
Share of intra-region trade (4)	8.89	11.11	14.32	18.43	19.45	20.48	22.75	13.85	15.21	16.28	16.77	19.20	18.39	20.49
Intensity (4)	10.15	11.33	11.70	12.20	13.28	13.81	13.73	10.34	11.95	12.47	11.78	13.37	13.43	14.62
Share of intra-region trade (6)	11.49	14.07	17.42	21.57	22.14	22.97	25.12	17.08	18.43	19.13	18.90	21.43	20.36	21.62
Intensity (6)	10.23	11.34	11.44	11.73	12.51	12.61	12.41	10.63	11.93	12.09	11.22	12.40	11.94	12.65

Source: IMF, Direction of Trade Statistics, Various Years.

Note:
1. '4' means Argentina, Brazil, Paraguay and Uruguay: '6' also includes Bolivia and Chile.
2. 'Intensity' is defined as the ratio of intra-regional exports (imports) to the region's share in total world imports (exports).

is still young, it would be unwise to take its current intentions as irrevocable, but at present it appears to be assuming a regional identity permitting deep integration among four countries, contrasting with more limited interests in its relations with other trading partners. It is not clear how long the PTA countries will accept this. Chile and Bolivia are increasingly pressing for greater participation in all committees and Chile is moving towards a request for full membership.

MERCOSUR dates from a declaration of intent between Argentina and Brazil in 1985, followed by a series of protocols in 1986-89 (Zormelo, 1995, p. 5). Even before that, Argentina had proposed a customs union with Brazil in 1939-1941 (Bernal, 1997, pp. 27-8). The 1989 treaty had the target of a common market by 1995. The two countries had a history of distrust and armies on borders (although no recent conflicts), but had acquired common interests in the 1980s as they returned to democracy and suffered from heavy foreign debts (Hirst, 1992, pp. 141-2). The agreement was seen as a way of defusing regional tension as each country tried to integrate into the international economy. Although intra-regional trade was low (see Table 4.1), both countries were liberalising trade and restructuring their economies. Argentina also wanted to reduce its dependence on primary exports (Hirst, 1992, p. 143). MERCOSUR, therefore, came at a time when both were changing development strategies; it was not seen as an institutionalisation of existing trends. Brazil also needed to reduce the distrust caused by its nuclear advances (Hirst, 1992, p. 142), and a nuclear agreement was part of the cooperation (Schiff and Winters, 1997, p. 6). This group was, therefore, formed in a very different context from regional integration schemes in Latin America in the 1960s, which rose out of traditional trading relationships or from national industrial planning objectives. While increasing trade and some sectoral objectives were important, and there were important changes in trade and other economic policies, it was very much led by political decisions, more specifically by the presidents and the foreign ministries, not by economic interests. Economic policies remained very different; Brazil had an industrial strategy, promoting particular industries (notably, in the context of MERCOSUR, automobiles), while Argentina had had a more open approach since the 1970s.

In 1991, MERCOSUR was extended to Paraguay and Uruguay, with the Treaty of Asunción. Uruguay had little alternative to joining its two neighbours. Paraguay saw possible problems from being the least developed and suffering from imports from the two principal members, but nevertheless chose to join. Both had a high degree of trade integration with their neighbours (see Table 4.1). The four members had cooperated with Bolivia on developing their rivers and other infrastructure, but deliberately excluded Bolivia and all new members except Chile for five years with a rule that members of other trading groups could not join. From 1993, however, Brazil proposed a possible link with the Andean Community (Oman, 1994, p. 123). With the expiry of the five years, Bolivia (a member of the Andean Community) joined in 1996. Chile has signed a free trade agreement with MERCOSUR, and also joined in some of the working groups and joint initiatives, but is not yet formally a member because it does not want to raise its tariff to the planned Common External Tariff (from about 8 per cent to 12 per cent) of

MERCOSUR. Bolivia's location and its trading interests are as tied to MERCOSUR as to the Andean Community, and its infrastructure is probably more closely related. Chile's declared interests were entirely in market opening.

The 1997 MERCOSUR summit brought major steps towards greater integration. A target date for liberalising services was finally agreed, and there were the first discussions of the possibility of transfer payments from the richer countries to the poorer. This is normal in customs unions, and probably essential to a common market. Chile was given observer status in the institutions, although still without a vote. In contrast, the summit saw little further progress towards broadening the associate membership to other Andean Community countries or to Mexico. Chile now no longer rules out full membership (van Klaveren, 1997), and it has sought MERCOSUR support in trade disputes with the USA outside current MERCOSUR obligations.

The Argentina-Brazil agreement coincided with the US initiatives for free trade with first Canada then Mexico, and the founding of MERCOSUR with the initiative for an FTAA; it could also be argued that the deepening has come with the setting up of FTAA working groups in 1996. There was certainly a move to regions in the late 1980s (not only in North and South America), and it is probable that a bilateral relation that might have been security, cultural, energy or joint-infrastructure-based in another decade was called a customs union because that was the fashion of the period. But the interests of Argentina and Brazil were in establishing a permanent institutional relationship with each other, not at that time with establishing a counter-bloc to NAFTA. The entry of the smaller members was inevitable once the trade between the others took off. The recent deepening may be more closely related to US policies, at least in timing. If the MERCOSUR countries are to have an effective negotiating position in the FTAA, they may need to go further faster than they otherwise would on areas like standards and services which are included in the agendas of both. The FTAA pressure is reinforced by advances in multilateral negotiations.

Table 4.2:
MERCOSUR'S Major Trading Partners

	EXPORTS				IMPORTS			
	1990		1996		1990		1996	
	Value	(%)	Value	(%)	Value	(%)	Value	(%)
ARGENTINA								
MERCOSUR	2361	19.1	9983	41.9	1224	30.0	6515	27.4
Latin America	3219	26.1	11296	47.4	1416	34.7	7402	31.2
FTAA	4999	40.5	13375	56.2	2317	56.8	12426	52.3
USA	1699	13.8	1974	8.3	876	21.5	4749	20.0
EU	3824	31.0	4562	19.2	1178	28.9	6898	29.0
All Industrial	6144	49.7	7315	30.7	2402	58.9	13098	55.1
World	12353	100.0	23811	100.0	4076	100.0	23762	100.0
BOLIVIA								
MERCOSUR	352	38.0	223	19.6	286	41.6	439	26.9
Latin America	413	44.6	501	44.1	329	47.9	610	37.3
FTAA	598	64.6	827	72.7	491	71.5	1080	66.1
USA	185	20.0	317	27.9	156	22.7	430	26.3
EU	268	28.9	271	23.8	113	16.4	246	15.0
All Industrial	476	51.4	700	61.6	348	50.7	934	57.1
World	926	100.0	1137	100.0	687	100.0	1635	100.0

Table 4.2: (cont.)
MERCOSUR'S Major Trading Partners

	EXPORTS				IMPORTS			
	1990		1996		1990		1996	
	Value	(%)	Value	(%)	Value	(%)	Value	(%)
BRAZIL								
MERCOSUR	1986	6.3	8893	18.6	2871	12.5	10161	17.8
Latin America	3570	11.4	11437	23.9	3733	16.3	12852	22.6
FTAA	11826	37.6	21255	44.5	8724	38.0	27251	47.9
USA	7734	24.6	9312	19.5	4505	19.6	13016	22.9
EU	10220	32.5	13135	27.5	5259	22.9	15497	27.2
All Industrial	21383	68.1	26496	55.5	12499	54.5	34486	60.6
World	31414	100.0	47762	100.0	22950	100.0	56947	100.0
CHILE								
MERCOSUR	725	8.7	1969	12.8	1145	14.9	2850	16.0
Latin America	1055	12.6	3019	19.7	1734	22.6	4722	26.5
FTAA	2600	31.1	5718	37.2	3331	43.4	9240	51.8
USA	1489	17.8	2559	16.7	1373	17.9	4110	23.1
EU	3322	39.7	3682	24.0	1884	24.5	3538	19.8
All Industrial	6303	75.3	9079	59.1	4209	54.8	9444	53.0
World	8373	100.0	15353	100.0	7678	100.0	17828	100.0
PARAGUAY								
MERCOSUR	413	43.1	783	61.1	393	32.9	1647	47.2
Latin America	465	48.5	810	63.2	395	33.1	1654	47.4
FTAA	507	52.9	854	66.6	550	46.1	2248	64.4
USA	41	4.3	43	3.4	152	12.7	590	16.9
EU	304	31.7	244	19.0	204	17.1	362	10.4
All Industrial	399	41.6	381	29.7	589	49.4	1466	42.0
World	959	100.0	1282	100.0	1193	100.0	3489	100.0
URUGUAY								
MERCOSUR	613	36.2	1198	50.0	560	41.7	1519	45.7
Latin America	673	39.8	1295	54.4	658	49.0	1709	51.4
FTAA	863	51.0	1480	61.7	809	60.2	2140	64.4
USA	164	9.7	170	7.1	138	10.3	406	12.2
EU	449	26.5	467	19.5	254	18.9	645	19.4
All Industrial	668	39.5	694	29.0	460	34.3	1189	35.8
World	1693	100.0	2397	100.0	1343	100.0	3323	100.0
MERCOSUR (4)								
MERCOSUR	5373	11.6	20857	27.7	5048	17.1	19842	22.7
Latin America	7927	17.1	24838	33.0	6202	21.0	23617	27.0
FTAA	18195	39.2	36964	49.1	12400	41.9	44065	50.3
USA	9638	20.8	11499	15.3	5671	19.2	18761	21.4
EU	14797	31.9	18408	24.5	6895	23.3	23402	26.7
All Industrial	28594	61.6	34886	46.4	15950	54.0	50239	57.4
World	46419	100.0	75252	100.0	29562	100.0	87521	100.0
MERCOSUR (6)								
MERCOSUR	6450	11.6	23049	25.1	6479	17.1	23131	21.6
Latin America	9395	16.9	28358	30.9	8265	21.8	28949	27.1
FTAA	21393	38.4	43509	47.4	16222	42.8	54385	50.8
USA	11312	20.3	14375	15.7	7200	19.0	23301	21.8
EU	18387	33.0	22361	24.4	8892	23.4	27186	25.4
All Industrial	35373	63.5	44665	48.7	20507	54.1	60617	56.7
World	55718	100.0	91742	100.0	37927	100.0	106984	100.0

Source: IMF, Direction of Trade Statistics, Various Years.

MERCOSURs internal trade now shows strong economic integration, but links to the rest of an FTAA are much weaker. Most of the share of regional trade is explained by MERCOSUR (Table 4.2). MERCOSUR seems, on the basis of present trade flows, to gain little from an FTAA region. Flows could increase with a removal of barriers, but the small current base of trade does not indicate large potential effects. The region, however, is more important for manufactures (as is also MERCOSUR). One simulation (Baumann and Carvalho, 1997, p. 6), found that most of the effect of an FTAA on Brazilian exports of manufactures would come from liberalisation within South America, not from extending this to the NAFTA countries; Brazil in turn would be an important market for the rest of the region.

For the MERCOSUR countries as a group, more than half of their current trade with a potential FTAA is with MERCOSUR, but total FTAA trade is only half their trade (see Table 4.2). Their trade with the EU is about the same as with non-MERCOSUR FTAA countries. This diversification of their trade helps to explain MERCOSUR policies towards the FTAA, which we consider in the next section.

The Free Trade Area of the Americas

At first glance the Americas appears to be a promising candidate for economic integration. The total exports of the 34 countries in 1996 amounted to $1083 billion, of which $594 billion were hemispheric exports, i.e. exports to other countries in the Americas (see Table 4.3). Thus, over half of all exports are intra-regional and this compares favourably with other regions of the world and is higher than western Europe when the Treaty of Rome was signed in 1957.

The figures, however, are dominated by the three NAFTA countries (Canada, Mexico and the USA). If these countries are excluded, the importance of intra-regional trade is much more modest (see Table 4.3). Total exports of the 31 countries reached $164 billion in 1996, of which $47 billion was intra-regional, i.e. exported to non-NAFTA countries in the Americas. Intra-regional exports for these 31 countries represent only 28.7 per cent of total exports – a much more modest proportion. Furthermore, intra-regional trade is highly concentrated, with bilateral trade between Argentina and Brazil representing almost 50 per cent of the total.

The low ratio of intra-regional trade for the non-NAFTA countries might not matter if there were strong links between them and the NAFTA countries. However, this appears not to be the case. The three NAFTA countries have total hemispheric exports of $502 billion, but only $65 billion is exported to the 31 non-NAFTA countries. This means that a mere 13 per cent of NAFTA hemispheric exports go to non-NAFTA countries in the Americas.

Table 4.3:
Trade Flows in the Americas, 1996

	Total Exports	Intraregional Exports	Percentage
(a) Exports of the Americas ($bn)	1083	594	54.9
(b) Exports of the Americas Excluding NAFTA Countries ($bn)	164	47	28.7

Source: IMF (1997).

It is worth exploring this in more detail, as the figures are so striking. In Table 4.4, the exports of each NAFTA country are recorded together with exports to NAFTA partners as well as other countries in the Americas. For Mexico 85 per cent of all exports and 93 per cent of hemispheric exports go to NAFTA partners. For Canada the proportions are 83 per cent and 96 per cent respectively. In the case of the USA the first ratio (share of all exports going to NAFTA partners) is much lower (30.4 per cent), but the share of hemispheric exports going to NAFTA partners (78 per cent) is also very high. Thus, in all three cases the vast majority of hemispheric exports go to NAFTA partners and only a small proportion go to non-NAFTA countries.

Table 4.4:
NAFTA Country Exports ($bn), 1996

MEXICO	Total Exports	96.0 bn
	to the United States	80.7 (83.6%)
	to Canada	1.2 (1.3%)
	to the rest of the Americas	5.9 (6.1%)

Note: 84.9% of total exports to NAFTA countries; 93.3% of hemispheric exports to NAFTA countries.

CANADA	Total Exports	200.1 bn
	to the United States	164.8 (82.4%)
	to Mexico	0.9 (0.4%)
	to the rest of the Americas	6.4 (3.2%)

Note: 82.8% of total exports to NAFTA countries; 96.3% of hemispheric exports to NAFTA countries.

THE UNITED STATES	Total Exports	622.9 bn
	to Canada	132.6 (21.3%)
	to Mexico	56.8 (9.1%)
	to the rest of the Americas	52.7 (8.4%)

Note: 30.4% of total exports to NAFTA countries; 78.2% of hemispheric exports to NAFTA countries.

Source: IMF (1997).

The sheer size of the US economy means that even a small proportion of exports destined to non-NAFTA countries is large in absolute terms. However, what matters for non-NAFTA countries is the absolute size of US *imports*. These are smaller than US non-NAFTA exports since the USA has recently been running a trade surplus with Latin American countries other than Mexico (since 1994 it has had a deficit with Mexico). Thus, US exports to non-NAFTA countries in the Americas reached $53 billion in 1996, while US imports from the same source were $52 billion.

This volume of imports is still large in absolute terms and has been growing. For most small countries in the Caribbean basin, the US market dominates all others and improved access remains an attractive prospect. However, there are huge differences among Latin American countries in the share of exports destined to the United States, as Figure 4.1 makes clear. At one extreme are countries with a very high dependence (more than half of all exports) and this group includes Mexico, Haiti and Honduras. At the other extreme are 12 countries (13 if we include Cuba) with only a modest dependence (less than 25 per cent). This latter group includes some of the largest and most important countries in the region (e.g. Argentina and Brazil).[11]

The proposed FTAA is a very asymmetric affair with NAFTA countries forming a largely self-contained bloc and non-NAFTA countries divided into three groups in terms of their dependence on the crucial US market: those with high dependence (more than 50 per cent of exports); those with moderate dependence (between 25 and 50 per cent) and those with low dependence (less than 25 per cent). There are therefore likely to be very different objectives behind each country's interest in the FTAA. In order to illustrate this, we will take a small number of countries and explore their interest in the proposed FTAA starting with the USA.

The United States of America

The FTAA concept originated in 1990 under a Republican, President Bush, and was taken up again at the end of 1994 by a Democrat, President Clinton. Thus, at least at the level of the executive, the project appears to have bipartisan support. How can we explain this?

If the *level* of trade between the USA and non-NAFTA countries in the Americas is modest, the same has not been true of the rate of growth. US exporters did exceptionally well from the spectacular growth of Latin American imports in 1990-6 and this is true even when Mexico is excluded from the figures. Non-NAFTA country imports from all sources, spurred on by trade liberalisation and economic recovery, jumped from $84 billion in 1990 to $216 billion in 1996 – an annual rate of growth of 17 per cent. US exports to these same countries grew at the same rate, leaving the USA with an unchanged share of the total. This was a considerable achievement given the steps taken to promote regional integration among the 31 non-NAFTA countries.

Yet US success in retaining its share of a fast-growing market, however impressive, cannot explain US interest in the FTAA. First, the Bush initiative in 1990 predates the rapid growth in imports; secondly, the non-NAFTA market (as we have seen) remains of minor importance for US exporters; thirdly, the USA has demonstrated its ability to keep its share of this market without the need for a PTA.

The main interest of the US administration in the FTAA appears to lie in the opportunity to promote a new trade agenda. The FTAA originated at a time of deep frustration at the lack of progress in the Uruguay Round. This frustration helps to explain US interest in NAFTA, where the USA was able to place on the agenda its new concerns in international trade and investment. An extension of NAFTA to the rest of the Americas provides the USA with an opportunity to implement its agenda with less risk of losing control. For a country now ambivalent about the virtues of multi-lateralism, this is an attractive opportunity.

It might be argued that the completion of the Uruguay Round and the replacement of GATT by the WTO makes the FTAA unnecessary from the US

Figure 4.1:
US Share of Exports (%), 1996

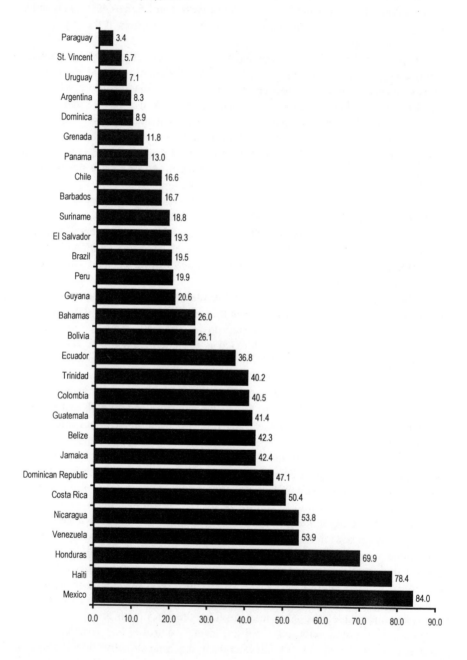

Source: Derived from IMF (1997).

point of view. It is, however, very difficult for the USA to control the WTO agenda and already several arbitration panels have ruled against the United States. Even small countries have secured rulings in their favour against the USA and the European Union has also explored the possibility of using the WTO to rule against the extra-territoriality of the Helms-Burton legislation. Thus, the WTO is not popular in many parts of the United States and the FTAA is seen as an easier route to promote the new US agenda.

This agenda has many elements, but it bears a striking resemblance to the working groups established within the framework of the FTAA in 1995. These include rules on foreign investment, public procurement, intellectual property and services – all areas where the USA has a strong interest and which are already covered by NAFTA. If US views on these sensitive issues prevail within the proposed FTAA, there is much more chance that they will be adopted globally within the WTO. Thus, the FTAA – from the US perspective – can be seen as a pioneer in US efforts to shape the next generation of WTO agreements. Perhaps that is one reason why the US administration has been less than enthusiastic about launching a new trade round within the WTO, since progress towards the FTAA is still very limited.

The US administration also has non-economic objectives it wishes to pursue through the negotiations for the FTAA. The asymmetry referred to above gives the USA a strong bargaining position over a whole range of issues with those countries that are keen to secure market access. That is why the US administration favours negotiations on a country by country basis and – despite the ministerial meetings in Belo Horizonte in May 1997 and Costa Rica in March 1998 – it has still not abandoned this position.[12]

The FTAA can also be seen, from the US perspective, as a 21st century version of the Monroe doctrine. It is a sophisticated and mutually beneficial US instrument for restricting European and even Asian influence. A successful conclusion to the FTAA negotiations would undoubtedly strengthen even further the economic, and probably political, ties between Latin American countries and the USA and further reduce the trade linkages with the European Union. Indeed, such a possibility is undoubtedly one of the factors behind European interest in Preferential Trade Agreements with Latin American countries (see next section).

It is not difficult, therefore, to see why the US administration continues to argue in favour of the FTAA. However, the obstacles it faces are considerable even within the USA. Congress is unwilling to grant 'fast-track', without which negotiations for the FTAA – formally launched at the Americas summit in April 1998 – will certainly stall. Public opinion has shifted against NAFTA as a result of Mexico's economic and political difficulties since December 1994 and the FTAA is seen as an extension of NAFTA. And the next US president may be much more sceptical about the benefits of free trade than either Bush or Clinton.

Costa Rica
Costa Rica, as Figure 4.1 shows, has a high trade dependence on the USA. Committed to export-led growth, it has put in place a series of reforms designed to

promote exports. The regional (i.e. Central American) market, to which Costa Rica is linked by the Central American Common Market (CACM), is too small to create many opportunities for long-run rapid growth of exports and the other Latin American countries produce goods with which Costa Rican products are in direct competition. Costa Rica is instead seeking to attract multinational investment that will use the country as a springboard for exports to the rest of the world. The best example is Intel, the computer company, whose exports from Costa Rica have already overtaken both coffee and bananas in gross value.

In this strategy access to the US market plays a crucial role. Costa Rica has already experienced the arbitrary nature of US trade rulings on anti-dumping and countervailing duties and would be willing to make many concessions to have more secure market access with lower tariffs and an elimination of non-tariff barriers. Costa Rica is a beneficiary of the Caribbean Basin Initiative, but this is seen as limited in scope, uncertain in duration and inadequate as a defence against NAFTA. Almost all Costa Rican exporters have experience of the US market through study abroad, family ties and vacations, and language is not a major problem.

Costa Rica is linked through regional integration schemes with the rest of Central America, Mexico and Panama, but she would happily abandon all these schemes tomorrow if there was a realistic chance of increased and secure market access to the USA. It is not true to say that Costa Rica would be willing to pay *any* price in order to gain such access, but the USA would certainly be able to extract many concessions if the negotiations for the FTAA were conducted on a country by country basis.

Costa Rica, which hosted in March 1998 the ministerial meeting that preceded the presidential summit in April, would like the negotiations for the FTAA to begin immediately and on all topics. The Costa Rican administrations – current and former – are not interested in extending the discussion over many years and would be happy to see partial implementation as agreements are reached rather than a postponement until all negotiations have been completed.

Brazil

Brazil did not propose the FTAA and for the first half of the 1990s had other priorities (e.g. MERCOSUR, inflation stabilisation). By the time Brazil began to take the project seriously, following the 1994 presidential summit, the FTAA was already taking shape as a US-inspired project. Thus, Brazil has found itself having to react to events rather than leading them – the exact opposite of its experience with MERCOSUR.

The FTAA has taken shape at a difficult time for Brazil. It has coincided with the shift from a large balance of trade surplus in 1993 to a severe deficit after 1995. Thus, Brazil is not in a strong position to contemplate a further round of tariff reductions and is already facing serious domestic opposition to the trade liberalisation measures already adopted. This position has not been made any easier by the Asian financial crisis, since Asian exports are competing with Brazilian products both in the domestic market and in third countries.

Brazil is wary of the new US trade agenda and needs allies to block some of its more radical features. These allies (e.g. India) can be found in the WTO, but Brazil cannot be so confident of the support of other American countries. That is why Brazil is determined that MERCOSUR should negotiate as a bloc in the FTAA. Just as the FTAA is a US-inspired scheme, so MERCOSUR appears increasingly as a Brazilian project with Itamaraty (the Brazilian foreign ministry) firmly in control of the agenda. The latter includes agreements by MERCOSUR with other countries, leading to Brazil's dream of a South American Free Trade Area (SAFTA), but not expansion of MERCOSUR itself as this could dilute Brazil's leadership.

A SAFTA with Brazil as its undisputed leader, and negotiating as a bloc, would be a formidable force in the FTAA negotiations. That is why Brazil has an interest in delaying both the start of the negotiations and the implementation of any agreement. Brazil's position on this has been consistent and effective, but it is not shared by all Latin American countries (e.g. Costa Rica) and is certainly not supported by the United States.

The presidential summit in Santiago and the preceding ministerial meeting in Costa Rica have gone some way towards bridging the gap between the different parties in terms of what they seek from the proposed FTAA. While the absence of fast-track is a serious blow to the successful conclusion of negotiations, the Asian crisis may prove to be a strong stimulus. Many countries in the Americas will face direct and indirect competition from Asian exports as a result of the recent devaluations and the FTAA can be seen as a way of recovering lost ground. However, the fact that the FTAA is not even due to *start* until 2005 – let alone be completed – means that it is not a short-term solution to the Asian threat.

Relations with the European Union

Its size, level of development, and now age have given the EU a particular role in relation to other regions, not only as a model (or anti-model), but as a trading partner and aid donor with a strong commitment to a regional approach (see Chapter 3). The EU, as a region itself, takes a strong view that economic linkages should be, perhaps need to be, reinforced by institutional linkages. This means that it not only accepts regions as trading partners, or joint recipients for aid, but encourages their institutional strengthening. The EU also applies its interpretation of its own experience – that forming a region promoted growth, efficiency, and also intra-regional security and peace – to other regions, and therefore sees this as a reason to encourage countries to form regions. 'The community – perhaps not surprisingly given its own history – has always regarded this [regional cooperation] as a key area. It is viewed as one of the most promising ways of contributing to growth in the developing countries' (Smidt, 1996, p. 8). In a recent statement (Commission, 1995, p. 1), it pointed out that the EU has encouraged, partly by example, partly through direct support, many of the new regional groupings in the developing world, and 'all major strategy documents and undertakings of the

European Commission addressing the problems of developing countries and the EU's relations with them, place a high priority on the support of regional initiatives'. In the 1970s and 1980s, the European Community (EC), as it was then called, defined its priority in cooperation agreements with Latin America as promoting regional integration. Assistance to Latin America began with the first EC/Latin America Joint Committee in 1970, following which the EC established direct relations with the Andean Pact in 1983. This was regarded by the Commission as potentially similar to the EC, and projects to help regional integration accounted for 85 per cent of the funding of the Pact (Commission, 1995); a third of the total bilateral aid for Latin America was directed to the Andean Pact countries.

It is only recently, however, that this long-standing policy has moved beyond encouragement of regional integration among developing countries to advocating region-to-region trading arrangements between the EU and developing regions. Now agreements have been signed with the Central American countries as a group and with the Andean Community and MERCOSUR organisations.

The importance of regions is mentioned in all current EU agreements with Latin American countries and regions, and provision is made for technical assistance in implementing them in most. It is most explicit in the agreement with MERCOSUR (Commission, 1995), which emphasises the importance of regionalism in promoting international integration and notes the common interests and experiences of the EU and MERCOSUR, and makes it a priority for development cooperation. It provides specifically for the EU to give technical assistance in the implementation of the MERCOSUR institutions. Assistance for countries attempting to meet their regional commitments is potentially also important.

There are, however, strict limits to the regionalism which the EU promotes. The agreement with Mexico (Commission, 1995) explicitly mentions only existing regional agreements (which would include those with other Latin American countries, but not, at the time of agreement, NAFTA), and both the Brazil and the Paraguay agreements explicitly encourage agreements only in their region. This is not defined, but it seems clear that it is intended to exclude arrangements with the USA. It is argued that such agreements would reduce member countries' interest in purely Latin American agreements, and thus potentially reduce the benefits of these.

In the agreement with MERCOSUR, preparing the conditions for an inter-regional association between it and the EU is one of the declared objectives, with a mention of the possibility for an EU-MERCOSUR free trade area. The idea of PTAs between the EU and MERCOSUR or EU and Mexico would be a significant extension of inter-regional links with the EU, but it not clear if this is feasible. Sensitive products on both sides, as well as commitments by MERCOSUR and Mexico,[13] which should preclude external agreements, suggest that these are more expressions of encouragement than practical proposals. Although an agreement between the EU and Mexico entered the negotiation phase at the end of 1998, this in itself – as the long negotiations between the EU and South Africa has shown – is no guarantee of a successful outcome.

The history of Latin American regions and the EU suggests a question parallel to that of the relation of MERCOSUR to US initiatives: how far is the regional movement in Latin America the result of EU targeting? The Andean group (founded 1969) and the Central American Common Market (founded in 1960), both preceded Europe's move into assisting Latin America, so the only influence would be that of example. But in the late 1970s and early 1980s, EU encouragement and financial assistance probably preserved the regions long after they were effectively dead, and, at the least, made their revival in the late 1980s easier. The additional preferences which the EU offered to the Andean Community countries to encourage them away from exporting drugs were specified in terms of membership in the Community, and have thus had the effect of encouraging Peru to remain a member to receive the preferences, even when it was not participating actively in the region. MERCOSUR clearly was not a European initiative, although it has been strongly encouraged and assisted by Europe. Europe and Latin America are the two areas where regions have a long history, so what we see is probably a common interest, rather than direct causation.

Conclusions

Sub-regional integration schemes within the Americas are probably here to stay. The historical legacy of Latin America will always favour regions, at least when conditions are favourable. Economic reform and democratic consolidation have encouraged them in recent years. Recession may test them again now, and lead to a period like the 1970s and 1980s when they became dormant. The new schemes – MERCOSUR and NAFTA – have better prospects, as their design takes more account of the new circumstances and there are few, if any, impediments inherited from the past.

That said, it cannot be denied that regional integration is a stressful business. There is no such thing as a static equilibrium in integration schemes, as the European experience has shown so clearly. One stage leads inexorably to another. PTAs either break up or move towards customs unions. In the latter, the adoption of a common external tariff (CET) leads on to a single market; this in turn requires exchange rate harmonisation, which – in the presence of capital mobility – implies monetary union.[14] The process is only complete when – as in the case of Bismarck's Germany or the 19th century United States – economic integration leads to a single country. Since member states may resist this process, or at the very least will have different ideas about the speed of integration, there is plenty of scope for friction.

Integration in the Americas is not exempt from these processes and the friction is made worse by the absence of shared objectives. What eases the problem, paradoxically, is the slow progress towards the completion of each stage. Thus, MERCOSUR's difficulty in completing the CET allows the member states to postpone consideration of the next stage (the single market).

NAFTA is also not immune from these pressures with the result that the United States has found that regional integration is not costless in terms of national economic sovereignty. Whether it be a dispute with Canada on car assembly or an argument with Mexico about labour representation, the USA is learning the hard way that regional integration requires a change in the way economic policy is made. The financial rescue of Mexico in 1995, despite congressional opposition, was also a reminder that partners bring obligations as well as opportunities.

NAFTA will probably survive these stresses and strains. The process of economic integration among the three countries is almost certainly irreversible and the benefits are substantial (see Chapter 5). However, the deepening of NAFTA will not necessarily lead to a broadening through the FTAA or the inclusion of other members. On the contrary, the responsibilities associated with NAFTA (e.g. environmental improvements), coupled with the highly visible costs (e.g. job losses in labour-intensive industries), are likely to reduce even further the popular appeal of the FTAA and increase congressional resistance to fast-track. The coalition in favour of NAFTA, a bare majority in Congress even in 1993, will be hard to rebuild for other countries in the Americas.

The Clinton administration cannot abandon the FTAA and negotiations will take place as agreed at the Santiago summit. However, there will be no urgency to the discussions and Latin American countries will be reluctant to make any concessions in the absence of fast-track. As the clock ticks towards 2005, it will become increasingly difficult to weld together the different integration schemes in the Americas. The European experience in this respect is not a precedent: the competition between the European Free Trade Area (EFTA) and the EEC led to the absorption of the former by the latter. It is difficult to imagine something similar in the Americas.

If the FTAA falters, the prospect for PTAs between the European Union and the different countries/regions of the Americas will recede. It is possible that the PTA with Mexico may be concluded, because it is so much further advanced than the others. Yet even this is not certain and it is unlikely to set much of a precedent for MERCOSUR. For both Mexico and the EU, a PTA is largely symbolic; the volume of trade is small and is unlikely to increase by much even with a PTA. MERCOSUR is different and the EU would have to make painful concessions if an agreement were to be reached. The pain may seem unnecessary if the threat of exclusion from the Americas through an FTAA has receded.

Whatever happens, trade links between Latin American countries and the USA seem set to grow. The logic of globalisation, cultural ties and the erosion of language barriers are all pushing in the same direction. The United States has proven its ability to retain and even increase market share in adverse conditions. With or without the FTAA, the strengthening of economic ties between the USA and its hemispheric neighbours is a safe conclusion. And trade between the United States and Cuba – once a major partner – has only one direction in which it can go.

Notes

1. 'Latin America' in this chapter means Latin America and the Caribbean unless otherwise stated. This corresponds closely to 'western hemisphere' in the publications of the International Monetary Fund.
2. See Bulmer-Thomas (1994), Tables 3.6 and 3.7.
3. The shares of exports and imports in 1996 were 17.6 per cent and 15.4 per cent respectively. See IMF (1997), p. 454.
4. In this paper we use the term Preferential Trade Agreement (PTA) rather than Regional Trade Agreement (RTA) to refer to a legally binding arrangement in which countries offer trade concessions to each other, but not to third countries. We use Free Trade Agreement (FTA) only when it is part of the title of an agreement, e.g. the North American Free Trade Agreement (NAFTA).
5. When Mexico under President López Portillo (1976-82) was approached by the USA with a view to signing a PTA, the offer was rejected. No doubt old-fashioned nationalism was part of the explanation, but economics also played a large part.
6. Regions and regionalism have received considerable scholarly attention recently. See, for example, Bhagwati, Greenaway and Panagariya (1998), Ethier (1998) and Fernández and Portes (1998).
7. The ITO therefore never came into existence, leaving GATT – which at the time of its creation (1947) was assumed to be only temporary.
8. See Wonnacott (1994).
9. The only absentees from the Americas were Cuba and those territories which are colonies or departments of metropolitan powers.
10. Chile had been identified at the Summit of the Americas as the first country to be invited to negotiate to join an enlarged NAFTA.
11. Figure 4.1 includes observations for all 34 countries involved in the FTAA except Canada and the USA (not relevant) and Antigua, St Kitts and St Lucia (data not given in source).
12. At the Belo Horizonte meeting, countries in customs unions won the right to negotiate as a bloc. However, the USA reserved the right to negotiate as a single country and not as a member of NAFTA.
13. These commitments are to ALADI, the regional body created in 1980 as the successor to LAFTA (Latin America Free Trade Area).
14. See Wyplosz (1997).

CHAPTER 5

TRADE, INVESTMENT AND NAFTA:
THE ECONOMICS OF NEIGHBOURHOOD

E.V.K. FitzGerald[*]

In the field of world policy I would dedicate this Nation to the policy of the good neighbor.

Franklin D. Roosevelt, Inaugural address,
4 March 1933[1]

My apple trees will never get across
And eat the cones under his pines, I tell him.
He only says, 'Good fences make good neighbors.'

Robert Frost 'Mending Wall' (1914)

Whenever our neighbour's house is on fire, it cannot be amiss for the engines to play a little on our own.

Edmund Burke (1790)[2]

The North American Free Trade Agreement (NAFTA) represents a major departure in the economic and institutional relationship between the United States and the other nations of the Americas. On the one hand, it involves an explicit commitment to market integration – not only in goods but also in services and capital markets – with significant additional agreements in employment and environmental standards. On the other, it appears to involve an implicit step back from the traditional US commitment to multilateral agreements on free trade and open capital markets on a global scale, while not contemplating the free movement of labour.[3]

From the point of view of US-Latin American economic relations, the implications of the progress of NAFTA since its inception in 1994 are considerable, both for the integration of the region in general and for the nature of the proposed Free Trade Area of the Americas in particular.[4] Mexico accounts for over half of the trade between the USA and Latin America. Mexico is the destination for most US investment in the region, and the origin of the bulk of immigration – both legal and illegal. So the integration of the NAFTA economies will have profound consequences for not only the foreign trade of Latin America, but also its relationship with the USA.

Evaluating a trade agreement of such magnitude – in 1997 the three NAFTA countries generated one-fifth of world trade – would be no simple task so soon after its inception even without the major disruption caused by the 1995 peso collapse and the consequent macroeconomic shock in Mexico. Moreover, since signing in 1993 it has been clear that

> the NAFTA negotiations not only marked the virtual completion (rather than the negotiation) of a free trade area in North America, but also suggested that NAFTA itself may quite rapidly evolve through a customs union into a wider economic community – if not by design, then by institutional response to problems of regulatory practice. ...While the direct consequence of NAFTA itself should be quite modest trade creation and very limited trade diversion, the indirect consequences might include a considerable diversion of capital flows towards Mexico, to the possible detriment of productive investment elsewhere in the region. Further... the institutional consequences of NAFTA within North America may be much greater than is currently anticipated, and will probably be such as to delay further links between the USA and other Latin American countries.[5]

This chapter contains five elements. In Section 2, the original objectives and expectations of the interested parties are recalled, followed in Sections 3 and 4 by a necessarily incomplete evaluation of the initial trends in trade and factor market integration during the first five years of application. Section 5 then discusses the major disruptive incident of the period – the 1995 peso crisis – in terms of the mutual causalities involved and the institutional consequences of the resolution of cross-border monetary instability. The implications of NAFTA for trade and investment relations in the rest of Latin America are explored in Section 6. Finally, Section 7 concludes with some speculative remarks about the implications of NAFTA for constitutional change in the USA itself.

Origins and Objectives of NAFTA

In 1980 expectations of economic relations between Mexico and the USA were very different from what they were to become by 1990. Attempts to establish a 'New International Economic Order' that would overcome unequal exchange between industrialised and industrialising countries during the 1970s meant that secular integration between the Mexican and US economies was seen as problematic for both the Mexican national development project and social stability in the USA, each of which seemed to be threatened by growing capital and labour flows across the Rio Bravo.[6] Events did not turn out that way, for at least three reasons: the Mexican debt crisis of 1982, which forced a policy shift away from the concept of an independent state-led industrialisation model; the change in the economic paradigm in Latin America during the 1980s in Latin America, and the world as a whole after 1989; and the domestic reaction against multilateralism within the USA itself, accompanied by a perceived threat from the European Union and Asian industrial exporters.

By the early 1990s two historical trends had converged in US politics. On the one hand, the 'free trade alliance' of multi-national corporations, investment banks, trade unions and consumer groups which had dominated US trade policy since World War II had broken up. On the other hand, a strong strain of populist isolationism had reappeared as a major force in local and congressional politics. The free trade alliance had been formed in the 1920s as a reaction against the high US tariffs of the previous hundred years of import-substituting industrialisation; these were now felt to be unnecessary because US manufactures were now internationally competitive. This view was clearly reinforced by the destruction of Europe and Japan during World War II: with the USA the dominant force in the world economy, there was a clear benefit from expanding global trade as her share was unlikely to rise further. Initially a Democrat policy[7] backed by labour unions in search of export-based jobs, trade liberalisation had become bipartisan by the 1960s as Republicans came to reflect the interest of large business. Nonetheless, US policy-makers were continually forced to construct domestic political coalitions to support freer world trade[8] as well as putting pressure on trade partners.

By the 1970s the USA was felt to be losing ground in world trade and technological innovation compared to Europe and Japan; both labour unions and firms in vulnerable sectors shifted back towards protectionism. Indeed, from 1970 onwards the Nixon Administration could not pass trade liberalisation legislation; and no new trade bill was in fact achieved until the end of the 1980s. Support for full free trade was now mainly confined to a narrow yet powerful coalition of multinational corporations and banks, neo-liberal economic experts and foreign government representatives seeking access to the US market. Technological change and the shift of production overseas alarmed both labour unions and small business, which in turn affected both political parties at the state and congressional level. Finally, the US strategic perception of external threat shifted towards economic competition after the end of the Cold War.

The NAFTA negotiations logically became an occasion for this political conflict, despite the fact that

> ...NAFTA is not really about global free trade. It does remove trade and investment barriers among the United States, Canada and Mexico, but it maintains and erects (in the form of 'rules of origin') barriers between the three countries and the rest of the world. Appearances aside, NAFTA is a prudent step towards creating a regional trading bloc that would withstand the devolution of Western Europe and Asia into rival blocs. The treaty's free trade proponents would never admit this, but NAFTA's underlying thrust is toward managed trade and investment.[9]

At the level of US policy-making,

> NAFTA was originally seen by its promoters as an opportunity to
> reward the Mexican government for its sweeping economic reforms
> (and) consolidate its neighbour's political and social stability (and)
> an opportunity to gain access to Mexico's rich natural resources,
> particularly oil, and to take advantage of its large cheap labour
> market. (Moreover) ... the Salinas administration overwhelmed the
> Bush administration with its commitment to 'leave the past behind'
> and make the USA an offer it could not refuse: to accept a
> partnership with the USA no Mexican government had wanted since
> 1910.[10]

Meanwhile, Mexico itself had abandoned its attempt at independent national industrialisation along the 'East Asian' model by the mid-1980s – largely as a consequence of the 1982 debt crisis. The de la Madrid administration unexpectedly entered GATT in 1985 – effectively lowering its trade barriers with the USA without demanding or receiving reciprocal concessions. NAFTA was thus regarded by Mexico not just – or even principally – as a channel for privileged access to the US market, but also as a means of 'locking in' Mexican macroeconomic policy and thus ensuring the confidence of the domestic and foreign investors required for industrial modernisation. Beyond these general aims, 'Mexico entered the NAFTA negotiations and the parallel agreements with virtually no agenda of its own'.[11]

The North American Free Trade Agreement is clearly a remarkable step forward in the long-term process of economic integration between the USA and its two neighbours. However, NAFTA does not really constitute a full customs union as there is no common external tariff structure even though trade barriers have been more or less eliminated between the three partners. Still less is it a 'common market' because, although there is free movement of goods and capital in the treaty, there is no free movement of labour and there are few if any common regulatory institutions.

Moreover, NAFTA negotiations were conducted in the framework of the closing stages of the GATT Uruguay Round, which in any case required considerable reduction of trade barriers of all member countries. As we have seen, trade liberalisation had in fact been started by Mexico with unilateral entry to GATT in 1985 in an effort to restructure the domestic economy through external trade and investment competition, so that by 1993 it had become one of the most open markets in Latin America. Canada, of course, already had a free trade agreement with the USA. In other words, NAFTA represented a recognition of a developing integration process rather than its cause.

Moreover, the emerging relationship between the three economies is not one of specialisation along the lines of 'comparative advantage' based on factor endowments in the textbook sense. In that case we would expect the USA to specialise in capital- and skill-intensive production, Canada to focus on natural resource- and skill-intensive products, and Mexico to rely on natural resources and unskilled labour. In fact, manufacturing trade is expanding most rapidly between Mexico and North America, particularly intra-industry trade between (or within) firms in the same sector. In the case of Mexico, the dynamic sectors are not the labour-intensive ones[12] but rather the relatively heavy industries where scale and transport effects are important – such as steel, cement, glass, paper – and integrated production systems such as automobiles and electronics.

The key advantage of NAFTA for Mexico – and by implication for any other Latin American country which eventually joins – is not the tariff reductions but rather the 'rules of origin' which grant preferential access to the US market.[13] By extension this advantage permits the relocation of US industry and makes investment from the rest of the world in Mexico extremely attractive – although a number of clauses in the agreement are intended to keep NAFTA preferences exclusive to the parties. In relation to goods these preferences are explicitly expressed in the form of rules of origin and the gradual elimination of temporary import provisions (to 2001); for services and foreign investment, there is a general equivalence to the origin rule. NAFTA does not exhibit any directions on the harmonisation of financial services regulation, in marked contrast with the explicit agreements on the unification of financial services in the European Union.[14] In fact, NAFTA focuses on types of financial intermediation rather than on financial products – an approach that is more congruent with Mexico's regulatory practice rather than that of the USA or Canada – while the stability of the financial system in each country remains the responsibility of the authorities of the receiving country, independently of the degree of participation of foreign intermediaries.[15]

One of the most noteworthy aspects of NAFTA is the lack of any common institutional arrangements between the member countries. The only provision is for arbitration commissions in trade disputes: there is no provision for joint supervision of standards or competition, nor for any means of easing the adjustment of declining sectors or poorer regions. The separate initiative of the 'North American Development Bank' to fund border transport, water and environmental projects was still-born. In consequence NAFTA itself has no explicit provision for joint intergovernmental action, and even the dispute settlement mechanisms are somewhat imprecise. However, historical precedent indicates that the practice of trade relations will eventually lead to a felt need for a formal coordination mechanism, and the gradual harmonisation of commercial legislation. The scale of private capital flows between the three countries will also lead to a need for tax coordination and mutual bank regulation, both of which will require more legislative change on the part of the USA than on that of Canada or Mexico due to the federal nature of the former.

This is all the more surprising when one of the partners (Mexico) has a very different economic structure, income level and administrative framework from the other two. Incomes *per capita*, output per worker and wage levels are comparable in the USA and Canada; but productivity is three times greater than in Mexico, and wages four times higher. In terms of relative bargaining power, moreover, another partner (the USA) has an aggregate output level ten times the size of the other two combined, and over twice their population. These asymmetries – summarised in Table 5.1 below – logically imply that the implementation of a common market would require complex institutional arrangements to ensure smooth integration.

Table 5.1:
Structural Heterogeneity within NAFTA

	USA	Canada	Mexico
Population (mn, 1995)	260.7	29.3	88.4
GDP (US$bn, 1995)	6,981	565	235
GDP/head (US$ PPP[a], 1995)	26,525	21,002	6,780
Manufacturers' gross output per worker (US$, 1995)	202,793	180,485	68,057
Manufacturers' wages per worker (US$, 1995)	31,803	28,001	5,080

(a) PPP – Purchasing Power Parity exchange rates used.
Source: UNIDO (1997).

The contingent fiscal liability for the USA in assuming explicit responsibility for social and institutional adjustment in Mexico was an obvious deterrent and one to which the US legislature could not agree.[16] This essentially political decision was supported by the view of mainstream US economists that markets do not need institutions anyway. In particular, it was felt that a central NAFTA secretariat and compensation provisions would only lead to a Brussels-style bureaucracy and controlled markets.

Nonetheless, the institutional responsibilities implicit in economic integration undoubtedly explain why further extension of NAFTA towards Latin America has been stalled. The US Congress has refused to grant 'fast-track' negotiating authority, despite the desire of many Latin American countries – particularly Chile – to accede, and the support of the US executive for such initiatives.[17] NAFTA itself has signed no trade agreements and indeed it does not really possess the institutionality, let alone the secretariat, necessary to conduct such negotiations with third parties. The EU, for instance, has had to negotiate trade agreements with the three members separately.

Political considerations within the USA have also stalled the concession of NAFTA parity to Central American and Caribbean states, despite the commitments under the Caribbean Basin Initiative since the mid-1980s. In consequence, both Canada and Mexico have pursued bilateral arrangements similar in many ways to NAFTA.[18] In contrast, the USA has limited its offer to Latin America to the very general proposals of the Free Trade Area of the Americas (FTAA) which contains little more than what is already available under the WTO.[19]

Trends in NAFTA Trade

Since 1990, the main gains in trading volume within NAFTA have clearly been made by Mexico and Canada in terms of increased exports to the USA and thus an increased share of that market. Table 5.2 shows the ratios of exports in 1996 to those of 1990 for the three members; we take 1990 as the base year because the integration process was well under way before the formal initiation of NAFTA in 1994. Mexican exports to the USA have more than doubled while those to Canada have increased more than tenfold.[20] Exports of all three countries to other NAFTA members have increased significantly more than to the rest of the world (RoW). Thus, NAFTA has become somewhat more 'closed' in trade terms – a point to which we will return in Table 5.2 below.

Table 5.2:
NAFTA Trade Expansion Ratios 1996/1990

	Destination					
	USA	Canada	Mexico	NAFTA	RoW	World
Origin:						
USA	—	1.60	2.01	1.70	1.54	1.59
Canada	2.52	—	1.80	1.73	1.16	1.59
Mexico	2.49	11.00	—	2.54	1.75	2.39
NAFTA	1.92	1.62	1.99	1.83	1.51	1.64

Source: Calculated from Appendix Table 5.A.1.

The key issue is whether this remarkable increase is due to trade creation or trade diversion: in other words, is it due to higher-cost producers within NAFTA being protected from competitive exporters from the rest of the world; or is it the result of new efficiency brought about by the larger market? To resolve this conundrum we would have to examine individual commodity groups (as the new trade pattern might reflect a change in the commodity composition of trade itself due to industrial restructuring) and areas of the world to see whether any trade diversion (allowing for relative exchange rate shifts) has been at the expense of Latin America or of Europe and Japan. Broadly, Table 5.3 indicates that Latin America appears to have maintained its position as an export destination for the USA and Canada, but has lost ground as an import source relative to Mexico. Europe appears to be the real loser from the expansion of trade with Mexico, while Asia has retained its share.[21]

Table 5.3:
North America – Export and Import Shares (%)

	1990 Exports	1996 Exports	1990 Imports	1996 Imports
Asia	25.5	26.4	34.8	34.9
EU	21.9	16.8	18.6	16.6
Latin America	10.7	13.7	11.2	13.5
Mexico	5.5	7.0	5.1	7.9
Rest	5.2	6.7	6.1	5.6
Intra-NAFTA	34.2	36.0	26.6	27.8
RoW	7.7	7.1	8.8	7.2

Source: WTO (1997).

A clearer illustration of this trend in trade patterns can be detected by examining the respective income elasticities of demand, because this allows for the effect of market growth.[22] Table 5.4 shows the 'implicit trade demand elasticity', which relates GDP growth in the importing region to the growth of its imports from another region. The higher this elasticity, the more 'competitive' that supplier region is, due to improved quality or relative prices – these in turn reflecting costs or protective barriers. The 'implicit export elasticities' in Table 5.4 suggest that it is much 'easier' for North America to export to itself or to Latin America than to Asia, Europe or the rest of the world, and within Latin America to Mexico. This is what we would expect from a customs union, but to the extent that the extra-union elasticities are still unitary or more, trade creation rather than diversion seems to be the main explanation. Similarly, the import elasticities into North America are much higher for Mexico and Latin America than for other regions, but these latter are significantly greater than unity – again suggesting trade creation rather than trade diversion. On balance, therefore, it is probable that trade integration within NAFTA has not been at the expense of other regions.[23]

Table 5.4:
Implicit Trade Demand Elasticities

	NAFTA export growth 1990-96 (% per year)	NAFTA import growth 1990-96 (% per year)	GDP growth rate, 1990-96 (% per year)	Implicit export elasticity	Implicit import elasticity
Asia	9	8	8.7	1.0	5.0
EU	3	6	1.5	2.0	3.8
Latin America	12	11	3.5	3.4	6.9
Mexico	12	16	2.2	5.5	10.0
Intra-NAFTA	9	7	1.6	5.6	4.4
RoW	8	8	3.1	2.6	5.0

Source: Calculated from WTO (1997), IMF (1998).

Nonetheless, regional 'openness' – that is, the proportion of trade outside the region – of the three NAFTA members has declined considerably since 1990, as Table 5.A.1 indicates (see Appendix for Tables 5.A.1 to 5.A.4). In 1996 NAFTA members sent 47 per cent of their exports to each other, compared to 43 per cent in 1990. Indeed the trade integration for the Western Hemisphere as a whole has risen too so that over 50 per cent of Western Hemisphere exports are intra-regional (see Table 4.3 in previous chapter). Taking NAFTA as a whole, the proportion of the merchandise exports of the three members going to the rest of the world has fallen from 58 per cent in 1988 to 53 per cent in 1996 so that, if current trends continue, the main source of US trade dynamism will lie within the Western Hemisphere – with NAFTA itself the core of this driving force. Averaging the import and export shares yields an intra-regional trade coefficient in 1996 of 43 per cent for NAFTA compared to 21 per cent for MERCOSUR and 63 per cent for the

EU.[24] Yet the relative importance of NAFTA trade to the three partners is very different: in 1996 it accounted for 86 per cent of Mexican exports, and 82 per cent of Canadian exports, but only 30 per cent of US exports; while Mexico-Canada trade is very limited – only 2 per cent and 1 per cent of their respective exports (see Table 4.4 in previous chapter).

The departure of NAFTA from textbook notions of comparative advantage is underlined by the composition of Mexican merchandise exports to North America shown in Table 5.5. In 1996 some 79 per cent were manufactures and only 7 per cent and 11 per cent agriculture and mining respectively; within manufactures, textiles and clothing (the journalistic image of the border sweatshop) account for only 1 per cent; some three-quarters of manufactured exports are in fact machinery and transport equipment.[25] The Mexican share of North American imports has risen spectacularly over time in key industrial categories: by 1996 Mexico accounted for 12 per cent of automotive imports and 22 per cent of electrical machinery imported into the USA and Canada.[26] Only one half of Mexican imports from North America are intermediate goods; and Mexico not only accounts for 21 per cent of all North American exports of electrical machinery but also a surprising 20 per cent of clothing exports. In value terms, imports and exports of agricultural products are more or less balanced.

In other words, NAFTA is 'about' the promotion of inter-sectoral specialisation. The leading products traded both ways are in fact automotive components, followed by electrical goods. A consequence is that a large part of the trade is *within* firms: about half of the total exports to the USA from Mexico are believed to be of this kind; while the proportion for USA-Canada is even higher.

Table 5.5:
Merchandise Imports of North America from Mexico by Product, 1980-96

	US$bn 1996	per cent of NAFTA Imports 1980	1985	1990	1996
Total merchandise imports	78.5	4.1	4.6	5.1	7.9
Manufactures	62.0	2.2	2.8	4.4	8.0
Machinery and Transport Equipment	44.3	2.4	3.3	5.5	9.7
Electrical machinery	9.5	11.7	11.9	16.1	21.6
Automotive products	17.9	0.6	2.4	4.8	12.2

Source: WTO (1997).

In mid-1997, the US administration was required to present an evaluation of NAFTA trade to Congress. This was clearly a difficult task because of the intervening devaluation of the peso and the simultaneous reduction of tariffs with other nations under GATT. NAFTA had been explicitly presented by Clinton as part of his three-part economic strategy of fiscal deficit elimination, investment in education and training, and competitive market opening to the global economy. Canada had already become the major US trade partner; and by early 1997, due to the major 1996-97 increase after devaluation, US exports to Mexico made it nearly equal to Japan as the second trade partner. Mexico was said to have reduced tariffs from a 10 per cent average in 1992 (they had fallen precipitously in 1985 on GATT entry) down to 3 per cent on average in 1997, while the USA had reduced average tariffs from 2 per cent to 1 per cent in the same period. Although much of these reductions (as is the case with Mexico) would have been achieved under the Uruguay Round even without NAFTA, US exports to Mexico grew faster than vice-versa – partly because Mexico cut its tariffs much more than the USA – allowing US firms to displace other suppliers. In this context, it is interesting to note that despite the fears of competitive devaluation by Mexico in order to penetrate US markets, and the explicit provisions in NAFTA for emergency powers to block such 'import surges', after the 1995 devaluation the sharp increase in Mexican exports did not encounter significant resistance within the USA.

Factor Market Integration

The main economic simulations of the economic impact of NAFTA made as part of the negotiations all showed that the aggregate economic benefits would come from capital flows rather than from trade as such. Expected GDP growth gains from investment reallocation were projected to four times greater than those from trade reallocation:

> It is in the domain of capital movements, rather than trade, that one should look for the real levers behind the integration movement. (However) the capital inflows (could) lead to a strong appreciation of the peso, causing severe damage to large parts of Mexican industry, followed by a period of acute balance of payments difficulties as capital outflows decline sharply.[27]

Indeed, it can convincingly be argued that the importance of NAFTA is not the exchange of merchandise as such but rather the guarantees it offers to traders and investors.[28]

The growth in the stock of inward foreign direct investment (FDI) in Mexico in recent years is notable, as Table 5.A.2 indicates. The increase up to 1995 is strongly affected by major privatisations such as Telmex, and until 1997 figures are available it will not be possible to assess the effect of the 1995 crisis or the diversion effect relative to the rest of Latin America. Nonetheless, the ratio of the Mexican FDI inward stock to GDP (the most appropriate scaling factor) shown in Table 5.6 is not only higher than the average for the world, developing countries and Latin America but also rising over time. This would seem to indicate that the Mexican productive structure is increasingly coming under foreign control (albeit in some cases by expatriate Mexican firms), a feature which is reflected by the fact that half of the stock of Mexican financial securities are now traded on the New York stock exchange.

Table 5.6:
Inward Foreign Direct Investment Stock as a percentage of GDP

	1980	1985	1990	1995
World	4.6	6.4	8.3	10.1
Developing Countries (Dev C)	4.3	8.1	8.7	15.4
LAC[(a)]	6.4	10.8	11.6	18.4
Mexico	4.2	10.2	13.2	25.6
Mex/world (%)	91	159	159	253
Mex/DevC (%)	98	126	152	166
Mex/LAC (%)	66	94	114	139

(a) LAC – Latin America and Caribbean.

Source: UNCTAD (1997).

Turning to the flows of FDI, the Mexican average for 1995-96 was US$ 7.2 billion per year – much greater than the 1991-93 average of US$ 4.5 billion. The decline from the 1994 peak shown in Table 5.A.3 is clearly due to the peso crisis – although FDI is generally much less volatile than portfolio capital flows by its very nature.[29] What the FDI inflows would have been in the absence of the peso crisis can only be guessed, but would presumably have approached US$ 15 billion and represented a considerable diversion from investment elsewhere in the region.

The importance of FDI has three dimensions: the contribution to investable resources and increased access to bank credit; the flow of new technology and management techniques; and the access to export markets. Table 5.7 shows that the contribution of FDI to gross fixed capital formation (GFCF) in Mexico is higher than elsewhere. In fact, corporate investment probably accounts for about half of GFCF in Mexico, and if FDI finances one half of affiliates' investment,[30] then the ratio of foreign affiliates' investment to corporate GFCF in Mexico is of the order of 60 per cent.

Table 5.7:
Inward Foreign Direct Investment as Percentage of Gross Fixed Capital Formation (GFCF)

	1985-90	1991	1993	1995
World	5.4	3.1	4.4	5.2
Developing Countries (DevC)	8.0	4.4	6.6	8.2
LAC[(a)]	11.3	7.8	7.2	11.0
Mexico	16.9	13.6	5.8	13.5
Mex/world (%)	313	439	132	260
Mex/DevC (%)	211	309	88	165
Mex/LAC (%)	150	174	81	123

(a) LAC – Latin America and Caribbean.

Source: UNCTAD (1997).

Over half of all foreign investment in Mexico is believed to come from the USA, although this would include (say) Japanese firms with US affiliates. Thus, foreign investment involves large-scale reorganisation of production networks within the NAFTA countries, dominated by US firms, to supply all three markets from a single plant – in effect the 'southern movement of the rust belt'. This regional restructuring necessarily involves the transfer of management and technology as well as market access.

Labour market integration is perhaps the most contentious aspect of NAFTA. This is partly due to the illegal nature of much immigration across the Rio Bravo, but also to the fact that the US labour market is changing rapidly under the pressure of technological change. The underlying problem is that, although goods and capital can move freely across the border, labour cannot. In all three countries, rising industrial production has been accompanied by even more rapid decline in industrial employment. This implies that increasing productivity has come as much from shedding labour as from increasing the capital stock available for each worker. This is understandable in the case of Canada and Mexico, but much less so in the case of Mexico, and may indicate that the technology transferred is not the most appropriate in view of the high degree of underemployment of the workforce. In particular, it is difficult to see from these figures that industrial employment is being 'exported south'; indeed, aggregate industrial employment in the three member countries has fallen by about 13 per cent between 1980 and 1995 to 20.8 million.

In this context, confused and confusing arguments and data have been mobilised as to the effects of NAFTA on employment in the USA, and by implication Mexico too. According to the US administration, exports to NAFTA supported 2.3 million jobs in 1996; and as US exports have grown, so has the employment generated. The number of such jobs created between 1994 and 1996 (net of losses from increased imports) is estimated as 90-160,000; which is insignificant compared to an official estimate of 8.6 million jobs created in the USA during the same period. A coalition of labour unions, environmentalists, 'liberal' economists and isolationist Republicans argues that NAFTA has harmed workers and the environment on both sides of the US-Mexican border. The AFL-CIO claims that 400,000 jobs have been lost; but that only 100,000 were eligible for Labour Department special unemployment assistance and retraining and thus officially registered. The calculations are rendered even less meaningful by the effects of the peso crisis in 1995; and in any case it can plausibly be argued that the aggregate level of employment in the USA is continually adjusted upwards by the Federal Reserve's monetary fine-tuning.[31]

The US labour market is strongly segmented, with little direct competition between legal immigrants and native-born workers; nevertheless the supply of low-wage immigrant labour has helped to control aggregate wage costs in the economy. It has allowed native whites to move up the wage ladder, while increasing labour market flexibility and thus easing production adjustment. According to the US Census Bureau, of 24.6 million legal immigrants resident in the USA in 1996, 27 per cent were from Mexico, and 3 per cent from Canada. The average age of immigrants on arrival is 30 years, and just over half are female. 22 per cent live below the federal poverty line; a ratio similar to that for blacks and twice the rate for native-born population as a whole. Non-citizen legal residents earned considerably less than native-born workers in 1996: this 'immigrant wage discount' has widened steadily from 4 per cent in 1970 to 25 per cent in 1980 and 27 per cent in 1996. The cross-border wage and skill differentials thus remain large.

The political pressure to reduce immigration (an argument much used by President Bush to justify NAFTA) is led by local residents and labour unions (see Chapter 11). Business organisations have lobbied in favour of relatively unrestrictive policies on immigration: firms in the agribusiness, textile and meat packing sectors seek to ensure a steady supply of low-skill, low-wage but highly motivated workers from Mexico.[32] In contrast, firms in the high-technology sector have favoured the immigration of skilled workers from Asia. The 1996 Illegal Immigration Reform and Immigrant Responsibility Act stepped up measures against illegal migration including fines on employers. Also 1996 welfare reforms were intended to deter inward migration, as even new legal residents without citizenship are deprived of Supplemental Security Assistance.

Table 5.8:
Productivity, Wages and Unit Labour Costs Relative to the USA, 1980-95

	1980	1985	1990	1995
Canada				
Productivity	80%	73%	79%	70%
Wages	75%	69%	82%	88%
Unit labour costs	93%	94%	103%	126%
Mexico				
Productivity	44%	35%	26%	34%
Wages	28%	15%	12%	16%
Unit labour costs	64%	43%	45%	47%

Source: Calculated from Table 5.A.3.

Industrial productivity and manufacturing wages in Mexico and Canada relative to the USA exhibit contrary trends, as Table 5.8 indicates. Productivity in Canada is about two-thirds of that in the USA while in Mexico it is about one-third. Over the long term it appears to be rising faster in the USA than in either Mexico or Canada, so there is little sign of secular convergence. However, there does seem to have been some relative catching up by Mexico since 1990 which can be attributed to trade and investment integration.

Relative wages show a different story: Canadian wages have converged with those in the USA, presumably because there is fairly free labour movement between the two economies. In contrast, real wages in Mexico have fallen sharply relative to the USA since 1980, the ratio falling by about one half, due not only to relative productivity trends but also to deliberate labour market segmentation. Unit labour costs in the three countries[33] have thus moved in contrary directions. While unit labour costs in Canada have risen steadily in relation to those in the USA, in Mexico they declined strongly to about one-half in the mid-1980s and have remained there since. While it is not possible to claim that NAFTA has harmed US (or Canadian) workers in terms of wages or employment, it is difficult to claim that it has helped Mexican workers either.

The Peso Crisis as a Test for NAFTA[34]

The pre-announcement of NAFTA and the privatisation of state enterprises generated a large amount of foreign direct investment (mainly from the USA but also from the EU and Japan) to Mexico in the early 1990s, which was consistent with the strategic scenario of the negotiators. However, Mexico also attracted a wave of short-term investment from New York and London, which was attracted not only by the high real interest rates but also by the implicit guarantee to investors afforded by NAFTA. This implicit guarantee had two elements: first, that Mexico was now 'locked in' to a sound macroeconomic policy and that in particular it would not have to devalue as it could count on US support for the peso; and second, that US institutional investors of Mexican government bonds would be bailed out by the US authorities if anything went wrong. There was no legal or institutional basis for this market belief, but rather a general expectation as to the political behaviour of Washington and Mexico City.

The peso collapse of 1994/5 was thus a major test for the two governments, and thus by implication for NAFTA itself. In the event, the trade agreement held together well, despite fears that an export surge from Mexico would create lobby pressure from US producers for temporary protection measures. The lack of a proper framework for financial, monetary and exchange-rate coordination between the two countries led to near-disaster, however. There was no adequate means of policy coordination between the Bank of Mexico and the Federal Reserve, so that the exchange rate adjustment could not be properly managed. The US bondholders were correct in their expectations: Washington did have to act as lender of last resort so that they could be paid; but the Federal Reserve did not have the powers to do this, nor would Congress provide the funds. In the event, the IMF was forced by the USA to make an emergency loan to Mexico three times higher than its rules allow; the US Treasury was forced to allocate some of the reserves held for the defence of the dollar and commit European resources without prior consultation.[35] A regional – and possibly global – capital markets crisis was averted, but on an *ad hoc* basis.

The Mexican response was a draconian but orthodox stabilisation policy based on fiscal contraction and monetary expansion limited to the emergency fund needed to prevent retail banks from collapsing. Trade restrictions were not used to control the balance of payments deficit, but rather demand reductions. This can be considered a successful outcome of NAFTA in the sense that trade and investment liberalisation was not threatened nor payments suspended. The reduced domestic demand for Mexican output, plus the large real devaluation, meant that Mexican exports to the USA recovered very quickly. The fact that the import surge into the USA was not countered by any generalised trade restrictions – other than some long-standing sectional claims – can also be attributed to the successful implantation of NAFTA north of the border.

As a result Mexico recovered from the 1995 crisis comparatively quickly, in terms of both output and trade – although not in terms of employment or wages – and certainly much faster than after the debt shock of 1982. The confidence of longer-term investors was also maintained by the belief that Mexico would not abandon the economic reform programme – in part at least because of NAFTA. During the 1982-83 macroeconomic adjustment, US exports to Mexico fell by over 50 per cent; in 1994-95 they fell only 2 per cent – Mexico's 35 per cent adjustment was all from other import sources, particularly Japan and the EU. At least four linkages were involved. First, NAFTA trade provisions attracted investors to export to the USA at lower costs. Second, existing investors were reassured by the fact that NAFTA locked in Mexico's trade and payments policy. Third, the financial liberalisation enabled Mexico to attract longer-term funding in order to repay the last-resort lending rapidly. Fourth, automatic access to the US market allowed producers to switch sales rapidly from Mexican to US clients.

However, many of the attractions to invest in Mexico were emerging independently of NAFTA, or were only tangentially related to it. On the one hand, the massive privatisation programme attracted both FDI and portfolio inflows that made up the bulk of capital flows to Mexico in the early 1990s. On the other, the decision to switch from external to domestic borrowing opened up a large market in domestic treasury bills, at high real interest rates and eventually denominated in dollars. Both these attractions were underpinned by two changes in US capital markets. The first was the increasing importance of pension and mutual funds, for which Mexican securities became 'investment grade' and thus more attractive than both US treasury paper and other Latin American securities. The second was the fact that a large proportion of Mexican securities turnover (as much as one half in 1994) were traded in New York – usually as depository receipts (ADRs) – and thus represented a highly liquid asset at apparently low risk and high return.

By 1990 it was widely agreed that the highly restricted, government controlled and oligopolistic nature of the Mexican financial system was holding back both domestic and foreign investment. More and faster financial deregulation was urged by the Mexican authorities, the multilateral financial institutions and the US authorities. US banks and financial service companies were also eager to penetrate the large market south of the border. The financial services chapter of NAFTA was very important in this respect, and was expected to reduce the cost of credit to Mexican firms so they could compete better. The main concern of observers was with the efficiency effects of regulatory arbitrage and lack of sufficient competition.[36] The problem of systemic risk was ignored. Indeed, the NAFTA negotiators seem to have deliberately avoided the issue of monetary coordination between the Federal Reserve and the Banco de México (let alone the integration of the two systems for banking and securities regulation) on the tactical grounds that it would generate too much resistance in the US Congress. The lessons of financial integration, indicating an increased need for prudential coordination and last-resort lending as capital markets are opened up,[37] were ignored.

The combination of increased investor confidence and financial liberalisation attracted a flood of short-term capital into Mexico. This sustained the nominal exchange rate and overvalued the real exchange rate, and the trade gap opened as this capital was on-lent by Mexican banks in the form of consumer credit and Mexican firms accepted dollar liabilities in order to avoid high peso interest rates. The *absence* of any coordinated regulatory or monetary approach between the two countries increased the risk of systemic collapse at precisely the same time as investors believed that the Mexican and US authorities *would* act as lenders of last resort – even though there was no provision for this in the agreement and the respective authorities frequently claimed that they would not intervene in this way.

In the event, the bubble collapsed. The massive nominal devaluation reflected a sudden shift in investor perceptions about Mexican securities: it did not relate to relative prices in trade. Neither was it a fiscal crisis because there was no budgetary deficit. Although treasury bills were the object of speculative attack, this was only because it was felt that central bank reserves could not guarantee their immediate payment. In other words, this was a private sector crisis quite unlike that of 1982.[38] As the investors had anticipated, the US and Mexican governments were forced to intervene in order to take over the bad loans and provide new liquidity, thereby preventing a systemic collapse that would have brought down large banks and corporations on both sides of the border. To call this a problem of 'moral hazard' is not analytically useful because no commitment was made by the authorities; rather, a political bet was being made by the investors. If anything, the problem was the reverse: the *absence* in NAFTA of any provisions for creating an orderly capital market was at the root of the problem.

There has been no move to set up intergovernmental financial institutions since 1995, although there has been greater *de facto* coordination between central banks, treasuries and securities regulators in the three member countries. The cost of the peso crisis – whether measured in terms of the cost of the international bailout (US$ 50 billion) and the bad debts of Mexican banks (15 per cent of GDP) or in those of unemployment and wage cuts[39] – is certainly far greater than those of establishing adequate institutions in the first place.

The Implications of NAFTA for Latin America

The effects of NAFTA on the rest of Latin America depend upon the dynamics of the regional grouping. Regional groups, especially if they account for a significant share of world trade, can have a sizeable effect on non-members. A large regional group may shift substantial amounts of trade from suppliers outside the region, shifting terms of trade against non-members, and possibly driving producers in non-member countries out of markets where they may have a clear comparative advantage. When the union's external barrier is high or there is a *perceived* risk that the region may develop a 'fortress mentality' in the future, foreign direct investment that might otherwise have gone to non-members may now flow to the union.　However, non-members may reap gains if trade and investment discrimination is low and falling.　Through the economies of scale and efficiency induced by intensified competition, a large union may be able to export at lower cost: this would imply more favourable terms of trade for non-members, offsetting to an extent the deterioration in the terms of trade that non-members may experience as a result of trade diversion.　Non-members may also benefit from the spillovers of increased demand from outside imports by the regional grouping; and the reduced cost of access to a large market no longer segmented by differential regulations, technical standards and customs formalities.[40]

The emergence of regional trade groupings within a globalising world economy during the 1990s is not just an issue in Latin America.　Given the progress in multilateral trade liberalisation through the WTO, other 'new' regional arrangements are really more concerned with financial services and cross-border investment than with merchandise trade as such.　In this context regional regulatory systems, monetary coordination and even infrastructure provision constitute the 'public goods' that are required in order to create and sustain an orderly market. The experience of NAFTA – both positive and negative – is significant in this respect.

Regional trade agreements involving both industrialised and developing countries have responded to the growing importance of the latter group as an investment location.　Typically, these treaties include commitments on non-discriminatory treatment and investment restrictions.　This appears to be easiest where one of the partners has a clearly dominant position in the region and is committed to a liberalisation agreement.　Investment provisions in the rather loose and diverse group of APEC countries are non-binding; but those in NAFTA or in the EU Association Agreements with eastern European countries are both binding and stringent.　The investment provisions in the NAFTA treaty are in effect the blueprint for both the Multilateral Agreement on Investment currently under negotiation at the OECD and the possible WTO 'Millennium Round'.[41]

Investment provisions are contained in the NAFTA chapters on investment, on services and on financial services.　All three chapters provide for national treatment.　Where a signatory has lodged an exemption from these disciplines Most Favoured Nation (MFN) treatment acts as a minimum standard.　In this case, the host country may discriminate in favour of national firms, but must grant equal treatment to all foreign investors.　Conversely, where the host country government discriminates in favour of foreign firms, such preferential treatment will have to be extended to all foreign investors.　NAFTA also bans a comprehensive list of performance requirements and thereby provides disciplines that go well beyond multilateral disciplines in GATT/WTO.　Most performance requirements are also banned even if the investor agrees to comply with the restriction in return for accepting an investment incentive from the host country.　The dispute settlement mechanism in NAFTA is similarly innovative.　Private investors and not just states have the right to bring cases for arbitration under either ICSID or UNCITRAL, the two international bodies for the settlement of investment disputes – creating the prospect of international investor-state claims.[42]

To date the above provisions represent the strongest international standard with regard to investment liberalisation and protection. Even though the Mexican government needed to liberalise its investment policies significantly to conform with the agreement, it subsequently extended the substantive rights (Chapter 11:A) to investors from outside North America. Still, the agreement has been criticised for a number of shortcomings. Rules of origin could have a distorting effect on trade and investment flows. Disciplines on subsidies are weak and few provisions exist to deal with the competition aspects of inward investment in Mexico. Moreover, where parties were granted exemptions they are free to derogate from the above disciplines. This is the case for Mexican energy and transport sectors, Canadian cultural industries, maritime transport in the USA and for agriculture in all three parties.

NAFTA underscores the benefits of a comprehensive approach to trade and investment liberalisation. Provisions on intellectual property rights, services and technical standards are all integral elements of meaningful investment liberalisation. Nonetheless, the lessons learned from NAFTA are not fully applicable for a more comprehensive investment agreement in the developing world. The strong political interest of the USA in a treaty with Mexico and the previous liberalisation between the USA and Canada make this agreement unique. Nor has the traditional political desire for open export markets and closed import markets in the USA been overcome; but in the case of NAFTA at least this has been undermined by production sharing, and was particularly clear from the parallel agreements on labour standards and the environment.[43] Nonetheless NAFTA does reflect the long-term US goal of liberalising trade in services and foreign investment rules, and intellectual property rights (where the codification of national treatment may be the most significant provision of the whole agreement) – much more than the USA has yet achieved in a multilateral context.

Conclusions

Less than five years after implementation started, NAFTA is generally regarded as irreversible. The complex structure of trade, investment, production and distribution that has been established in the private sector cannot be dismantled without enormous political and economic cost. The process of Mexican, Canadian and US lobbying and negotiation for NAFTA changed inter-state relationships too, as Mexican and Canadian officials started to work directly with their counterparts in Washington and elsewhere rather than through the respective foreign ministries. No political party of any significance in the three countries now seriously opposes NAFTA. This is particularly notable in Mexico, despite the fact that *per capita* incomes are now below the 1980 level and poverty is at an all-time high. However, it is also true that NAFTA is the *result* of a trend towards trade and investment integration rather than the *cause* of one; and that the threats to its future arise from precisely the aspects that were left out of the agreement.

A major obstacle to greater economic policy coordination and regulatory harmonisation between Mexico, Canada and the USA lies in the constitutional and political process in the USA itself. At the inter-governmental level, the evident need for the formalisation of monetary coordination between the three central banks would require a major change in their traditional roles – in effect, there would have to be new thirteenth and fourteenth members of the Federal Reserve System, which in turn would be responsible for monetary stability throughout NAFTA. Federal courts and government agencies would have to recognise the regulatory legitimacy of their Canadian and Mexican counterparts,[44] which would require legislation that would rightly be regarded by opponents as having profound constitutional implications.

Moreover, NAFTA harmonisation of trade and financial services regulations will eventually require major changes at the level of individual US states, if only to prevent regulatory arbitrage and regulatory capture. These changes might be even more politically difficult than changes in federal legislation. There is an evident long term need in the USA for rationalisation of inter-state trade structure, including the introduction of a single retail tax system – probably a Value Added Tax. It may well be that this change will be accelerated by NAFTA.

In a sense, the USA is coming to terms with having neighbours for the first time. This does not just require alterations in external economic relations ('border controls'), but also in internal economic organisation – the fabric of civil society itself. After all, one must live with one's neighbours:

> Any one watching keenly the stealthy convergence of human lots, sees a slow preparation of effects from one life on another, which tells like a calculated irony on the indifference or the frozen stare with which we look at our unintroduced neighbour.

> George Eliot, *Middlemarch* (1871-2), bk. 2, ch. 11

Appendix

Table 5.A.1a:
Merchandise Exports US$bn, 1990

Destination:	USA	Canada	Mexico	NAFTA	RoW	World
Origin:						
USA	—	83.0	28.3	111.3	281.6	392.9
Canada	95.2	—	0.5	95.7	31.2	126.9
Mexico	32.3	0.2	—	32.6	7.6	40.2
NAFTA	127.6	83.2	28.9	239.6	320.4	560.0

Source: WTO (1997).

Table 5.A.1b:
Merchandise Exports US$bn, 1996

Destination:	USA	Canada	Mexico	NAFTA	RoW	World
Origin:						
USA	—	132.6	56.8	189.3	433.4	622.8
Canada	164.6	—	0.9	165.5	36.1	201.6
Mexico	80.5	2.2	—	82.7	13.3	96.0
NAFTA	245.1	134.8	57.6	437.5	482.8	920.4

Source: WTO (1997).

Table 5.A.2:
Inward FDI Stock

US$ billion	1980	1985	1990	1995
World	479.2	745.2	1726.2	3233.8
Developing Countries	106.2	207.3	352.8	917.6
LAC(a)	47.8	76.8	126.1	316.1
Mexico	8.1	18.8	32.5	71.5
Mex/world (%)	2	3	2	2
Mex/DevC (%)	8	9	9	8
Mex/LAC (%)	17	24	26	23

(a) Latin America and Caribbean.

Source: UNCTAD (1997).

Table 5.A.3:
Annual Inward FDI Flow

US$ billion	1985-90	1991	1994	1996
World	141.9	158.9	238.7	249.2
Developing Countries (DevC)	24.7	41.7	90.5	128.7
LAC(a)	8.1	15.3	27.0	38.6
Mexico	2.6	4.8	11.0	7.5
Mex/world (%)	1.8	3.0	4.6	3.0
Mex/DevC (%)	10.5	11.5	12.2	5.8
Mex/LAC (%)	32.1	31.4	40.7	19.4

(a) Latin America and Caribbean.

Source: UNCTAD (1997).

Table 5.A.4:
Manufacturing Productivity and Wages in NAFTA, 1980-95

	1980	1985	1990	1995
Productivity: value added per worker (US$ '000)				
Canada	32.2	42.0	60.0	68.6
Mexico	17.8	20.0	19.3	33.4
USA	40.1	57.2	75.5	98.2
Average Wage (including supplements, US $'000)				
Canada	15.3	19.2	27.5	28.0
Mexico	5.8	4.2	3.9	5.1
USA	20.4	27.9	33.6	31.8

Source: UNIDO (1997).

Notes

* The support of the MacArthur Foundation, for the research programme at Oxford University from which this chapter is derived, is gratefully acknowledged.
1. Franklin D. Roosevelt, *Public Papers* (1938), vol. 2, p. 11.
2. Edmund Burke, *Reflections on the Revolution in France* (1790), p. 10.
3. Indeed, one of the political justifications for NAFTA in the USA was that it would *prevent* labour movement from Mexico, by creating jobs south of the border. See Lustig et al. (1992).
4. Devlin and Garay (1996); see also Chapter 4.
5. FitzGerald (1994, p. 133); this was written in mid-1993.
6. Reynolds and Tello (1981, 1983), written in late 1980.
7. The USA under Truman joined GATT in 1947 against Republican opposition.
8. Such as the intensive lobbying by Kennedy in 1962 for the Trade Expansion Act.
9. 'The Divide', *The New Republic*, 11 October 1993.
10. Aguilar (1994), p. 126.
11. *Ibid.*
12. Where external competition from the Asia/Pacific area is intense.
13. Schettino (1994).
14. FitzGerald and Grabbe (1997).
15. Trigueros (1994).
16. Puerto Rico constituting an alarming precedent.
17. IDB (1998).
18. For instance: Canada with Chile in 1996; Mexico already with Costa Rica, Chile, Bolivia, Ecuador, Venezuela and Colombia, and now with the rest of Central America.
19. Devlin and Garay (1996); see also Chapter 4.
20. Note that all the data are in current US dollars; real exchange rate fluctuations would yield slightly different physical volumes – Mexican exports would increase nearly three-fold in consequence.
21. It remains to be seen what the effect of the East Asian crisis of 1997-98 will be upon NAFTA trade patterns. In the short run (i.e. 1998) the effect appears to have been to reduce exports to the region, but subsequent recovery, based on a much depreciated real exchange rate and considerable excess capacity derived from depressed domestic demand, will presumably lead to an export surge *from* East Asia, and thus an import surge *into* NAFTA. This in turn may well displace imports from the rest of the Western Hemisphere and possibly Europe.
22. In other words, the share of exports going to Europe might have fallen due to European income growth being slower than the rest of the world while the degree of market penetration and competitiveness remained the same.

23. A more sophisticated approach would involve econometric estimation of import functions, and then testing for structural breaks.
24. See WTO (1997).
25. *Ibid.*, Table III.15.
26. The US automobile industry has consolidated plants in Mexico for particular cars (e.g. Ford makes Thunderbirds in Cuautitlán and Mercury Cougars in Ohio) while the autoparts trade has consequently increased both ways. Between 1993 and 1996 investment by the 'big three' automakers was $39 billion in the USA and $3 billion in Mexico.
27. Ros (1994), p. 24. The models are surveyed in USITC (1993).
28. FitzGerald (1994). This of course is a general feature of preferential trade agreements (PTAs), on which see Fernández (1997).
29. World Bank (1997).
30. US affiliates worldwide financed their investment as follows: own funds (25 per cent); host-country sources (28 per cent) other foreign sources (47 per cent). The own sources were made up of equity outflows (6 per cent), reinvested earnings (16 per cent) and intra-firm loans (3 per cent). UNCTAD (1997), p. 27.
31. Weintraub (1997).
32. Logically, smaller employers prefer a regular supply of *undocumented* labour, which accepts lower wages, cannot unionise, and bears no social security costs; thus, they would support neither free immigration nor effective barriers to entry.
33. That is, the ratio of relative wages to relative productivity.
34. The object of this section is not to dissect the Mexican currency crisis as such, but rather to analyse its relationship to the NAFTA.
35. See Griffith-Jones (forthcoming) for a detailed account of these events.
36. Trigueros (1994).
37. FitzGerald (1997).
38. In 1982 the debt was fundamentally public, and owed to foreign banks, so that when higher US interest rates and lower oil prices forced a moratorium it could be negotiated over an extended period and gradually addressed by fiscal consolidation and the sale of public assets (privatisation).
39. See FitzGerald (forthcoming) for an analysis of the 'real economy' effects of capital surges.
40. De la Torre and Kelly (1992), p. 6.
41. Rugman and Gestrin (1995).
42. FitzGerald et al. (1998).
43. Gruben and Welch (1994).
44. In essence, this is the European 'passport' system for mutual recognition agreements (MRAs) applied to trans-border supply of financial services. FitzGerald and Grabbe (1997) explain this system and derive the implications for Latin America.

CHAPTER 6

UNITED STATES FOREIGN RELATIONS AND THE PROMOTION OF DEMOCRACY IN LATIN AMERICA*

Rodolfo Cerdas Cruz

This chapter examines relations between the United States, Latin America and the Caribbean. It does so by placing them in the new context of international politics and by relating them to the promotion and defence of human rights and democratic values in the continent. Given that the United States plays such a predominant and decisive role in the region and has a significant presence on many levels in the institutional and political life of the region, it would seem appropriate to pose several key questions. What is the real purpose and scope of the promotion of democracy and democratic development that the United States government is attempting? What are the contributions, limits and dangers that go with the present policy? And what suggestions can be made to promote more coherent and institutionalised democratic initiatives?

For this reason I have decided to abandon the traditional practice of dealing with the subject in such a global manner that the regional differences, which objectively do exist and which mark the diverse realities of the hemisphere, end up being effaced. This heterogeneous and complex whole that is Latin America has therefore been divided into zones or regions, specifying the criteria to which these divisions are subject.

The guidelines that mark the profile of United States foreign policy and the main areas of interest in each one of the different regions are identified below. There is then an analysis of the traditional methods used up to now before I outline my preferred approach to these questions. This will be done bearing in mind both the positive and the negative aspects of these policies, which in many cases are concomitant with the way in which foreign policy decisions are made in the United States.

Latin America and the Caribbean: Regional Differentiation and Promotion of Democracy

There is no doubt that the end of the Cold War, the demise of the Soviet Union and the communist threat, as well as the accelerated processes of contemporary globalisation, have given rise to important changes in Inter-American relations, both among the Latin American countries themselves, and between them and the United States, the European Union and the Asia-Pacific region. In this changing world, the promotion of democracy from outside, unless effected through military means by a hegemonic power, requires careful specifications and procedures in order to have any chance of success.[1]

In terms of US policy towards the Caribbean and Latin America with regard to the promotion of democracy, one has to recognise the existence of a high degree of regional differentiation, which has generated specific socio-political patterns in each area. These different characteristics range from the demographic and social composition of countries and regions, to the levels of institutionalisation and the particular way in which the processes of transition to democracy have developed.

The application of US policy in each of these different regions requires the adoption of a varying set of specifications in order to respond to the particular characteristics of each area. This inevitably introduces substantial variations in the common objectives of this foreign policy which cannot be ignored.

These characteristics, which help to shape the different regions around which this study is structured, come to light from the moment that factors of a diverse nature are taken into consideration. Examples of such are the different economic and demographic weight of the countries that comprise the region; their financial, economic and commercial links at the subregional and global level; their geographical location; their strategic military potentiality and value, and their specific socio-political problems.

In other words, the starting point is the idea that these different levels of development, and the different socio-political conditions of the countries that make up each region, impose individual and differentiated treatments on the concrete application of US policy towards Latin America, which for their part require specific analysis.

For the purposes of analysis, let us distinguish four main regions:

1.   The first region comprises Mexico and Canada, which together constitute an area where, among other objectives, one of the most immediate concerns is linked to border security. Politically, historically and culturally this represents a whole set of problems and questions that cannot be dealt with here and which are therefore excluded from this chapter (US policy towards Mexico is analysed in Chapter 7 of this book).

2.   The second region is the one comprising the countries of the Caribbean, Central America and Panama. All of them, by extension, share the US notion of extended border security. All these nations are on the whole characterised by a very limited national capacity, due to the size of their populations and national territories, the strength of their economies and their military and technological capability. This puts them in a position of great weakness in resisting certain pressures that, over and above the subjective intentions of the United States, objectively emanate from its hegemonic pretensions and its natural way of relating to national entities as small as those that make up this region.

As in the Mexican case, US interest in the region is related to various factors of US internal political concern. Among these, the following stand out:

a)   These are countries of transit for the movement of drugs and for the laundering of money.

b)   They send large numbers of migrants to the United States, particularly from El Salvador[2] and Nicaragua in Central America, and from Haiti and the

Dominican Republic in the Caribbean (see also Chapter 11).

c) They are very recent nation states, despite the fact that they acquired independence in the 19th century, and are still in the process of implementing peace accords and/or consolidating democratic practice. This is the case in the Central American isthmus with Guatemala,[3] El Salvador and Nicaragua. And it is the case in the Caribbean with the Dominican Republic and Haiti. (In the case of the Dominican Republic, because, with the assumption of office of President Leonel Fernández in 1996, important changes and developments of a democratic nature are occurring;[4] and in the case of Haiti, because the lack of maturity and the fragile nature of the most recent institutional and political changes are evident there.)[5]

d) In the case of Panama, this constitutes not only an important international financial centre, but also the core of an entire geo-strategic subject of particular interest to the United States, linked to the problems of implementing the final stages of the Torrijos/Carter Canal Treaties.

Thus, an official USAID document states that: 'The principal justification... remains as it was... in early 1990: to support U.S. foreign policy objectives aimed at successful implementation of the Panama Canal treaties... Assistance to Panama at this critical juncture is clearly in the U.S. national interest. A substantial amount of US (12%-14%) and world (4%) ocean going cargo transits the Panama Canal. A democratic, transparent, prosperous and stable Panama will help ensure smooth transfer of Canal ownership and control, contributing to efficient Canal operations well into the 21st Century. Environmental protection of the Panama Canal Watershed is vital to safeguarding the fresh water resources upon which Canal hydrology depends.'[6]

In all of these countries, where the capacity for manoeuvring and possible political resistance is considerably limited, it is inevitable that external influences have a much greater impact. The pressures that can be applied to influence their governments and political forces to adopt certain directions, promoted from the exterior, are much more effective than in countries with a greater economic, military and political potential.

However, the fact that it is easier to exert external pressures in this region does not mean that the task of resolving the problems of promoting democracy is a straightforward or easy one. It may be helped by international support, and external influences may be very useful and convenient in advancing democratic transition and consolidation, but we must not forget that securing solid and positive results in this area ultimately continues to depend on the internal actors and processes.[7]

The US government's definition of national interest in this area is quite clear, as can be seen in an official document which states: 'We have major strategic and economic interests in the countries of Central America and the Caribbean, which are among our closest neighbors and with whom we share many historical and social ties.'[8]

There is no doubt that, defined in those terms, US interest in this region seems to fit in much better than in other regions, given the means at the United States's disposal to promote, and even to impose, in the case of Panama and Haiti, certain types of policies which directly correspond to its foreign policy objectives.

3.   The third region comprises the so-called Andean countries, where – at least in the cases of Bolivia, Colombia and Peru – the problems of drug trafficking and violence are endemic and have led to the adoption of policies that, on the one hand, entail various types of sanctions and pressures, but which on the other all too frequently lead to critical situations with regard to democracy and respect for human rights. Often these violations of democratic life and human rights have been overlooked in the interests of achieving other objectives. This introduces serious limitations with regard to the consistency of certain aspects of foreign policy.

Apart from these three countries, which will form the nucleus of the Andean group, we have partially to include Ecuador and, to a much lesser degree, Venezuela, where the question of raw materials, primarily oil, continues to be a key concern.

More recently, in the case of Ecuador and Peru, the border tensions between the two countries and the possible destabilising effects of their armed conflict, which could generate undesirable and dangerous arms races in the whole of South America, have occupied an important position on the US agenda for this region.[9]

4.   The fourth region is made up of Brazil, Argentina and Chile, with the additional and subsidiary inclusion of two further countries: Uruguay, particularly because of its participation in MERCOSUR; and Paraguay, not only because of its participation in the regional integration process, but also because the fragile nature of its transition to democracy has become evident.

The latter was clearly testified to by the growth of political tensions generated during the 1998 electoral process between President Wasmosy, various sectors of the military, factions of the Colorado Party and General Lino Oviedo. A US government document points out that 'Paraguay is a young and emerging free market democracy of 4.6 million people facing formidable political, economic, environmental, and social challenges. The country has suffered a long history of war with its neighbors followed by subsequent extensive periods of isolation and authoritarian rule. *The US Government's overriding policy objective in Paraguay is to consolidate and strengthen democracy...* While an impressive beginning has been made in Paraguay's democratic transition, there are still many obstacles in the way of further progress. With its tradition of a strong central executive, judicial, legislative and local government institutions are notably weak. The country suffers from a legacy of weak democratic institutions, values, and practices that are under constant threat of the military, the country's strongest institution... *Strong and effective democratic institutions will guarantee human rights, social justice, and enhance US investment.*'[10]

In the case of Brazil, it is interesting to note US appreciation of that country's importance, which differs substantially from the focus of interest in the other Latin American countries. Effectively it is said that 'Brazil is critically important to the U.S. national interest because of its vast size, a population of 155 million, and an economy of $550 billion. Brazil is a pivotal state and the predominant power in Latin America, a strategic ally to the United States, and a valuable trading partner with over $20 billion in bilateral trade. The U.S. interest in long-term, sustainable bilateral development in Brazil is hampered by Brazil's past performance in poor economic management, an extremely uneven distribution of income, and serious problems in issues of global importance such as the environment, population, and health care. In 1996, the Government of Brazil continued its commitment to modernize Brazil through social, economic, and democratic reforms and the pursuit of growth. Within this context, modest U.S. assistance on global issues can play a catalytic role in accelerating this modernization in Brazil.'[11]

On the other hand, Brazil has been identified as a possible centre of subregional hegemony[12] and is the MERCOSUR country leading the resistance to US initiatives for the creation of a Free Trade Area of the Americas by the year 2005 (see Chapter 4). As has been pointed out, Brazil and Argentina are the countries that could most effectively oppose United States hegemony. 'Some countries of Latin America, in some situations, were better prepared than others to confront the United States. Variations in capability reflected the impact of four related factors: 1) size and strength, 2) geographical proximity, 3) links to extra-hemispheric powers, and 4) intellectual and cultural resources. In terms of population size, economic output, and military capability, some nations of Latin America were stronger than others. Argentina and Brazil possessed resources that Honduras, Haiti and Cuba did not. Such capabilities enabled these countries not only to avert outright US interventionism but also, at times, to entertain visions of continental grandeur and subregional hegemony.'[13]

Let me repeat that these groupings of countries do not in any way exhaust the numerous and varying regional interrelations and ties. However, in spite of its relative value, it is my opinion that such a regionalised focus is useful in understanding more clearly the nature, scope, limitation and perspective of US policy in the different regions of Latin America; and the relationship between the promotion of democracy and the defence of human rights to the other US foreign policy objectives.

Thus, it is clear that promotion of democracy, defence and protection of human rights and external support for civilian control over the military, is not, and cannot be, of the same nature or scope in Haiti, El Salvador, Guatemala, Honduras and Nicaragua as in Chile, Argentina or Brazil. For their part, the requirements for achieving these objectives in countries like Colombia, Bolivia and Peru, contrary to what is occurring in the nations of the Southern Cone, are determined by the need for implementing an effective anti-drugs policy in the Andean region; for not encouraging the insurrectional movements active there; and for preventing social and political instability from reaching uncontrollable levels.

The United States, Latin America and the Caribbean

The present international political climate has allowed for an environment favourable to the development of democracy on the entire Latin American continent.[14] Broadly speaking the peace agreements seem to have generated an important consensus in favour of democratic development.

As the statement of a high-ranking US State Department official reads: 'The commitment in Latin America to democracy and market economics gives us an unusually solid foundation on which to build our policies.'[15] Or, as the same official had previously indicated, 'it's not just that we have an unprecedented hemispheric consensus on the broad goals of democracy, economic integration, protection of the environment, and combating poverty. What is most impressive is the depth of the commitment to those general goals not only by the hemisphere's governments, but also by private sector leaders and the public.'[16]

Thus, in the United States it is considered that 'the Summit of the Americas [in Miami, December 1994] ratified a hemispheric consensus that advances US national security interests as never before. The 34 heads of state... agreed that democracy is the touchstone for partnership in the Americas; that stable economies based on competition, open markets and regional economic integration will lead to the creation of a Free Trade Area of the Americas by 2005; that poverty, which still affects 40% of the population, must be eliminated; and that nothing is sustainable unless the environment is respected and natural resources are managed wisely... This shared vision for the Western Hemisphere would have been inconceivable only twenty years ago, when with the exception of North America and the English-speaking Caribbean, only four countries had elected civilian governments. Military dictatorships and state-directed economic systems were the norm, and respect for fundamental human rights under those regimes was non-existent... USAID [US Agency for International Development] programmes have been critical in the transformation: from dictatorship to democracy; from closed economies to open markets; and from conflict to peace in Central America.'[17]

It is worth pointing out here that, although the US government's effort in promoting democracy cannot be denied, USAID's perception of its own role in the establishment of democracy in the region as decisive is, at the very least, disproportionate. If we were to agree with this opinion, we would have to accept that neither the Argentine military defeat in the Falklands/Malvinas War; nor the years of guerrilla warfare in El Salvador, Guatemala and Nicaragua; nor the Chilean people's continuous struggle to restore democracy, to cite but a few examples, played any role at all. In addition, as has been shown elsewhere,[18] any successes the export of democracy has had, have been very limited – and, in any case, have required as a *sine qua non* the effective participation of internal political forces in the process.

Although the Miami Summit of the Americas in December 1994 has not had the same spectacular quality and impact in political and propaganda terms as, for example, the Alliance for Progress in the 1960s, it is important to stress that the Clinton administration had to acknowledge that: 'the United States' national interests are vitally linked to making the vision of the Summit of the Americas a reality. As the Summit's Action Plan highlights, *representative democracy is indispensable for the stability, peace and development of the region... Democracy and development reinforce one another.* By promoting democratic peace in

Central America, by supporting emerging democracies such as Haiti, and by strengthening the region's commitment to democratic government, *the United States promotes its basic values and provides an environment for long-term development and stability.* The pressure on Latin Americans to flee their homes and come to the United States has sharply decreased. *Democratic governments with shared values are key to making significant progress on many issues of interest to the United States,* such as economic integration, pollution reduction, global warming, biological diversity, narcotics trafficking, public health, and Acquired Immunodeficiency Syndrome (AIDS) prevention. Strong democracies also will lead to reduce emergency assistance and lower U.S. defense expenditures in the region over the long run.'[19] (The emphasis in that quotation is my own.)

These themes are recurrent in the official statements of the US government,[20] which has officially defined its national interest in the entire area in the following way: 'Our policy toward Latin America is derived from three basic objectives established by the President and the Secretary of State for our overall foreign policy: First, to keep the United States economically strong, internationally competitive and prosperous, and to preserve its position as the hub of an expanding global economy. Secondly, to preserve and advance freedom by promoting the principles and values upon which this nation's democracy and identity are based. Third, to establish a framework of co-operation that protects our citizens and our friends from the new transnational threats of environmental degradation, narcotics trafficking, migration, smuggling, terrorism, and international crime.'[21]

This political will, however, does not seem to be accompanied by sufficient consistency. In fact, the moment the authorities in charge of assigning resources have the necessary financial and political means at their disposal to achieve the aims and objectives proposed in their foreign policy design, they apply them in such a limited way that it is difficult to find an acceptable and rational link between the proposed aims and the available means. 'Most often it is said that the United States no longer has the resources that it once devoted to foreign policy. But how can that be? America is the richest country the world has ever known, and its resources have been expanding. There is no resource problem; there is a budget problem based on the American public's failure to reconcile its aversion to taxes with its appetite for benefits.'[22] This has led to a situation whereby 'the share (of federal revenue) actually spent on US foreign aid amounts to less than one per cent; zeroing it would scarcely dent the deficit... The trend of diminishing spending on foreign policy has accelerated since the end of the Cold War. Foreign policy spending absorbed about 10 per cent of GDP during the Kennedy years, about 7 per cent during the Reagan years, and 4.5 per cent in 1994. In 1995 it was scheduled to drop to 4.2 per cent and in 1996 to 3.8 per cent, with further decreases as far as the projections reach. Since 1989, the year the Soviet empire dissolved, foreign policy spending as a share of GDP has fallen by more than a third... The US Information Agency has had to eliminate nearly 900 positions, or about ten per cent of its personnel, in the last three years, and another ten per cent will be cut this year. The State Department and the National Endowment for Democracy have also been slashed... The State Department was forced to close 22 of some 275 foreign posts from 1992 through 1994 and schedule 19 more for closing since then, although a few of them have so far been spared. Some of those closed have been in pivotal countries such as ...Mexico..., Venezuela, Brazil...'[23]

Clearly, when the plurality of objectives – the promotion of democracy, the curbing of immigration, the fight against drug-trafficking and poverty, and the promotion of integrated development in the region – is compared with the total of funds allocated to achieve these ends, a marked shortage becomes evident. Without including Mexico, total aid to the region in 1996 amounted to only US$613,845,000 which is equivalent to approximately $1.50 for each Latin American (excluding Mexico). Of this sum a total of US$65,525,000 (10.67%) was dedicated to military assistance and combating drug-trafficking; US$241,452,000 (39.33%) to development assistance; US$125,883,000 (20.50%) to the Economic Support Fund; US$146,831,000 (23.9%) to the PL-480 (agricultural supply programme); and US$34,154,000 (5.56%) to the Peace Corps.

Since a differentiated analysis of US-Latin American relations has been proposed here, it would seem appropriate to show the total of US assistance broken down by region. This is done in Table 6.1 both for the total as well as military assistance (including combating drug traffickers) and development assistance. What is striking is the modest amount allocated to the Southern Cone (including Brazil and Paraguay) compared with the other regions.

Table 6.1:
US Assistance to Latin America and the Caribbean: Totals by Region (Fiscal Year 1996 in $ 000)

Region	Total	Military Assistance and Combatting Drug Trafficking	Development Assistance
Southern Cone, Brazil and Paraguay	24,745 = 4.03%	2,400 = 3.66%	16,438 = 6.81%
Andes and Venezuela	214,812 = 34.99%	50,000 = 76.30%	63.755 = 26.40%
Central America	159,687 = 26.1%	4,050 = 6.18%	80,863 = 33.49%
Caribbean and Guyana	164,937 = 26.86%	5,375 = 8.20%	47,742 = 19.77%
Regional	49,664 = 8.09%	3,700 = 5.64%	32,654 = 13.52%
Total	613,845	65,525	241,452

Source: USAID, Congressional Presentation, Financial Year 1996.

Despite these modest totals (reduced even further in 1998/9) it is important to point out, as a relevant factor in the better understanding of Latin American interests and perceptions regarding the construction of democracy,[24] the significant change in the conceptualisation of what is understood by a democratic political system on the subcontinent today.

This concept, at last, seems to have moved on from the old simplified approach to democracy as reduced to the ritual holding of elections. The problem of democratic transition and consolidation is beginning to be recognised as a process that is far more complex than the mere staging of electoral tournaments. Thus, at least in certain spheres, a more enriched vision is gaining ground, which tries to include in the subject of regional democracy areas such as the real division of powers, the creation of institutions, the rule of law, civilian control of the armed forces, an end to exclusion and marginalisation, the issue of ethnic groups, and questions of gender and extreme poverty.[25]

An example of the previously mentioned tendency can be inferred from an official document published by the US government. The emphasis in the following quoted passage is my own:

> The region made significant advances in democratization in 1996, particularly with Peace Accords signed in Guatemala, and fair elections in the Dominican Republic that mark an historic step towards full democracy.   National elections in Ecuador and Nicaragua continued the region's steadfast adherence to democratic electoral procedures.   Nonetheless, important challenges to fulfilment of democratic aspirations persist. Strong leadership by the United States and other hemispheric partners only narrowly halted a military coup attempt in Paraguay. In many Latin America nations, military and police retain *reserved* powers not susceptible to civilian elected oversight. While democratic procedures in elections and rule of law are improving, *many citizens in the region cannot yet effectively participate in their political systems.* Indigenous groups in Guatemala, southern Mexico, and the Andean region are still largely excluded from political life. *Regardless of electoral reform, political systems will not be truly democratic until the indigenous majority are included.*[26]

Towards a New Perception of Inter-American Relations

Within a short period of time inter-American relations have undergone important changes which are of great significance in terms of political practice. Broadly speaking, these can be synthesised into three different stages, bearing in mind certain conditions that, although varying with time, have to do with the 'before' and 'after' of the Cold War.[27] They are:

a)   From hegemony to imposition.

This first stage saw a shift away from a clear position of US hegemony towards a general questioning, not only of internal hegemonies, but also of US hegemony in the region. In addition, there was also a last attempt at destabilisation by the former Soviet Union, which sought to take advantage of the objective conflicts occurring in various parts of the globe, and particularly in Central America.[28]

b)   From imposition to indifference.

This second stage came about in the period immediately after the signing of the Peace Accords, the treaties in Cambodia and Angola, the 'fall' of the Berlin

Wall, the dissolution of the Soviet Union and the supposed establishment of a 'New World Order'. Here, faced with the profound changes in the international situation, the United States government came to place the region at the bottom of its foreign policy agenda. There was a marked shift of United States priority interests to other regions of the world, above all to Eastern Europe.[29]

c)   *From indifference to conditional collaboration.*

Not much time passed before it became evident that this approach suffered from an overvaluation of what was occurring in global politics. The US authorities soon came to recognise that their indifference to the Latin American and Caribbean region was not only negative, but also dangerous to US national interests. If these were to be protected and defended, then a more active co-operation with Latin America, and a meeting of responsibilities at the global level, would be necessary. In the words of President Clinton 'We cannot become the world's policeman. But where our values and our interests are at stake and where we can make a difference, we must act and we must lead. That is our job and we are better, stronger and safer because we are doing it.'[30]

However, in many countries there was strong internal resistance to some of the democratic changes, above all from the civilian and political elites who had benefited from the previous authoritarian regimes, but also from certain sectors of the armed forces. It was therefore decided to apply in the political sphere the experience gained in the economic sphere, where, through the application of various forms of financial pressure, countries in economic disarray had successfully been forced to rationalise their finances and economic systems. In this way the system of cross-conditionality was being imposed in order to support and strengthen democratic changes in the region from the exterior.[31]

It would seem that the latter is the stage at which we currently find ourselves. Thus, various types of political conditions are now being imposed in the promotion of democracy. These have further reduced the degree of national autonomy, which in the past had been used to curb support for the development of democracy and the promotion of human rights. In addition, as numerous analysts have upheld,[32] we have seen the participation of multinational institutions, such as the United Nations, which have facilitated collective actions in areas like peacekeeping and restoration of political order. This has made it possible, for example, despite the notion of national sovereignty and the principle of non-intervention, for external assistance to help quash the coup attempt in Paraguay, or send troops into Haiti in order to restore democracy, if the result there can be described as such.[33]

On the other hand, the central US objectives in the region demand not only a policy of pressure or imposition, but above all one of co-operation. The fight against drug trafficking, money laundering, illegal migration and so forth, requires democratic political organisation, the rule of law, an independent judicial power, a modern police force that respects human rights, and armed forces that are subordinate to the civil power. All these democratic elements have, to a certain degree, become necessary conditions for the success of US foreign policy in the region.

For this reason it is important to understand the construction of democracy as something more than the holding of elections. Its complexity demonstrates the negative and counter-productive nature of certain attempts at external imposition which do not fit in with the internal reality of each country, or of certain attitudes of indifference which in the end lead to political paralysis. A correct conceptualisation of democracy leads to the adoption of a prudent and progressive policy of conditioned collaboration, both in the achievement of common goals, and in favour of the consolidation of democratic change.

One of the characteristics of this latest period is the US effort to contribute to the strengthening of regional organisations, in particular of the Organisation of American States (OAS) as one of the useful instruments for the reinforcement of human rights and the upholding of representative democracy. Even though the value and applicability of democratic rights were set out in the preamble and the regulations of the OAS Charter, the *Realpolitik* of the Cold War allowed authoritarian regimes to thrive, protected by the Charter itself. Now, in contrast, the Organisation's commitment to democracy has been strengthened and mechanisms have been established to make it operationally effective in the event of a breach of constitutional order or of threats to democratic institutionality.

As Acevedo and Grossman have shown, 'the OAS's commitment to upholding representative democracy appeared to have finally become operational when, in 1991, the members approved the Santiago Commitment to Democracy and the Renewal of the Inter-American System and Resolution AG/Res.1080 (XXI-o/91) on Representative Democracy. The resolution, a brief and simple document, calls for an automatic meeting of the OAS Permanent Council 'in the event of any occurrences giving rise to the sudden or irregular interruption of the democratic political institutional process or of the legitimate exercise of power by the democratically elected government in any of the Organisation's member states, in order, within the framework of the Charter, to examine the situation, decide on and convene an ad hoc meeting of the Ministers of Foreign Affairs, or a special session of the General Assembly, all of which must take place within a ten-day period'.[34]

Although the results obtained by the OAS are in the end little more than modest ones in which the United States's influence has almost always been decisive, as in the cases of Haiti and Panama, the fact is that the predominant tendency at present is to increase its authority and its role in the management of certain initiatives and critical political situations in the region. In spite of this, the emphasis on the promotion of democracy continues to be on the side of bilateral relations between the United States and Latin America and the Caribbean.

It should be noted that the abuses and errors in this area of the promotion of democracy generally have a long-lasting and seriously negative significance. Indeed, errors here will tend to weaken internal efforts at constructing democracy and a state governed by the rule of law at the national level. Policies such as the decertification of countries involved in the drug trade; the protection of nationals involved in questionable or even illegal activities *via* various types of pressure, taking bilateral relations back to the time of impositions, and the desire of US politicians and government employees to impose institutional and legal practices and methods characteristic of the Anglo-Saxon system, which differ from and are even at odds with local judicial traditions and institutions, all weaken democracy and delay the introduction of a modern state governed by the rule of law.

For this reason the past US record in inter-American relations should not be condemned to obscurity. As Larry Diamond has pointed out, 'The US record in promoting democracy in the hemisphere has been mixed at best, and much policy has been promulgated in the name of democracy that in fact has weakened, undermined, or failed to strengthen it... Most of all, the United States needs to craft a pro-democracy policy that has the coherent backing of all foreign policy branches of the government and bipartisan support that can be sustained across administrations. It must then take care to provide unambiguous and consistent signals about the high priority it attaches to the maintenance of democracy and human rights. The concern for human rights (codified in aid conditionality) must be vigorously pressed with formally democratic regimes no less than with undemocratic ones... A particular point of caution for the United States involves relations with Latin American militaries... It would be tragic if, in the name of fighting the drug trade or building democracy, the United States were to repeat its previous mistakes of aggrandizing Latin American militaries at the expense of democracy.'[35]

However, in spite of warnings such as Diamond's, such conduct and attempts at imposition from the outside, without consideration for internal legal, institutional, political and cultural features, have not been long in coming. This has been the case, even though it is clear that such acts subvert the state governed by the rule of law, erode constitutions and national sovereignty, irritate the region's population, and, in their totality, weaken the process of democratic consolidation.

Because of their negative effects, the actions of senators like Jesse Helms and Republican presidential ex-candidate Robert Dole are in this sense paradigmatic. These and other US senators issue threats and carry out actions that infringe on the dignity, the rights and the security of small countries in order to protect some companies involved in the banana trade or in the telecommunications industry; or anonymous businessmen who in some way were linked to the CIA in the contra war in Nicaragua; or others involved in judicial problems related to properties which were being used for drug trafficking. Inter-American relations are inevitably and negatively affected.

The same happens when, in the effort to fight drug trafficking, actions are undertaken on foreign soil on the fringes of the national state concerned. Negative developments also arise when initiatives are organised – as, for example, in the fight against the drug trade in Bolivia – that end up generating conflicts of loyalty as a result of the emergence among government officials of various kinds of dependencies (financial and others).

Another example is the US attempt to impose certain extradition rules that are characteristic of its own system, but which in the light of the judicial traditions more highly valued in the region are not acceptable within the constitutional systems there. This is the case with the US intention to apply retroactively the new laws to extradite Colombian nationals, to legitimise the action of private bounty hunters, or to involve the executive power in order to guarantee certain results on issues that are in the exclusive sphere of the judicial power.

Democratic transition and consolidation in Latin America do not mean the adoption of the US political and institutional model, nor of any other imported model. They mean no less than the deliberate and conscious effort of each country to build its own political regime of rights and guarantees, in accordance with its specific socio-political, cultural and historical conditions.

Conclusions

United States foreign policy includes, as one of its principal aims, the promotion of democracy in Latin America. As is only natural, this is done in a way that is closely linked to its other objectives in the region. In one sense, this is very positive, since it helps to understand US policy towards the region in an integrated way; this in turn ensures that mutual support afforded in different areas amounts to a favourable factor in the consolidation and strengthening of democracy.

Nevertheless, this same interconnection, as has already been pointed out, can be counterproductive in several ways, above all if its implementation is effected unilaterally and with hegemonic pretensions by the United States. There is no doubt that linking the fight against poverty with support for sustainable development, as two decisive facets in the consolidation of democracy and the construction of citizenship, amounts to a breakthrough. In contrast, the association and imposition of forms of business organisation and of state involvement in the economy, of directly or indirectly influencing the design of policies regarding wages, health, pensions and public services, all give rise to the appearance of very negative reactions, Requesting co-operation in the fight against drug trafficking is positive, which cannot be said for the imposition of foreign judicial styles, methods and criteria to the detriment of national ones, because this weakens the power of and respect for the constitution, the law and the judicial bodies, at a time when their operation and prestige need to be strengthened and improved.

On the other hand, if there is not an adequate correspondence between the instruments employed in the promotion of democracy and the tasks that this implies, the shortfall can be so great that the investment made could become purely symbolic. In that case, what tends to remain is only the negative part of the US protection of its national interests.

Thus, for example, there is a clearly negative side to key US policies towards the region in the following areas:

- No to drug trafficking.
- No to money laundering.
- No to immigration.
- No to 'fast track'.
- No to entry into NAFTA
- No to the renewal of the Caribbean Basin Initiative.
- No to public sector assistance for development.

The positives, by contrast, are relatively few although each is very important:

- Yes to democracy.
- Yes to human rights.
- Yes to a distant and partial integration into the Free Trade Area of the Americas.

The overlap of negatives and positives generates numerous contradictions and tensions that require a constant revision of US actions with regard to the region. This is made even more difficult because of the complexity of the process of formulating foreign policy in the USA, the important role played by public opinion in this process and the proliferation of various actors and influences that intervene in its formations.

Finally, it has to be acknowledged that the promotion of democracy has had notable, albeit partial, successes in several important areas which are worth mentioning:

- The provision of support to electoral bodies and giving impetus to their development and consolidation. In addition to the Central American countries that have signed the Tikal Protocol, there are the other countries of Latin America that signed the Quito Protocol. This has brought to life a regional body of electoral tribunals and committees involved in democratic transition and consolidation.
- Support to international electoral observation, as a mechanism for guaranteeing the holding of free, competitive and fair elections.
- Support for the modernisation of the state and the processes of democratic institutionalisation.
- Support for improvement in the administration of justice.
- Support for the transformation and education of those agencies in charge of safeguarding the security of citizens and the fight against crime.
- Support for changing the nature and character of the military doctrine of the Latin American armed forces and the strengthening of their training with regard to human rights, democratic values and, in particular, the subordination of the military to civilian power.

There is, then, a *chiaroscuro* in the value and effect of the promotion of democracy from the outside. With regard to surmounting the ambivalences entailed in the promotion of democracy, the final result will greatly depend on the internal efforts of each country to construct democracy on its own terms. On this will also depend whether the positive aspects of democratic development will in the end prevail over the negative aspects of the existing objective asymmetry between the global hegemonic power of the United States and the relative weakness of Latin America and the Caribbean.

Notes

* Translated by Pam Decho.
1. In this respect Martz (1994), is very useful, in particular the chapters by Joseph

Tulchin about the United States and Latin America, and the chapter by John Martz himself about the United States as champions of democracy.

2. Thus, an official US document provides the following revealing assessment of El Salvador: 'Located in the center of a region that, with Mexico, borders the United States, El Salvador's political and economic stability are important to US interests in the region. Any instability in El Salvador would directly affect its neighbors –undermining their economic development and transitions towards peace, democracy and the rule of law... The threat from illegal immigration is particularly relevant to US interests in El Salvador. Salvadorans, primarily as a consequence of the civil war, account for well over 300,000 illegal immigrants; the second largest group of illegal immigrants after those from Mexico. Renewed instability in El Salvador would, no doubt, lead to another wave of illegal Salvadoran immigration. Finally, humanitarian interests compel the US to address the widespread poverty in one of the least developed countries in the hemisphere.' USAID, *FY 1998 Development Assistance Request. El Salvador.* Introduction, p. 1.

3. While in the cases of El Salvador and Nicaragua, quite different from each other, the process of applying the peace accords has been going on for a number of years, in Guatemala a peace accord was only signed at the end of 1996. The situation there is still very fragile and the process of democratisation – which includes the incorporation of the great mass of Indians into national life – very recent. USAID, *FY 1998 Development Assistance Request. Guatemala.* Introduction, p. 1 *et seq.*

4. Cerdas Cruz (1996), p. 263 *et seq.*

5. See Maingot (1992), p. 123 *et seq.*; Maingot (1996), p. 189 *et seq.*

6. USAID, *FY 1998 Development Assistance Request. Panama*, Introduction, p. 1.

7. I have addressed the subject of the conditionality of promoting democracy from the exterior, its limitations and perils, in Cerdas Cruz (1996). Also of interest on the subject of the limitations of external promotion and the decisive weight of internal factors is the study by Whitehead (1991). For a very favourable view of external influence as a means of promoting democracy, see: Nelson and Eglinton (1992). See also Nelson and Eglinton (1996), p. 169 *et seq.*

8. Davidow, Jeffrey, Assistant Secretary for Inter-American Affairs, *Testimony before the Trade Subcommittee of the House Ways and Means Committee*, Washington D.C., 22 July 1997, p. 3.

9. 'The U.S. national interests in Ecuador are centered around the following themes: a mutual interest of both countries to preserve political stability and peace in the region, in view of the armed confrontation between Ecuador and Peru in 1995; the strengthening of democratic institutions and the streamlining of procedures for the administration of justice...' etc.. USAID, *FY 1998 Development Assistance Request. Ecuador*, Introduction, p. 1.

10. USAID, *FY 1998 Development Assistance Request. Paraguay*, Introduction, p. 1. Emphasis added by author.

11. USAID, *FY 1998 Development Assistance Request. Brazil*, Introduction, p. 1.
12. This is the perception presented by Smith (1996), p. 331, Table 5, Strategic Options for Latin America.
13. Smith (1996), p. 330 *et seq.*
14. See Albright, Madeleine K., Secretary of State, *Welcoming Remarks to the Council of the Americas*, Washington, D.C., 28 April 1997.
15. Davidow, Jeffrey, Assistant Secretary for Inter-American Affairs, '*U.S. Foreign Policy Toward Latin America and the Caribbean in the Clinton Administration's Second Term.*' Address before the Council of the Americas, Washington D.C., 28 April 1997.
16. See *U.S. Policy Toward Latin America and the Caribbean. Building Upon A Solid Foundation.* Remarks by Assistant Secretary of State Jeffrey Davidow to the Miami Conference on the Caribbean and Latin America, Miami, Florida, 9 December 1996, p. 1.
17. USAID, *FY1998, Development Assistance Request. Latin America and the Caribbean*, p. 1 *et seq.*
18. See Lowenthal (1991).
19. USAID, *FY1998, Development Assistance Request. Latin America and the Caribbean*, p. 2.
20. 'The Summit of the Americas was a dramatic expression of this new era of cooperation... The consensus on the specific initiatives of the Summit's Action Plan may be even more impressive than consensus on overall philosophical goals. The Plan's 23 initiatives and over 100 specific action items mobilize national governments, international financial institutions and non-governmental organizations. They involve work in areas which were in many countries considered too sensitive domestically (such as human rights and problems of corruption) to even discuss multilaterally – much less act on multilaterally.' See Watson, Alexander F., *Mutual Interest and Cooperation in Latin America,* Remarks by Assistant Secretary of State for Inter-American Affairs to the Latin American Association of Japan, Marsuya Salon, Tokyo, Japan, February 21, 1996, p. 4.
21. Jeffrey Davidow, Assistant Secretary of State for Inter-American Affairs, *Testimony before the House Ways and Means Committee*, Washington, D.C., July 22, 1997, p. 1.
22. Muravchik (1996), p. 8.
23. *Ibid.*, pp. 9, 10 *et seq.*
24. The final document of the Third Summit of Latin American Heads of State and Government, held in Salvador, Brazil, 15-16 July 1993, states: 'We have to bear in mind... the mutual relationship between the consolidation of democracy and the promotion of development. Political stability favours the realisation of effective economic and social programmes. On the other hand, the absence of prospects for growth with social justice hinders the consolidation of democracy and the protection of human rights. If in today's world it is no longer acceptable to make the observance of civil and political rights conditional on the prior achievement of development objectives, then it is also not plausible to

imagine that the full realization of human rights can be abstracted from the socio-economic situation of the populations involved.' See Contributions (1993), p. 149 *et seq.*

25. Thus, Jeffrey Davidow, Assistant Secretary for Inter-American Affairs, has pointed out that: 'without broadly shared growth, citizens' trust in their governments and institutions deteriorates, state legitimacy erodes, the rule of law weakens and social ills propagate.' See *Testimony before the Trade Subcommittee of the House Ways and Means Committee*, Washington, D.C., 22 July 1997, p. 2.
26. *Ibid.*, p. 4.
27. Although adapting it to the purposes of this study, I draw inspiration from the proposal by Augusto Varas (1991).
28. See Cerdas Cruz (1989), p. 1 *et seq.*
29. See LeoGrande (1990).
30. Cited by Omestad (1996-7), pp. 38 and 51.
31 See Cerdas Cruz (1992); and Whitehead (1991), p. 356 *et seq.*
32. See Hoffmann (1994), p. 43.
33. See Fauriol (1995), chapter 1.
34. Acevedo and Grossman (1996), p. 137. After examining the cases of Guatemala, Peru and Haiti, the authors conclude that 'the role of the OAS has been insufficient. It seems that national democratic elites have not yet fully understood to what extent their future is linked to the protection and promotion of democracy in other countries. As a result, the OAS expresses a vision of national interests that limits its potential. The challenge for the future is to strengthen those shared values, giving shape and content to a hemispheric community organized on the basis of democratic values, along with the institutions and mechanisms needed for its protection and development.' Acevedo and Grossman (1996), p. 149.
35. Diamond (1996), p. 102.

CHAPTER 7

THE UNITED STATES AND DEMOCRACY IN MEXICO

John H. Coatsworth

The United States has always exercised, and continues to exercise, a deep, at times decisive, and always disproportionate impact on the evolution of Mexican politics and society. It is not surprising, therefore, that Mexico's transition to democracy has as much to do with the United States as the authoritarianism it is slowly eroding. The purpose of this chapter is to analyse that influence in the perspective of the past century for what insight history can provide for the present and future.

By democracy, I refer here to three related but distinct characteristics of a society's organisation. By electoral democracy I mean open, competitive elections on a more or less level playing field. By civic democracy, I refer to an ensemble of rights, entitlements and policies that encourage citizens to speak, assemble and organise freely (whether for electoral or other purposes). By social democracy, I refer to the availability of jobs, housing, education, health services and other modern necessities, usually as a result of economic growth and government policies that reduce inequalities in the distribution of individual (or collective) income. Authoritarian political regimes lack (and democratic regimes embody) the first two of these dimensions, but not necessarily the last. It is probably true, though there is surprisingly little research to show it, that the sustainability (*ex ante*) or longevity (*ex post*) of either kind of regime is positively related to improvements in social conditions. Similarly debatable is the putative causal link between democratic political regimes and social democracy.[1]

The extent to which Mexico has achieved progress or failed to advance in expanding democracy in any of these three dimensions has always depended critically on four external variables:

1.   The domestic welfare and productivity effects of the country's evolving external economic relations.

2.   The competitiveness of the external economic and strategic environment the country faces.

3.   The constraints imposed on Mexican governments by the impact, direct or indirect, of the actions and policies of external powers, particularly the United States.

4.   The nature and influence of external non-governmental actors on Mexican politics and social life.

Mexico's external economic relations are important because for much of the country's modern history, the magnitude, timing, and sectoral or spatial impact of external trade, capital, and technology flows have helped to determine the pace and pattern of economic growth as well as such crucial derived consequences as employment and wage levels, the distribution of income and assets, the perceived legitimacy of governing authorities, and the opportunity costs of different policies. The United States has been Mexico's principal trading partner and main source of external capital and technology for more than a century.

The competitiveness of the international environment Mexico faces has proved crucial at key moments in Mexican history because it has helped to determine the potential costs and benefits of alternative domestic policies and policy strategies. In general, Mexican authorities have enjoyed greater freedom of action when dependence on US economic ties has been smaller and the power of the US government in Mexican affairs diminished by the competing pressures of other important external actors.

Foreign governments, particularly that of the United States, have exerted continuous, and often irresistible, influence on Mexican politics and society throughout the 20th century. This is not to say that US administrations always achieve in Mexico what they set out to accomplish. On the contrary, US influence has often been greatest when its policies have provoked negative responses or when its inaction or lack of clear objectives has shaped political outcomes that would not otherwise have occurred.

Finally, external non-governmental actors have shaped political developments in Mexico throughout the 20th century, though never before to the extent that they do now. Foreign (mostly US) business corporations, labour unions, universities, print and electronic media, private foundations, election monitoring, human rights and environmental organisations, and religious and charitable groups now produce a mosaic of political pressures and effects that are as complex and even as contradictory as they are pervasive. These external variables shape not only the extent to which Mexico democratises its electoral practices, civil society and economic opportunities, but also the pace and pattern of the process and the results.

This chapter argues that crucial developments in Mexican history were shaped by the four external variables sketched above and supports the argument by looking at key periods and episodes. It concludes with an attempt to assess the current influence and likely near- to medium-term impact of these four variables on Mexico's seemingly interminable – but now perhaps accelerating – transition to democracy. I have deliberately avoided the temptation to give useful advice.

First, however, a disclaimer. The extent to which Mexico has achieved competitive elections, vibrant civic institutions and more equitable social outcomes has always depended fundamentally on what Mexicans themselves do or fail to do. Moreover, diverse elements of Mexican society, including Mexican governments, have often managed to mediate or manipulate the impact of external forces to achieve some national or sectional purpose. Occasionally, Mexican governments or other entities have even succeeded in externalising domestic interests, that is, in bending external forces to serve some domestic need or 'national' interest. In short, I do not contest the perfectly obvious fact that Mexicans make their own history. My point is simply that Mexicans have never made their own history just as they pleased.

The Porfirian Era (1876-1911)

The Mexican economy experienced its first period of sustained growth between the early 1870s and 1907. Beginning in 1876, the federal government was dominated by the perpetually re-elected Porfirio Díaz and his collaborators. For most of this period Mexico faced a moderately competitive international economic and strategic environment. The main goals of the Díaz regime – consolidation of national sovereignty and export-led economic growth – were consistent with the interests of all the major external powers, including the United States. None, therefore, sought to impose significant constraints on Mexican policy-makers. Internal and external non-governmental actors, apart from private business, played relatively minor roles in the country's domestic politics and external relations.[2] The market worked its magic more or less unfettered.

The rapid economic growth of the Mexican economy in the Porfirian era could not have been sustained without substantial flows of capital and technology, mostly from the United States. In turn, the achievement of high growth rates helped to legitimate and then to consolidate and prolong Díaz's rule. Three aspects of the external economic impact are less well understood, but particularly helpful for understanding the violent *dénouement* of the Porfirian regime.

First, the growth of the Mexican economy during the Porfirian era was 'export-led' in the classic sense. Exports grew more rapidly than the rest of the economy and tended to pull more backward and less dynamic sectors along. In 1877, exports accounted for only 6 per cent of Mexico's Gross Domestic Product (GDP). By 1910, they had risen to 17 per cent. Total foreign trade (exports plus imports) grew from 11 to 31 per cent.[3] This pattern of development linked the macroeconomic health of the economy to the world and particularly the US market as never before. Growth was more rapid than it would otherwise have been, but the impact of external shocks, like the recession of 1907-8, tended to spread across the economy more widely and deeply than ever before. External disequilibrium was the main cause of the economic difficulties that undermined the Porfirian regime between 1907 and 1911.[4]

Second, it is likely that income and wealth distribution worsened, particularly in the countryside, during the Porfirian era. The conventional historiography tended to see Mexico's late 19th-century concentration of landownership as an evil inherited from the colonial era, exacerbated perhaps by the Porfirian regime's well-known disposition to encourage brutality and rapaciousness. But landownership became dramatically *more* concentrated during the Porfirian era for two reasons: (1) the government sold off vast tracts of public land at low prices to individual entrepreneurs and land companies mainly in the sparsely populated North; and (2) it permitted the widespread purchase and frequent usurpation of lands from individual peasants and free villages throughout the Centre and the South. Federal agencies and the president himself tried, though inconsistently, to slow the process of concentration in the Centre and South whenever it threatened social peace, but because railroad construction and the modernisation it promoted suddenly made hitherto isolated lands worth buying or stealing, these efforts, even when they were more than half-hearted, proved futile. In any case, it was the sharply regressive redistribution of landownership during the *Porfiriato*, rather than inherited inequalities, that produced the explosive discontent that wracked Chihuahua, Morelos, and several other key states in 1910-11.

Third, the external capital that flowed to Mexico during the *Porfiriato* consisted mainly of foreign (largely US) direct investment, that is investment in land, railroads, factories, banks and other enterprises, rather than in portfolio or indirect investment in sovereign or corporate debt. Direct investors want low taxes. Portfolio investors in government securities want fiscal revenues sufficiently robust as to guarantee debt service.[5] In Mexico, the government's capacity to tax deteriorated during the *Porfiriato*. Central government revenues as a proportion of GDP fell from 11 to just over 5 per cent between 1877 and 1910.[6] In Brazil, a contrasting case where (the mainly European) foreign investors sank their funds disproportionately in government and (government-guaranteed) railroad bonds, the central government increased its extractive capacity dramatically and by the early 20th century was routinely collecting 15 per cent of GDP in fiscal revenues.[7] Both Mexico and republican Brazil (after 1889) had nominally decentralised federal systems of governance, but in Mexico the Porfirian government never managed to overcome the fiscal constraints built into the 1857 Constitution, in part because it was not pressured to do so by the foreign economic interests it worried about most.[8] In the end, Díaz did not command resources sufficient either to coopt or to suppress serious social discontent.

Finally, the traditions of peasant political mobilisation and militancy in the Centre and parts of the South of the country, which were reactivated in the turmoil of the Revolution, owed much to the conditions created by the loss of Texas (1837), the disastrous war with the United States (1846-48), and the long and bitter struggle against Maximillian and the French army that supported him (1862-67).[9]

In the North, as Katz points out, the majority of the Chihuahuan irregular forces that provoked Díaz's resignation by seizing Ciudad Juárez in 1911 were drawn from the ranks of peasants in former military colonies, established to defend the region from marauding nomads like the Apaches driven south into Mexico by the US army. The Mexican government's interest in promoting the exploitation of the North's valuable mineral and agricultural resources led it to give priority to pacifying the border area, beginning in the 1880s. With the Apache threat gone and land prices rising, especially in areas along the new rail lines, the state government adopted legislation in 1905 that facilitated elite assaults on peasant landownership.[10] When Madero issued his call for rebellion (from San Antonio), the victims of these assaults were the first to take up arms and constituted a majority of the troops in the revolutionary army that took Ciudad Juárez and precipitated Díaz's resignation in 1911.

In short, the economic vulnerability, regressive social outcomes, fiscal incapacities, peasant militancy, and precipitating events that pushed Mexico into revolution owe so much to Mexico's external ties that it is easy to conclude that Mexicans would not have set about killing each other on so large a scale without them. The end of the dictatorship brought a brief interlude of advances in electoral and civic democracy, but did not reverse the concentration of land and income that had proved to be the Díaz regime's Achilles heel.

The Revolution (1911-46)

The Revolutionary era bears witness to the crucial impact of three of the four variables mentioned above. External economic conditions structured the opportunity costs of divergent public policies throughout the era. The competitiveness of the international environment shifted in ways that heightened the Mexican government's capacity for independent action at key points in time. The United States government failed to intervene massively to impose a Caribbean-style protectorate along the lines urged by some private interests, politicians and interest groups and thus excluded a wide range of potentially radical outcomes in Mexico. Non-governmental actors increased in number, noise-level, and influence, especially during the revolutionary decade, but their combined effects within Mexico or on the Mexican policy of the United States were small.

External economic conditions were important in two ways. First, external demand for Mexican exports due to World War I kept key sectors of the Mexican economy booming even during the worst of the fighting from 1914 to 1916. Losses there were, but exporters understood that profits awaited anyone who could find a way to produce and ship. Other sectors of the Mexican economy, especially domestic-use agriculture, suffered greater temporary disruption (partly from unusually bad weather), but except for a few months of paper-money inflation, the economy rode out the violence without experiencing a great crisis.[11] This in turn reduced the scope for social polarisation and created fiscal incentives for political moderation. Mexico's revolutionaries understood, Carranza as well as anyone else, that external demand for Mexican exports guaranteed the survival of any government stable enough to impose order and collect taxes. Unionisation, agrarian reform, new tax schemes, even entire articles of the 1917 Constitution were set aside or moderated in the interest of promoting an economy recovery that could help to consolidate the new regime.[12]

Second, the Great Depression altered the domestic political environment in Mexico by lowering the economic opportunity costs of radical reform. Trade fell sharply with little hope of quick recovery while external capital flows stopped altogether. Mexico actually exported capital to the United States and other creditor nations during the 1930s in the form of debt payments and profit remittances on external capital investments made in earlier decades. The Calles strategy of 1929-34 was to move sharply to the right in an effort to restore the confidence of potential external (as well as domestic) investors, but this policy carried high political costs and produced no positive economic results. In short, the depression removed the external inducement to moderation. Mexico suffered all the external economic costs of the coming round of agrarian, labour, and nationalist reforms in advance, as it were.[13]

During the period of violent revolutionary upheaval (1911-17) and the Cárdenas presidency (1934-40), Mexico faced an international environment more competitive than it would ever be again. The Carranza government benefited directly, because the Wilson administration's preoccupation with the European war limited its interest and capacity for intervention in Mexico.[14] During the Cárdenas administration, competition in the international arena cemented the US commitment to its new 'Good Neighbor Policy' in the Caribbean and reduced Mexican fears of military intervention. The Cárdenas government was thus better able to implement social and agrarian reforms, and even to nationalise the petroleum industry and weather the international boycott that followed, than it would otherwise have been.

US policy during the Revolution often pursued impossible goals on the basis of poor intelligence and even worse analysis. The complicity of the US ambassador, Henry Lane Wilson, in the military coup that martyred the country's democratically elected president, Francisco I. Madero in 1913; the occupation of Veracruz the following year; the Pershing expedition to capture Pancho Villa in 1916-17, and other less spectacular blunders diminished as Mexico became more predictable. In the end, the most important and consequential aspect of US policy in the revolutionary era was the caution imposed on it by events outside the hemisphere. US administrations repeatedly faced enormous domestic pressures for military intervention in Mexico and repeatedly decided not to mount a full-scale military intervention during the Revolution and in the years that followed. This was crucial because, as Katz has pointed out, the radicalisation of such major upheavals as the French and Russian revolutions occurred in the context of foreign invasions.[15] Had Mexico faced a full-scale US invasion for the purpose of installing a new more pliant government or even a more limited but prolonged US occupation of the oil fields along the Gulf coast, the mobilisation of human and material resources to meet such a challenge would have pushed the Revolution sharply to the left, with long lasting consequences. Instead, when President Wilson faced in 1917 the stark choice between mobilising a huge army of occupation to join General Pershing's 6,000 troops in northern Mexico or a unilateral withdrawal of the expeditionary force without Mexican concessions of any kind, he brought the troops home.

Once the US troops had left and the world war had ended, the United States and Mexico experienced what Alan Knight has called 'oddly congruent governments and policies' in the 1920s and parallel commitments to social reformism in the 1930s, resulting in US policies that were 'unusually benign'.[16] Good relations between the United States and Mexico throughout this period, and especially during the Cárdenas era, played an important role in the consolidation of Mexico's post-revolutionary state. The quality of US decision-making reached a high point during the administration of Franklin Roosevelt and his ambassador Josephus Daniels.

Non-governmental groups supported or denounced the Mexican Revolution, but did not have much impact either in Mexico or on US policy towards Mexico in this era. The oil companies and the Roman Catholic Church in the United States were the most vociferous and influential of the Revolution's enemies, but they failed to push the US government into military adventures. The enthusiasm of socialists, Wobblies, and less consistently, the American Federation of Labor was equally ineffectual. Probably most influential were journalists and academics, like John Reed and later Frank Tanenbaum, who wrote of the Revolution and its goals sympathetically, and major banks, such as Morgan, which lobbied consistently and effectively against intervention.

In the revolutionary era, then, external economic conditions and US policy provoked moderation in the 1910s and 1920s and aided reformism in the 1930s. International competition for economic and political influence in Mexico virtually disappeared between 1918 and the early 1930s, but returned in time to help Mexico in the Cárdenas years. In the end, the advances in social democracy during the 1930s helped to establish 'revolutionary nationalism' as the defining national ideology, promoted the incorporation of elements of the population previously excluded from politics into the dominant ruling party, and helped to consolidate the power of the presidency.

The Post-War 'Miracle' (1946-82)

In the post-war era, Mexico adjusted to a new set of external economic and political conditions. The flow of capital and technology resumed, but with the United States as the country's only significant source of supply. Mexico and the other larger countries in Latin America (and elsewhere) embraced import substituting industrialisation (ISI). The bipolar division of the world left the United States unchallenged in its dominance in the western hemisphere. US policy-makers sought to extirpate the influence of Communist and other left-wing parties from the region and made it clear that their sympathy for popular movements and populist reforms, such as those of the Cárdenas era, had ended. Non-governmental actors receded in importance.

As a strategy, ISI could not have succeeded without external, mainly US, capital and technology. An important proportion of the post-war external capital flows passed through Mexican government agencies, such as Nacional Financiera, the national development bank that provided subsidised credit for new industrial projects. The United States endorsed ISI in the less developed world in part, as Nolt and Maxfield have shown,[17] because the Eisenhower and Kennedy administrations lacked congressional support for more aggressive efforts to achieve reciprocal reductions in tariffs and other obstacles to freer trade. Without freer trade, the major US industrial firms could not increase their exports to the developing world, but they could and did leap over tariff walls to build production facilities there. Later on, some of the great smokestack industries created in this era, including many owned by US and other foreign firms, resisted the dismantling of the strategy that protected them from imports, including imports from the US and Asian branches of the same companies. In short, ISI was not a 'national' (much less a 'revolutionary nationalist') strategy that helped Mexico resist foreign domination. On the contrary, it was the economic strategy most consistent with the rebuilding of close economic ties to the United States.

The ISI strategy of this era had two additional significant consequences for Mexican politics and society worth emphasising. First, it required an across-the-board reversal of the reformism of the Cárdenas era. The Cardenista emphasis on improving rural living standards through agrarian reform and the spread of education and health services was abandoned. Rapid industrialisation meant that resources had to be extracted *from* the countryside, not invested *in* it. Even in urban areas, basic government services often fell behind as rural to urban migration skyrocketed and demographic growth reached unprecedented rates. Similar reversals occurred in government support for the labour movement; industrialisation required a disciplined and loyal labour force, not a militant working class mobilised to seek new conquests. The economic growth of this period brought with it renewed inequality, in large part the result of government policies that kept salaries in the public sector high and protected privileged industries (and the wage levels of their workers) at the expense of the wages and living standards of the rest of the population.

Second, the ISI strategy required the creation of new public institutions and placed large new areas of discretionary power in the hands of the Mexican president and his subordinates. The list of state-owned companies increased, slowly in the 1950s, but more rapidly thereafter. In the increasingly unstable economic climate of the 1970s, the list exploded. The expansion of the state sector created new sources of inequality and strained the fiscal resources of the government to cover the accumulating deficits of public enterprises. Ironically, as the state expanded, it grew weaker and in its weakness began to yield some limited political spaces to opposition parties.

In the post-World War II era, US-Mexican relations, as Lorenzo Meyer put it, 'entered into a period of great normality'.[18] The United States wanted a stable and friendly country on its border; Mexico wanted to attract capital and technology and to avoid trouble and intervention. Both countries succeeded admirably in achieving their main foreign policy goals. The US government did not object to the authoritarian aspects of the Mexican political system, not even in 1968 when the Mexican government violently suppressed a nation-wide student movement that demanded greater democracy. Tensions arose in the 1970s under the successive administrations of Presidents Luis Echeverría and José López Portillo, in both cases because of Mexican foreign policy initiatives, in collaboration with other regional and extra-hemispheric powers, that challenged aspects of US dominance in the Caribbean and Central America. Aside from strengthening the two presidents' approval ratings, especially on the left, the minor confrontations of this era had no lasting impact.

Mexico's shift to ISI and the more conservative social policies this strategy required after World War II was not painless, but in contrast to many other countries in Latin America, the Mexican transition went rather smoothly. The one-party state with its highly authoritarian institutions managed to retain the credibility and legitimacy it had earned in the 1930s for another three decades before serious fissures appeared.[19]   This success depended far more on external resources to achieve high rates of economic growth than Mexico's leaders acknowledged. In any case, the ISI strategy did not experience serious problems until the early 1970s, when the international economic environment, and US economic policy-making in particular, turned unstable. New petroleum discoveries generated sufficient income (and credit) to keep the model running for several more years until the financial and economic crisis of 1982. By then, the contradictions and problems inherent in the model had already begun generating serious political problems, including demands for greater democracy to which the regime could no longer avoid responding.

The Long Transition (1982-98)

Following the 1982 crisis, Mexican authorities moved quickly to alter the country's fundamental economic policy orientation, but moved much more slowly to open its political system or improve social conditions.   Indeed, prolonged economic stagnation and reduced government spending have combined to produce some deterioration in levels of physical welfare, health care, education and the like since the early 1980s. Since income distribution has become more unequal, poverty has actually increased on some measures even through short-lived episodes of economic upswing.

The nature and timing of the changes Mexico has experienced over the past decade and a half were determined largely by the increasingly complex interplay of the four external variables identified above.   External economic conditions precipitated the 1982 crisis as well as the subsequent crises of 1987 and 1994, punishing Mexican decision-makers for failing to recognise the country's economic vulnerability. The economy has yet to recover its 1981 level of GDP *per capita*, making the 1982-98 period the longest epoch of economic stagnation in Mexican history since the catastrophic first half of the 19th century.   Mexico's new economic strategy of openness, deregulation, privatisation and fiscal restraint as well as the political changes that have accompanied it have been shaped by the policy preferences and political needs of key US actors. Mexico has found no potential external competitors with which to balance the influence of the United States, in part because the end of the Cold War turned the attention of European and Asian economic powers away from the Americas and towards Eastern Europe. US government policy, which became erratic and undisciplined in the early to mid-1980s, returned to its traditional concern for stability in 1988. For the first time in Mexican history, non-governmental organisations (NGOs), especially US NGOs linked to political and social organisations within Mexico, have begun to play a consequential role in US-Mexican relations and in the democratisation of its political system.

Mexico, like the other large countries that pursued ISI strategies after World War II, began to experience serious economic difficulties in the 1970s. Mexican authorities initially worked to improve the competitiveness of the country's major industries, such as automobiles, and gave them incentives to export, but the oil boom of the late 1970s led to overvaluation of the Mexican peso and a steep decline in the export of non-petroleum products. Nonetheless, had the US monetary authorities and economic policy-makers not miscalculated in 1981 and plunged the USA into a much sharper and more prolonged recession than anticipated, Mexico might well have muddled into the 1980s without the collapse of 1982 and the dramatic shift in strategy taken by the de la Madrid administration (1982-88) in 1985-86. The abrupt opening of the economy in the mid-1980s and the North American Free Trade Agreement (NAFTA) that went into effect in 1994 reversed nearly a century of Mexican efforts to avoid tying the country's economy too closely to that of the United States. NAFTA privileges Mexico's economic relationship with the United States, though the Mexican government has sought to regain some balance by seeking free (or freer) trade agreements with other countries and regional blocs, most notably the European Union.[20]

NAFTA has probably worked to accelerate electoral democratisation while simultaneously depriving future elected leaders of economic policy options they or their constituents might favour. The two effects are linked. NAFTA's principal impact has been to make the potential cost of any new shift in fundamental economic policy orientation prohibitively high. Confidence that the current open economy strategy will be sustained is high both in Mexico and abroad. Elite opinion in the United States and Mexico has now shifted decisively in favour of electoral democracy and greater transparency and accountability in economic policy-making. In Mexico, the shift was intensified at all levels of society by the collapse of the peso in December 1994 and the ensuing recession.

The US government interest in Mexican electoral democracy peaked between 1982 and 1988, when some in the Reagan administration openly embraced the conservative opposition party, the Partido de Acción Nacional (PAN), as an alternative to the ruling Partido Revolucionario Institucional (PRI). The US embrace of the PAN diminished after the Mexican government opened the economy and was abandoned in July 1988 when a Centre-Left coalition proved to be the country's second largest political force and the likely beneficiary of US pressures to open the electoral system to greater competition.[21] The Bush and Clinton administrations have not made electoral democratisation a significant issue in US-Mexican relations, in part because the electoral reforms of the Salinas (1988-94) and Zedillo (1994-) administrations have resulted in relatively free and fair federal elections in the 1990s. Greater integration of the two economies may also intensify efforts to reform the police and judicial systems, though this subject is now linked to a separate set of pressures related to drug trafficking. US authorities have little interest in questions of social democracy.

Mexico's new economic strategy has made its political leaders far more sensitive to US political pressures than they anticipated. One of Mexico's chief motives for pursuing NAFTA was to gain more secure access to the US market for Mexican exports. NAFTA was supposed to eliminate the discretionary power of US authorities to impose arbitrary limits and prohibitions on Mexico's exports. To an extent this has occurred, though the United States has failed to implement NAFTA provisions in a number of fields. The residual discretionary power of the

US executive, however, remains higher than the Mexican government anticipated when it signed the treaty.

A far more important constraint on the freedom of action of Mexican policy-makers is the persistent threat of a recurrence of circumstances such as those that led to the December 1994 crisis and its aftermath. In the narrowest sense, the 1994 events cannot recur because Mexico now publishes the fiscal and monetary data, the lack of which permitted the government to delay corrective action in 1994 until it was too late. Nonetheless, the events in Asia during the 1997-98 crisis have demonstrated how vulnerable even well-managed economies may become to short-term international capital flows and currency fluctuations. In the Mexican case, this vulnerability has two consequences. It forces the government to be sensitive to the image it projects to key opinion leaders and fund managers in external capital markets, particularly in the United States. It also makes Mexican leaders more sensitive than ever before to currents of opinion in the US executive and Congress, where Mexico's economic fate was fixed in 1995 and on whom, in the absence of adequate NAFTA, inter-American, or global institutions, the country's economic fate may again come to depend.

If short-term capital movements can be worrisome, the cumulative effects of long-term foreign direct investment raise other issues. The Revolution of 1910 and the depression of the 1930s reduced foreign ownership of assets in Mexico to a small proportion of the nation's capital stock. The economic opening and privatisations of the past decade have pushed foreign ownership back towards the levels of a century ago. For the first time since the 1930s, foreign companies have again become crucial players in Mexican politics and economic life. The extent and nature of the impact of this change in ownership patterns on Mexican politics and policy-makers is as yet impossible to predict.

Since the NAFTA debate began in the United States, Mexico's rulers have also come to appreciate the significant role of non-governmental actors in the formation of public and elite opinion in the United States. The Salinas administration, for example, cultivated US print and electronic media as never before. The impact of US non-governmental actors from private foundations, think tanks and universities to various NGOs, lobbying and interest groups on Mexico and on US-Mexican relations has increased dramatically over the past two decades. Moreover, this impact has proved to be cumulative. The number of Mexican organisations from cultural institutions to all manner of NGOs supported by US foundations, the 'stock' of human capital represented by Mexicans educated in US universities, the cross border cooperation between labour unions and environmental groups, have all grown larger and more important. The large and fast-growing population of Mexicans and Mexican-Americans in the United States has also emerged as an important political force to be reckoned with on both sides of the border.

The Future

Mexico faces the 21st century with an economic strategy that is theoretically superior to ISI but has yet to produce comparable rates of economic growth.[22] So long as the US economy is growing, Mexico's leaders and Mexican public opinion are likely to continue to respect the NAFTA consensus. The costs of abandoning the current economic strategy appear to be higher than the potential benefits of returning to the past or experimenting with some ill-defined alternative. A future US recession could change these calculations, particularly if trade and investment flows were to decline significantly over an extended period of time. For the presently foreseeable future, however, the terms of Mexico's external economic relations and therefore the broad outlines of domestic economic policy are not likely to change.

The end of the Cold War and the effects of freer trade have consolidated the position of the United States as the only significant star in Mexico's external firmament. Mexican authorities persist, nonetheless, in their efforts to 'diversify' the country's external relations. Recent initiatives have focused on the European Union (EU). In July 1997, Mexico signed an agreement to become an economic and political 'Associate' of the EU. To do so, Mexico had to overcome its long-standing reluctance to signing the EU's 'democracy clause',[23] but did so when EU negotiators agreed to make the clause apply to all the signatories. The 1997 agreement also committed the EU to reduce barriers to imports from Mexico. Even if this and other diversification efforts succeed, however, the United States will continue to dominate Mexico's external environment for many years to come. Mexico is reduced, in effect, to balancing selectively against US influence in policy arenas vital to neither country.

As the century ends, the impact of US government policy on Mexican politics and society is increasing and with it the temptation in Washington to deal unilaterally with problems in US-Mexican relations, especially those that resonate in US domestic politics, such as drug trafficking. Since Mexican policy-makers cannot balance effectively in the international arena, their capacity to evade external constraints will depend chiefly on the domestic institutional and political resources they can mobilise. Democracy has become crucial to defending the nation's sovereignty.

Mexico's transition to electoral democracy, at least at the level of federal elections, seems well in hand. So long as the major presidential candidates appear unlikely to abandon the NAFTA constraints, it is even conceivable that the next president will not be the candidate of the PRI. Elite and popular opinion in Mexico, as well as informed and self-interested opinion abroad, now seems to view such an outcome, in principle at least, as acceptable and possibly even desirable. External non-governmental actors, including the media and a broad array of US and European election monitoring, human rights, environmental, trade union and other organisations, appear committed to such a transition. In these circumstances, the Mexican government would have to be prepared to pay a high price, at least in external public opinion and possibly also in external capital lost to projects in other countries, were it to reverse the progress of recent years towards free and fair elections. Even in a close contest, the PRI is much more likely to exploit the advantages of incumbency in ways that shift votes at the margin than to return to the grosser exploits of the past.

It also seems likely that Mexico will continue to experience greater civic democracy, in part because of external flows of information and aid to Mexican civic associations and NGOs of all kinds. As in the case of electoral practices, conditions will continue to vary from place to place – more favourably in the north and in the cities, less favourably in the rural South.

This trend towards enhanced electoral democracy and a more vibrant civil society could be reversed by narco-corruption and violence on the Colombian model. It could also be threatened by some of the measures the Mexican government has adopted or will be pressured to take by the United States to combat the drug trade. Regulated decriminalisation of trade and consumption of currently prohibited substances is not likely to occur in the United States for another generation. Many analysts believe, however, that chemical substances produced within the United States will soon begin to substitute for imported cocaine and heroine. If this occurs, the Mexican connection may lose some of its political salience in the United States. In the meantime, however, Mexico will face continued and even escalating US pressure to help keep drugs away from US consumers.

US policy currently supports the militarisation of public security and law enforcement in Mexico, mainly because the United States views the Mexican military as less corrupted by the drug lords than Mexico's federal or local police forces. Militarisation poses three important potential threats to Mexican democracy. First, there is the long-term danger that as the Mexican military becomes ever more indispensable to public order, its officer corps will become ever more frustrated with the corruption, incompetence, and pretensions of the civilian authorities they serve. Second, there is the short- to medium-term danger that the military will become as corrupt as the federal and local police they displace; and the military is far better equipped, now with new US weapons and training, to defend its impunity. Finally, there is the problem of human rights, now and in the future. Credible and confirmed reports of abuses, in both anti-drug and counter-insurgency operations, have increased substantially in recent years.[24]

Mexico is one of only three Latin American countries that did not experience a military coup and the prolonged nightmare of military rule between the 1960s and the 1980s. It will be tragic if short-sighted blunders on both sides of the US-Mexican border were to produce conditions that pushed Mexico towards militarism at the dawn of the new millennium.

Finally, Mexico's ever closer economic and political relationship with the United States does not seem likely to contribute much to promote social progress. The historic failure of Mexican governments since the colonial era to invest adequately in the country's human resources is consistent with the NAFTA strategy as a whole and with current trends in government policy as well as long standing cultural biases in the United States. Many non-governmental organisations in the United States, from labour unions to foundations and universities, have taken an interest in social conditions in Mexico, some in the wake of NAFTA or the January 1994 Chiapas revolt, others, like the Ford Foundation, over many years. These activities often contribute to strengthening community and advocacy organisations and may thus, in the longer run, help focus attention on the country's appalling social deficit.   But if Mexico is to become healthier, better educated and less unequal, it will need to develop the domestic political, institutional, and economic resources to do so.

Notes

1. Theoretically, there should be a link between political democracy and government policies that make income distribution more equal. In Latin America, however, Cuba has one of the least competitive political regimes, but ranks among the most democratic in social outcomes. Throughout Latin America, income distribution appears to have worsened since the early 1980s, despite the restoration of democratic regimes. It is not clear that a continuation of authoritarian rule would have caused inequality to increase any faster than it did in the past decade. Maravall among others has suggested that the increases in inequality due to structural adjustment were mitigated in southern European countries transiting to democracy by increases in progressive taxation and social expenditures that might not have occurred under authoritarian auspices. This did not happen in the Latin American transitions. See Maravall (1993), pp. 77-131.
2. The most important external NGOs of this period were Protestant missionaries and the Wobblies. On the Protestants, see Baldwin (1990); on the International Workers of the World (IWW or 'Wobblies') in Mexico, see Caulfield (1987).
3. See Coatsworth (1985), pp. 40-54.
4. To this list I would add the transformation of the northern reaches of the country from an unexploited and largely unpopulated frontier into a border zone of ever more intense economic interaction with the United States, which played a vital role, as Katz has argued, in creating conditions that precipitated and sustained revolutionary movements after 1910. See Katz (1998), chapter 2. Katz and others have also pointed to the 1908-9 drought as an aggravating factor, though most of its direct effects (on food prices, for example) had disappeared by the outbreak of violence.
5. During the Mexican Revolution and the 1920s, this difference mattered for US policy, as oil interests (not for the last time) agitated for intervention (to reverse provisions of the 1917 Constitution that 'expropriated' their oil) and banks urged caution and moderation, hoping for a resumption of payments. See Smith (1972).
6. See Coatsworth (1985), p. 43.
7. Topik (1987), pp. 20-21.
8. For a somewhat different focus on this issue, see Carmagnani (1994), chapter 1.
9. Coatsworth (1988), pp. 21-62.
10. Katz (1998), chapter 1.

11. See Womack (1978), pp. 80-123. Womack's conclusions are reaffirmed in Haber and Rozo (forthcoming). Haber and Rozo focus particular attention on industrial production and productivity during the Revolution. See also Gómez (1998), chapter 13.

12. When the war ended and the 1919 recession hit, the Mexican government had little choice but to move quickly to settle its differences with the United States. The domestic trade-off was Obregón's (modest) tilt to the left in domestic policy.

13. On economic conditions and policies during the Cárdenas era, see Cárdenas (1987).

14. The Pershing invasion that followed Pancho Villa's raid on Columbus, New Mexico, seems to have been motivated in part by the calculation that it would help secure increased war appropriations through Congress – a unique case in which international competition may have worked to Mexico's disadvantage. The humiliating US withdrawal from Mexico some months later fits the historic pattern better, since it was due entirely to the impending US decision to enter the World War. See Katz (1981), chapter 8.

15. See Katz (1978), pp. 95-101.

16. Knight (1987), pp. 8-11.

17. See Nolt and Maxfield (1990), pp. 49-82.

18. Meyer (1991), p. 220.

19. Even when opposition to the regime multiplied, the PRI's grip on power eroded far more slowly than most observers thought possible. Friedrich Katz has pointed out how the Mexican Revolution retains a degree of popular affirmation and legitimacy that the Bolshevik and Chinese revolutions appear to have lost. See Katz (1998), chapter 1.

20. Chen (1996), pp. 149-58. See also chapter 3 in this volume.

21. See Meyer (1991), p. 217.

22. Except, of course, during recoveries from periodic crises provoked by the very external disequilibria the new model is supposed to avert. For a recent, critical survey of Mexico's economy and economic policies in the past ten years, see Peters (1997).

23. Until recently, Mexico has always opposed references to internal political arrangements in international treaties. The modern first breach of this principle was Mexico's endorsement of the Esquipulas II Accords of 1987 in which the governments of El Salvador, Guatemala and Nicaragua agreed to negotiate with armed rebels and to accommodate their electoral systems to incorporate them. Long negotiations with the European Union from 1994 to 1997 resulted in a new framework agreement signed by Mexico and the EU on 23 July 1997. For an excellent account of EU-Mexican relations in the recent past, see Sanahuja (1997).

24. For an excellent discussion of these issues, see Schulz (1997).

PART III

DRUGS AND MIGRATION

CHAPTER 8

HOOKED ON DRUGS: COLOMBIAN-US RELATIONS

Roberto Steiner

'Offhand, it's hard to think of any country anywhere that spells more trouble for the United States than Colombia, which produces most of the heroin and cocaine Americans voraciously consume'

Washington Post, 11 October 1997

'Colombia and the US share long-term economic, cultural, and political interests. However, in the short-run drugs have to dominate the bilateral agenda'

US drug czar General McCaffrey,
quoted in *El Tiempo*, 12 October 1997 (my translation).

The United States is the world's largest consumer of illicit drugs. Colombia is the largest supplier of refined cocaine, an important producer of marijuana and plays a small but increasing role in the supply of heroin to the USA. Notwithstanding the fact that after Brazil, and alternating with Venezuela, Colombia is the United States's most important South American trading partner, and that it is one of the region's longest lasting democracies, during the last decade the drug issue has come to dominate the bilateral Colombia-US relationship. That relationship, which used to be one of confidence and cooperation, has become one of mistrust, threat of trade sanctions and outright condemnation of Colombia on the part of the USA. Even though matters were made particularly complicated due to allegations that the electoral campaign of President Samper (1994-98) was financed with drug money, there are fundamental aspects which make for a particularly strained relationship. Relations between Colombia and the USA improved with the victory of Andrés Pastrana in the 1998 presidential elections, but this was mainly due to the US sense of relief that his rival, Horacio Serpa, had been defeated.

In this chapter we analyse key aspects of Colombian-US relations in regard to drugs. We will argue that both in good times and in bad, the bilateral anti-drug agenda has proven to be remarkably unsuccessful. Drug availability has increased while Colombia's income from drugs has stabilised. By making extradition a key element to combat drugs, narco-terrorism and narco-nationalism have been boosted and corruption exacerbated. As a result, Colombia's institutions are in shambles, with an enhanced role for the military at the expense of civilian democratic institutions. Both countries are responsible for this sad state of affairs. While the USA bullies Colombia and advances policies whose main virtue is to suggest to the US public that 'something is being done', Colombia's policies have been short-term, and adopted as a reaction to US policies.

In the first section we present a schematic summary of the evolution of bilateral relations since the early 1970s. We show that they have evolved from friendly cooperation to outright imposition, from trade incentives to threats of sanctions, and this has, perhaps inadvertently, brought an increase in the role of the military. In section two we provide scattered evidence that suggests that policies have failed, at least in the sense of reducing the supply of and demand for drugs. In addition, we review previous work on the economics of drugs, and show that while the impact of drugs on the Colombian economy is not negligible, it is a gross exaggeration to suggest that the Colombian economy has been all but over-taken by the drug trade. In the third section we evaluate three important features of current US policy towards Colombia: certification, extradition and support for militarisation of anti-drug efforts. We will argue that certification – though unilateral, unfair and insulting – might have been useful in advancing key aspects of the US agenda (see also Chapter 10). Extradition has certainly been ineffective, creating all types of problems, with few positive results. And militarisation, though justified as a tool to combat the drug trade, might weaken democratic institutions and facilitate human rights abuses if unchecked.

US-Colombian Relations since the mid-1970s

Colombia played a positive role in the construction of a new world order following World War II. Its strong opposition to a communist regime in Cuba made it a show-case within US foreign policy, as witnessed by the close cooperation with the US Agency for International Development (USAID). Under the auspices of the UN, Colombian combat troops were active during the Korean war, and were part of the Peace Force in Suez after 1956. Colombia has always been true to its legalist tradition, has never been considered a threat by its neighbours and has never undertaken expropriation of foreign assets (see Comisión de Análisis, 1997). During the Cold War, Colombia was never marginalised because of drugs.

Drugs became an issue in US foreign policy in the 1970s, when President Nixon announced the first 'war against drugs'. Under President López Michelsen (1974-78) Colombia was fostering the repatriation of financial assets held abroad by Colombian nationals – and presumed by many to be linked to drug proceeds. In addition, López re-established relations with Cuba and declined financial assistance from USAID. While public perception of drugs within the USA was increasing, the political and economic penetration of drugs in Colombia commanded little attention.

In 1978 Julio César Turbay was elected President. His image had been tarnished after a TV programme in the USA accused him and two of his ministers of having connections with the drug industry. In its 12 September 1978 edition,

Esquire magazine argued that Attorney General Serrano was the only high-ranking official that the USA fully trusted. Turbay then went on an all-out campaign to recover US support. With the Security Statute (*Estatuto de Seguridad*) he intensified the fight against those in the political left. During the 1982 Falklands war Colombia acted in tandem with the USA at a crucial OAS vote, very much against the interests of Argentina. Furthermore, relations with Cuba were suspended. As if all this was not enough, Turbay signed an extradition treaty with the USA.

According to Tokatlian and Botero (1990), with regard to extradition both countries opted for a 'quiet and reserved diplomacy': few actors, concealment and no publicity. Conversations began in late 1978. There are no indications of 'hot' debates between the national representations. In Colombia neither the press nor Congress nor the political parties discussed the matter. There is no evidence that either the USA or Colombia conditioned the bilateral agenda to the signing of the treaty, which was passed into law on 3 November 1980. In retrospect, this was a swift passage for what eventually became a crucial element of the bilateral relationship and the main, but certainly not the only, cause of drug-supported violence within Colombia.

When Ronald Reagan became President in 1981, he faced rising pressure to combat what was seen as a drug 'epidemic'. In 1982 he declared another war on drugs and unveiled plans to launch a 'full-scale' attack against abuse at home and production, processing, and trafficking abroad (Bagley, 1995). Public health issues, though relevant, were not his only concern. National Security Directive 221 of April, 1986, stated that 'drug production and trafficking comprised a threat to the security of the Americas' (Walker, 1995, p. 3).

Belisario Betancur became Colombia's President in 1982. He envisaged a more autonomous foreign policy than his predecessor. During his administration, Colombia became a member of the non-aligned movement and actively participated in the search for a peaceful solution to the Central American conflict. During the presidential campaign he criticised the repressive practices of the Turbay administration, and made peace with the guerrillas his top priority. Betancur was pressured throughout his term by the USA to apply the extradition treaty. In April 1983 a verbal request for extradition led the government's legal experts to say that the treaty was unconstitutional, as it had fundamental flaws. In October the Supreme Court expressed the opposite view. Based on judicial arguments, and with a profound nationalist tone, Betancur denied this specific extradition request. As a result, US actions to engage the Colombian government shifted emphasis: exporters of cut-flowers and other perishable goods, as well as Colombian airlines, were targeted. The intermittent use of trade policy as a 'carrot and stick' was surreptitiously initiated.

In spite of not favouring extradition, the Betancur administration took strong actions against the drug business. As a result, on 30 April 1984, Justice Minister Rodrigo Lara was assassinated. He had been an outspoken critic of drug money in politics and in professional sports and was involved in a heated debate with Pablo Escobar, at the time an alternate in the House of Representatives, and soon to be recognised as the head of the infamous Medellín cartel. Lara's assassination brought about a radical change in Betancur's policies. At his funeral, the president back-tracked on his opposition to extradition. He acknowledged that the enemy was too powerful, and that all instruments at hand should be used against it. The first four Colombian nationals were handed to US authorities in January 1985. The year 1984 was a breaking-point in Colombian-US relations. On the one hand, they became definitely 'narcotised'. On the other, organised crime began a ten year blood-bath.

In June 1984, and notwithstanding popular protest, aerial spraying of marijuana began. Tokatlian and Botero (1990) argue that by accepting the use of this US sponsored tactic, Betancur was acknowledging the argument that the drug problem lay essentially within producing countries. Even though the military preferred a more discrete involvement, Betancur – much to the liking of the USA – was interested in enhancing their role in anti-drug efforts. A May 1984 decree established that military penal justice should deal with drug related crimes. The limitations of both the executive and legislative branches became evident, while military autonomy to control public order was enhanced. As pointed out elsewhere (see Steiner, 1997), few political experiments have ended on such a different note as they began than that of Belisario Betancur.

In 1986 the USA implemented operation 'Blast Furnace' in Bolivia. According to Walker (1995, p. 3), this was a good example of a 'quick fix: raid now, reflect later'. Soon after those events and on the day of his inauguration in 1986, President Virgilio Barco said the presence of a foreign army within Colombia was unthinkable, although he was in favour of extradition. However, much to his disdain, on 12 December 1986, the Supreme Court ruled the extradition treaty was unconstitutional. Barco was left without what to him was the most effective instrument to deal with drug-trafficking.

In 1988 there was an important change of emphasis in Colombia's policies towards drugs. Though spraying and eradication were not completely phased out, the new targets would be rural and urban drug processing laboratories, the Medellín-paid assassins, and the cartel leaders themselves. In March 1989 Colombia agreed to the installation of a complex radar system. President Barco paid a heavy political toll, as he was accused of yielding the nation's sovereignty and 'Vietnamising' Colombia. The involvement of the military in these endeavours was not well received. In particular, in late 1988 the minister of defence stated that the army would obtain much better results in its anti-guerrilla activities were it not involved in drug-related operations.

As Colombia's military involvement in anti-drug activities was escalating, the US Congress, frustrated by the ineffectiveness of Reagan's policies, enacted the Anti-Drug Abuse Act of 1988, complementing supply-side programmes overseas with a second front, directed at curtailing domestic demand. Whatever the emphasis on demand reduction, on September 1989 the US Secretary of Defense publicly stated that detecting and countering the production and trafficking of illegal drugs was a 'high-priority, national security mission' for the Pentagon (Bagley, 1995, p. 63).

The 18 August 1989 killing of Luis Carlos Galán was the last ingredient in Colombia's escalation of the 'war on drugs'. Galán was a presidential candidate, who was expected to win the 1990 elections. He was an outspoken enemy of the drug cartels and a close political associate of Rodrigo Lara, who had been gunned down in 1984. Following Galán's death, increased militarisation of anti-drug activities would be the salient feature of drug policy. In addition, President Barco instituted extradition of Colombian nationals 'through administrative procedure'.[1]

With regard to US policy, 1989-90 marked the explicit establishment of a 'carrot and stick' approach. On the one hand, there was the Andean strategy, adopted in Cartagena in 1990. It consisted of a three-prong programme of military support, law enforcement advice, and economic assistance. The latter was based on the ATPA (Andean Trade Preference Agreement). According to Tokatlian (1995, p. 133), for the USA ATPA was politically meritorious and economically inexpensive. For Colombia, at most it made up for the lost revenue resulting from the US-sponsored collapse of the International Coffee Agreement. On the other hand, in December 1989 the USA invaded Panama. It was the first full-scale military operation undertaken to combat narco-trafficking. More than ever before, the USA was sending a clear message to countries involved in the drug business: economic benefits and military assistance if you cooperate, trade sanctions and perhaps military intervention if you do not. In early January 1990 US warships were dispatched to the Colombian Caribbean. This explicit violation of the principle of non-intervention was emphatically rejected by Colombia. The Bush administration (1989-93) regretted the incident, and said there had been a 'misunderstanding' between Washington and Bogotá.

Just as Bush had done four years before, during the 1992 campaign Bill Clinton pledged that he would redirect drug policy away from the Reagan-Bush emphasis on supply-side strategies towards a comprehensive crusade against drug abuse. According to Bagley (1995), once Clinton was in office, his new budget contained no fundamental change in policies or priorities.

US-Colombian relations entered a new phase with the election of César Gaviria as President in 1990. With regard to the drug issue, two issues are worth highlighting: (i) the constitutional banning of extradition by a popularly elected Constitutional Assembly in early 1991; (ii) the establishment of a very generous plea-bargaining system with regard to organised crime. These two facts led to the surrender of Pablo Escobar and the highest echelons of the Medellín cartel. In spite of living in great comfort, – having a saying on the selection of prison guards, allegedly leaving prison at will in order to attend soccer matches and the like – Pablo Escobar escaped from prison in 1992. Apparently, his excesses had reached such proportions that the government was determined to move him into a real prison. According to the Comisión de Análisis (1997), Escobar's escape turned Washington's doubts and expectations with regard to Colombia into deep concerns and suspicions.

Even if it had wanted to act otherwise, the embarrassment following the escape of Escobar left the government no other choice but to hunt him down. An all-out effort by the police proved successful in late 1993, when he was gunned down in

Table 8.1:
Teenagers and Drugs in the USA

Year	Lifetime Prevalence for High School Seniors (a)			Disapproval of Drug Use by Twelfth Graders (b)			Teenage Perception of Availability (c)			Teenage Perception of Harmfulness (d)		
	Marijuana*	Cocaine	Heroin	Marijuana	Cocaine	Heroin	Marijuana	Cocaine	Heroin	Marijuana	Cocaine	Heroin
1975	47.3	9.0	2.2	47.0	81.3	91.5	87.8	37.0	24.2	18.1	-	75.6
1976	52.8	9.7	1.8	38.4	82.4	92.6	87.4	34.0	18.4	15.0	-	75.6
1977	56.4	10.8	1.8	33.4	79.1	92.5	87.9	33.0	17.9	13.4	-	71.9
1978	59.2	12.9	1.6	33.4	77.0	92.0	87.8	37.8	16.4	12.4	-	71.4
1979	60.4	15.4	1.1	34.2	74.7	93.4	90.1	45.5	18.9	13.5	-	70.9
1980	60.3	15.7	1.1	39.0	76.3	93.5	89.0	47.9	21.2	14.7	-	70.9
1981	59.5	16.5	1.1	40.0	74.6	93.5	89.2	47.5	19.2	19.1	-	72.2
1982	58.7	16.0	1.2	45.5	76.6	94.6	88.5	47.4	20.8	18.3	-	69.8
1983	57.0	16.2	1.2	46.3	77.0	94.3	86.2	43.1	19.3	20.6	-	71.8
1984	54.9	16.1	1.3	49.3	79.7	94.0	84.6	45.0	19.9	22.6	-	70.7
1985	54.2	17.3	1.2	51.4	79.3	94.0	85.5	48.9	21.0	24.5	-	69.8
1986	50.9	16.9	1.1	54.6	80.2	93.3	85.2	51.5	22.0	25.0	54.3	68.2
1987	50.2	15.2	1.2	56.6	87.3	96.2	84.8	54.2	23.7	30.4	66.8	74.6
1988	47.2	12.1	1.1	60.8	89.1	95.0	85.0	55.0	28.0	31.7	69.2	73.8
1989	43.7	10.3	1.3	64.6	90.5	95.4	84.3	58.7	31.4	36.5	71.8	75.5
1990	40.7	9.4	1.3	67.8	91.5	95.1	84.4	54.5	31.9	36.9	73.9	76.6
1991	36.6	7.8	0.9	68.7	93.6	96.0	83.3	51.0	30.6	40.6	75.5	74.9
1992	32.6	6.1	1.2	69.9	93.0	94.9	82.7	52.7	34.9	39.6	75.1	74.2
1993	35.3	6.1	1.1	63.3	92.7	94.4	83.0	48.5	33.7	35.6	73.3	72.0
1994	38.2	5.9	1.2	57.6	91.6	93.2	85.5	46.6	34.1	30.1	73.7	72.1
1995	41.7	6.0	1.6	56.7	90.3	92.8	88.5	47.7	35.1	25.6	70.8	71.0
1996	44.9	7.1	1.8	52.5	90.0	92.1	88.7	48.1	32.2	25.9	72.1	74.8

* or hashish

(a) % who have ever used them

(b) % disapproving use 'once or twice'

(c) % saying 'fairly easy' or 'very easy' to get

(d) % saying 'great risk' from occasional use

Source: NIDA, Drug Abuse Survey, 1996.

his Medellín hide-out. There is no doubt that Gaviria at least commanded absolute trust from the USA. The USA led a successful effort in having Gaviria elected as Secretary General of the OAS following the completion of his four-year term as president. To be sure, Colombians had a right to interpret this gesture as evidence that – in spite of the banning of extradition and notwithstanding a most curious plea-bargaining system – the country's role in the fight against drugs still commanded some respect.

Following the 1994 scandal surrounding the financing by drug-traffickers of various political campaigns – including that of President Samper (1994-98) himself – bilateral relations deteriorated in a way only comparable with the situation at the turn of the century, when Panama seceded from Colombia.[2] Whether this reflected a fundamental shift in the bilateral relationship, or whether it was highly influenced by the figure of Samper himself, is still not clear. According to Tokatlian (1996), as a result of the surfacing of explicit ties between organised crime and elected officials at the highest levels within Colombia, it is no longer drug-traffickers – either individually or collectively – but the country as a whole that could be identified by the USA as the epicentre of security threats to the international community.

The Drug Trade

In a celebrated 1973 statement, President Nixon claimed that 'we have turned the corner on drug addiction in the US' (Matthiesen, 1997). Table 8.1 tells a rather different story. Panel (a) shows that drug 'usage' among teenagers peaked in 1979-80, went on a declining trend throughout the 1980s, and has increased since 1992. A similar pattern emerges with regard to 'disapproval' of drug use (panel b). Regarding 'availability' (panel c), marijuana has always been easily available; cocaine was less easily found in 1996 than in 1989, but more available than in 1975; heroin's availability has been increasing over the last decade. The perception of 'harmfulness' has decreased in the case of marijuana and has been stable for cocaine and heroin during the 1990s (panel d).

Table 8.2:
Estimated Number of Drug Users in the USA (thousands)

| Year | Occasional | | Hardcore | |
	Cocaine	Heroin	Cocaine	Heroin
1988	6,000	170	3,600	875
1989	5,300	150	3,400	880
1990	4,600	140	3,200	780
1991	4,500	170	3,000	730
1992	3,500	210	3,100	690
1993	3,300	200	3,300	790
1994	2,900	210	3,200	800
1995	3,000	320	3,300	810

Source: Office of National Drug Control Policy (1997).

Table 8.2 suggests that, while the number of occasional cocaine users has been declining since 1988, the number of occasional heroin users has increased. In 1995 there were more hardcore users of both than in 1990. According to Reuter (1998, p. 24) 'the severity of problems caused by drugs has not declined ... because those who use drugs most heavily and experience the most severe health and behavioural consequences have continued to take narcotics.' Table 8.3 shows time series for wholesale prices of cocaine. They have been continuously falling in nominal terms, again reflecting increased availability. If anti-drug policy is measured in terms of reductions in availability, or of reductions in public health problems associated with drugs, then it is clear that it has not been successful over the past two decades.

There are several reasons why it is important to have a good estimate of the income appropriated by Colombians through this involvement in the drug trade. First, it provides useful information for Colombia's economic authorities. Second, it gives insights regarding the possibility of committing Colombia in multilateral anti-drug efforts.[3] Finally, by showing that profits are made mostly within consuming countries, it discredits the xenophobic approach to the problem.[4]

Table 8.3:
Cocaine: Wholesale Prices (US$000/kg)

| Year | US National Average | |
	Min.	Max.
1980	55.0	65.0
1981	55.0	65.0
1982	55.0	65.0
1983	45.0	55.0
1984	40.0	50.0
1985	30.0	50.0
1986	22.0	45.0
1987	12.0	40.0
1988	11.0	34.0
1989	11.0	35.0
1990	11.0	40.0
1991	11.0	40.0
1992	11.0	42.0
1993	10.5	40.0
1994	10.5	40.0
1995	10.5	36.0

Source: Steiner (1998), based on DEA.

All estimates of an illegal activity are highly speculative. Given the lack of reliable information, implausible numbers are offered under the premise that any estimate is as good as any other. In its 2 September 1989 issue *The Economist* (p. 21) stated that a subcommittee of the US Senate put yearly US cocaine imports at around 2,500 tons. Recent studies have estimated yearly US cocaine consumption at 250 tons (Office of National Drug Policy, 1995 and 1997). The subcommittee missed the mark by a factor of ten.

Whynes (1991, p. 484) stated that 'it is thought that at least \$7 billion per annum eventually returns to Colombia'. This figure falls short of the one reported by MacDonald (1989) according to whom drugs could be Colombia's biggest source of national income – nearly 36 per cent of its total gross national product. And he tries to dissipate doubts by pointing out that 'sources interviewed in Colombia in 1988 indicated that the assessment was relatively accurate' (p. 141). With a GDP of around \$50 billion, MacDonald is suggesting that Colombia receives \$18 billion a year from drug exports. Andelman (1994, p. 98) went even further, implicitly suggesting that yearly revenues for the Colombian cartels in the USA could reach \$25 billion, i.e. 50 per cent of GDP.

No wonder an important Colombian weekly (*Semana*, 30 July 1996, pp. 36-46) suggested that two Colombians had a fortune of around \$12 billion. The list of Colombian billionaires was impressive: one had \$11 billion; another \$8 billion: five had \$6 billion. In a US survey (*Forbes 400*, September 1996), Bill Gates led the field with a net worth of \$18.5 billion. Mr Knight of Nike (\$5.3 billion) came in 6th; he would have been 10th in Colombia.

In none of the above estimates is there an explicit methodology; in most cases there is no mention of the reference period; and in several instances we have estimates based on other estimates. In Steiner (1998) I summarise some previous work on the economics of drugs and estimate the net income received by Colombian residents from their involvement in the drug trade, using the most recent information regarding drug production as compiled by US authorities.[5]

Figure 8.1:
Net Total Drug Income: As Percentage of Exports and GDP

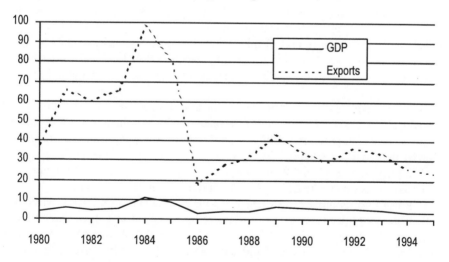

Source: Steiner (1998).

Colombia's net total income from illicit drugs – i.e. including marijuana and heroin – could have been 7 per cent of GDP and 70 per cent of exports at its peak during the first half of the 1980s (see Figure 8.1). For the recent past it represented close to 3 per cent of GDP and around 25 per cent of legal exports. Even though these estimates give no support to the claim that the Colombian economy has been taken over by the drug trade, it is still the case that a small group of outlaws is receiving yearly income to the tune of 3 per cent of GDP. This is not a negligible amount, particularly given that it is concentrated in a few hands. While yearly revenues from coffee also stand at around 3 per cent of GDP, they provide for the livelihood of 300,000 families. It seems fair to conclude that, while drugs do not seem to represent a crucial element in Colombia's economic well-being, they have implied a huge transfer of power to a small group of individuals involved in organised crime.

Three Critical Issues

Several issues of Colombian-US relations demand particular attention. Some, including the rationale behind aerial spraying and the possibilities of legalisation, are not addressed here. In reversed order of importance, these issues are:

(a) Certification[6]
In 1986 the USA established a unilateral certification mechanism according to which the president must report to Congress in regard to the cooperation in drug-related matters of those countries which grow, transform or ship drugs or are suspected of being involved in money-laundering activities. A 'decertified' country cannot receive credit from any US government agency and faces a negative US vote in multilateral financial institutions. A routinely decertified country is likely to face trade sanctions. Thanks to a 'national waiver interest', Colombia was certified in 1995 and 1998, but it was fully decertified in 1996 and 1997. By US standards, it has joined the 'pariah nations' club, that includes, among others, Iran and Libya.

It goes without saying that the certification process is unilateral, unfair and insulting. Acknowledging there are problems with a unilateral mechanism, the USA is considering the possibility of participating in a joint evaluation procedure led by the OAS (see Chapter 10). Whether a Republican-dominated Congress will subscribe to the idea is a different matter. In any event, it is highly unlikely that a multilateral evaluation would *replace* the current unilateral certification.

Regarding its unfairness, when US drug czar General McCaffrey was asked about the 1997 decision to certify Mexico, he conceded that there was 'creative hypocrisy' (*The Economist*, 8 March 1997).[7] Currently, Mexico's involvement in the drug trade might be more significant than that of Colombia. According to the head of the US Drug Enforcement Administration (DEA), Thomas Constantine, 'sophisticated drug syndicates from Mexico have eclipsed organised crime groups from Colombia as the premier law enforcement threat facing the US today...' (*The Economist*, 15 November 1997).

And it is obviously insulting. Not so much because of the position adopted by the USA, but because of the submissive attitude of the Colombian authorities. It is worth contrasting two quotations that exemplify this point. While Mexican President Zedillo was quoted as saying 'Certify us? They should compensate us for the filthy mess they leave us' (*The Economist*, 15 November 1997), Colombian Foreign Minister Mejía argued that 'If this year's decision is based on objective criteria, then the least we can expect is certification based on a US national interest waiver' (*Portafolio*, 12 February 1998, my translation). It seems that in certification matters, you actually do get what you bargained for. It should be acknowledged, however, that Colombia did not do any better when it had a more dignified position.

Apart from being unilateral, unfair and insulting, for some the mechanism has been counter-productive. It has been criticised everywhere, including in the USA itself. In February 1997 a *New York Times* editorial stated that

> The politicisation of the debate is only one example of what is wrong with the whole certification process. It has not been successful and should be abolished... When Colombia was decertified, President Samper rallied Colombian nationalism and his popularity rose... Certification is ultimately dangerous because it contributes to the myth that America's drug problems can best be fought overseas. In both Colombia and Mexico, this task is shifting to the military. As relations with Colombia's civilian Government have deteriorated, Washington has increased aid and weapon sales to the country's military, which has the worst human rights record in the hemisphere and strong ties to paramilitary leaders who traffic in cocaine (26 February 1997).

It is unilateral, it is unfair, it is insulting, but has it necessarily been counter-productive? It has certainly exacerbated nationalism in Colombia and Mexico; it might even have provided President Samper with much needed political support. But who is to deny that it was pressure from the USA – including quite prominently the certification process – that prompted action by Samper's administration to incarcerate drug-dealers, increase penalties for drug-related offences, advance money-laundering and asset-forfeiture legislation, and support the re-instatement of extradition? From the point of view of the USA, it is not at all clear that certification has been ineffective. From the Colombian perspective, that is precisely the bad news.

(b) Extradition
Several analysts have suggested that Colombia has no long-term, well-planned strategy to confront the drug problem. As a result, policy has been reactive, heavily influenced by immediate economic, political, social and international

pressure. In no aspect is this characterisation more appropriate than in the case of extradition.

It was introduced in the late 1970s, with no significant social or political opposition within Colombia, and under no undue pressure from the USA. It was not presented as the panacea against drugs. And it could not have been otherwise. Thoumi (1995) has made an in-depth analysis of the industry's structure and has argued that illegality is an obstacle to vertical integration, with two implications: (i) jailing or extraditing a major trafficker has at best a minor short-term impact; (ii) negotiations with industry leaders who do not have enough control over the industry in order to enforce any agreement are deemed to fail.

Even though 'when' and 'why' are a matter of debate, by the mid-1980s extradition had become the cornerstone of Colombia's drug policy and its suppression the principal objective of drug traffickers. The several rounds of extraditions – in particular, by Betancur following the assassination of Lara and by Barco following the death of Galán – have not made a dent on the drug business, and have not deterred others from participating in the business. In the words of Thoumi (1995, p. 282), 'the increasingly violent reaction to this policy was totally out of proportion to the benefits it produced'.

While it is evident that the 1997 re-establishment of extradition was done because of relentless pressure from the USA, the same cannot be said of its application during the second half of the 1980s. To be sure, and in sharp contrast to Samper, both Betancur and Barco thought it was the right thing to do. Why? It seems reasonable to argue that while the public discourse now makes reference to extradition as a key component in the fight against drugs, in reality it has been a useful mechanism for quite different reasons. In the case of the USA, it is an inexpensive way of showing the US people that 'something' is being done. In the case of Colombia, it is a way of pleasing the USA, and, presumably, an effective way of telling prominent traffickers that there are limits to what they can do. While few presume that because of extradition Colombians will abandon the drug trade, many do believe that it acts as an effective deterrent to those prominent drug-dealers who, apart from making money through drugs, might also have the idea of subduing the country as a whole. At the very least, extradition seems to be a good way of 'getting even' with criminals. Needless to say, this positive feature comes at a huge price.

Colombia's ambivalent position with regard to extradition – from Betancur's use of an instrument he 'philosophically opposed', to the popular support given to the Constitutional Assembly that killed it in 1991, to the relentless public pressure on Congress to re-instate it in 1997 – is partially related to shifts in what Colombians perceive to be the importance given to extradition by different US administrations. Clearly, the USA has not sent a consistent message in that regard. In the early 1980s Betancur announced he would not extradite Colombian nationals, and the US reaction was not extremely negative. A decade later, the US Congress approved ATPA *after* extradition was barred from Colombia's constitution. Furthermore, the USA was instrumental in having César Gaviria elected as OAS Secretary General, in spite of the fact that it was during his administration that extradition was constitutionally precluded.

Colombia's ambivalent position is also related to the violent reaction from drug organisations. What in 'peaceful' times might be understood as the correct policy to have in place – one that deters criminals and assures the international community that Colombia is a reliable ally in the fight against drugs – is easily seen as a 'concession to imperialism' when bombs start exploding in aeroplanes, shopping-malls and street corners.

Thousands of Colombians have been killed because of drugs in general, and because of extradition in particular. Given the industry's structure, it is a mechanism that has no chance of effectively diminishing the production of drugs. Presidents philosophically opposed to it have either applied it or re-instated it. The President who never used it, and who made no significant attempts at keeping it alive, César Gaviria, was a US favourite. The principal merits of the mechanism seem to rest in that it helps the USA save face with regard to the US public and the Colombian government save face with regard to its US counterpart. It has certainly been very expensive for Colombia. However, eliminating it could cost even more. It would alienate the international community and facilitate matters for cartel leaders. It is an unfair deal, one with which Colombia has to live, particularly after the embarrassment following disclosure of the financial dealings in the 1994 election and after the lack of 'teeth' of the country's extremely generous plea-bargaining system became evident.[8]

(c) Militarisation

It is hard to imagine a more sensitive issue with regard to drugs and Colombian-US relations than the increased use of the Colombian military in the fight against drugs.[9] On top of being an important drug producer, Colombia has Latin America's longest lasting guerrilla movement. During the Reagan years, military involvement in anti-drug efforts took place amidst accusations from many corners within the USA that US aid was being partially diverted to anti-guerrilla activities, undertaken by people not extremely concerned with human rights issues. To justify what was being done, a former US ambassador coined the term *narco-guerrillas*.

The problem is that the links between guerrillas and drugs is not obvious at all. There is little evidence of actual trafficking by any guerrilla organisation. Their involvement in the business is related to some crop growing, a lot of crop and laboratory protection, and routine extortion of landowners, many of them with direct ties to the drug trade. While there might be ties between guerrillas and coca and poppy growers – a socially sensitive issue – their relationship with traffickers and organised crime is mainly one of confrontation. If there was any doubt about this, it has been dissipated by the recent bloody war between guerrillas and paramilitary organisations, the latter with close ties to drug-traffickers.

During the Cold War, US involvement in Latin America was more closely linked to containing the spread of communism than to combating drugs. The focus now lies in containing drugs, not communists. Calls for militarisation of the war on drugs have emanated from the US Congress at least since 1981. Events within Colombia in the late 1980s opened the door for a greater US-sponsored military role, as narco-terrorism provided the rationale for using military resources to smother the drug business. A benevolent interpretation of the new emphasis is offered by Perl (1995), according to whom some have argued that, by promoting military involvement in the fight against drugs, the USA is 'inadvertently strengthening the power of the military at the expense of often fragile, civilian democratic institutions in the region' (p. 34). The strengthening of the military would then be a side effect of an otherwise well-intended policy.

A different line of reasoning is offered by Mabry, according to whom supporting the use of the military to combat drugs is problematic at best. It presumes a mutuality of interests between the US and Andean militaries, which does not exist. In addition, it incorrectly links traffickers and guerrillas and threatens democracy in the region. In fact, 'the US, by insisting that the civilian police forces in these nations are incompetent to destroy what the US itself terms criminal organizations, has telegraphed the message that militaries are more important than civilian institutions' (Mabry, 1995, p. 51).[10]

Of late, attitudes in the USA regarding the involvement of the military have shifted somewhat. If the emphasis was on combating communists during the Cold War, and in dealing with drug dealers in the last decade, human rights issues are now an integral part of the agenda. And rightly so, because if the blood-bath of the 1980s was provoked by traffickers mainly fighting to over-turn extradition, the more recent one is to a great extent explained by the relentless pursue of the guerrillas by paramilitary organisations, sometimes linked to drug-traffickers, sometimes linked to the military, and on occasions linked to both.

Recently *El Tiempo* (4 January 1998) quoted a *New York Times* editorial according to which the US government should pressure the Colombian military to respect civil authority and to arrest the members of the paramilitary groups. Respect for human rights and concerns for the activities of the paramilitaries in no way implies a change in US conception regarding links between guerrillas and drugs. According to *The Washington Post* (as transcribed in *El Tiempo*, 28 December 1997), the Clinton administration is concerned that the Marxist guerrillas, allied with drug traffickers, will pose a major threat to the Colombian government and to the entire region. *The Post* quotes General McCaffrey as saying that the guerrillas 'are moving away from their ideological struggle, in the direction of criminal activities'.

Important US constituencies and the vast majority of Colombians resent any US intervention in the conflict with the guerrillas. However, if it is actually true, as we have argued, that links between guerrillas and traffickers are weak, the implications of allowing the USA and the Colombian military to advance policies as if those links were strong could be disastrous. It enhances the relative power of the military and weakens democratic institutions, even if it is far fetched to suggest that the USA has the explicit objective of strengthening the Colombian military *vis-à-vis* civilian institutions. In fact, without wanting to, that policy might end up supporting the worst type of elements in the drug business (the paramilitaries), if not in their drug-related endeavours, certainly in their plans of extending control over vast portions of the country. The good news is, of course, that whatever the actual links between guerrillas and drugs might be, human rights abuses now rank very high in the US agenda.

Conclusions

Today, illicit drugs are as easily available within the USA as they have ever been. They are less expensive and of higher quality. Income from drugs continues to be an important source of foreign revenue for Colombia. While narco-terrorism has abated, drug money and drug interests have infiltrated Colombian politics. Bilateral relations are at their worst in almost a century. After 15 years of a drug-dominated agenda, both countries have little, if anything, to show in the fight against drugs. At the very best, Colombia can claim to have 'exported' part of its drug problems to Mexico – small comfort for the USA.

Colombia has been left with many dead people. Some were killed because of extradition, a mechanism that can hardly play an important role in diminishing the drug trade. It has a narco-infiltrated political class and a ruthlessly violent narco-sponsored paramilitary. The role of the military has been enhanced, in spite of its bleak record with respect to human rights. Thanks to the certification mechanism, it is now a 'pariah' nation. It is difficult to imagine a worse combination of results. Though economically in reasonable shape, Colombia is in institutional shambles.

Was it the drugs, or the unintentional consequence of policies against them? Probably a combination of both. The mere presence of drugs and the huge profits associated with them were bound to influence institutional development, as those involved in the drug trade would strive for social and political recognition. But there should be no doubt that the weakness of Colombia with respect to the USA determined that what should have been a multilateral issue has for the most part been treated as a problem generated by a few Colombian thugs.

The discourse is about a multilateral problem, about supply and demand. Actual policies are different. Regardless of its good intentions, US-sponsored initiatives to confront the drug problem have made a bad situation even worse. Instead of having reasonable political representation, drug organisations have corrupted the entire political process, the judicial system, and almost any other institution one cares to mention. Colombians have been alienated from the USA. Narco-nationalism is a political reality. As Tokatlian and Botero foresaw in 1990, and as Bagley (1995) has recently suggested, Washington's coercive diplomacy was bound to exacerbate moral imperialism on the side of the USA and narco-nationalism within Colombia. Moderate sectors on both sides have lost their capacity to influence the shaping of policy.

In the context of the post-Cold War, the current Colombian situation is not only a matter of utmost concern for all Colombians, it is also a big problem for the USA. The weakness of democratic institutions, the enhanced role of the military, and the terrible record on human rights are now unacceptable within the USA. It might be the right time to acknowledge past failures and structure a new bilateral relation that is based on cooperation and not confrontation; on drug-related policies that can truly be effective in the long-run, even if they do not make the headlines; on institutional strengthening, not on worthless finger-pointing. In short, a policy that is reasonable enough not to make drugs more of a problem than they already are. Issues regarding money laundering and the international trade in chemical inputs are multilateral by definition. While Colombian criminals sell the drugs, legal corporations profit from selling them chemicals. The USA's number one brand of cigarettes (Marlboro) dominates the Colombian market; it has been claimed that not one single cigarette is legally imported. They arrive through contraband, a most efficient way for traffickers to launder their money. As if it were not enough to have Colombia's judicial system in disarray, the USA is generally unwilling to share evidence with Colombian authorities. Finally, and granting the need to involve the military in anti-drug efforts, multilateral cooperation is essential in order to keep the military doing what they are supposed to do, and not allowing them to become involved in what does not concern them.

Notes

1. In late 1989 the House of Representatives wanted to include the banning of extradition in a proposed constitutional reform. The president had to withdraw the entire project. By February 1990, his administration had performed 14 extraditions through administrative procedure.
2. To exemplify the deterioration in the relationship, it is useful to quote Robert Gelbard, a high-ranking State Department official. According to *The Economist* (23 November 1996), he testified before Congress that Mr Samper was a 'truly corrupt president who has had a clear history of co-operating with drug dealers.' The same publication went on to say that 'few diplomats have worked as hard to anger their hosts as Myles Frechette, the American ambassador in Bogota'.
3. According to Perl (1995), producing countries – particularly Bolivia and Peru – would be 'committing economic suicide' if they accepted a multilateral strategy without some kind of economic compensation.
4. Matthiesen (1997) argues that a dominant guiding force in US drug policy has been the perception among broad segments of the population that drugs are produced overseas and consumed and distributed within the USA mainly by minorities.
5. Data on prices are from US Department of Justice, Drug Enforcement Administration, *Illegal Drug Price/Purity Report* and *From the Source to the Street*. Data on production and seizures are from National Narcotics Intelligence Consumers Committee (NNICC), *The Supply of Illicit Drugs to the United States* and from US Department of State, *International Narcotics Control Strategy Report*.
6. A comprehensive analysis of the certification process is found in Elizabeth

Joyce's contribution in this volume. She emphasises the fact that US domestic issues dominate the whole process.

7. Much to his embarrassment, in early 1997 General McCaffrey had referred to General Gutiérrez, then chief of Mexico's anti-drug force, as 'a guy of absolute, unquestioned integrity'. Soon afterwards, Gutiérrez was found to have been in the pay of Mexican drug traffickers.

8. Not everybody agrees with extradition. *El Tiempo* (9 November 1997) reports on a survey of 600 people in the six largest cities. To the question 'do you agree or not with the extradition of Colombian nationals?' 43.1 per cent said no, 46.1 per cent said yes, 7.8 per cent were indifferent, and 3 per cent did not respond.

9. The involvement of the US military apparently is a less complicated issue. According to Mabry (1995), between the collapse of the Soviet empire and the beginning of the Gulf crisis, many in the USA thought the military had little use for its enormous installed capacity and sought a 'peace dividend'. For some, involving the military in anti-drug efforts was a way to collect.

10. It should be noted that Colombia's police is not civilian. Rather, it is the fourth branch of the armed forces, together with the army, navy and air force.

CHAPTER 9

THE UNITED STATES AND BOLIVIA: FIGHTING THE DRUG WAR

Eduardo A. Gamarra

The USA has been a significant actor in Bolivia since at least the early 1940s.[1] On at least five occasions Washington has paid relatively close attention to events in Bolivia.[2] During these moments of high US interest, despite the very small presence of US investment, Bolivia commanded a proportionately high share of US assistance to the region. At the same time, however, Bolivia has been a relatively minor player in the western hemisphere and has rarely had any influence in the international arena. Most important, Bolivia has rarely been able to design or articulate a specific US policy. For the most part, it has been forced to react to US initiatives.

In the post-World War II period, the overwhelming concern with containment relegated all other issues, especially the trafficking of drugs. In the early 1980s, the logic of the Cold War clashed directly with an incipient 'drug war', in the midst of a transition from military rule to civilian-elected governments. With the collapse of the Soviet Union and the end of the Cold War, US drug policy has failed to transcend Cold War institutions, strategies, and tactics.

US-Bolivian relations are characterised by nine basic traits which transcend the specificity of the Cold War period. First, Bolivia's central geographical location in South America became the principal focus of US policy towards this Andean country. While Bolivia has long considered its geographical location as a disadvantage, for strategic reasons, US policy has perceived it as a crucial 'hinge country' in South America. The logic behind Che Guevara's failed guerrilla experiment in 1967, for example, ratified this logic. In the context of today's war on drugs, the hinge analogy is even more powerful, as Bolivia has become a central player in South America's narco-geopolitics.

A second characteristic of US policy towards Bolivia has been the overwhelming presence of bureaucratic politics. Bureaucratic infighting amongst and between the multiple agencies charged with implementing US policy undermined the very logic of the US foreign policy agenda. As the Cold War unfolded and as US policy towards Bolivia became more complex, a larger number of agencies became involved. At times, these agencies worked at cross purposes while ostensibly pursuing the same broad set of policy objectives. The basic logic of US policy has been that as the intensity of the problem grows so does the number of agencies involved in attempting to resolve it. As Jorge Malamud and others have shown, bureaucracies tend to expand and attempt to command their share of resources often to the detriment of others involved.[3] To this end, bureaucracies involved in security matters have tended to exaggerate the nature of any problem – redefining a problem as a national security threat – in their attempt to capture greater resources.

As agency involvement increases, so too do the problems of bureaucratic politics. As numerous General Accounting Office (GAO) reports have noted, there is a lack of coordination between agencies, intelligence sharing is minimal and different US agencies may even have conflicting objectives. Joint US-Bolivia counternarcotics strategies have been plagued by the lack of coordination between US and Bolivian agencies and bureaucratic infighting within agencies of both governments.[4]

Thirdly, US policy in Bolivia has often been trapped in the vicissitudes of domestic politics. This trait is especially evident in instances of US congressional involvement. In the main, although with important exceptions, members of Congress have pushed for harsher terms of conditionality for US-Bolivian policy. This is largely the result of constituent-driven demands to target countries where the threat has been identified. Since at least the early 1980s, US congressional delegations have visited Bolivia to verify first-hand the nature of the threat. The flip side of this trait is that Bolivia has historically had little or no capacity to influence members of Congress. While this may be explained away by the lack of resources of Bolivia's foreign ministry, the fact is that few Bolivian ambassadors in Washington have understood the basic logic of US foreign policy-making.

Fourthly, the US embassy, especially the US ambassador, has always had a significant degree of influence in Bolivian politics. Every ambassador in Bolivia since World War II has become an important figure in domestic politics, sometimes even determining the direction of policy. A key point to understand is that US policy towards Bolivia – or for that matter anywhere else in the region – is made in Washington, but the individual style of each ambassador has been crucial in terms of policy implementation.

A few individual ambassadors are noteworthy. Ben Stephansky in the early 1960s was accused of campaigning for the MNR (Movimiento Nacionalista Revolucionario) during elections. Edwin Corr (1981-85) was a crucial actor in Bolivia's transition to democracy, holding off military coups and supporting a weak civilian president. Finally, Robert Gelbard (1989-91), whose style was most proconsular, was accused of adding his own clauses to policy without clearance from Washington. The crucial point about the overwhelming significance of US ambassadors is that successive Bolivian governments have had no capacity to respond to ambassadorial tactics which have ranged from threats to suspend assistance, to certification ultimatums, to the denial of visas to questionable politicians.

Fifthly, to secure specific objectives in Bolivia ambassadors have often relied upon individuals deemed trustworthy or honest. The paradox is that US Cold War policy-makers worked closely with individuals who would later become the targets of the logic of the war on drugs. This final trait became very obvious in Bolivia in the late 1970s and early 1980s when charges of drug-trafficking were brought against members of the armed forces who had been close allies of the USA. In this sense, one of the paradoxes of the drug war is that some Cold War champions have been brought to justice for involvement in drug-trafficking activities that were tolerated in the past. As Luis Arce Gómez, the infamous former minister of interior who is currently serving a 30-year sentence in a Memphis Federal Penitentiary noted, the USA betrayed him and the rest of his military comrades who had fought to keep communists out of Bolivia.[5]

The sixth trait concerns the asymmetries in USA-Bolivia relations and this does not require much analysis. It is important to note, however, that the weakness of the Bolivian state and its inherent characteristics set the direction of relations. Several issues must be noted:

a)   Bolivia's foreign ministry is trapped by the clientelistic logic of Bolivian politics and has no capacity to articulate any coherent set of US policy options, especially in the context of the Drug War. As a result, Bolivian policy-makers have little autonomy in foreign policy decision-making. Foreign policy-making in Bolivia is limited by parameters imposed by an international environment which includes the USA and international financial institutions.

b)   By the same token, other ministries, have no capacity to design effective policies. They are simply forced to respond to US policy initiatives and/or impositions.

c)   The USA has multiple points of access into the bureaucratic apparatus. Often US representatives ignore diplomatic protocol and bypass the foreign ministry to deal directly with whatever ministry may be relevant for a specific policy goal. This works out well for the USA but says very little about Bolivia's capacity to respond to foreign initiatives.

d)   Finally, the extreme vulnerability and lack of capacity of Bolivia's state institutions often results in the carrying out of activities without the knowledge of any government authority. At times, some activities might even be carried out with the complicity of a Bolivian bureaucracy which believes it will further its own interests by going along with US policy interests.

The seventh characteristic is Bolivia's temporary and periodic importance to US policy objectives, which twice resulted in the country commanding the lion's share of economic and military resources (late 1950s to early 1960s and 1988 through 1991). This has exacerbated the extreme degree of dependence on the USA. Few in Bolivia understand, however, that US interests change even in the context of long-term strategies such as the drug war. A recurring issue has been that as US policy interests shift so do the flows of US aid. In the context of the drug war it is not uncommon to hear the DEA chief lament the shifting of resources to Colombia or elsewhere in the world. This fact has become even more pronounced in the context of severe cutbacks in US foreign assistance.

In the context of the war on drugs, it is important to note that while successive Bolivian governments faced extensive US and other international pressures, they also faced intense domestic demands from myriad social forces and actors affected not only by counternarcotics policies but also by a troubled transition to democratic governance in the context of the country's gravest economic crisis in history. This is the eighth feature of the bilateral relation. Bolivia's elected civilian governments of the 1980s and early 1990s not only were trapped by external demands for greater efficiency in fighting drug lords and reducing the size of coca crops, but also faced intense domestic pressures. Organised labour, political institutions, such as parties and legislatures, peasant coca growers' unions, and regional organisations, which faced severe economic hardship stemming from both reduced profits from the drug industry and harsh austerity measures imposed by democratic governments, rallied against government programmes.

Successive Bolivian governments were able only to postpone or defuse conflictive situations with particular social groups. Bolivian governments responded first to US and other international pressures and bypassed, repressed or simply ignored domestic groups. Domestic actors and forces were often neglected even on issues which directly affected them, as the battle for the so-called militarisation of the drug war and forced coca eradication illustrates. Once policies were in place, the Bolivian government faced the task of negotiating separate deals with each social group. Agreements reached with these groups, in turn, were respected only to the extent that they did not conflict with external demands.

A final trait that colours US-Bolivian relations involves the perceptions of the coca-cocaine problem and of each other. For US actors drug trafficking is a major security threat not only to Bolivian democracy, but also to the United States and the rest of hemisphere – some even argue that it is a graver threat than the Soviet Union during the Cold War. Drug trafficking is seen as a borderless problem which cannot be viewed under previous notions of national sovereignty. For US policy-makers, the actions of a coca grower or cocaine manufacturer in Bolivia have a direct impact on the international environment and on US national security.

Historically, Bolivians have not viewed cocaine traffickers as a national security threat. Most defined the problem as either a law enforcement or a public health issue. In either case, Bolivians believe that the industry is driven by US demand for cocaine and that Washington is not doing enough to attack the consumption problem which drives the industry. Moreover, Bolivians reject the argument that national sovereignty notions are no longer valid. While the Bolivian government has made a pitch for multilateralising the drug war to lift the burden from Bolivia, in general a sense exists that US activities in the country have undermined national sovereignty and dignity.

The most serious problem in defining a common counternarcotics strategy, however, is the perception each government has of the other. Each views the other with suspicion and distrust. US policy-makers in Bolivia perceive Bolivian officials as corrupt and lacking the correct set of values to combat drugs. Bolivians, in turn, view US embassy officials as arrogant, condescending and as generally disrespectful of the country's national sovereignty.[6] These perceptions gave rise to growing anti-Americanism in Bolivia and to increasing cynicism on the part of the US mission.

This chapter traces the evolution of US-Bolivian relations from the post-World War II period to the post-Cold War era. In the following section an attempt is made to understand the logic of US Cold War policy and the structural legacy it left behind. Then the chapter analyses Bolivia-US relations between 1982 and 1998 – a period when Bolivia was forced to confront the multiple challenges of democratisation, economic reform and the proliferation of narcotics trafficking. The underlying theme in this section is that the war on drugs in Bolivia has relied extensively on strategies developed during the Cold War. As a result, the drug war, like the Cold War, is likely to become a decades-long, costly affair.

Drugs and US Cold War Policy

Bolivia has occasionally occupied a prominent position in the hierarchy of US foreign policy interests in Latin America. During those times Bolivia commanded a comparatively high level of US resources. The Bolivian Revolution of 1952, for example, drew Washington's interest owing to the perception that the Nationalist Revolutionary Movement (MNR) was Marxist. In sharp contrast to other social revolutions in the hemisphere, however, the USA did not fund any counterrevolutionary group; instead it underwrote the MNR government after 1954, redirecting and controlling the outcome.[7]

Because the 1952 Revolution reduced the size of the armed forces, in the mid-1950s US policy conditioned economic aid to Bolivia on the reconstruction of the Bolivian military. By the early 1960s Bolivia had become one of South America's largest *per capita* recipients of US military assistance. As the MNR succumbed to factional disputes, in the mid-1960s – and largely by virtue of US assistance – the military took over the reigns of power. Concerned that it could lose control over the direction of the Revolution through a shift of power towards the left, US State Department analysts crafted a policy aimed at strengthening the armed forces. A declassified State Department memorandum spelled out the basic thrust of the policy.

> That [the U.S. government] adopt and put into effect a line of action with respect to the Bolivian army for the deliberate purpose of seeing the formal military so strengthened that there would be some responsible body from which leadership might emerge should political chaos come to Bolivia through a collapse of or an unfavorable reorientation of the MNR regime. This would provide a form of secondary insurance for the achievement of our objectives in Bolivia, especially should hopes with respect to our present policies not materialize, and should the situation deteriorate against our interests.[8]

The State Department's line of action involved a five-step approach aimed primarily at strengthening the Bolivian army at the expense of civilian militia mobilised by the MNR:

1. Strengthening the US military mission.
2. Increasing programmes for the training of Bolivian officers in the USA.
3. Granting military aid for Bolivia in order to provide a rejuvenating military with the strength required for internal security.
4. Devising effective means for US civilians and military officials to

influence MNR leadership, particularly those in responsible positions of government, to rely on the military and to weaken the civilian militia

5.   Devising means to enhance the prestige of the Bolivian military such as decorating high officials where possible; scheduling visits to Bolivia of high ranking US military figures; inviting Bolivian military figures to the USA as official visitors, etc.[9]

By the end of the 1950s, US assistance had effectively built up the Bolivian military while the MNR was mired in internal conflict that would lead to its overthrow in 1964. At the same time, the US presence in Bolivia increased not only in terms of military personnel but also through a small number of agencies. The end of the decade also brought a more serious challenge, the Cuban Revolution. Almost immediately, Bolivia became the testing ground for the Alliance for Progress. At one level, the Alliance for Progress stressed building democracy and economic reform. The core of the Alliance, however, was an anticommunist counterinsurgency strategy. The overall net impact of the Alliance for Progress in Bolivia was the tripling of the US bureaucratic presence in Bolivia resulting from the increasing sophistication of Cold War efforts.

A key component of US policy to Bolivia during the Alliance for Progress years came under the rubric of *civic action*. Officers such as General René Barrientos Ortuño, who would go on to become president of Bolivia, were important participants in civic action programmes, which involved the armed forces in community projects. As some have noted, civic action programmes enabled the military to develop a significant base of support from the very same *campesinos* mobilised by the 1952 Revolution.[10] This base of support played an important role in the *coup* headed by General Barrientos that overthrew the MNR in November 1964. For the next eighteen years, with the exception of the Alfredo Ovando Candia and Juan José Torres period (1969-1971), the armed forces were to run the country with the overt support of the United States.

US involvement in Bolivia peaked in the mid-1960s with the arrival of the small guerrilla force headed by Ernesto 'Che' Guevara and the efforts to capture the Argentine Cuban revolutionary. Trained by the United States, Bolivian soldiers gradually hunted down the small band of revolutionaries. The multiple US agencies in the counterinsurgency effort included CIA-trained Cuban exiles and military advisers who played a significant role in the campaign to capture Guevara. The failed Guevara experiment proved to the USA that Bolivia was a strategic target for the spread of communism in South America. US intelligence analysts saw Bolivia's geographic location as vital to US strategic interests in the hemisphere. As a result, by the mid-1960s, the USA had developed an important multi-agency presence in Bolivia.[11]

Obscured by the Cold War, drug trafficking was largely unimportant in the overall scheme of US policy towards Bolivia. Thus, there was no serious US effort in the 1950s or 1960s to target known drug-traffickers and corrupt government officials with well-known linkages to the industry. A brief overview of Bolivian trafficking reveals that it had been present for a number of decades and had been an important source of wealth. US policy, however, paid little attention to this phenomenon in the early years. Important linkages between government officials and international smuggling organisations can be traced to the 1950s.[12]

According to one account:

> By about 1955 as communication and air transportation to Bolivia improved, organized Cuban narcotics traffickers had, in concert with elements in La Paz and Cochabamba, brought on line a significant coca paste conversion capability and an embryo illicit cocaine manufacturing capability. By the late 1950s, Bolivia and more specifically La Paz and Cochabamba had become the major source for coca paste for the clandestine manufacture of cocaine in Cuba. This traffick with Cuba gradually ended between 1959 and 1960 when the Cuban narcotic traffickers in Havana and Santiago fled to the United States, Mexico and Colombia following the Castro takeover.[13]

The Cuban Revolution produced an important shift in trafficking routes from Bolivia. In the early 1960s, Chile became one of the most important transit zones for Bolivian cocaine. Cuban traffickers picked up right where they had left off, establishing their new headquarters in Chile and Colombia.[14] Interviewees in Miami claim the Allende period in Chile reduced the trafficking of Bolivian cocaine owing largely to the fact that anti-communist Cubans had a difficult time operating under a Socialist government. They also claim that trafficking came to a complete standstill following General Augusto Pinochet's coup in 1973.[15]

While drug-related corruption appears to have had little visible impact on US policy, by the late 1960s and early 1970s traffickers began to influence the course of Bolivian politics.[16] Domestic political battles made it increasingly necessary for actors to tap into the revenues provided by the illicit drug industry. The problem was exacerbated as military governments either turned a blind eye to emerging trafficking organisations or actively sought their support to take and/or retain power. While the empirical data is scant, anecdotal evidence gathered through interviews with key actors suggests that US officials in Bolivia made little effort to target anticommunist officials who engaged in illicit drug smuggling activities. In short, going after corrupt drug-tainted officials undermined the ultimate objective of combating communists.

Nearly all stories about drugs tend to prove the adage that reality is stranger than fiction. Consider the plausible story about an alleged relationship between drug trafficking and Cuban exiles and Bay of Pigs veterans. After playing a role in Che Guevara's capture, a few allegedly became engaged in cocaine smuggling activities to fund Miami-based anti-Castro activities with the full knowledge of US intelligence agencies.[17]

In the early 1970s, cocaine trafficking shifted to Santa Cruz and was largely the domain of a few prominent families from Santa Cruz who pioneered contacts with the emerging Colombian cartels, their Cuban mentors, and also developed direct trafficking links into the United States. In other words, Bolivia's relatively small cocaine trafficking networks developed in the early 1970s, long before the boom years of the Colombian cocaine cartels. According to some accounts, these families were among the many private sector financiers of the coup that brought General Hugo Banzer Suárez to power on 21 August 1971.

The military-organised crime connection matured in the 1970s during the Banzer period (1971-78) and was apparently of some concern to Washington. Reports of increasing cocaine trafficking activities prompted the Nixon administration in 1973 to open a Drug Enforcement Administration (DEA) office in the US embassy in La Paz staffed by two agents. The presence of the newly founded DEA in Bolivia responded to Richard Nixon's own domestic agenda to demonstrate that he was indeed carrying out the war on drugs he had declared in 1972.

But the presence of the DEA in Bolivia did little to deter the politically connected drug organisations. Infatuated with Banzer's implementation of a national security doctrine to purge leftists, for most of the 1970s US officials looked the other way when charges surfaced that prominent members of the government were linked to the cocaine industry.[18] Moreover, US assistance was unaffected. Between 1972 and 1974 US assistance totalled nearly $150 million, which was exceptionally high considering the period and Bolivia's small population. The USA provided grant-in-aid military equipment to Bolivia of about $3 million annually to finance the maintenance of internal security. A GAO audit endorsed the nature of US assistance on broader geopolitical grounds:

> Developments within Bolivia, due to its central location in South America, have a great impact on the Latin American community. Political stability has been the overall US objective in Bolivia and since the August 1971 revolution this stability has increased.

The military government did pursue a counternarcotics strategy which satisfied US examiners. In 1974, it established the first National Directorate for the Control of Dangerous Substances (DNCSP). Housed in the Ministry of Interior, the DNCSP centralised all counternarcotics efforts ranging from controlling the cultivation of coca leaf to drug abuse prevention programmes. Between 1972 and 1974 Bolivia received $200,000 in US assistance as part of a USAID Public Safety Program aimed at teaching police organisations methods to control drug trafficking.

A GAO report concluded that the government had:

> Strengthen[ed] its [counternarcotics] organization structure and increased measures to control the trafficking of narcotics. It has issued a new drug law providing stiff penalties for drug offenders. These efforts, while significant, are inadequate to control the manufacture of cocaine from coca. Improved Bolivian financial support and coordinated efforts between the Bolivian government and its agencies are needed.

In 1975, based on the premise that coca farmers would substitute legal crops for coca if these were properly identified and funded, the State Department funded a pilot programme to identify viable crops. In 1977, the Bolivian government established an agency called Proyecto de Desarrollo (PRODES) Chapare-Yungas that, in conjunction with the University of Florida at Gainesville, established a number of experimental nurseries for the production of plant seedlings to be distributed to farmers.

During a visit by Secretary of State Henry Kissinger in September 1976, the Banzer government agreed to expand investigations into alternative crops in exchange for economic assistance and Bolivia's ratification of the Single Convention on Narcotic Drugs of 1961, a key event from the perspective of future efforts to eradicate coca. In signing the convention, the Bolivian government committed itself to the eradication of all coca crops, except for those used by the pharmaceutical industry, by the year 1990.

The late 1970s, however, did not witness a reduction in the production of coca. Instead between 1976 and 1981 farmers in the Chapare and elsewhere abandoned traditional food crops to grow coca as the production of coca increased from 15,600 hectares to 55,000. An inverse relationship appeared to exist between crop substitution programmes and the proliferation of coca cultivation.

The focus on crop substitution dominated Banzer's counternarcotics efforts in the 1970s. Interdiction efforts clearly took a back seat. In 1976, for example, the DEA still had only two agents in La Paz to assist the Bolivian government in its narcotics control enforcement measures. Based mainly in La Paz, the two agents were no match for the cocaine industry, which had multiple direct lines to the Bolivian government and to the elite of the eastern city of Santa Cruz de la Sierra.

A retrospective examination of US counternarcotics efforts in Bolivia in the 1970s demonstrates an important pattern. First, US ambassadors in the 1970s showed some concern over drugs, but not sufficient to warrant alarm. Then, as now, ambassadors commanded much presence and attention in La Paz. Yet, at least publicly, they steered away from the drug issue. Second, the logic of the drug war during the Cold War was based on the premise that the supply of coca had to be targeted through a combination of interdiction and crop substitution efforts. In other words, the conceptual and practical basis of contemporary drug policy was developed during this period. Third, US policy recognised that Bolivia was a producer of cocaine hydrochloride and that native drug-trafficking organisations with international connections existed. Significantly, the Colombian connection was rarely made. Fourth, US policy-makers turned a blind eye to accusations that high ranking Banzer government officials were involved in the illicit trade. As a result, the military-drug trafficking relationship developed as corrupt officials assumed that the USA would always look the other way as long as anti-communism was the ultimate objective. Finally, turf feuds between US agencies developed as more became involved in Bolivia. As will be seen, these would result in a rather tragic outcome with the advent of the García Meza government in 1980.

President Carter's administration (1977-81) was the first to establish a narcotics focused unit within the State Department. Under the leadership of

Mathea Falco, the Bureau of International Narcotics Matters initiated a more direct serious counternarcotics effort in Bolivia. Between 1976 and 1980 the Bureau provided $9.5 million in assistance to Bolivia for interdiction and crop substitution activities, a high figure even by contemporary standards.

Under Carter, Washington became concerned with human rights violations by the military government. These pressures were partially responsible for the call to elections in late 1977 by the Banzer government. Insisting on elections and respect for human rights, the Carter administration played an important role at least in helping set in motion the process of democratisation that eventually led to civilian rule in 1982. Allegations of involvement of several military officers and numerous civilians linked to the various uniformed rulers between 1978 and 1980, however, were secondary to the concern with human rights violations. Moreover, the multiple agencies present in Bolivia during this period appeared disconcerted by the change of emphasis directed primarily by the Department of State and the Department of Justice. The CIA and the military group, which had worked closely with Banzer, had a difficult time turning on the individuals with whom they had both trained and worked.

The narco-military link did not become public until the brief democratic interlude in 1979-80. These connections were not revealed, however, as a result of accusations or revelations from the US embassy. In the early months of 1980, paramilitary squads linked to the armed forces kidnapped Luis Espinal, a Catholic priest, who as director of the weekly *Aquí* had threatened to reveal names of officers involved in the cocaine industry and other forms of corruption.

Pressure on the two weak civilian governments that ruled Bolivia between August 1979 and July 1980 to prosecute human rights violators by both the Carter administration and numerous political and social groups triggered the 17 July 1980 coup that brought General Luis García Meza and his infamous minister of interior, Colonel Luis Arce Gómez, to power.[19] Financed by Roberto Suárez, one of Bolivia's most significant drug barons, the coup was significant for delaying Bolivia's short-lived attempt at democratising and for becoming the first true narco-military government in Latin America.[20] In response, the Carter administration suspended all relations with Bolivia until and unless democracy was restored. With the advent of the Reagan era, however, non-diplomatic ties between the two nations continued. Official diplomatic relations were suspended between July 1980 and November 1981.[21] In the two-year period that followed the coup, the García Meza-Arce Gómez faction of the Bolivian military provided protection to traffickers linked to Colombia's Medellín cartel while persecuting, jailing and torturing competitors.

Recent accounts suggest that, despite the efforts of the State Department and the DEA, other US agencies may have been involved in the García Meza coup to prevent the leftist Unidad Democrática y Popular (UDP) coalition, which had won the June 1980 elections, from coming to power.[22] According to some of its key participants, the coup received some encouragement from members of the Department of Defense mission in Bolivia and assistance from the Argentine military.[23] Moreover, members of Senator Jesse Helms's staff allegedly also promised that US assistance would be renewed once President Reagan took office in January 1991.[24] Owing to its numerous ties to the Argentine military, to cocaine traffickers, and to Italian, Argentine and German neofascist mercenaries (including Klaus Barbie), the García Meza government became an international outcast. In the year and a half that this isolation lasted, the economy of the country began a roller coaster ride down the precipice of hyperinflation.

In August 1981, General García Meza was overthrown by a three-man junta which was primarily interested in obtaining an honourable exit from the political arena for the armed forces. Although they were also suspected of providing protection for traffickers in September 1981, one of the junta members, General Celso Torrelio, took over as president largely because he was perceived by the United States embassy as having fewer ties to the drug industry. As US pressures increased, a larger DEA mission returned to support the military's counternarcotics efforts.[25]

By 1982 the USA had re-established leverage over the Bolivian military. A congressional delegation that visited Bolivia in December 1981 concluded that while there:

> ...does not appear to be an intelligent and coherent Bolivian strategy on enforcement, [...] the Bolivians do not appear to have any problem with allowing US enforcement experts to work closely as advisors with their enforcement people?[26]

The congressional study mission's view of Bolivian coca control efforts in 1981-82 are worth noting. Responding to the military junta's resistance to forced eradication in the Chapare region, the mission made an observation that became a dogma in US congressional circles:

> It is difficult to believe that the coca growers of the Chapare could constitute much of a political force as is claimed by the military junta. These new settlers of mostly Indian stock appear on the surface to be humble and passive subsistence farmers, and were known as such before the recent coca bonanza. It is more probable that the political pressure is coming from the traffickers.

In November 1981, the USA renewed diplomatic relations with Bolivia and dispatched Edwin Corr, a State Department specialist on narcotics matters and former ambassador to Peru, to La Paz. With Corr playing an important role, the military agreed to hand over the government to the winner of the 1980 elections.[27]

The Drug War and Bolivian Democracy

The General Pattern
Following the transition to democracy in 1982, US counternarcotics policy intensified, but its conceptual basis changed little. The basic elements of

interdiction and crop substitution were still the principal pillars of a supply side strategy technically initiated in the early 1970s when President Nixon founded the Drug Enforcement Administration and declared the 'War on Drugs'. A decade later, Ronald Reagan would re-declare a war and target the Andean region in particular.

On the US side two Reagan terms (1981-9), a single term by George Bush (1989-93) and six years under President Clinton did little to change the fundamental supply side emphasis of the drug war. In the sixteen years since Reagan declared this new war on drugs, over forty US agencies have become involved in the crusade and nearly $100 billion dollars have been committed by the US Congress. The drug threat has been declared the principal threat to Latin American democracies and to US national security. Finally, the US military, through the now Miami-based Southern Command, has become one of the principal institutions fighting drugs in the Andean region. On the diplomatic side, the most important dimension of US policy has been the passage in 1986 of a certification law forcing the US president to 'certify' that Bolivia and other countries in Latin America have fulfilled their obligations under the terms of bilateral accords and, since 1988, the terms of the UN Vienna Convention. Since 1986, Bolivia was nearly decertified in 1987, given a national interest waiver in 1995, and certified with flying colours the rest of the time (see Chapter 10).

On the Bolivian side, five elected presidents (Hernán Siles Zuazo, 1982-85; Víctor Paz Estenssoro, 1985-89; Jaime Paz Zamora, 1989-93; Gonzalo Sánchez de Lozada, 1993-97; and Hugo Banzer Suárez, 1997 to present) have also been incapable of altering the essence of US policy in fundamental ways. From Siles Zuazo's weak attempts to negotiate with Roberto Suárez, Bolivia's former drug chief, to Paz Zamora's feeble 'Coca Diplomacy' strategy, to Sánchez de Lozada's *Opción Cero*, to General Banzer's ¡*Plan Dignidad!*, which claims it will eradicate the production of coca in the Chapare Valley in five years, Bolivian governments have offered no real alternatives. At the same time, Bolivia has become an increasingly 'narcotised' society: polity and economy trapped in an escalating drug war logic that has undermined the basis of its incipient democracy.

Since 1982, Bolivia has become a quasi-laboratory for US drug war strategies that were later to be implemented in the broader Andean region. As a result of relentless US pressure, Bolivia had to deal simultaneously with the challenges of democratisation, economic crises and the coca-cocaine boom. Bolivia's democratic governments have given less priority to tackling the drug issue as attempts to bring it under control could threaten the process of economic reform and undermine the political system.[28] This trade-off, however, has rarely been recognised in Washington, which sees Bolivia's efforts as meek and uncommitted to the objective of ending the flow of drugs out of the country. The reality is that on a *per capita* basis, Bolivia has spent more on fighting drugs than the United States. In the context of a democratising and very poor economy, the resources spent on fighting drugs are also resources that are not being spent on education, health, and/or responding to other multiple needs.

At the same time, the drug war has strengthened units of the police and the armed forces which have been given *carte blanche* to carry out interdictive strategies throughout Bolivia's coca growing and trafficking regions. As an Americas Watch report noted, these units have engaged in human rights violations in coca growing regions. In short, the trade-off between drugs and democracy in Bolivia is clear. Drug trafficking and related crimes do undermine democracy, but so do unchecked police and military units charged with stopping the flow.

Hernán Siles Zuazo (1982-85)

When Siles Suazo came into office in October 1982 in the midst of the worst ever political and economic crisis, the narcotics industry in Bolivia was booming. This boom coincided with the explosion of demand in the United States for cocaine, a major drought in the Andean highlands resulting from the El Niño current, and the exhaustion of a state-centred development strategy. Trapped between the pent-up demands of key groups such as organised labour and the private sector, Siles Zuazo lacked the muscle to deal effectively with the economic crisis. In Congress he faced a coalition between the two major opposition parties that constantly questioned the legitimacy of his government. As the government failed to deal with the economic crisis and as the political crisis deepened, the only healthy sector appeared to be the booming coca-cocaine economy. Despite Siles Zuazo's good intentions to carry out a counternarcotics campaign, the industry proliferated and reached enormous proportions. According to US sources, hectarage under cultivation, for example, doubled between 1982 and 1985.[29]

Siles Zuazo did respond to US demands as best he could. In 1983 he established a specialised police unit, named Unidad Móvil de Patrullaje Rural (UMOPAR), to direct counternarcotics operations. The government also agreed to eradicate 10,000 hectares of coca in return for $14.1 million in US aid. Considered high by the standards of the time, this amount did little to offset the gains made by the illicit drugs industry.

In June 1984, in a rather pathetic turn of events and much to the chagrin of US ambassador Edwin Corr, several UMOPAR officers were involved in the kidnapping of President Siles Zuazo. Although Siles was released unharmed, this incident demonstrated the fragility of the situation and the fact that the Bolivian government could do very little either to govern or to resolve the key issues of the day.

Nevertheless Siles attempted to demonstrate his government's commitment to combat the drug war. In August 1984, he ordered the army into Cochabamba's Chapare region which had become for all intents and purposes a haven for coca growing and for the manufacturing of coca paste. Almost immediately critics charged that the publicity which characterised the operation had served only to warn the drug traffickers. The sad irony was that Siles Zuazo's weak government had to confront charges that, like the corrupt military government it had replaced, it was also providing protection to drug traffickers.

Any discussion of the coca-cocaine industry during this period would be incomplete without a reference to the 'Otazo affair' which was partially responsible for the shortening of Siles Zuazo's mandate. Rafael Otazo, the president of the

National Counternarcotics Office (Consejo Nacional de Lucha contra el Narcotráfico) and one of Siles's closest friends, revealed that he had met with Roberto Suárez, one the most sought after international drug traffickers, in June 1983 under express orders from Siles Zuazo.[30] Otazo subsequently revealed that Suárez, Bolivia's alleged 'King of Cocaine', had offered the government a two billion dollar low interest loan to help the government solve the economic crisis.[31]

The Congreso Nacional ordered an immediate investigation of Otazo's allegations. Otazo and several key cabinet members were subpoenaed by the Constitution and Judicial Police commissions of both chambers. Otazo testified, in addition, that Mario Roncal and Raúl Cardona, two MNRI deputies who had served as minister of interior and head of presidential security respectively, were part of an international drug operation.[32] Already, in January 1983, Roncal had been accused by the opposition of having links to the drug trade.

Siles's reaction was to sack Otazo on 7 September 1984 and to accuse him of being mentally unstable. In an attempt to cover-up the government's role in the Suárez interview, Mario Rueda Peña, the minister of information, argued that Otazo had been sent to meet Suárez in order to find the trafficker's hiding place.[33]

The Otazo affair became the final straw for the Siles government. The opposition requested a joint session of Congress to hear the reports of the congressional commissions that had investigated the case. Before the evidence against the regime could be weighed, it was clear that the only feasible outcome would be the revocation of Siles's mandate.[34] Through constitutional succession the presidency would fall on Julio Garret, the opposition's president of the Senate. This idea came to be known as the 'Garretazo'. On 18 September, another bill was presented to the Chamber of Deputies that called for the temporary revocation of Siles mandate until the president could demonstrate his innocence in the Otazo affair.[35] The opposition had already tried and convicted the Siles regime. In the end Siles was forced to cut his period in office by one year and to leave Bolivia in the midst of a record hyperinflation.

A final point about the Siles period concerns the role of the United States, especially that of Ambassador Edwin Corr, a career foreign service officer who had developed an expertise in narcotrafficking. Corr, who had supervised the State Department's crop substitution programme in Peru, was moved to Bolivia in November 1991 to pressure the Bolivian military to relinquish power. Corr's strategy in Bolivia included four major policy goals: asserting Bolivian and US control over cocaine production and trade; reinstituting formal democracy; stabilising and reactivating the Bolivian economy; and enhancing the organisation and political activities of the private sector.[36]

Corr became one of the most active ambassadors ever assigned to Bolivia. He not only helped steer the process of transition that culminated in October 1982, but was also instrumental in preventing the overthrow of Siles. On the drugs front, Corr was largely responsible for laying the foundations of all future US counternarcotics actions in Bolivia. In many ways, Corr became a protagonist in the political drama and even his critics note his role in the preservation of Bolivia's democracy.

Corr's role during the Otazo affair is important to note. In contrast to what was to occur in subsequent periods, Corr worked with Siles and little pressure was exerted on the Bolivian government. According to Corr, if the USA had joined the chorus to end Siles's tenure, Bolivia's fragile democracy would have collapsed.[37] That was not the case, however, with the US Congress. The Siles government became the first to play host to a series of roving fact-finding congressional delegations, which called for everything including economic sanctions.[38]

Víctor Paz Estenssoro (1985-89)

The elections of 1985 brought Víctor Paz Estenssoro, arguably the most important statesman of 20th century Bolivia, back to the presidency. Paz Estenssoro's government successfully introduced the Nueva Política Económica (NPE) one of the most profound stabilisation programmes in Latin America. After sustaining the NPE for four years and ending the country's hyperinflation, Paz Estenssoro handed power over to a newly elected government headed by Jaime Paz Zamora.[39]

The Paz Estenssoro administration was responsible for the implementation of a set of counternarcotics policies which, during Operation Blast Furnace (July-November 1986), included the use of US military troops. A landmark bilateral agreement, signed in February 1987, produced even greater Bolivian reliance on US assistance and ushered in a period of significant US military presence without congressional authorisation. Simultaneously, under extensive US pressure, in 1988 the Paz Estenssoro government signed Law 1008, a more stringent version of zero tolerance ordinances in use throughout the United States. The signing of two annexes to Law 1008 (1988 and 1989) tied US assistance to progress on crop substitution and legitimised the Bolivian government's alternative development proposal.

Beginning in 1987 under the name of Operation Snow Cap, DEA officers became directly involved in drug seizures and arrests throughout Bolivia. US military personnel engaged in civic action or nation-building exercises tied to counternarcotics efforts throughout Bolivia; the Pact for Democracy allowed the government to secure congressional approval for the arrival of US troops to work on airports and other facilities. US border patrol members guarded roads into and out of the Bolivian Yungas and Chapare Valleys. Members of the US Navy Seals and Coast Guard officers trained their Bolivian counterparts in Bolivia's vast network of Amazon tributaries. Finally, Bolivia's elite rural counternarcotics police (UMOPAR) received extensive US special forces training, and the Bolivian navy and air force became engaged in support activities throughout the Beni department.[40] By any measure, this was the largest build-up of counternarcotics efforts in Bolivian history.

Between 1985 and 1989, the Paz Estenssoro government convinced two successive Republican administration of its commitment to fighting drugs. Although it faced a constant uphill battle with the US Congress, in the end even the most recalcitrant US legislators were convinced that Bolivia's octogenarian president, who had presided over a remarkable transformation of the Bolivian economy, would press ahead with US counternarcotics initiatives. In retrospect,

Paz Estenssoro ushered in policies which inevitably increased US presence in Bolivia. When Paz Estenssoro left office in 1989, the US mission to Bolivia was the second largest in Latin America.

Like Blast Furnace in 1986, Snow Cap yielded few positive long-term results. A few drug lords were captured, tons of cocaine were seized and coca crops were eradicated. Yet cocaine continued to flow out of Bolivia as the Andean country became the world's second producer of cocaine hydrochloride. Moreover, corruption eroded the integrity of all institutions charged with fighting the drug war, especially UMOPAR. The usual accusations of connections of leading politicians to the drug trade surfaced daily.[41] The policy also created inter- and intra-bureaucratic feuding as competition escalated between branches of the police and the armed forces to enter into the drug war. On the US side, similar bureaucratic 'turf' disputes involving the numerous agencies involved in Bolivia undermined all counternarcotics efforts.[42]

In 1988, the Bolivian government played an important role in Vienna. Headed by Foreign Minister Guillermo Bedregal, Bolivia joined the international community in Vienna at the United Nations Convention on Narcotics. The final document which emerged from Vienna had widespread repercussions for future US-Bolivia relations. Bolivia signed the Vienna Convention in 1990. Under the terms of this agreement, Bolivia agreed to items such as the extradition of nationals accused of narcotics trafficking.

Washington claimed positive outcomes despite the overwhelming signs of failure; for the USA the Paz Estenssoro government was, after all, a showcase of sound economic policies and democratic principles. Pushing ahead too quickly on counternarcotics matters could undermine the progress made in terms of bilateral agreements, but could also threaten the progress on economic reform. In 1989, the New Economic Policy was still considered one of the most significant structural reform programmes in Latin America. Similarly, US-Bolivia counternarcotics efforts were also seen as extremely successful.

When Paz Estenssoro left office in 1989 Bolivia had committed itself to the US drug war on US terms. Incoming government officials claimed that several promises were made to the US government in his finals days in office. Some claimed that the Paz Estenssoro government promised to engage the Bolivian army in the drug war.[43] Others claimed that the government had agreed to an extradition treaty. In any event, the newly elected government would have to deal with US demands and would have to honour all agreements signed by the Paz Estenssoro government.

Jaime Paz Zamora (1989-93)

Jaime Paz Zamora's experience in office highlighted the contradictions and dilemmas of the drug war. The Bolivian military became a full participant in the war on drugs with the establishment of a specialised army unit that joined similar Navy and Air Force units in Bolivia's vast Amazon region. The Paz Zamora period revealed the overwhelming importance of the US embassy and of 'activist' ambassadors. Robert S. Gelbard became the most significant political figure in the country, deciding not only the extent of US assistance but also inserting himself into daily domestic squabbles between political parties. Gelbard also presided over the establishment of a huge US bureaucratic enforcement complex housed in the US embassy.

The general pattern of US-Bolivian relations under Paz Zamora became evident in 1990. After vainly resisting pressures from the US State Department, Paz Zamora signed Annex III to a 1987 US-Bolivia anti-drug agreement in return for \$33.2 million in US military assistance and promises that economic aid would also be disbursed.[44] Even as Paz Zamora denied the 'militarisation' of the drug war, he ordered two regiments to initiate anti-drug operations.[45] Already a large anti-militarisation effort had been mounted by opposition political parties, labour, and *campesino* groups who feared the consequences of such a policy. Upon returning to Bolivia this was Paz Zamora's response to protesters:

> When I arrived in Bolivia after my trip to the United States and announced the victory of dignity and the negotiating capacity [of our government], I was surprised [to find] that every day militarisation is spoken about. This has obstructed the dignified way in which Bolivia has achieved these results without realising that militarisation had not been achieved and that the training and equipping of our armed forces is an unseparable part of the global strategy of alternative development. He who continues to speak about [militarisation] is either stupid or anti-Bolivian, because without a doubt it is a way of damaging the dignity of the nation and its armed forces.[46]

In July, August and November 1990 *campesino* unions carried out road blockades and strikes, announced the establishment of armed *campesino* defence committees, and called on *campesinos* in general to dodge compulsory military service. In August, after signing an agreement with *campesino* unions promising not to militarise its anti-drug efforts, the government announced that instead of ordering troops into the Chapare where confrontation with peasants was inevitable, US military aid would be used to deploy army units to monitor and prevent ecological damage caused by the processing of coca paste in the Bolivian jungles.

Throughout 1990 official Bolivian claims that the solution to the drug war required more than guns, radar and helicopters enraged many in the US State Department's Bureau of International Narcotics Matters, who believed that Bolivians had reneged on previous commitments.[47] Robert Gelbard, the outspoken US ambassador, publicly reminded the Bolivian government that economic aid would be disbursed only if the military entered the drug war. Gelbard also headed efforts to hold up the signing of trade and investment agreements as a way to pressure the Bolivian government into signing an extradition agreement.[48] Faced with a no win situation, Paz Zamora's government engaged in a bit of double speak: he complied with US requirements, but also attempted to convince Bolivians that his government was not capitulating.

The mood surrounding the formulation of anti-narcotics policy in Bolivia was intolerant of opposing or dissident voices. Egged on by the US embassy, the Bolivian government labelled any opposition to the militarisation policy as cooperation with narcotics traffickers. Leaders of the Coca Grower's Federation, for example, were accused of trafficking in cocaine or providing traffickers with protection. Members of political parties who opposed the policy suffered the same fate.

A surreal situation developed in late February 1991 when the Bolivian government named retired Colonel Faustino Rico Toro to head the National Council Against Drug Abuse and Trafficking. Rico Toro headed the infamous G-2 intelligence service under the drug-tainted government of General Luis García Meza, was widely suspected of providing protection to narcotics traffickers and was reportedly linked to Klaus Barbie, the infamous 'Butcher of Lyon' who served as adviser to the Bolivian military. When the USA announced its intention to cut off $100 million dollars in economic and military assistance, Rico Toro resigned. Under fire from the United States, Guillermo Capobianco, the minister of interior, and Colonel Felipe Carvajal, the chief of police, were also forced to step down before US aid was restored.

The US charge that Capobianco, Rico Toro and Carvajal were involved in a conspiracy to secure the appointment of corrupt persons, who would protect traffickers, to high government positions is also pure speculation. Capobianco was later charged but never convicted. Rico Toro was extradited to the USA and served three years in a Florida jail. Carvajal was never charged. The paradox of this situation is that Capobianco was involved in the December 1989 expulsion of former minister of interior Colonel Luis Arce Gómez to the United States where he was tried and convicted in January 1991.[49]

In late March 1991 the Paz Zamora government confirmed what had been public knowledge in the United States for over ten months, but which had been kept from most Bolivians. According to the government two light infantry battalions would be ordered into the Chapare to carry out 'logistical and operative support functions'. These battalions would previously undergo two 10-week training sessions under the guidance of 112 US advisers.[50] After overcoming stiff opposition from the opposition in Congress the ruling coalition, dubbed the Acuerdo Patriótico, approved the presence of US advisers. A few hours after the debate concluded in Congress a Galaxy plane loaded with 90 tons of ammunition landed at La Paz airport. The first contingent of US military advisers was scheduled to arrive in Bolivia on 22 April.[51]

At about the same time (the last days of March 1991) *campesino* leaders from Bolivia and Peru met for four days at a so-called Encuentro Andino de Productores de Coca to plan a joint strategy to counter the militarisation of counternarcotics efforts in both countries. As the meeting ended, it became increasingly clear that Bolivian peasant leaders, in particular, were willing and able to mobilise in opposition to the government's planned militarisation campaign. *Campesino* leaders repeatedly warned that militarisation would lead to 'generalised violence throughout the coca growing regions'.[52]

Paz Zamora responded to this challenge and outlined a six-year timetable for the 'substitution of the coca economy'. Between 1990 and 1995 this programme claimed it would eradicate 43,735 hectares of excess coca production. The Bolivian government was also quick to point to success in meeting crop eradication targets mandated by bilateral agreements with the United States.[53] In the same period the economy would lose $385.9 million in production, 175,300 jobs, and $195.6 million in revenue. Bolivian government officials claimed that $1.8 billion in the same period would be required to carry out its coca for development project.[54] Securing financing for these programmes proved elusive, especially given the US focus on militarised solutions.

One of obstacles to the alternative development strategy is that payments to peasants in exchange for voluntarily eradicating coca crops have been very slow. As coca prices recover, the attractiveness of substitution is not great to peasants who cannot make a living from other crops. Additionally, coca substitutes, such as macadamia nuts, take years to generate profitable returns. Other crops have high start-up costs; moreover, *campesinos* are not guaranteed a market for new products. Without a great infusion of foreign investment or aid and a coherent and long-term rural development component, Paz Zamora's Coca for Development thesis was doomed to failure. In the Bush administration, few embraced this approach where it was perceived only as a delaying tactic. The US Congress, in turn, continuously regretted Bolivia's decision to ban the use of herbicides for the eradication of coca plantations and found little political use for alternative development programmes. Consequently, Bolivia's only choice during Paz Zamora's rule may have been to accept military assistance and push ahead with ordering the army into the drug fray.

The reality under Paz Zamora was that the Bolivian government had painted itself into a corner. The Rico Toro incident and the government's bumbling attempts to resist US pressures to engage the military proved very costly. The permission granted to US military advisers and the entry of the military into the Chapare aggravated tensions in coca growing regions and showed the futility of any attempts to put forward a Bolivian strategy. Above all, the Paz Zamora period showed the absolute lack of trust between the USA and Bolivia that resulted in mutually exclusive perceptions.[55] US mistrust was partially justified when it became obvious that major figures in the government were also corrupt. In 1994, the USA finally admitted that it had evidence as early as 1988 that Paz Zamora and others in his political party, the Movimiento de Izquierda Revolucionaria (MIR), had received funds to support the party's 1989 campaign from Isaac 'Oso' Chavarría, a major figure in the drug industry. Paz Zamora was also accused of providing cover for Chavarría during his tenure as president of Bolivia. Moreover, in 1997 the USA was further embarrassed when its 'golden boy', Gonzalo Torrico, was accused of involvement in the trafficking business.[56] Paz Zamora, Torrico and the five others had their US visas withdrawn.

Gonzalo Sánchez de Lozada (1993-97)
Sánchez de Lozada devoted little time to any conceptualisation of Bolivia's coca-cocaine issue.[57] He spent his four years in office carrying out one of the most

profound institutional transformations in the country's history. Given the interesting and provocative innovations carried out by this government, it is a shame that more time was not given to thinking through this issue in a more dedicated manner. Instead, the government was trapped by the legacy and the strength of the policies implemented since at least 1985. Sánchez repeated the dogma of alternative development, interdiction and added a meek notion of prevention and social reinsertion. The thrust of the policy, however, remained unchanged.[58]

Sánchez de Lozada's only attempt radically to alter the narcotics issue came under the rubric of Opción Cero (Option Zero), a strategy developed with the assistance of Harvard University's Jeffrey Sachs. The proposal's basic argument was that the solution to the drug problem is economic and not military. Given the fragility of the Bolivian economy and society, Sachs argued, it was unwise to run the risk of provoking guerrilla groups and terrorism into action by forcefully eradicating coca fields. Presented in 1993, the strategy was simple. There was a need to implement a short-term shock therapy in place of a long-term strategy. Option Zero proposed that all land used for the production of coca should revert to the state for the establishment of either a huge national park or a labour intensive industrial zone. Peasants would receive compensation for their land and would be encouraged through some funding to colonise other production regions of Bolivia where coca is not cultivated. The entire programme would cost around one billion dollars, and it also called on the United States to increase Bolivia's export quotas for sugar, cotton, and soya – the industries that would theoretically absorb peasant labour.[59]

Option Zero called for a long and complicated process to negotiate not only with the United States and multilateral agencies, but also with the very domestic groups affected by this proposal. In the end, Option Zero generated zero support internally and externally. Sánchez de Lozada was left with no option other than to implement the same policy as his predecessor.

Sánchez de Lozada presided over the escalation of military involvement in the drug war owing primarily to US threats to decertify Bolivia. In March 1995, the USA granted Bolivia a national interest waiver certification and shortly thereafter sent a secret ultimatum to Sánchez de Lozada threatening to decertify the country by 30 June if coca eradication targets were not met. Faced with this inevitable fate, the Bolivian government crossed an important threshold. It not only initiated the forceful eradication of coca fields in the Chapare, but the government also admitted for the first time that the coca grown in the Chapare was exclusively for use by the cocaine industry.[60]

Whether the threat of decertification and the ultimatum were responsible, the fact is that the Sánchez de Lozada government achieved things that others had been unable to do. One of the most important was the signing of an extradition treaty with the United States in 1995. Extradition had been one of the most significant US demands since the escalation of the war on drugs in the mid-1980s. The Paz Zamora government negotiated a treaty, but arguing that it feared the 'Colombianisation' of Bolivia, it refused to submit it to the Bolivian Senate for consideration. Sánchez de Lozada's team negotiated a new treaty and achieved Senate approval. The US Senate approved it shortly thereafter.[61] With this treaty the path was paved for continued US certification of Bolivian efforts. The USA rewarded Bolivia in 1997 with an important increase in assistance. At the same time, however, the USA began to shift resources from Bolivia to Colombia.

Hugo Banzer Suárez (1997-present)

General Banzer's return to power as a Democrat involved a number of significant and recurring themes in US-Bolivia relations. First, often suspected of having had ties with the drug industry, especially during the 1970s, Banzer had never publicly been accused by the United States. On the contrary, US agencies have sometimes gone out of their way to state that Banzer has always been a drug war ally. Be that as it may, when Banzer allied his party Acción Democrática Nacionalista with Jaime Paz Zamora and the MIR for the 1997 elections, the US embassy issued a stern warning that it would not look kindly on the naming of visa-less MIR members to high-ranking positions. Moreover, in July, in a statement before the US Congress, Acting Assistant Secretary of State Jane Becker warned that Bolivia faced almost certain decertification in March 1998 if it did not meet its eradication targets. At that point it appeared unlikely that Bolivia would meet the target.[62]

The Banzer government has unveiled an ambitious plan (*¡Por la Dignidad!*) that calls for the complete and total eradication of 38,000 hectares of coca, to provide an alternative to the 35,000 families dependent on the coca-cocaine cycle, to carry out a strong interdiction effort, and to implement an aggressive prevention and rehabilitation strategy within a five-year period.

The plan's introductory paragraph states:

> The narco trafficking phenomenon in Bolivia has reached a crucial point: either it is destroyed immediately and definitively or Bolivian society must forever live with it side by side and face all the internal and external consequences that situation implies.[63]

The plan's total cost in five years will be $952 million: $108 million for eradication; $700 million for alternative development; $129 million for interdiction; and, $15 million for prevention and rehabilitation. The Bolivian government has pledged to finance at least 15 per cent of the cost. To finance the rest, the government has embarked on an international strategy to obtain support from the USA and multilateral agencies.[64]

Facing the prospect of decertification, the Banzer government set off on a race against time to meet the eradication targets. In mid-December 1997, the government announced that owing to its intensive and costly involuntary eradication programme it had surpassed the 7,000 hectare goal. It also announced that narcotics related arrests had increased considerably. In return, Bolivia did not face the anxiety of other Andean nations as the certification date drew near (see Chapter 10).

Bolivia's plan *¡Por la Dignidad!* has been well received internationally. The

United Nations Drug Control Programme in particular has lavished praise on it. And the annual certification statement also praises the strategy. In fact, the overall statement praises Bolivia for successes in alternative development, in reducing the production and distribution of cocaine, in asset seizures, in extradition, and the like.[65]

Given Bolivia's apparent commitment to comply with US and international agreements on narcotics, the US decision to cut counternarcotics assistance to Bolivia by nearly 70 per cent came as a tremendous surprise. In part, the reduction represents the lack of understanding by Bolivian government officials about the budget process, executive legislative relations, and bureaucratic politics in the United States. In 1997, the US Congress ordered the Office of International Narcotics and Law Enforcement Matters (INL) to provide the means for Colombia to purchase Black Hawk and Hughey Helicopters. At the same time the US Congress approved a $17 million increase in INL's budget. To complicate matters, former Assistant Secretary of State and also former ambassador to Bolivia, Robert S. Gelbard, who is currently serving as President Clinton's Special Envoy to the Balkans, essentially raided the INL budget taking $25 million to provide assistance to the police in Bosnia. Gelbard's request for the same amount from Congress had apparently been denied.

The following exchange is illustrative of how other foreign policy priorities can affect US- Bolivia drug policy. In a letter dated 26 February to General Barry McCaffrey, Congressman Mark Souder (R-Indiana), the author of the Colombia BlackHawk Amendment, states:

> I am somewhat perplexed by comments in the press that the Colombian BlackHawk amendment, which I authored, is decimating the International Narcotics Control Program for Bolivia.
>
> The genesis of the amendment, frankly, was the House Report language on the Foreign Operations bill which would have permitted a shift of $25 million in funds from the INL account to police training in Bosnia. The language was deleted, but it is an open secret that a high executive at the State Department lobbied for this raid on the INL account. I hope that you agree with me that the influx of illegal narcotics is a higher national security priority than the conflict in the former Yugoslavia. Moreover, the House approved $17 million more for the INL account that the Senate wanted to spend, and the overall account is up more than 100% since 1994. If the House had ceded to the Senate number and retained the Bosnia language, the account would have had a $42 million shortfall.

On 3 March, in a press release Representative Ben A. Gilman, Chair of the House International Relations Committee stated:

> The Administration is not cutting anti-narcotics funds to Bolivia as a result of any Congressional pressure. We support full funding for all

countries which are working with us and doing their share to combat the scourge of narcotics. The facts of the situation are these:

The Administration is 'robbing Peter to pay Paul' trying to take fund from Bolivia to pay for police training in Bosnia and making Congress the scapegoat. The same Administration that dropped the ball in Colombia in the first place is now trying to suspend a carefully targeted appropriation earmark as an excuse for chopping support for Bolivia, a Latin American ally in our war on drugs.[66]

Finally, it is important to make a comment about the feasibility of the Bolivian strategy. This is not the first time, and is unlikely to be the last, that Bolivia has pledged to end the production of illicit coca within a given time frame. This is, however, the first time that such an objective has become part of a Bolivian strategy. Even if the $1 billion request were to materialise, it is highly unlikely that the goals will be met. US funding cuts provide a convenient excuse for the current government for not meeting its own goals. At the same time, however, it provides a new unrealistic benchmark that the USA may use to gauge all future counternarcotics progress.

Conclusions

The basic dilemma of the drug war in Bolivia is not whether it is being won or lost. Instead, it has to do with its impact on the still incipient process of democratisation. On the one hand, it is certainly true that drug trafficking and related crimes have affected and further weakened Bolivia's institutions. But it is also true that the logic of the war has resulted in the strengthening of police and military institutions, the violation of human rights in certain areas, and other unconstitutional behaviour. In short, the dilemma is that the greatest threat to democracy in Bolivia may not necessarily be the 'drug threat' as US and Bolivian government agencies have proclaimed, but the very policies used to combat the problem.

Despite the end of the Cold War, the drug war is still dominated by a Cold War strategy and this factor has much to do with a Vietnam-like mentality. Driven by a body-count logic, success has been difficult to gauge, much less define. While every year more people are arrested and more drugs confiscated, it is also evident that more coca is cultivated, more cocaine is refined – and more traffickers appear. Since drug 'body-counts' do not work, policy-makers have turned to ubiquitous declarations about political will and calls for more resources essentially to do more of the same.

The budget for the drug war has increased from less than $1 billion in 1982 to $16.5 billion in 1998. Less than two per cent of that amount has been spent in Latin America. Clearly, much less was spent on Bolivia. As former president Sánchez de Lozada noted, as a percentage of its budget, Bolivia spends more fighting drugs than the United States. The USA has spent over a billion dollars in

Bolivia since 1984 and the country has commanded the lion's share of US resources destined for the Andes.

The point is that US political will has been measured by the dedication of monetary resources and the proliferation of drug fighting institutions. On the other hand, US policy has been tied to questionable measures of Bolivian political will. In my view, political will is not the central issue. The most significant factor has to do with Bolivia's lack of capacity to implement any type of counternarcotics policy. Incapacity refers to three factors. First, in the last fifteen years, Bolivian governments have faced serious domestic political conditions with regard to the coca question. The mobilisation and unionisation of coca growers is just one of the major problems. Corruption within political parties, including linkages by prominent politicians to the drug industry, is another. Second, Bolivia's fragile institutions, especially its administration of justice, has made fighting drugs a futile exercise. Police, courts and prisons have been essentially narcotised and no amount of will appears enough to reverse this trend. Finally, the absence of resources has been a fundamental issue. While Bolivia has enjoyed a relatively high level of US assistance, it has not been enough to make a significant difference. Moreover, the fact that resources are disproportionately assigned to the interdiction efforts has meant that less punitive, more long-term strategies, such as alternative development, are underfunded. And when alternative development programmes show few results, these suffer cutbacks.

The incremental nature of the policy has also led to a proliferation of bureaucracies that derive their income from annual drug budgets. If during the military period, the USA had only a few DEA agents, by the early 1990s at least 12 agencies, from the DEA to the US Coast Guard were performing some type of drug duty in Bolivia. At the same time, Bolivian agencies had also become trapped by the drug war logic. For Raúl Barrios, the perverse nature of the relationship with the drug budget meant that multiple Bolivian and US agencies had become 'addicted' to the drug war.

The driving factors of US policy in Bolivia have been fundamentally domestic and local. As the drug problem spread throughout the United States and as Colombian cartels fought turf battles in cities like Miami, the supply side explanation of the problem prevailed. Increasingly, members of Congress called for greater interdictive action abroad. The local basis of drug policy is a factor often overlooked. Members of Congress have had to demonstrate to their constituencies that effective strategies against drugs have been designed. In this sense, long-term, less punitive strategies are politically unfeasible. Thus, members of Congress have often demanded greater interdiction programmes and sometimes more.

As occurred during Vietnam and elsewhere throughout the Cold War period, Bolivia and the rest of the Andean region played host to congressional missions sent to evaluate the progress of the war on drugs. In the early and mid-1980s, for example, Senator Paula Hawkins and Representative Larry Smith either visited Bolivia or made grandiloquent statements on the floor of the House about the need for more punitive policies. Smith even argued for a full-scale US invasion of

Bolivia to put an end to the flow of cocaine. A recent debate following the visit of a ten-member delegation to Bolivia, Colombia, Panama, Peru and Mexico is illustrative. Representative Dan Burton, who did not make the trip, argued:

> So I said to my colleagues this morning and I say to the administration and anybody else, Mr. Speaker, that might be paying attention, that if there is a war on drugs, I missed it. And if we do not really have a war on drugs, let us declare a war on drugs. We could put an aircraft carrier off the coast of Peru, load it up with a herbicide called tebucyron, or spike, and at five o'clock in the morning take off and fly up and down the Upper (sic) Yuagua Valley and drop these little pellets that are environmentally safe. We could do the same thing in Bolivia. We would have to fly a little bit further. But we could knock out 90 per cent of the world's coca production in a week. I hope everybody is listening. In one week we could knock out 90 per cent of the world's coca production.[67]

When a State Department official noted that this tactic would violate Bolivian and Peruvian sovereignty, Burton rebutted: 'What are they going to do, shoot down our planes? Of course they would not do that.'[68]

US counternarcotics policy in Bolivia is likely to continue along the same path, with a few occasional nuances. With current Bolivian pledges sounding very much like those in Washington, it is worth pondering over Jeffrey Sachs's warning in articulating the ill-fated Option Zero. While Bolivia may not have guerrillas and terrorism, it has a highly organised coca growers' sector that has rejected Bolivia's current plan *¡Por la Dignidad!*. Escalating the punitive side of the drug war in Bolivia could unravel the delicate balance between growers and Bolivian democracy.

Notes

1. See Blasier (1978).
2. These periods were: the late 1930s when Bolivian nationalised the Standard Oil Company; the early 1940s when Bolivia was forced to sell tin to the allies at below market prices; the Bolivian Revolution of 1952; the 1967 Che Guevara-led guerrilla in Nancahuazú; the Ovando-Torres interlude between 1969 and 1971 which included the nationalisation of Gulf Oil; and the current drug war period, which for our purposes, began with the 17 July 1980 coup by General Luis García Meza. For an analysis of those periods see: Blasier (1978); Malloy (1970); Dunkerley (1984); Klein (1982); Barrios Morón (1989); and Gamarra (1994).
3. See Malamud Goti (1991).
4. See *ibid.* and Office of Inspector General (1991) for an in-depth discussion of the problems of coordination between US anti-drug agencies.

5. Interview (February 1991) with former Colonel Luis Arce Gómez in the Federal Metropolitan Correctional Center in Miami where he was being held following his expulsion from Bolivia in December 1989 and his December 1990 trial. Arce Gómez was sentenced to a 30 year prison term.

6. For a similar conclusion about US policy in Latin America see Schoultz (1998).

7. See: Blasier (1978); Dunkerley (1984); and Malloy (1970) for discussions of US policy and the Bolivian Revolution.

8. Memorandum from the Officer in Charge of West Coast Affairs (Ernest Siracusa) to the Director of the Office of South American Affairs, 2 February 1956. *Foreign Relations of the United States 1955-1957*. Volume VII (Washington, D.C.: US Government Printing Office, 1987).

9. *Ibid.*

10. See Malloy (1970). Malloy notes that involving the Bolivian military in nation-building efforts, such as civic action, politicised the armed forces and made them compete with civilian authorities for scarce public funds.

11. Between 1969 and 1971, during the Ovando and Torres interlude, US presence declined considerably as the two military governments adopted anti-US nationalistic policies. It is widely recognised, however, that US intelligence agencies played an important role in bringing down the Torres government.

12. Interviews with retired members of the Bolivian police who served during the MNR period, La Paz, July 1991.

13. House of Representatives, Select Committee on Narcotics Abuse and Control, International Narcotics Control Study Missions to Latin America and Jamaica (6-21 August 1983), Hawaii, Hong Kong, Thailand, Burma, Pakistan, Turkey, and Italy (4-22 January 1984).

14. Anecdotal evidence gathered from numerous interviews with members of political parties and the Bolivian armed forces suggests that cocaine trafficking was directed by Luis Gayán, a Chilean national who commanded the MNR's secret police.

15. Anonymous interviews May 1993 and June 1994, Miami, Florida.

16. Bolivian governments, including that of General Barrientos, were engaged in other types of corruption, including arms smuggling. One of the most notable individuals involved in these government-sanctioned schemes during the Barrientos period was Klaus Altman, also known as Klaus Barbie.

17. Interviews in Miami (May 1993 and June 1994). Respondent requested anonymity.

18. Dunkerley (1984) provides a long list of the individuals linked to narcotics who allegedly enjoyed the protection of the Banzer government. The best known case was that of Luis Alberto Valle, Banzer's son-in-law who was expelled from Canada in 1974 after facing accusations of cocaine trafficking. However one examines the Banzer period, it is highly unlikely that these stories were unknown to the US embassy and the DEA personnel in Bolivia. Yet, at least publicly, the Banzer government was never admonished by the USA.

19. In one instance, in June 1980 the military high command declared US ambassador Marvin Weissman persona non grata for his warnings that the USA would suspend all assistance to Bolivia if the military launched a coup. The same month, in the city of Santa Cruz members of the right wing Falange Socialista Boliviana torched the binational centre. The main reason for the coup, in my view, was the indictment of General Banzer and 50 of his collaborators handed down by the National Congress in mid-July 1980 after nearly a year of hearings in Congress. If the coup had not occurred, the Supreme Court would have been forced to initiate a so-called Juicio de Responsabilidades (malfeasance trial) against the former president. For an extension of this analysis see Gamarra (1987).

20. See Gamarra (1997a) for a more in depth examination of the Suárez organisation.

21. The best account of US-Bolivia relations during this period is Barrios Morón (1989).

22. See Levine (1993) for the account of a former DEA agent involved in undercover operations aimed at bringing down Roberto Suárez. Although Levine's account is largely anecdotal, and a few of his interpretations arguable, this book points out that US international law enforcement agencies have more often than not worked at cross purposes. In this instance, fighting communism was a priority for the CIA that undermined DEA and to a lesser extent State Department concerns about drug trafficking.

23. See the testimony of Leandro Sánchez Reisse, an Argentine intelligence operative, before the Subcommittee on Terrorism, Narcotics, and International Operations of the Committee on Foreign Relations (23 July 1987).

24. Arce Gómez claimed that US intelligence agencies encouraged the coup. He also complained that the USA had betrayed him and the Bolivian military. In his view, in launching the July 1980 coup the military had done nothing more than to prevent communists from taking power. Arce could not understand when the shift in US priorities had occurred. (Interview, February 1991, in Federal Correctional Center, Miami.)

25. The number of DEA agents in Bolivia increased from 3 to 10.

26. US House of Representatives, Committee on Foreign Affairs, International Narcotics Control, Report of Staff Study Mission to Latin America, Southeast Asia and Pakistan 22 October 1981, 3 April 1982, pp. 23-4.

27. These events are analysed in Dunkerley (1984) and Malloy and Gamarra (1988).

28. A more detailed account of this period can be found in Gamarra (1994a).

29. This section is based on Gamarra (1994a) and Gamarra (1987).

30. *El Diario*, 17 August 1984 p. 1.

31. *El Diario*, 8 September 1984, p. 1.

32. *El Diario*, 7 September 1984, p. 1.

33. *Presencia*, 12 September 1984, p. 9. Rueda Peña subsequently denied making that statement. For another account of the Otazo-Suárez interview, see Mario Alarcón Lahore's (secretary to Siles) testimony before the congressional

commission, reprinted in *El Diario*, 19 September 1984, pp. 1 and 5.

34. *El Diario*, 18 September 1984, p. 1.

35. *El Diario*, 19 September 1984, p. 4.

36. See Malloy and Gamarra (1988) p. 150.

37. Interview with Ambassador Edwin Corr, Oklahoma City, May 1994.

38. See, for example, Committee on Foreign Affairs, US House of Representatives, *Report of Staff Study Mission to Latin America, Southeast Asia and Pakistan, 22 October 1981, 3 April 1982* and Committee on Foreign Affairs, US House of Representatives, *US Narcotics Control Programs Overseas: An Assessment. Report of the Staff Study Mission to South East Asia, South America, Central America and the Caribbean, August-January 1985.*

39. For an in-depth examination of this period see Gamarra (1994b).

40. For a brief history of the Paz Estenssoro government's counternarcotics strategy, see Gamarra (1997b). US counternarcotics strategies also dominated programmes administered by USAID, especially those aimed at strengthening political institutions. Assistance to the judiciary, for example, was tied to counternarcotics strategies. See Gamarra (1991).

41. None was more problematic to the Paz Estenssoro government than charges against Fernando Barthelemy, the minister of interior during Operation Blast Furnace, of links to the narcotics industry. Barthelemy's role in the investigation of the September 1986 murder of Noel Kempff Mercado, a prominent scientist, in the Huanchaca region of eastern Bolivia became the main issue.

42. For an in-depth examination of these disputes consult, Malamud Goti (1991). See also, US Congress (1995).

43. Interview with officials at the Bolivian foreign ministry, La Paz, December 1992.

44. While most of the aid would go towards equipping and training, Annex III claimed that a substantial, but unspecified, portion of this amount would go to civic action programmes. The army would obtain training and equipment for two infantry battalions for anti-narcotics operations; training and equipment for two engineering battalions for civic action programmes; training and equipment for a transport battalion; and training and equipment for a supply and services section. The air force would receive helicopter and airplane parts, six new UH-1H helicopters, and maintenance and repairs for its entire air fleet. Additionally, the air military police would receive training and equipment. The navy would obtain up to eight Piraña patrol boats and four additional 36 foot patrol boats. Navy personnel would also receive training and equipment.

45. See, 'Paz Zamora anuncia ingreso de FF.AA. a la lucha antidroga', *Ultima Hora*, 19 May 1990, p. 20.

46. *Ibid.*

47. Jorge Crespo, Bolivia's ambassador to the United States, spearheaded efforts in Washington to counter the momentum towards full scale militarisation. In interviews with Bolivian embassy officials they noted that the ambassador's

efforts in Washington proved costly. In an ironic twist of events, Ambassador Gelbard reportedly accused Crespo of 'involvement in the internal affairs of the United States' and allegedly exerted pressure on the Paz Zamora government to secure his resignation.

48. Interviews with members of the Ministry of Industry and Trade and with members of the Bolivian embassy staff in Washington confirmed this view.

49. Because Arce Gómez's expulsion from Bolivia took place without an extradition treaty and despite the fact that warrants were out for his arrest on human rights charges, a major institutional crisis was initiated pitting the Supreme Court against the executive branch. The fall-out of this conflict was felt throughout 1990; in fact, the attempted impeachment of two-thirds of the Supreme Court magistrates by the government-controlled Senate can be seen as an extension of this conflict. For an expansion of this analysis consult Gamarra (1991).

50. 'Militares combatirán drogas, reitera Bolivia', *El Nuevo Herald*, 28 March 1991, p. 3a.

51. Governmental intolerance of dissident groups escalated considerably as opposition to the presence of US military adivisers and the ordering of the army into the Chapare mounted. The Paz Zamora government initiated a campaign in the local media accusing peasant groups and opposition parties of inadvertently collaborating with drug traffickers. A full page announcement from the ministry of information stated boldly: 'The enemy is astute and there are those who, without knowing it, help the enemy.' See *Presencia*, 3 April 1991, p. 9.

52. 'Productores de coca de tres países discuten estrategia ante gobiernos', *El Nuevo Herald*, 28 March 1991, p. 3a. and 'Cocaleros reacios a política antidrogas', *El Nuevo Herald*, 30 March 1991, p. 3a.

53. The Bolivian government, however, does not acknowledge that voluntary eradication targets may have been successful only because of temporarily low coca prices resulting from both the disruption of trafficking operations in Colombia and a glut in the coca market. Because of the lack of alternative crops Bolivian *campesinos* who voluntarily eradicated their crops have also planted new coca fields. Moreover, the price for coca leaves rebounded in late 1990 and early 1991 from the low of $10 to around $47 per hundred pounds. These signs do not bode well for alternative development goals.

54. In 1990 the Bolivian government presented a list of 75 alternative development projects to the World Bank requiring $611.4 million dollars in investment. Clearly the potential for carrying out a great number of projects is there; however, financing has been slow to come.

55. On this point see Gamarra (1997b)

56. Gonzalo Torrico was often described by US embassy officials as the only trustworthy person in the government. (Interviews with US embassy personnel, including Ambassador Bowers, December 1992.) Torrico wrote a self serving book entitled *Un desafío para el siglo XXI* (1993) in which he highlights his accomplishments as Undersecretary for Social Defence in the

Ministry of Interior.

57. Sánchez de Lozada's lack of attention to the drug issue provoked angry comments from US State Department officials. (Interviews April 1996 with Robert S. Gelbard. See also Gamarra, 1998.)

58. See Sucre Guzmán (1995).

59. *Opción Cero* (1994)

60. According to Law 1008, in 1995 the Bolivian government had to initiate the forceful eradication of coca in the so-called transition zones.

61. United States Congress, Extradition Treaty with Bolivia: Message from the President of the United States (104th Congress 1st Sessión, 10 October 1995).

62. Statement of Jane Becker, Acting Assistant Secretary of State, Office of International Narcotics and Law Enforcement Matters, July 16, 1997.

63. República de Bolivia, *¡Por la Dignidad! Estrategia Boliviana de la Lucha Contra el Narcotráfico: 1998-2002.*

64. One of the most arguable assertions of the plan is the idea that 'a majority of coca growing peasants have joined the production of cocaine'.

65. According to the statement, [alternative development] 'has yielded significant results. Prior to 1992, coca was the principal crop grown in the Chapare. The hectarage in licit crops in the Chapare is now three times greater than coca cultivation, and 127 per cent greater than 1986. Licit agricultural production in the Chapare now represents 1.5 per cent of Bolivia's gross domestic product. The success of this programme has enabled the Government of Bolivia to effectively counter arguments that coca eradication impoverishes poor farmers and makes the goal of total coca eradication political unfeasible.' *International Counternarcotics Strategy Report* (INCSR) 1998 Report, Office of International Narcotics and Law Enforcement Matters, 28 February 1998.

66. Press Release, 'News from the House International Relations Committee, Gilman Says Administration is "Punishing" Congressional Support of Colombia by Cutting Funds to Bolivia', 3 March 1998.

67. US House of Representatives (1996), p. H5264.

68. *Ibid.*

CHAPTER 10

PACKAGING DRUGS:
CERTIFICATION AND THE ACQUISITION OF LEVERAGE

Elizabeth Joyce[*]

In November 1997, the White House announced that Syria and Lebanon were to be dropped from the list of 32 countries classed as major producers or traffickers of illicit drugs. US aid to the two countries would no longer be dependent on their having cooperated effectively with the USA on drugs under the annual certification process that reviews countries' drug control performance. The reason given for the decision to drop them from the process, that they had promised to undertake joint crop eradication programmes, was far from convincing. Neither country had ever won US approval for drug control, and Syria was one of the few countries that had been completely decertified for non-cooperation every year since the process began in 1986. Such apparent inconsistencies in the drug certification process can usually be explained by reference to the larger US foreign policy agenda. Though there was no significant progress on drug control, at the time of the announcement the administration was urgently seeking support in the Middle East for an air strike against Iraq. Certification, it appeared, had become a bargaining tool in diplomatic negotiations that had nothing to do with drugs.

Certification is not simply a review of drug control in foreign countries, but an instrument of US foreign policy that serves a wide variety of purposes. The process cannot be dismissed as a blunt instrument designed to bludgeon other countries into compliance with a range of narrow short-term objectives, nor as a public relations exercise that positions the United States as the leader in global drug control, nor can it be characterised simply as a congressional measure that forces the administration to account for its actions. US foreign drug policy is embedded in the broader context of foreign relations, the certification process itself only one of a wide range of sanctions that the USA currently applies to some two-thirds of the world's population, which cost US exporters billions of dollars a year. Despite this, US foreign drug policy is frequently, even usually, considered as a single issue, as if it existed independently of other domestic and foreign policy concerns. The way in which US foreign drug policy is articulated encourages this approach, and the certification process itself is a crucial means of promoting the idea that US foreign drug policy exists in a world apart from economic relations and more traditional security concerns. The fact that transnational crime has recently been defined as a 'new' security issue, requiring original ways of thinking about national and regional security, has encouraged this view. Detaching drugs from other foreign policy considerations for the purposes of analytical clarity has its uses, but the conclusions that follow from this detachment – that drug policy decisions tend towards caprice, and that outcomes systematically fall short of the one overriding objective of effecting a reduction in the supply of drugs to the United States – are inadequate and even disingenuous. Only by considering US relations on drugs with Latin America as an important issue in hemispheric affairs, but one that is embedded in relations on transnational crime and in the wider context of hemispheric relations, can accurate conclusions be drawn about its effects.

Understanding how the certification process works can explain much about the relative importance of drugs in US foreign policy, the degree of effectiveness that Washington has in its bilateral relations with other countries on drugs, and the development of global drug control given that the certification process is a key part of the international drug regime.[1] In light of recent interest in the promotion of a multilateral approach to hemispheric drug control, following the Summit of the Americas in April 1998 (see below), analysing the process can also offer insight into the possibility of its eventually being replaced by a more cooperative approach to this aspect of security.

For the USA, success in controlling imports of illicit foreign drugs partly hinges on its ability to persuade other countries in the western hemisphere to address drug control within their territory in ways that they and the USA perceive to be compatible with US interests and sometimes, but not always, their own. US policy-makers label this persuasive or coercive capacity 'leverage'. The acquisition and use of leverage in US relations with its neighbours is, of course, nothing new. Yet leverage in drug control differs in its complexity from other more traditional forms of influence. Rather than seeking to influence a specific event or set of circumstances, or a single policy, the USA must seek to bring pressure to bear on an extremely wide range of circumstances while engaging in sustained operational cooperation. The potential uses of leverage in foreign drug control go far beyond the ability to influence a neighbour's criminal justice arrangements or the activities of its policemen. To achieve its drug policy objectives, the USA requires leverage to persuade countries to effect major political change, expend massive state resources, adjust agricultural and social welfare policies, change constitutions, rewrite legislation, modify judicial systems, revise the terms of public sector employment, restructure banking and deploy their armed forces and law enforcement in ways compatible with US interests. No other facet of US foreign policy would, if pursued conscientiously to its logical ends, demand such transformation of another sovereign state.

During the last 15 years, the USA has tested its own capacity to acquire and use leverage in foreign drug control. Pressure is effected by a panoply of bilateral means ranging from the unreservedly positive (the promise of aid, diplomatic benediction and other benefits) to the negative (the threat of trade sanctions, aid withheld and international opprobrium). A supporting pillar of US drug diplomacy which helps give the impression that a strong state is not bullying some weaker states has been the promotion of multilateral drug control regimes and institutions, particularly the 1988 UN Convention against Illicit Traffic in Narcotic Drugs and Psychotropic Substances (also known as the Vienna Convention). Yet such is the dominance of the USA on drugs that its policy influences the way other countries and institutions plan and implement drug cooperation in Latin America even when that is not its explicit purpose. At the operational level, other actors, recognising the USA as the predominant source of aid and expertise on drug control in the western hemisphere, consistently tailor their programmes and policies in response to those of Washington, often to fill the gaps left unfunded by the USA. In the mid-1990s, the United Nations International Drug Control Programme (UNDCP) – seeking to provide 'maximum value-added' or assistance only where it was not provided by other sources – did not bother with law enforcement programmes in Colombia because of the size and scope of US law enforcement cooperation there.[2]

Latin American drug control policies can never, therefore, be fully disaggregated from those of their northern neighbour. The drug trade in Latin America is fuelled by US demand for cocaine, and drug control in Latin America is largely driven by the imperative that cocaine (and other drugs) must be prevented from penetrating US borders. US perceptions, policies and strategies prevail in western hemispheric drug control. Latin American governments, scholars and NGOs frequently question the existing drug regime, particularly the proscription of coca. However, there is some evidence that in Latin America public perceptions of drugs, particularly among the middle classes, reflect US public perceptions more than before, a similarity that has been ascribed to publication of the US point of view, the close working relations on drugs that Latin American governments have with the USA, and a growing domestic demand for drugs (Lerner, 1998, p. 127).

US drug control in Latin America and the Caribbean is not simply the most recent and wide-ranging undertaking in an American tradition of international crime control designed to serve a variety of US interests on matters ranging from arms trafficking to the regulation of international securities markets. It is by far the most intense and sustained effort the USA has ever made on transnational crime control. Almost three-quarters of the budget of the State Department's Bureau for International Narcotics and Law Enforcement Affairs (INL), which coordinates overseas drug control, is spent in Latin America, the bulk of it on material support to foreign police and military. Moreover, to secure an outcome favourable to US interests, a far wider range of policies has been implemented than for other matters and at other times. In Latin America, the deployment of US troops, the offer of military aid and the forceful pressure on other countries to use their troops in law enforcement operations also makes this facet of US international law enforcement substantively different from others.

Washington has never had any intention of handing over the lion's share of its foreign drug budget to Latin American countries and relinquishing control over how it was spent. The importance of US principles of international drug control is not simply the spontaneous consequence of a US willingness to spend more and do more. The USA has made strenuous efforts to influence the policies of other countries, although the intensity of these efforts varies over time and according to the region or country concerned. As the certification process demonstrates, Washington has been willing, at least in principle, to make its foreign relations conditional with some countries upon drug control. And certification has given the USA leverage in its relations on drugs with certifiable countries, frequently leading those countries to take actions they would not otherwise have taken. The desired outcome of certification, and the other forms of diplomatic and operational interaction with the Latin American countries, is the acquisition and use of leverage.

The Certification Process

Since its introduction in 1986, the annual certification process has gradually become the fulcrum of US leverage on other countries' drug control policies, providing an immediate and tangible threat if countries fail to carry out successful drug control programmes. What began as a Congressional attempt to make the Executive take more notice of drug-related issues has become a well-established diplomatic tool that gives a certain annual rhythm to international drug control.[3] The outcome is awaited with far more interest than the deliberations of the UN's International Narcotics Control Board (INCB), whose annual report provides a more disinterested summary of global drug control. Timing had a clear role to play in establishing certification's importance in the international drug regime. The certification process was in place in 1986 prior to the establishment of the more formal international rules and procedures on drug control laid down in the Vienna Convention, which did not enter into force until four years later. By the time that the Vienna Convention emerged as the centre-piece of the international drug regime, certification's annual process of bargaining and review was already established.

Certification has also acquired dynamism over time as the instrument has been refined, and as actors have become accustomed to working with it. It brings together many of the disparate elements of US foreign policy on drugs. Although it does not (nor was it intended to) eliminate bureaucratic and operational 'turf battles' at the operational or budgetary levels, it does allow the several US institutions involved in foreign drug control to speak to the Latin American countries, in diplomatic terms, with one voice.[4] The vagueness of its requirements strengthen rather than diminish its importance. Within certain limits, it can be made to do whatever political exigencies demand.

Certification has acquired rules, structures, codes and organisational norms that have helped shape and even determine the choices of the Latin American countries in their relations on drugs with the USA, and for a few countries (Colombia being the clearest example – see Chapter 8), the process has at times helped determine the direction of bilateral relations with Washington in their entirety. The accumulated weight of past negative decisions has also reinforced its influence over time. Moreover, its application has become more complex since it was introduced. The rules of certification were more specific at first. The inclusion of the phrase requiring cooperation with the Vienna Convention rather than just the USA made the requirements far broader, and the original rules emphasised the reduction of drug production (i.e. crop eradication); within two years the emphasis had shifted to law enforcement cooperation.[5] Of course, the USA also exercised a high degree of influence on drug control policies before the introduction of certification and when certification was of relatively minor importance. In addition, operational cooperation between law enforcement, the military and development officials often appears to go on as always, somewhat independently of the 'high politics' of diplomacy. Yet, during its first decade, certification increasingly made a package of US influence and became, in many cases, an effective fulcrum of leverage.

Every year at the end of February, the White House announces the results of the certification process. Countries regarded by the USA as major drug producing or transit countries, the 'Majors' (there are currently 30 countries thus designated), are examined on their efficiency in drug control during the previous year. If their efforts are judged to have been unsatisfactory, the offending countries are 'decertified'. This may render them ineligible for most US aid (humanitarian aid and drug cooperation aid are not affected by the decision) and invoke a US boycott on loans from multilateral institutions such as the International Monetary Fund (IMF) and the Inter-American Development Bank (IDB).[6] Other possible sanctions include the withholding of tourist visas to the USA. The consequences of decertification are not all mandatory and, in practice, are highly negotiable.

The president sends from the White House a memorandum to the secretary of state containing three lists of countries: those that have been approved and certified; those that have not been approved but have been certified in the vital national interests of the USA; and those that have been decertified. The procedure, with its annual test and lists, is designed to appear as a dispassionate assessment of a country's efforts on drug control. It is also intended to show that drug control is a matter of such importance that it may override other considerations in US relations with another country. The criteria for certification as set out in the presidential memorandum are for those countries that 'have cooperated fully with the USA, or taken adequate steps on their own, to achieve full compliance with the goals and objectives of the [UN Vienna Convention]'. The impression that the USA may be acting as a self-appointed arbiter of global drug control is deceptive. The rest of the report makes clear that success is measured by the degree to which a country works with the USA on US policy objectives, that is, the reduction of drug flows into the USA.[7] Yet the process also helps confirm the central position of the USA in global cooperation on drugs. With the certification results, the US State Department publishes at the beginning of March its annual *International Narcotics Control Strategy Report*, a 500-page document which details in a country-by-country format the state of illicit drug production, trafficking and control in almost every country in the world and is an important source of data about international drug control used by other governments and the United Nations.

Approval Guaranteed

The State Department says that certification 'depends exclusively on... counternarcotics cooperation throughout the year',[8] but in practice a decision to decertify does not depend on the quality of a country's drug control alone. All aspects of a country's relations with the USA condition the decision; the quality of a country's drug control need not even be the deciding factor. Moreover, there are no standard criteria for judging the countries. Each case for certification is judged on its own merits. Broadly, however, certain conditions tend to determine that the quality of drug control is not the most important factor in whether a country is certified.

Regularly decertified countries tend already to have poor relations with the USA, often having pariah, near-pariah, or rogue-state status independent of their relative indifference to drug control. They have usually included Afghanistan, Burma, Iran, Nigeria and Syria. Of these countries, Iran is distinctive in having draconian anti-drug policies that include the massive forced eradication of illicit crops, large seizures of drugs, the execution of drug traffickers and the arrest of drug users. They would appear to go beyond satisfying the rubric of certification that a country must have taken 'adequate steps on its own to achieve compliance with the Vienna Convention'. Yet Washington annually decertifies Iran. Responding to an assertion that the USA 'decertified Iran because basically we don't like the country's leadership; we don't like their policies', a former senior State Department official admitted that 'there is a tendency to focus on countries like Iran... It's easy. You up your quota of decertification by adding countries that don't matter anyway and everybody hates' (Congressional Research Service, 1996, pp. 12, 21). In these cases, decertification is part of a package of sanctions directed at a single country. The quality of drug control in these countries is far less important than the message of general disapproval from Washington.

Countries of major importance for reasons other than drug control are usually certified and in 1995 and 1996 they included China, Taiwan, Vietnam, Mexico, Panama and Brazil. Some of these countries have remarkably low-quality drug control, yet virtually no failure on their part can guarantee decertification. This group has economic and political links of such enduring importance that their certification is virtually assured. Mexico's continued certification, despite its deeply flawed drug control system, tends to confirm the hypothesis that important and complex relations with the USA will guarantee certification. Thus, a country stands a better chance of certification if enduring facets to its relations with the USA include important trade ties, the potentially destabilising effect a negative outcome might have on the country concerned, or the need to strengthen general relations, support an unstable regime, or avoid further 'muddying the waters' of a complex but important bilateral relationship. In some cases, the decision makes this linkage of drug control to other political considerations explicit. Although the efforts of Pakistan, the primary conduit for opium from Afghanistan, were described as 'seriously deficient' in the 1997 report, the country was granted certification with a national interest waiver because it is 'a moderate Islamic state with a nuclear weapons capability...[and]...the largest contributor of troops for UN peacekeeping operations' (US Department of State, Bureau for International Narcotics and Law Enforcement Affairs, 1997).

A third group of countries, whose certification does not rest on the quality of drug control or cooperation with the USA, comprises those countries to which certification is explicitly given because other factors at the time of the review have outweighed the perceived importance of drug control. Some have special interests in their relations with the USA which may be transient and they may not, therefore, permanently belong to this group of inviolable countries whose certified status appears certain. They tend to be countries of only minor or, at most, intermediate political importance to the USA. Yet they may be countries of major concern with regard to drug control. In the 1996 report, this group included Paraguay and Peru, when the quality of drug control and cooperation in both countries was causing concern to the USA. Paraguay is a small state of little importance to the USA either in general terms or with regard to drug control. The country is a major entrepôt for trafficking of all kinds, including illicit drugs, but is insignificant relative to the Andean countries or Mexico as a transit country for drugs entering the USA. Paraguay was, therefore, approved because a 'denial of certification could undermine the transition to democracy and weaken support for President Wasmosy's reform process' (US Department of State, Bureau for International Narcotics and Law Enforcement Affairs, 1996, p. xlviii). Peru's case was rather different, given that it was acknowledged to produce more coca than any other country. Despite that fact that, according to the report, Peru's 'central role as the largest coca producer in the world' expanded in the previous year, 'a denial... would result in a significant disruption of the US role as one of the guarantors of the Peru-Ecuador peace process, would impede the economic restructuring currently underway in Peru, and reduce US influence in ensuring progress on human rights cooperation' (US Department of State, Bureau for International Narcotics and Law Enforcement Affairs, 1996, p. 1). The risks associated with denying certification were judged to be greater than the risks associated with Peru's failure to cooperate fully with the USA to reduce coca cultivation.

Packaging Certification for Congress

Although the illicit drug trade is frequently named as one of the great new post-Cold War security threats, drug control competes for priority with other factions of US foreign policy, and often loses, as the case of Syria and Lebanon shows. The government does not hesitate to distort the certification process if other more important priorities demand it.[9]

The impression that drug control is a matter of great foreign policy importance is partly a mirror of congressional aspirations for that piece of policy. There are high levels of public concern about, and media interest in, all aspects of drug control. Violence, crime and drugs were the top national concerns of respondents to a 1996 Gallup poll (Office of National Drug Control Policy, 1996, p. 98). This domestic concern about drugs tends to mask the fact that drug policy is seldom one of the administration's top foreign policy priorities. Popular interest in a relatively low foreign policy priority creates, therefore, a tension between the administration and members of Congress, who address directly their voters' concerns.[10]

The original impetus for certification was domestic. Certification was introduced in 1986 by the Senate in response to public concern at the torture and murder in Mexico of a Drug Enforcement Administration (DEA) agent, Enrique Camarena, and the apparent indifference of the Mexican government to investigating the circumstances of his death.[11] Both Democratic and Republican senators believed that the Reagan administration was not paying enough attention to the Camarena case or to drug control generally in the foreign countries whose narcotics supplied the US market, and certification was seen as a means to ensure that the administration was treating foreign drug control as a priority, by forcing it to account to Congress for its relations with drug producing countries. This domestic purpose remains crucial.

Certification is therefore a package for domestic consumption in which the Executive gives account to Congress of how the foreign drug budget is being spent. The group of decisions that comprises certification is a discrete entity, and decisions on the individual countries are linked for the purpose of presenting an acceptable package to a domestic audience. A decision to certify one country can, therefore, be influenced by the decision taken on another. This aspect of the process – the fact that a decision on a single country can be determined by the status of another country as part of the certification package – became explicit for the first time in 1996. In that year Colombia's chances of being decertified were linked to those of Mexico being certified.

Both countries had long had a high degree of cooperation with the USA on drugs, yet drug control in both countries was causing concern in Washington in terms of outcomes. Drugs were continuing to pour into the USA, and Mexico and Colombia were the focus of most attention. In the early 1990s, Mexico became the main transit route for drug shipments in Latin America.[12] Drug trafficking across the US-Mexican border had increased rapidly and evidence had emerged of official collusion with drug traffickers at high political levels. US relations with Colombia had been seriously strained since President Ernesto Samper took office in 1994.[13] Washington mistrusted Samper, believing that he had knowingly received a $6 million campaign contribution from the Cali cartel. Peru and Bolivia, in contrast, received virtually no public attention in the USA, although together as producers of coca they were the source of most of the cocaine entering the USA. The key to this seeming paradox is that corruption or the perception of drug-related corruption in foreign countries attracts more political and public attention in the USA than the outcome, whether successful or not, of cooperation on drug control. In as much as there were objective criteria for the certification of Colombia and Mexico, the debate in 1996 focused on official corruption.[14]

In advance of the 1996 presidential elections in November, the Republican-dominated Congress was accusing President Clinton of being 'soft' on drugs and he needed to be seen taking a hard line on Latin American drug control. The notion of being 'soft' on drugs referred largely to what Congress perceived as unacceptably high federal spending on demand reduction policies and community policing programmes within the USA, policies which President Clinton had championed. To many Republican members of Congress not only was this evidence of an insufficiently tough approach to drug control, it also smacked of the

'Big Government' they had committed themselves to eliminating. Demand reduction programmes presented for approval to Congress were consistently cut in the preceding year, eventually making untenable the position of former New York police commissioner Lee Brown as the head of the Office of National Drug Control Policy (ONDCP). He was replaced in February 1996 by General Barry McCaffrey, former commander of US Southern Command (Southcom) and the first military official to occupy the post of 'drug czar'. He was a popular appointment with Congress because his military background and international experience seemed to presage a hard line on foreign drug control.

For Congress, a hard line on foreign drug control involved the decertification of either Mexico or Colombia (and possibly both). Yet the administration wanted to avoid the decertification of Mexico. Mexico is more important to the USA than Colombia. The two countries share a 1500-mile border, and have long had a close and profitable economic relationship. Mexico has a far larger economy than Colombia, and 80-90 per cent of its imports are bought from the USA (by contrast, Colombia buys around 40 per cent of its imports from the USA). The launch of the North American Free Trade Agreement (NAFTA) in 1994 has made bilateral relations closer still. Given that relations with Mexico mattered far more than those with Colombia, the decision on Mexico received more attention than that on Colombia.

In 1996, the quality of US relations with Mexico was an important domestic political issue. The Clinton administration, in the teeth of some trenchant opposition from Congress, was seeking to preserve the credibility of its commitment to NAFTA. The Republicans in Congress were already critical of policy towards Mexico with regard to NAFTA and the multi-billion dollar US rescue in February 1995 of the Mexican peso. There was concern in Congress – Senators Jesse Helms and Dianne Feinstein were vocal in this regard – about the direct links between free trade and the greater opportunities it afforded for transnational crime, including drug trafficking. A hearing of the Senate Foreign Relations Committee in August 1995 discussed at length cases of alleged corruption involving Mexican members of government (United States, Committee on Foreign Relations, Senate 1995). Congressmen expressed concern that drug trafficking was not being accorded a sufficiently high priority relative to other aspects of bilateral relations (United States, Committee on Foreign Relations, Senate 1995, pp. 66-7, 74-5). Republican Senator Bob Dole wrote to the president in February 1996 urging him to decertify Mexico in the drug certification round, and the administration was keen to avoid a public admission that its new free trade partner was not up to the task of preventing drug shipments entering the USA under cover of a greatly increased volume of trade between the two countries. The administration did not want to be seen to be ignoring reasonable concerns.

At one stage, the State Department argued forcefully for the intermediate sanction: both Mexico and Colombia should be certified but only on grounds of US national interest. According to one observer, the Mexican embassy in Washington expressed horror at the suggestion of an intermediate sanction and, in a feat of diplomatic brinkmanship, announced that Mexico would accept full decertification rather than a national security waiver from the USA.[15]   Mexicans, the embassy argued, would be more humiliated by the intermediate sanction with its implication that Mexico was being given a paternal 'dressing down' by its more powerful neighbour than by outright decertification, which would provoke outrage and a sense of defiant nationalism; the Mexican government was better able to tackle the latter responses.   Full decertification was already ruled out and, once the Mexican position had been accepted, Colombia's fate was sealed.   The administration believed it would be impossible to win congressional approval for both countries and decided to 'give' Congress the decertification of Colombia in the hope that this would allow for the full certification of Mexico.

The basic tensions in bargaining over certification between the administration and Congress do not necessarily indicate much difference of opinion about the process itself.   Until recently, any qualms about the validity, fairness or long-term political costs of the process were far outweighed by the immediate effectiveness of the outcomes.   And as regards outcomes, most disagreements among members of Congress and the administration have been over the Executive's *failure* to decertify countries.   The main advocates for change have been those who would prefer that certification become an even more powerful instrument in US foreign relations.   Of the anti-drug agencies, the DEA has been the most willing to see the certification process used in this way as a means to obtain concessions from foreign governments.   However, the ONDCP under General McCaffrey has questioned publicly the appropriateness of the process itself.[16]

Although the outcomes of certification are conditioned by the perceptions of congressmen and the administration's predictions about how the results it has chosen will 'play' in Congress, judgements about the quality of drug control and bilateral cooperation are nevertheless important.   Here, the emphasis is not only on the effectiveness of relations in the past – although this is a consideration in the Executive's account to Congress of how drug budgets were being spent, as formally required in the rubric of the procedure – but on the potential effects of the decision on future cooperation.   The administration also considers how the outcome will be received in Latin America.

Packaging Certification for Latin America: the Acquisition of Leverage

The process has become a more powerful political instrument over the last decade partly because it neatly packages the US position on drugs for foreign consumption.   Certifiable countries experience annually both direct pressure and the more indirect pressure of seeing one of their neighbours decertified. Decertification of a key country increases the effectiveness of the entire process on other countries.   Colombia's decertification reduced the possibility that the process was seen by other countries in Latin America as a paper tiger.   The apparent element of caprice – Colombia decertified but not Mexico; Peru's certification in 1996 and 1997 despite grave US criticism of its drug cooperation – increases this pressure by reducing certainty, making the Latin American countries more inclined to act cautiously.

For this threat to be effective, it is important that US relations with each country concerned are bilateral. In 1996 and 1997, the USA was negotiating Maritime Counternarcotics Cooperation Agreements, or ship-rider agreements, with several of the Caribbean countries which would allow US law enforcement officers to board Caribbean ships to inspect them for drugs. In 1996, Jamaica and Barbados tried to limit the scope of the ship-rider agreements and to link them to negotiations on arms trafficking, deportees and trade, and Jamaica was threatened with decertification if it did not agree to the US terms (Griffith, 1997, pp. 21-2). The Caribbean countries accused the USA of insisting on separate bilateral negotiations with each country that maximised the US advantage when they would have preferred a multilateral approach through the Caribbean Community (CARICOM). They argued that the USA would not have threatened decertification of the entire group, whereas in bilateral talks they were far more vulnerable to the threat.

The certification process provides a focus for Latin American resentment. US leverage acquired through certification might force Latin American governments to take unpopular steps, but certification also provides a means to defuse public opposition. In this regard, Latin American perceptions of the process are crucial. The overt pressure, the apparent capriciousness, and the implicit threat of military force, perceptible in the drug war rhetoric and the more robust comments of some US congressmen reinforce every Latin American prejudice about US foreign policy, thus increasing the authenticity of the process and its status as a credible threat. This image can work against, as well as for, US interests. US disapproval of Colombian President Ernesto Samper, trenchantly expressed as the reason for Colombia's decertification in 1996, had precisely the opposite effect to that intended by creating a wave of popular nationalism that helped keep a generally unpopular president in power. Reactive nationalism is, of course, the traditional response to perceived national insult. As we have seen above, in 1996 Mexican diplomats told the State Department that the Mexican public would accept more readily complete decertification than the humiliation of a paternalistic-seeming decertification with the effects suspended by national security waiver.

How the process is packaged for Latin America is also important for US diplomats, law enforcement officials and military personnel directly involved in foreign drug control. For them, Latin American perceptions of the process as a ritual humiliation of America's neighbours can, in the short-term, have a practical utility. These perceptions allow those involved in US foreign drug control to appear to go behind the public face of certification in their dealings with their foreign counterparts, and soften or mitigate the 'official line', while using the leverage it produces. In this regard, it should be remembered that the process of acquiring leverage in US foreign relations on drugs is far subtler than it appears at the beginning of every March. In some respects certification is simply the most visible manifestation of a complex and sophisticated process that is individually tailored to the particular conditions that inform relations with a given country. The most immediate form of leverage is applied by the US embassy and officials based in the country concerned.

The Uses of Leverage

That decertification is threatened tends to be clearly signalled months in advance through diplomatic channels. A flurry of ministerial visits to Washington from the country concerned precede the action. The Andean governments know from experience that the USA is prepared to carry out the threat and that, further, the withdrawal of aid will bring in its wake an increase in US ability to dictate the terms of drug control in their country. In June 1986, the US Congress announced the suspension of $7.1 million in US aid to Bolivia because of a failure to eradicate 10,000 hectares of coca demanded by Washington in 1983. The suspension of aid was immediately followed by Operation Blast Furnace, the first significant deployment of US troops in the Andes for the purpose of drug control.

The nature of the threat that decertification poses to the object of the procedure varies. This is weighed when Washington considers whether Bolivia should be decertified even though, in 1994 and 1995, the USA was dissatisfied with Bolivia's efforts to eradicate coca crops. In 1995, the mere threat itself was sufficient for Bolivia to increase eradication, the measure that the USA regarded as inadequately implemented. US targets for the voluntary eradication of coca (under which growers were compensated $2,500 for every hectare of coca destroyed) had not been met for the previous two years. Following conditional certification because of this, Washington gave La Paz a deadline (30 June) and a target (1,750 hectares) and said if the target was not met by that date $87.4 million in economic aid would be suspended. Such was the urgency this deadline created in La Paz that the government threatened to send in the army to destroy the coca by force.[17] As well as the threat of aid withdrawal, the USA can exercise influence on a host country by the promise, implied or explicit, of more support if cooperation on drugs is deemed satisfactory. Between 1986 and 1988, the Reagan administration supported Bolivia in its debt reduction negotiations with the multilateral financial institutions and promised to increase aid to help stabilise the country's economy.

In 1997, with President Samper still in power, the USA was almost obliged to decertify Colombia, or risk diminishing the credibility of its previous decision. Nevertheless, in hopes of staving off such an outcome, Colombia capitulated to just about every US demand. Less than two weeks before the certification announcement, the Colombian congress passed legislation that would increase the maximum penalty for drug trafficking from 24 to 60 years. On 20 February, Colombia signed a maritime interdiction accord with the USA that would allow the US Coast Guard to board Colombian ships, and even promised to lift the constitutional ban on extradition (see Chapter 8). Colombia was once again the only country on the list of decertified countries that had cooperated closely with the USA on drug control. These agreements were reached despite the fact that, in contrast to Bolivia, Colombia does not rely heavily on multilateral credits, and most US aid to Colombia is related to drug control to which certification sanctions do not apply. The opprobrium and inconvenience that certification implies were enough to produce compliance.

In contrast, Mexico was certified again in 1997, despite reports of corruption in its drug control system, including the firing of Mexico's most senior drug control officer, General Jesús Gutiérrez Rebollo, director of the Instituto Nacional Contra las Drogas (INCD), having been accused of taking payments from Amado Carrillo Fuentes, head of the Juárez cartel. This was only the most scandalous of a string of problems in the Mexican drug control system which suggested it might be inherently flawed and systemically corrupted.[18] Thus, although the differences between US treatment of the two countries appeared particularly stark in 1997, the two decisions were not specifically linked. Rather, the outcome in 1997 was largely dependent on the outcome of the previous year when they had been linked. The apparent incongruities, however, captured public attention to an unprecedented degree. Congress considered rejecting the administration's recommendation for Mexico, but was eventually persuaded to agree.[19]

The USA won a great deal of ground in the process. From Washington's perspective, the process had proved its worth. It had acquired a year of close cooperation from a Colombian president it considered corrupt and, in the final weeks of the process in early 1997, the almost total acquiescence of Colombia to US demands. These immediate gains were so great that the US administration was not only willing for the first time to admit publicly the inconsistencies of the process, but also to justify it. Gen. Barry McCaffrey, director of the White House ONDCP, described the process as 'creative hypocrisy'.[20]

Alternatives to Certification

The incongruous decisions on Mexico and Colombia in 1996 and 1997 captured public attention, and acquired emblematic significance as instances of foreign policy inconsistency comparable with the granting of privileged trading status to China despite its poor human rights record and the US commitment to upholding human rights through annual review. Only after the 1996 and 1997 drug certifications were serious questions raised in the USA about the process itself. General McCaffrey regretted publicly that it could be interpreted as 'unilateral arrogance'.[21] Frequent newspaper editorials expressed similar views and, in July 1997, two leading senators won a great deal of support in Congress when they proposed the suspension of drug certification for an experimental two years and its replacement by a multilateral arrangement.[22] Discussion of the senators' proposal was the first time that the process of certification rather than its outcomes was seriously questioned in Congress. Nevertheless, there has also been criticism in Congress of sanctions more generally, based largely on recognition that such measures can be extremely costly for US companies.

On drugs, General McCaffrey emerged in 1997 as a moderate yet influential sceptic of the certification process. A supporter of multilateral initiatives, he appeared to have become convinced by his experience as head of Southcom in Panama that joint law enforcement operations with Latin American allies could be effectively developed. In November 1997 McCaffrey promised that a range of multilateral initiatives would be announced the following year at the April 1998

Santiago summit, including a multilateral drug control centre at Howard Air Base in Panama after the US withdrawal at the end of the century. These, he promised, would guarantee that the certification process would 'become buried under a higher order cooperative effort'.[23] Although in the event little emerged from the summit, one proposal was that the Organisation of American States (OAS) might take a greater role in drug cooperation by requiring countries to submit annually their national drug strategies to the OAS for assessment.

The Latin American governments were already taking every opportunity to call for multilateral approaches to the hemispheric drug problem and, therefore, received such proposals with enthusiasm. Mexico had proposed the holding of a global conference on drugs, which eventually became the United Nations General Assembly Special Session on drugs, held in New York on 8-10 June 1998, and together with Colombia had repeatedly rejected the validity of the certification process. Yet Washington's putative new approach to hemispheric drug cooperation was unlikely to offer much change. The administration's stated rationale for supporting the OAS and other 'regional counternarcotics organisations and consultative groups' was to deflect attention from the certification process rather than to improve implementation of drug policies.[24] The USA has preferred to retain the control over its foreign anti-drug activities that bilateral relations better afford and has been reluctant to fund or relinquish control to external organisations concerned with drug control.

The USA has also been reluctant to relinquish operational control. European law enforcement officers have long complained about the USA's reluctance to share intelligence with the Lyons-based International Criminal Police Organisation (Interpol) despite holding many of the key positions within the organisation.[25] Successful multilateral drug operations involving the USA – like Operation Green Ice in the early 1990s which involved police from nine different countries and resulted in the seizure of millions of pounds of drugs and money – have usually been conceived, planned and coordinated by the DEA with the cooperation of other countries. In this case, the USA even managed to influence how the assets seized in the operation were allocated within the countries which participated in the initiative.[26]

The USA does not fund many UNDCP projects and tends to concentrate on law enforcement initiatives and support for the Latin American judiciaries rather than alternative development, to which the UNDCP is strongly committed but with which the USA has become recently disillusioned.[27] The UNDCP's commitment to an approach which the USA no longer believes can be effective partially explains the lack of US funding, although the UNDCP has always been willing to run law enforcement projects. In general, US funding for multilateral drug cooperation is minimal. The USA has tended to set aside for multilateral cooperation only around $5 million from an annual federal drug budget that now amounts to almost $17 billion.[28] The explanation as to why the world's leader in international drug control has a level of funding for organisations including the UNDCP that is roughly equivalent to that of one of the smaller European countries is partly a bureaucratic one: there is no separate budget line for multilateral initiatives, and the

State Department has to scrape away funding for UNDCP projects from budgets that fund US projects. That the State Department has had no separate budget line for multilateral cooperation is eloquent testimony to its place in the US foreign drug policy agenda.

The OAS is a convenient focus for multilateral cooperation in the western hemisphere, but it lacks the authority to act as a coordinator of hemispheric drug control, or as an arbiter of its member states' drug control efforts. The OAS's drug control institution, the Inter-American Commission for Drug Abuse Control (CICAD), has fared even worse from the western hemisphere's indifference to multilateral cooperation than the UNDCP, which also relies on donations from Europe and elsewhere. In the last decade, CICAD has often almost withered away for lack of attention and funding. When CICAD wanted to set up a network of 26 drug information centres in the western hemisphere in the late 1980s, it turned to the European Union (EU) for part of the funding because it could not raise enough interest among its own member states (Joyce, 1997, pp. 112-14). Thus, the Latin American governments have also demonstrated that their own commitment to multilateral cooperation does not extend much beyond rhetoric. It is unlikely therefore that member states could invest the OAS with the authority required to make it an effective motor of hemispheric cooperation on drugs. This level of commitment to multilateral cooperation is an extremely long way from the circumstances that exist in Europe, where EU member states are developing meaningful multilateral law enforcement instruments, and are required to take considerable political and institutional risks in order to do so. ·

Conclusions

The certification case shows that the threat of sanctions can significantly alter US foreign policy by giving added weight to a policy like drugs which, although reasonably important relative to other aspects of external relations with some countries, would otherwise be a far lower priority. Far from being based exclusively on standards of drug cooperation, the outcomes of the process are conditioned by, and often dependent on, other US foreign policy considerations, and on circumstances unrelated to drug control in the countries concerned. Certification can even be just one of a wide range of sanctions available to express disapproval of a country. As such, it is a form of US foreign policy-making that has proliferated in recent years: more than half of the 115 sanctions imposed by the USA since World War I have been initiated in the last four years.[29] However, although the certification case illustrates some of the ways in which the demands of domestic politics influence foreign policy-making, domestic politics do not determine the outcomes, because these demands have to be reconciled with what the more important countries on the list are prepared to accept. The president's decisions on certification are conditioned by what both Congress and countries like Mexico will tolerate.

Despite its embeddedness in a broader US foreign policy process, certification nevertheless has the capacity to influence and sometimes determine the choices and actions of a large number of countries on drug control and, given the relative lack of effective international enforcement mechanisms, the certification process has become a powerful instrument of the international regime on drugs, influencing the way in which countries formulate their own foreign drug policies but also how they consider cooperation on drugs in principle.

Certification has acquired such importance in relations with some countries that it changes not just the formal mechanisms of cooperation but also the environment in which policy is implemented. Although certification has proved an effective means of influencing the formulation of other countries' policies, such influence might in some spheres be bought at the price of effective implementation. This flaw in the process might explain why otherwise committed drug warriors like General McCaffrey have been willing to criticise it. Unlike many other areas of foreign relations, agreeing on the formal cooperative mechanisms of bilateral drug control is only the beginning of a long process of operational cooperation that occurs between non-diplomats in both countries and that depends for its success on complex, informal and often delicately-balanced social and professional relations that are informed by many of the perceptions and prejudices about the policy that are present in society at large. Thus, while diplomats and statesmen must engage in diplomacy as if immune from such responses, judges, police officers and development workers, whose cooperation is essential for the success of bilateral drug control, need not. Perceptions that the process is unfair or that one country is trying to exercise undue influence over another might, in these cases, materially affect the way cooperation occurs. Operational law enforcement cooperation with a number of countries, particularly Mexico, is said to be poor and rapidly deteriorating.[30] The complexity alone of the range of policies that Washington calls on in its attempts to control drugs is evidence that the foundation of effective hemispheric cooperation in this field should probably rely on something more complex and subtle than certification.

The USA might well decide at some point that the process has done its work and should be decently buried beneath a 'higher order cooperative effort', whatever this might be, although it would relinquish this leverage only with the greatest reluctance. The greatest threat to the certification process, however, lies outside the sphere of drug control in the US anti-sanctions lobby. As sanctions proliferate, cutting off sources of income to US business, companies have rallied to the cause of sanctions reform, and the support of influential legislators might make possible a major review of the use of sanctions generally. The drug certification process itself is conditioned to a great degree by non-drug considerations. Similarly, reform of the process, should it occur, will very likely be undertaken for reasons unrelated to the demands of drug control.

Notes

*   Research for this chapter was undertaken at the Government Department of Georgetown University and the Center for International and Strategic Studies at the University of Maryland thanks to an EU-US Senior Scholarship from the

Brussels office of the Fulbright Program. The author would also like to thank Charles King and Peter Reuter for their valuable comments on an earlier version.

1. The term international regime is used here in the sense defined by Krasner as 'explicit or implicit principles, norms, rules and decision-making procedures around which actors' experience converge in a given area of international relations'. Krasner (1983), p. 1.

2. Interview, UNDCP, Bogotá, 17 January 1995.

3. That certification should be a focal point in a calendar of cooperation was intended from the start. An early set of guidelines contains a timetable of certification-related events (the submission of reports, comments meetings and hearings) which takes up the whole year. See Congressional Research Service (1988), p. 11.

4. For a discussion of the bureaucratic politics in US drug policy and how inter-agency rivalry can affect US drug enforcement operations, see Bertram et al. (1996), pp. 102-33. For an argument that US and Bolivian law enforcement officials work together to essentially bureaucratic ends that often conflict with national policies, see Malamud-Goti (1992).

5. For a summary of the original procedures, see Congressional Research Service (1988).

6. The enabling legislation is Section 490 of the Foreign Assistance Act (FAA) of 1961, as amended. The USA withholds half of most foreign assistance to each of the countries that appear on the list of major illicit drug producing and transit countries that the State Department produces every year by 1 November. If countries are fully certified, the assistance is released. If a country is decertified, there is a complete cut-off of sales or financing under the Arms Export Control Act, non-food assistance under Public Law 480, financing by the Export-Import Bank, and most assistance under the FAA with the exception of specified types of humanitarian and counter-narcotics assistance. In addition, the USA must vote against any loans from six multilateral banks to the country concerned. The president also has the discretion during the year to impose trade and other economic sanctions under Section 802 of the Narcotics Control Trade Act. See State Department Website, February 1998.

7. United States, Department of State, Bureau for International Narcotics and Law Enforcement Affairs (1996, p. xii). The reference to the UN Convention did not appear in the early versions of certification.

8. US Department of State, Bureau of International Narcotics Matters and Law Enforcement Affairs, 'Country Certifications, The Certification Process', State Department Website, February 1998.

9. Syria had been completely and consistently decertified every year since 1986, Washington alleging that troops were protecting drug cultivation and trafficking; Lebanon was always granted certification only with a national interest waiver. The drug-related justification for removing them completely from the process – that they had jointly begun a campaign to eradicate opium

poppy cultivation in the Bekaa Valley – was very weak. Although no linkage was officially made between the certification decision and bargaining over Iraq, a security issue of such strategic regional importance is likely to have been one of the few circumstances that might warrant the gesture.

10. A senior House staff member who was involved in the certification process from its inception described the situation: 'Drugs is a messy issue; it is not one that most diplomats like to deal with... There are a lot of competing interests out there ... [drugs] is one that tends to get shunted aside a lot of times by other, maybe bigger or more important, interests.' Remarks of Marian Chambers, Professional Staff Member of the House International Relations Committee and former Staff Director of the Congressional Task Force on International Narcotics Control. See Congressional Research Service (1996), pp. 8-9.

11. Its legislative history is slightly longer. In 1974, the Rodino Amendment to the Foreign Assistance Act required the president to think about drug issues in giving foreign aid. In 1983, the Gilman-Hawkins-Rangel Amendment established that Congress should receive an annual report on drug control in other countries. This report was to become the State Department's annual *International Narcotics Control Strategy Report*, whose publication coincides with the announcement of the president's certification recommendations. The Senate originated the legislation for the certification process, and persuaded a more reluctant House to adopt it.

12. This has been widely attributed to the concentration on interdiction in the Caribbean that the USA had made in the late 1980s and early 1990s. Traffickers switched to Mexico as a safer route. By 1996, the DEA was claiming that as much as 75 per cent of cocaine was shipped to the USA via Mexico.

13. US-Colombian relations were strained even before Samper was elected (see Chapter 8). While his predecessor President Gaviria was still in office, Washington was concerned *inter alia* about the constitutional ban on extradition and about the way that a senior official, Prosecutor-General Gustavo De Grieff, was allowing traffickers to surrender on generous terms. De Grieff was also in favour of legalising cocaine consumption in Colombia, which did not endear him to the US government.

14. There is legal authority for this concern. Section 487 of the Foreign Assistance Act requires the president to take reasonable steps to ensure that assistance is not provided to or through officials or entities that the president has reason to believe have knowingly assisted or colluded with drug traffickers. See Congressional Research Service (1996), p. 2. For the legislation, see Congressional Research Service (1994), p. 20.

15. The observer arranged a meeting between Mexican and State Department officials in an effort to negotiate a compromise between the two parties. He also attempted to convey to the State Department the reasonableness of Mexico's 'all or nothing' attitude. Interview, Washington D.C., 19 February 1997.

16. General McCaffrey and DEA Director Thomas Constantine clashed directly over the certification of Mexico in 1998. The DEA had become dissatisfied with the standard of Mexico's operational commitment to anti-drug law enforcement and hoped that sanctions would improve performance. See *Washington Post*, 27 February 1998, p. A33.

17. Reuters, 5 June 1995.

18. Mexico had had seven Attorney-Generals in eight years (the Attorney-General's Office is responsible for the implementation of drug policy), including one who was sacked in December 1996 after he fired 737 members of the national federal police and announced that it would take at least 15 years to rid the *federales* of endemic drug-related corruption. The federal police were increasingly being replaced by the army in many states because of corruption. In addition to operational problems, political scandals within the most senior reaches of the Partido Revolucionario Institucional (PRI) apparently involving assassinations and vast sums of cash were causing concern.

19. *Washington Post*, 21 March 1997.

20. *The Economist*, 8 March 1997, p. 47.

21. Reuters, 20 November 1997.

22. The plan put forward by Senators Christopher Dodd and John McCain to Congress in July 1997 was defeated, but was nevertheless taken seriously.

23. Reuters, 20 November 1997.

24. The current counternarcotics strategy for the western hemisphere notes that multilateral cooperation 'lowers the US profile and blunts concerns about the threat US-backed antidrug programs pose to the national sovereignty of participating countries'. See US State Department, Bureau of International Narcotics Matters and Law Enforcement Affairs, 'FY Country Programs', State Department Website, July 1998.

25. Interviews, European police officers, 1995.

26. Interview, British police officer, September 1995.

27. In 1997, the USA decided to cut by half its funding for the compensation scheme that encouraged Bolivian farmers to grow crops other than coca, and to reduce aid for alternative development programmes generally. See *Latin American Weekly Report*, 2 September 1997, p. 416.

28. See Joyce (1997), p. 180. Funding for Interpol comes separately from the Department of Justice and amounted to $2.2 million in 1996.

29. *Financial Times*, 21 July 1998, p. 15.

30. For a recent account, see the *Washington Post*, 5 November 1997, p. 1.

CHAPTER 11

LATIN AMERICAN IMMIGRATION TO THE UNITED STATES

Marcelo M. Suárez-Orozco

Large scale immigration from Mexico, Central America and the Caribbean defines the central tendencies of what US scholars of immigration now call 'the new immigration' (Edmonston and Passel, 1994; Hing 1993). In this chapter, first I review some of the recently available data on new patterns of Latin American immigration to the United States. Second, I explore the dominant features of an emerging Interamerican Immigration System (IIS) attempting to demarcate this phenomenon from earlier experiences of immigration in the United States. Third, I offer some preliminary thoughts on a research agenda for the next generation of scholars of immigration.

Data on the new immigration are plentiful – the Immigration and Naturalization Service (INS) generates large data sets on a variety of indicators, so do, *inter alia*, the Bureau of the Census, the Department of Justice, the Department of Labor, and the Department of Commerce. While in general the data on legal immigration are quite robust – though large scale data sets share a number of limitations – the quality of the data deteriorates rapidly as we enter the more murky, but quite substantial, world of illegal or undocumented immigration.

In the early 1990s, as immigration to the United States became increasingly politicised (Suárez-Orozco, 1998), extravagant numbers began to circulate in media, policy and quasi-scholarly circles. The focus of these claims was illegal immigration from Latin America (especially from Mexico and Central America), the Caribbean (especially from Haiti and the Dominican Republic) and Asia (especially from China).

It was claimed that 'millions' of illegal immigrants were entering the USA every year. It was claimed that the total number of illegal immigrants living in the USA was well over 10 million and expanding at a geometric ratio. It was claimed that border controls, especially in the US-Mexico southern sector, had literally collapsed. Most of these claims turn out to be distortions.

After an exhaustive review of the data, the blue-ribbon National Research Council (NRC) panel on the new immigration concluded that an average 200,000 to 400,000 new illegal immigrants enter the USA every year. The panel estimates that the total population of illegal immigrants in the USA today is between 2 and 4 million people (National Research Council, 1997).

In recent years it is estimated that about half of all illegal aliens in the United States enter through the US-Mexico southern sector. Among those who 'enter without inspection', the great majority are Mexicans and Central Americans (Gonzalez Baker et al., 1998). The other half are 'visa over-stayers'. They typically fly into US international airports with proper documents and simply overstay their permits. This is an extremely heterogeneous population. Most US citizens would find it surprising that today Canadians constitute an important group of illegal immigrants in the USA. Other new data suggest that far from having 'fallen', the southern sector of the international border is, indeed, the most heavily guarded sector in the world (Andreas, 1998).

Table 11.1:
Number and Percentage of Foreign-Born Persons, 1980-1994/5 ('000)

Place of Birth	1980		1990		1994/45	
	Number	%	Number	%	Number	%
Central/South America	4,021	28.6	7,407	37.5	10,299	46.2
Mexico	2,108	15.0	4,098	20.7	6,322	28.4
Cuba	588	4.2	698	3.5	768	3.4
Other	1,325	9.4	2,611	13.2	3,209	14.4
Dominican Republic	160	1.1	321	1.6	478	2.1
Central America*	252	1.8	941	4.8	1,312	5.9
Colombia	136	1.0	249	1.3	170	0.8
Other	777	5.5	1,100	5.6	1,249	5.6
Asia/Pacific Islanders	2,540	18.0	4,979	25.2	5,855**	26.3
Other	7,519	53.4	7,381	37.3	6,116	27.5
Total Foreign Born	14,080	100.0	19,767	100.0	22,270	100.0

* *El Salvador, Guatemala, Honduras, Nicaragua and Panama*

** *Asian/Pacific Islanders tabulated from 1996 March Current Population Survey (CPS)*

Sources: 1980 and 1990 Public Use Microdata Samples (PUMS), 1994 and 1995 March CPS

From Gonzalez-Baker et al. 1998.

Latin Americans are now the largest immigrant group in the United States (see Table 11.1). They are highly heterogeneous. Three distinct social formations are the constituent units of what I call in this chapter the new Interamerican Immigration System (IIS): 1) a more or less uninterrupted flow of large scale legal and illegal immigration from Mexico (rapidly intensifying after 1980, see Figure 11.1), structured by powerful economic forces and socio-cultural practices, which seems unaffected by unilateral policy initiatives; 2) more time-limited 'waves' (as opposed to uninterrupted flows) of large-scale immigration from Central America – by the early 1980s replacing Cuba as the largest source of asylum seekers from the Spanish-speaking world; and 3) a Caribbean pattern of intense circular migration typified by the Dominican experience in New York – where they are now the largest immigrant group.

Figure 11.1:
Immigrants Admitted to the United States: 1821-1996

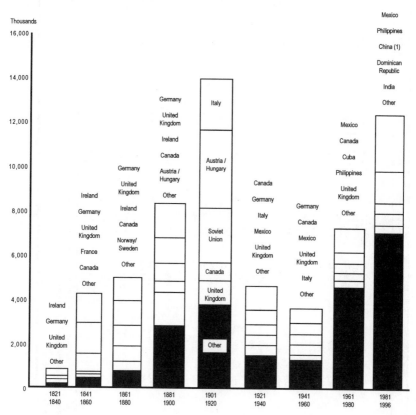

Includes People's Republic of China and Taiwan.
Adapted from Immigration and Naturalization Service, Statistical Yearbook, 1998.

In the case of Mexican immigration, the joint US-Mexico border, the critical mass of Mexican citizens now residing on the US side of 'the line', (generating, *inter alia*, a powerful Spanish-language market and mass media), and their heavy concentration in a handful of states suggest a phenomenon that is quite distinct from other immigration to the United States. The large presence of undocumented Mexican immigrants (it is estimated that nearly 40 per cent of illegal immigrants in the USA today are Mexicans) also separates their case from that of other immigrant groups – though perhaps not from the new arrivals from Central America.

By the early 1980s, the intensification of Cold War tensions in the Central American theatre generated large-scale population displacements. While during the 1960s – and again briefly in 1980[1] – Cubans had dominated the Latin America refugee experience, the 1980s were characterised by large-scale emigration from war-torn areas in El Salvador, Guatemala and Nicaragua. It is believed that during the early 1980s well over a million Central Americans settled in the United States.

Table 11.2:
Immigration to the United States: Fiscal Years 1820-1996

Year	Number	Year	Number	Year	Number	Year	Number	Year	Number	Year	Number
1820-1996	63,140,233										
1820	8,385										
1821-30	143,439	**1851-60**	2,598,214	**1881-90**	5,246,613	**1911-20**	5,735,811	**1941-50**	1,035,039	**1971-80**	4,493,320
1821	9,127	1851	379,466	1881	669,431	1911	878,587	1941	51,776	1971	370,478
1822	6,911	1852	371,603	1882	788,992	1912	838,172	1942	28,781	1972	384,685
1823	6,354	1853	368,645	1883	603,322	1913	1,197,892	1943	23,725	1973	400,063
1824	7,912	1854	427,833	1884	518,592	1914	1,218,480	1944	28,551	1974	394,861
1825	10,199	1855	200,877	1885	395,346	1915	326,700	1945	38,119	1975	386,194
1826	10,837	1856	200,436	1886	334,203	1916	298,826	1946	108,721	1976	398,619
1827	18,875	1857	251,306	1887	490,109	1917	295,403	1947	147,292	1976, TQ	103,676
1828	27,382	1858	123,126	1888	546,889	1918	110,618	1948	170,570	1977	462,315
1829	22,520	1859	121,282	1889	444,427	1919	141,132	1949	188,317	1978	601,442
1830	23,322	1860	153,640	1890	455,302	1920	430,001	1950	249,187	1979	460,348
1831-40	599,125	**1861-70**	2,314,824	**1891-1900**	3,687,564	**1921-30**	4,107,209	**1951-60**	2,515,479	1980	530,639
1831	22,633	1861	91,918	1891	560,319	1921	805,228	1951	205,717	**1981-90**	7,338,062
1832	60,482	1862	91,985	1892	579,663	1922	309,558	1952	265,520	1981	596,600
1833	58,640	1863	176,282	1893	439,730	1923	522,919	1953	170,434	1982	594,131
1834	65,365	1864	193,418	1894	285,631	1924	706,896	1954	208,177	1983	559,763
1835	45,374	1865	248,120	1895	258,536	1925	294,314	1955	237,790	1984	543,903
1836	76,242	1866	318,568	1896	343,267	1926	304,488	1956	321,625	1985	570,009
1837	79,340	1867	315,722	1897	230,832	1927	335,175	1957	326,867	1986	601,708
1838	38,914	1868	138,840	1898	229,299	1928	307,255	1958	253,265	1987	601,516
1839	68,069	1869	352,768	1899	311,715	1929	279,678	1959	260,686	1988	643,025
1840	84,066	1870	387,203	1900	448,572	1930	241,700	1960	265,398	1989	1,090,924
1841-50	1,713,251	**1871-80**	2,812,191	**1901-10**	8,795,386	**1931-40**	528,431	**1961-70**	3,321,677	1990	1,536,483
1841	80,289	1871	321,350	1901	487,918	1931	97,139	1961	271,344	**1991-96**	6,146,213
1842	104,565	1872	404,806	1902	648,743	1932	35,576	1962	283,763	1991	1,827,167
1843	52,496	1873	459,803	1903	857,046	1933	23,068	1963	306,260	1992	973,977
1844	78,615	1874	313,339	1904	812,870	1934	29,470	1964	292,248	1993	904,292
1845	114,371	1875	227,498	1905	1,026,499	1935	34,956	1965	296,697	1994	804,416
1846	154,416	1876	169,986	1906	1,100,735	1936	36,329	1966	323,040	1995	720,461
1847	234,968	1877	141,857	1907	1,285,349	1937	50,244	1967	361,972	1996	915,900
1848	226,527	1878	138,469	1908	782,870	1938	67,895	1968	454,448		
1849	297,024	1879	177,826	1909	751,786	1939	82,998	1969	358,579		
1850	369,980	1880	457,257	1910	1,041,570	1940	70,756	1970	373,326		

Note: From 1820-67, figures represent alien passengers arrived at seaports; from 1868-92 and 1895-97, immigrant aliens arrived; from 1892-94 and 1898-1996, immigrant aliens admitted for permanent residence; from 1892-1903, aliens entering by cabin class were not counted as immigrants. Land arrivals were not completely enumerated until 1908.

Adapted from Immigration and Naturalization Service, Statistical Yearbook, 1998 (Corrected Data).

By one estimate 'one in every six Salvadoreans now lives in the United States' (Mahler, 1997, p. 37).

During the Cold War US asylum policy was often used as an instrument to punish enemies and to reward friends. The vast majority of the asylum seekers from war-torn Central America were never granted formal refugee status by the US government (Suárez-Orozco, 1998). On the other hand, Cubans fleeing Castro, until very recently, were more or less automatically granted formal refugee status. Because large numbers of Salvadoreans and Guatemalans were fleeing US-sponsored regimes, they were quickly labelled 'economic refugees'. In the 1990s, many Central Americans remain in a legal limbo – some of them as illegal aliens, others having temporary protected status against deportation. Family reunification now drives a relatively small – but persistent – flow of Central American immigration to the United States.

The Dominican-Caribbean experience is paradigmatic of what sociologists and anthropologists of immigration now call transnational migratory circuits (see Basch et al., 1995). This pattern of immigration is typified by intensive back and forth movement – not only of people but also of goods and information – principally between the islands of Hispaniola and Manhattan where Dominicans are now the largest immigrant group.

Background

Immigration is the driving force behind a significant transformation of US society. Few other social phenomena are likely to have the same impact on the future character of US culture and society as much as the ongoing wave of 'new immigration'. In 1945, just fifty years ago, the US population was 87 per cent white, 10 per cent black, 2.5 per cent Latino and 0.5 per cent Asian. Fifty years from now, in the year 2050, demographic projections suggest a strikingly different population profile: 52.8 per cent of the population will be white, 13.6 per cent of the population will be black, 24.5 per cent of the population will be Latino and 8.3 per cent of the population will be of Asian ancestry (Bureau of the Census 1996; National Research Council, 1997). These census projections are quite problematic – they assume that ethnic categories (such as 'Hispanic') are enduring and more or less static. Given changing social practices and cultural models of ethnicity, along with the high rate of inter-ethnic marriage in the United States, there is reason to suspect that these categories are quite fluid constructs in constant formation and transformation. It is simply impossible to predict, therefore, who will consider himself or herself 'Hispanic' by the year 2050. It is, however, safe to assume that by then the United States will be a major post-industrial nation with ethnic minorities constituting a substantial portion of the total population.

In the United States immigration is at once history and destiny. It is a dominant theme in the foundational narrative which accounts for how the country came into existence.[2] It is foreordained, therefore, that all subsequent immigration shall be framed by this quasi-sacred narrative.[3] This, then, suggests the broad question that will guide much of the labour of the next generation of immigration researchers: Just how is the current IIS both like and unlike the large-scale immigration of a century ago?   Are today's Mexicans, Dominicans, and Salvadoreans simply replicating the grammar of a narrative already told – albeit with different accents – by Irish, Italians, and Russian immigrants a century ago (see Figure 11.1)? Or are the experiences of today's immigrants an entirely different phenomenon, requiring new categories of understanding and new policy responses?[4]

Since 1965 the United States has formally admitted over 20 million new immigrants. From the year 1990 onward the rate of immigration has intensified to an average of about a million new immigrants per annum (see Table 11.2). Mexicans and Central Americans – along with Caribbeans from Cuba and the Dominican Republic – are the key Latin American players in the 'new immigration'.

By the year 1990, there were more legal immigrants from Mexico *alone* than from all of Europe combined. Today, there are nearly as many 'Latinos' (a construct of the US Census Bureau which includes not only immigrants, but also US-born citizens of Hispanic origin) in the USA as there are citizens in Argentina (about 30 million people). In 1997, there were 7 million Mexican immigrants residing in the United States, constituting roughly a *third* of the total foreign-born population of the country (Gonzalez Baker et al., 1998). More than one quarter of all Mexican immigrants to the United States arrived in the last five years (Binational Study on Migration, 1997, p. ii). Mexican immigrants now constitute 40 per cent of the total Mexican-origin population of the United States.

Talk of 'the new immigration' refers largely to immigration from Latin America, the Caribbean, and Asia.   Latin American immigration now fully dominates the new immigration to the United States. By the 1980s over 47 per cent of all immigrants to the United States were Latin Americans or Caribbeans. In the rapidly growing area of immigration studies, Latin American immigration is where some of the most important basic research and theory is now taking shape.

Three preliminary observations might help us frame the nature of the new IIS. First, a growing body of research suggests that the deep economic and sociocultural changes taking place in the Americas virtually ensure that Latin American Immigration to the United States will be a long-term phenomenon. On the US side of 'the line' there is an enduring demand – indeed, 'addiction' might be a more appropriate term – for immigrant workers (Cornelius, 1998). While it is likely that the extremely high flows of Latin American immigration – especially Mexican and Central American immigration – to the United States during the 1980s and 1990s will eventually decrease (see Binational Study on Migration, 1997), we must assume that Latin American immigration will continue to dominate immigration to the United States over the next decades.

Second, new data suggest that the immigration momentum we are currently witnessing is structured by powerful economic and sociocultural forces not easily contained by unilateral policy initiatives – such as the various border control efforts now taking place. Transnational labour recruiting networks, family reunification, and wage differentials continue to act as powerful contexts for Latin American immigration to the United States.

Third, new data suggest that Latin American immigrants are in the USA to stay. Latin American immigrants today, especially Mexicans and Central Americans, are more likely to settle permanently in the United States than in previous eras of immigration (Suárez-Orozco, 1998). Indeed, until recently, the Mexican experience was dominated by a 'sojourner pattern' of male-initiated, target-earning, circular migration. US policies and the social practices of Mexican immigrants did not favour their long term settlement in the United States (Durand, 1998). This is no longer true. It is too early to predict whether the now cyclical Dominican-Caribbean migratory pattern will remain or whether, over time, Dominicans will join Mexicans in generating a momentum towards increasing embeddedness in the US mainland.

Given these three fundamental features of the new immigration, two basic areas of enquiry will become increasingly relevant in the study of the IIS. First, we need to know more about how this unprecedented pattern of Latin American immigration is changing the US side of 'the line'. In many parts of the country it is now obvious that the demographic momentum generated by Latin American immigration is visibly transforming the texture of the US fabric. Soon the United States will have the second largest number of Spanish-speakers in the world.[5] Ethnic life in the United States will no longer be dominated by 'black' and 'white' headlines. Latin American immigration is palpably changing the public space (see Ainslie, 1998; Gutiérrez, 1998) and social institutions – including schools (Trueba, 1996; Orfield, 1995), places of work (Waldinger, 1997), businesses (Cornelius, 1998) and places of worship (Eck, 1996).[6]

Second, we need to know more about how the immigrants themselves change over time. Immigration is an open-ended process which affects in distinct ways the experiences not only of the immigrants themselves but their children and their children's children. The permanence of Latin American immigrant life on the US side of the border will require that we develop more sophisticated models for understanding the long-term adaptations of immigrants and especially their children.

What is 'New' about the IIS?

In the scholarly literature, new immigrants generally means post-1965 immigrants (Portes and Rumbaut, 1996; Hing, 1993). The vast majority are non-white, non-English-speaking, non-Europeans emigrating from 'developing' countries in Latin America, the Caribbean and Asia (Edmonston and Passel, 1994, p. 41). In recent years, 'family reunification' (see Figure 11.2) and to a lesser extent 'employment-based preference' (Table 11.3) have fuelled the United States immigration momentum.

Immigrants today are a highly diverse population. Public schools in the two largest US cities (New York and Los Angeles) enrol children who speak well over

100 different languages – just thirty years ago, and indeed for most of this century, a smaller number of European languages dominated immigrant schools.

Figure 11.2:
Immigrants Admitted as Immediate Relatives of US Citizens: Fiscal Years 1970-96 ('000)

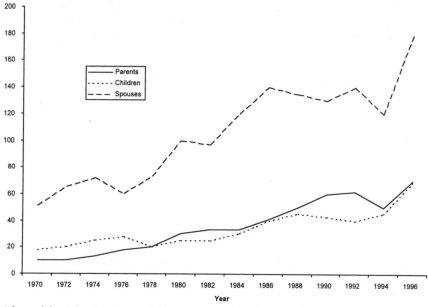

Adapted from Immigration and Naturalization Service, Statistical Yearbook, 1998.

In terms of educational background and skills, immigrants today are a much more complex group than ever before. They are at once among the most educated and skilled and least.educated and skilled people in the United States. Immigrants tend to be over-represented in the category of people with doctorates – or, indeed, winners of the Nobel Prize – just as they are over-represented in the category of people without a high school diploma. Latin American immigrants are an extremely heterogeneous group. While most are low-skilled workers, entering a highly segmented US labour market, many are professionals – over one-seventh of all Mexican immigrants in the USA, for example (Binational Study on Migration, 1977, p. iv). In technical language, immigrants today tend to be much more 'bimodal' in their socio-economic profile than ever before.[7]

In recent years, anthropologists and sociologists have claimed that what is most novel about the 'new immigrants' is that they are actors on a new transnational stage (Levitt, 1997); (Mahler, 1997); (Basch et al., 1995). The ease of mass transportation and new communication technologies seem to conspire to structure the journeys of the new immigrants into US society in ways that are not comparable to the patterns characteristic of the old trans-oceanic immigrants from Europe.

Table 11.3:
Immigrants Admitted by Major Cateogry of Admission,
Fiscal Years 1994-96

Category of Admission	1996	1995	1994	Change, 1995-96 Number	Per cent
All immigrants	915,900	720,461	804,416	195,439	27.1
Family-sponsored immigrants	594,604	458,482	461,725	136,122	29.7
Family-sponsored preferences	294,174	238,122	211,961	56,052	23.5
Unmarried sons/daughters of US citizens	20,909	15,182	13,181	5,727	37.7
Spouses & children of alien residents	182,834	144,535	115,000	38,299	26.5
Married sons/daughters of US citizens	25,452	20,876	22,191	4,576	21.9
Siblings of US citizens	64,979	57,529	61,589	7,450	12.9
Immediate relatives of US citizens	300,430	220,360	249,764	80,070	36.3
Spouses	169,760	123,238	145,247	46,522	37.7
Parents	66,699	48,382	56,370	18,317	37.9
Children	63,971	48,740	48,147	15,231	31.2
Legalisation dependents	184	277	34,074	-93	-33.6
Employment-based preferences	117,499	85,336	123,291	32,163	37.7
Priority workers	27,501	17,339	21,053	10,162	58.6
Professionals with advanced degrees or of exceptional ability	18,462	10,475	14,432	7,987	76.2
Skilled, professional unskilled	62,756	50,245	76,956	12,511	24.9
Chinese Student Protection Act	401	4,213	21,297	-3,812	-90.5
Needed unskilled workers	11,849	7,884	9,390	3,965	50.3
Special immigrants	7,844	6,737	10,406	1,107	16.4
Investors	936	540	444	396	73.3
Diversity programmes	58,790	47,245	41,056	11,545	24.4
Permanent	58,245	40,301	—	17,944	44.55
Transition	545	6,944	41,056	-6,399	92.2
Other categories	144,823	129,121	144,270	15,702	12.2
Amerasians	956	939	2,822	17	1.8
Children born abroad to alien residents	1,660	1,894	1,883	-234	-12.4
Parolees (Soviet & Indochinese)	2,269	3,086	8,253	-817	-26.5
Refugees and asylees	128,565	114,664	13,901	13,901	12.1
Refugee adjustments	118,528	106,827	115,451	11,701	11.0
Asylee adjustments	10,037	7,837	5,983	2,200	28.0
Suspension of Deportation	5,811	3,168	2,220	2,643	83.4
Total, IRCA[a] legalisation	4,635	4,267	6,022	368	8.6
Resident since 1982	3,286	3,124	4,436	162	5.2
Special Agricultural Workers	1,349	1,143	1,586	206	18.0
Other	927	1,103	1,636	-176	-16.0

(a) Immigration Reform and Control Act.

Adapted from Immigration and Naturalization Service, Statistical Yearbook, 1998.

Today, there is much more massive back-and-forth movement of people, goods, information and symbols than ever before.[8] Compared to Mexican or Dominican immigrants today, the Irish immigrants of last century simply could not maintain the level and intensity of contact with the 'old country' that is now possible (see Ainslie, 1998). Furthermore, a number of studies suggest that the ongoing nature of Latin America immigration to the USA constantly 'replenishes' social practices and cultural models that would otherwise tend to ossify (see for example Gutiérrez, 1998). Indeed, in certain areas of the Southwest, Latin American immigration – especially from Mexico – is generating a powerful infrastructure dominated by a growing Spanish-speaking media (radio, TV, and print), new market dynamics[9] and new cultural identities.

Another relevant feature of the new transnational framework is that even as they enmesh themselves in the social, economic and political life in their new lands (see Cornelius, 1998; Durand, 1998), immigrants remain powerful protagonists in the economic, political and cultural spheres back home. Immigrant remittances and investments have become vital to the economies of varied countries of emigration such as El Salvador – where in 1996 remittances were the largest source of foreign exchange at over $1 billion – the Dominican Republic and Mexico. The Binational Study on Immigration estimates that remittances to Mexico were 'equivalent to 57 per cent of the foreign exchange available through direct investment in 1995, and 5 per cent of the total income supplied by exports' (Binational Study on Migration, 1997, p. vii).[10]

Politically, immigrants are emerging as increasingly relevant actors with influence in political processes both 'here' and 'there'. Some observers have noted that the outcome of the 1994 Dominican presidential election was largely determined in New York City – where Dominicans are the largest group of new immigrants (Pessar, 1995). Likewise, Mexican politicians – especially those in the opposition – have recently 'discovered' the political value of the 7 million Mexican immigrants living in the United States. The new Mexican dual nationality initiative – whereby Mexican immigrants who become nationalised US citizens would retain a host of political and other rights in Mexico – is also the product of this emerging transnational framework.

Culturally, immigrants not only significantly reshape the ethos of their new communities, but they are also responsible for significant social transformations 'back home'. Peggy Levitt has argued that Dominican 'social remittances' affect the values, cultural models and social practices of those left behind (Levitt, 1997). Because of a new ease of mass transportation and because of new communication technologies, the IIS is not structured around the 'sharp break' with the country of origin that once characterised the trans-oceanic experience. Immigrants today are more likely to be at once 'here' and 'there' – bridging increasingly unbounded national spaces (Basch et al., 1995) and in the process transform both home and host countries.

Another feature of the IIS is that immigrants today are entering a country which is economically, socially and culturally unlike the country that absorbed – however ambivalently – previous waves of immigrants. Economically, the previous large wave of immigrants arrived on the eve of the great industrial expansion in which immigrant workers and consumers played a key role (Higham, 1955).

Immigrants now are actors in a thoroughly globalised and rapidly changing economy which is increasingly taking an 'hour-glass' shape. High-skilled immigrants are moving into well remunerated knowledge-intensive industries at a previously unprecedented rate (Waldinger and Bozorgmehr, 1996). Meanwhile, low-skilled immigrants, many of them from Latin America, are locking themselves into the low-wage sector in large numbers. Some scholars have argued that unlike the low-skilled industry jobs of yesterday, the kinds of jobs typically available to low-skilled new immigrants today do not offer prospects of upward mobility (Portes, 1996).[11]

Another defining aspect of the IIS is the increasingly segregated concentration of large numbers of immigrants in a handful of states in large urban areas polarised by racial tensions. Some 85 per cent of all Mexican immigrants in the United States reside in three states (California, Texas, and Illinois). A number of distinguished sociologists have argued that as a result of an increasing segmentation of the economy and society, many low-skilled Latin American immigrants 'have become more, not less, likely to live and work in environments that have grown increasingly segregated from whites' (Waldinger and Bozorgmehr, 1996, p. 20).[12]

The Future of Immigration Research

Although immigration has been gathering momentum over the last three decades, only recently has it become a sharply focused policy and research issue. Before the 1990s, immigration as a concern seemed to be limited mostly to ethnic politicians and to powerful business interests – largely in California (and limited, therefore, to Californian politicians) – attentive to the need to maintain a large pool of foreign workers to do the impossible jobs natives do not want to do. Other than that, the general attitude towards immigration was one of 'benign neglect' (Martin, 1994, p. 83). Immigration, as US as apple pie, was simply not a big deal: immigrants came, immigrants assimilated, and in a couple of generations or so they become proud and loyal US citizens.

By the early 1990s all of this began to change. A number of developments contributed to a sudden shift in public attention. The economic recession generated strong anti-immigration sentiment feeding isolationist and nativist impulses in a post-Cold War ethos. During the 1991 presidential primaries, Pat Buchanan – then challenging President George Bush for the Republican nomination – began a nationwide debate when he claimed that the US borders were being overwhelmed by illegal immigrants from Latin America and that 'Zulu immigrants' – surely a code word for the new immigrants of colour – did not fit into US culture as well as Anglo-Saxon Europeans.

Another wave of public debate over immigration began when Zoë Baird, President Clinton's first nominee for the office of Attorney General, removed herself from consideration when it was revealed that she had hired two undocumented migrants from Latin America as domestic workers. A few months later, the participation of illegal immigrants in the terrorist bombing of Manhattan's World Trade Center injected another dosage of anxiety into the public debate. By then, immigration began to dominate the headlines that both reflect and foment public discourse.

In the area of basic research, immigration went from being a low status field of enquiry, mostly generating 'low theory' in a handful of disciplines – prominent among them, labour economics, demography, sociology and cultural anthropology – to a place of high priority in the scientific agenda of many influential national and international agencies. By 1996 the National Research Council had created a blue-ribbon commission of leading scholars to examine the relevant data on the socio-economic and demographic consequences of immigration. In 1997, the Binational Study on Immigration – with funding from the Mexican and US governments as well as the private sector – was working on its binational study of migration between Mexico and the United States. Likewise, the National Science Foundation, the National Institutes of Health, as well as a number of influential private foundations such as the Spencer Foundation, suddenly gave immigration research a high priority.

Why this change? Surely, the numbers involved are impressive: since 1990 the United States has been accepting, on average, nearly 1 million new legal immigrants each year. The economic downturn of the early 1990s, which hurt traditional immigrant destinations such as California and Texas, contributed to a concern about the economic consequences of immigration. Suddenly many began asking: have immigrants become redundant, taking away jobs from native workers and contributing to unemployment? Are immigrants depressing the wages of native workers? And what about the fiscal implications of large-scale immigration? Do immigrants 'pay their way' tax-wise? Or are they simply a load that must be carried by native taxpayers? All of these questions, and many others, found various ways into public debate, political positions and scientific and quasi-scientific research.

In addition to the absolute numbers of new immigrants and the complex economic consequences of immigration, a third fact may help account for the sudden change in attention. Immigration to the United States has over the last three decades been thoroughly dominated by the non-English speaking developing world. Many are anxiously asking how will these non-Europeans adapt to US culture and its public institutions? And, perhaps more importantly, how is the USA going to be changed by them? Because of history, geography, economics and demography, Latin American immigration has become the dominant focus of concern.

The study of Latin American migration to the United States reveals a number of analytically delicious paradoxes. It is an issue that at once unites and divides a deeply asymmetrical continent. While powerful interests in the USA have achieved significant gains by large scale immigration, Latin American migration also generates a great deal of ambivalence in terms of US public opinion and attitudes. While immigration spawns substantial wealth for Latin America – particularly in countries of high emigration to the United States such as Mexico, El Salvador, the Dominican Republic – Latin America loses important human capital as many of its more ambitious and entrepreneurial citizens choose to pursue their fortunes north of 'the line'. Policy initiatives making crossing the border more difficult – in theory to deter the substantial flows of undocumented Mexican immigration to the United States – seem to be slowing down the number of Mexican immigrants *returning home* after trying their fortunes in the USA (for an overview of recent US policies and Mexican immigration, see Bean et al., 1997).

Mexican immigration to the United States is at once paradigmatic of the new immigration – particularly of low-skilled, non-European, non-English speaking people from the South moving in large numbers to the North – and a unique case that must be set apart from all other immigration. Mexicans in the USA are at once immigrants and non-immigrants – the original Mexican-origin population in the USA did not move to the USA but rather the USA moved to them when Mexico lost an enormous portion of its northern territories to the United States.

Newly arrived Mexican immigrants are, in the apt metaphor used by Douglas Massey and colleagues, 'returning to Aztlan'. No other immigrant group shares this unique historical fact with Mexicans – though, of course, Native Americans and African-Americans share with them the fact that their earliest experiences in the USA were as 'involuntary minorities', not as voluntary immigrants (Ogbu, 1997). These groups found themselves in a subordinate position of power *vis-à-vis* a dominant Euro-American majority which not only exploited them economically but disparaged them psychologically and culturally as inferior, violent and lazy.

A version of this symbolic apparatus very much colours how many in the United States view Latin American immigrants. In recent years, it has taken the form of a near-hysterical anti-immigrant sentiment very much focused on the southern border. Such forms of what George De Vos has called 'psychological disparagement' (De Vos, 1992) generate impossible cultural double-binds especially for many Latin American immigrant children who are being asked to 'Americanise' just as they face toxic dosages of emotional and symbolic violence. The anti-immigrant ethos in many parts of the United States is making the psychologically complicated process of Americanisation even more difficult for many Latin American immigrant children. Many Mexican immigrant youth responded to what they saw as an attack by Proposition 187 (the ballot that seeks to deny illegal immigrants an array of social services, including schooling to children) by proudly – some said defiantly – displaying the Mexican flag in street demonstrations in Los Angeles, San Diego, and San Francisco. Some observers noted that the 'Mexican flag' incident generated a backlash and ensured passage of the controversial proposition.

The huge US-Mexican border connects two vastly unequal regions. It is both – the paradoxes are endless – the most porous border in the world and the most heavily guarded. It is a line that at once separates and unites two cultures, two languages, two economies. Another way in which Latin American immigration is a unique phenomenon – unlike all other immigration to United States today – is that both proximity and size matter. There is now a critical mass of Latin American immigrants in the United States generating a demographic and cultural momentum, the effects of which will be felt for decades to come. They tend to settle, in great numbers, in a handful of states – Mexicans in California, Texas, and Illinois; Cubans, Dominicans, and Central Americans in Florida and New York.

The explosive growth of the Spanish-speaking mass media, new communication technologies that instantaneously connect large numbers of Latin American immigrants to their areas of origin, the seasonal back and forth movement between Latin America and the USA among those immigrants who can afford it, the more or less uninterrupted flow of new arrivals – along with changing cultural models and social practices regarding ethnicity – structure the cultural adaptations and identities of Latin American immigrants in unique ways. Some data suggest that Latin American immigrants (especially Mexicans – but I think this is also true of Dominicans and Central Americans) tend to retain their home language more systematically than other immigrants – such as new immigrants from Asia (Portes and Hao, 1997). Rather than following a unilineal path of assimilation towards Americanisation, large numbers of Latin American immigrants and their children are crafting new hybrid cultural identities and styles of adaptation.

The large number of undocumented Latin American immigrants in the United States also distinguishes their experience from that of other immigrant groups. Today there are between 2 and 2.5 million undocumented Mexican immigrants in the United States – the data on the other Latin American groups are less robust. During the 1980s, fully 2 million undocumented Mexican immigrants legalised their status under the Immigration Reform and Control Act (IRCA) of 1986.

The anaemic employer sanctions under IRCA, the continued demand for immigrant labour in various sectors of the US economy (Cornelius, 1998), the enduring North/South wage differential,[13] the powerful transnational social networks linking Latin American towns and cities to the USA (Durand, 1998), the failure of the Latin American liberalisation efforts to generate jobs at reasonable wages (today there are over 15 million working age Mexicans looking for work – see Dussel, 1998) generate a strong momentum towards ongoing unauthorised immigration – a momentum which has not so far been deterred by the massive border control build up at the international sector.

It is another paradox that the new border control initiatives are making it more likely that undocumented Latin American immigrants, who might have returned home, now seem to stay longer in the USA (Gonzalez Baker et al., 1998). Large numbers of poor and low-skilled undocumented immigrants are marginalised and forced to live, in the words of Leo Chavez, 'shadowed lives' with no prospect for integration into the mainstream (Chavez, 1992). Particularly worrisome is the marginalisation of large numbers of immigrant children in the light of recent legislation that would exclude them from publicly funded services (Suárez-Orozco, Roos and Suárez-Orozco, 1998). The long-term consequences of the marginalisation of large numbers of immigrants are likely to be quite negative – in economic, social, and human terms.

The pattern of marginalisation is not only affecting undocumented immigrants. While Latin American immigrants are an extremely heterogeneous group, large numbers of Latin American immigrants are low-skilled workers. These workers are entering a US economy facing profound transformations – including massive losses in the manufacturing sector. It is an economy characterised by growing inequality where large numbers of low-skilled and unskilled redundant workers have little or no prospect for status mobility. This new economic landscape – along with deepening patterns of ethnic and racial segregation – will shape the long-term adaptations of a large number of unskilled and low-skilled Latin American workers.

A critical but understudied and undertheorised aspect of Latin American immigration to the United States is the experience of children. Immigrant children are the fastest growing sector of the US child population. Today 48 per cent of all children enrolled in New York City schools come from immigrant-headed household. In California today there are nearly 1.5 million school age children classified as LEP (Limited English Proficient). Latin American immigrant children are entering US public schools when many large inner city districts are collapsing. Immigrant Latin American children tend to enrol in highly segregated, poor and violent inner city schools. These schools are overpopulated and understaffed. Qualified teachers are needed. Bi-lingual education – eternally controversial in the USA – has faced a head-on challenge in California in 1998 – the state most heavily impacted by Latin American immigration. While many Latin American immigrant children do extraordinarily well in schools, as a group they tend to receive lower grades and lower scores in standardised achievement tests than other immigrant children (Carter and Segura, 1979). They also tend to have higher suspension rates and drop out rates than other immigrant children (Portes, 1996). While most immigrant youngsters who give up on school before graduating will join their relatives in the ethnic economy and service sector, others are sure to gravitate towards a gang culture ready quickly to socialise new arrivals into a lucrative alternative economy – where drug taking and dealing is a growing part of the economic and cultural ethos.

The current research on immigration is quite uneven. During the 1960s there was concentrated research effort on issues of race, poverty, and education, mostly focused on African Americans and poor whites. Since the 1980s, at a time when immigration to US cities was growing, there has been a lack of further progress in basic research on urban issues. We know much about some topics and next to nothing about others. Much of the work on immigration today is superficial and contradictory – such as the work on the fiscal consequences of immigration. In the area of children the research is quite scattered: there is a little on bilingual education, a little on the law, a little on health, a little on students in high school, and a little on the transition to college and the world of work. There is a lack of basic research on a variety of problems. Why do immigrant girls do better than boys in schools? Why do some schools have a better record in educating immigrant children than other schools? Why is it that over time many immigrant children seem to experience a dampening of their optimism and faith in schools as the primary avenue for status mobility?

Another area in need of basic research relates to questions of immigration and citizenship. Latin American immigrants are taking up US citizenship – and registering to vote – in unprecedented numbers. The political implications of this trend over the long term are far from clear. With population growth, will there be a commensurable growth of Latin American participation in US electoral politics? What will the political process be like in regions of the country where Latino-origin US citizens will soon be majorities? Will the growth of the Latino population necessarily equate with increased political power? How will the culturally conservative Latino voters behave in the context of bipartisan US politics?[14] Will there be new forms of transnational alliances involving, for example, recent immigrants from Mexico, more established Mexican-Americans, and Mexicans in Mexico? How will the Mexican dual nationality initiative affect, if at all, the long-term political behaviour of naturalised Mexican immigrants in the USA? With increasing transnationalism has the political appeal of citizenship and nationhood diminished? Is the growth of citizenship applications among Latino immigrants the result of instrumental need in the light of new punitive legislation limiting immigrant access to certain publicly funded services? What, then, of the emotional or expressive appeal of citizenship? Such questions will surely preoccupy the next generation of observers of the Latino political experience in the United States.[15]

Because immigration from Latin America to the United States is likely to be a long-term phenomenon, we need to know more about public attitudes towards immigration. The recent work of Espenshade and Belanger (1998) at Princeton University suggests that in recent years US citizens have experienced a 'growing anxiety over the presence of immigrants in the United States' (for a classic study of US attitudes towards immigration, see Higham, 1955). Indeed, their data reveal that by the year 1990 over 60 per cent of the US public wanted to see immigration decreased. They found that Mexicans – along with other Latin Americans and Caribbeans – rank among the least favoured immigrants in US public opinion. They are perceived by many as less likely to work hard and more likely to use welfare than other immigrants such as Asians or Europeans. While most US citizens – by a 2 to 1 ratio – say that the US government should do more to control immigration, the Princeton researchers note that African-Americans, Asian-Americans, and Hispanic-Americans tend to have more pro-immigrant views than whites.

The Princeton study suggests that the public is very concerned about illegal immigration. However, while the US public thinks immigration is a serious issue – and wants the government to take action, especially against illegal immigration – they rank immigration way below other concerns such as crime, jobs and the economy.

Public anxieties over immigration – especially illegal immigration –have inspired a great deal of new legislative and policy initiatives. These include the new welfare law – barring new immigrants from a host of publicly funded services, the 1997 immigration legislation – requiring that a person sponsoring a family member from abroad demonstrate earnings of 125 per cent of the poverty level ($19,500 a year for a family of four), and a number of border control initiatives to deter illegal immigration. We need longitudinal data to examine the long-term consequences of these policy initiatives.

Immigration will continue to be powerful vector of change in both sides of the border. We need better understanding of how immigration is transforming both sides of 'the line'. If job availability on the US side decreases and Latin American wages improve, the recent historically high flows may decrease but are not likely to cease – family reunification and transnational networks will continue to play a part in immigration. We need a major research agenda to examine the long-term causes and consequences of Latin American immigration to the United States. We need better theoretical understanding of multiple paths taken by Latin American immigrants in their long-term adaptations. In short, we need more interdisciplinary dialogue.

Notes

1. In 1980 over 129,000 *Marielitos* arrived in Florida over the course of a few weeks (see Chapter 14).
2. Arguably all of the defining themes in the US experience, including the landing at Plymouth Rock, the involuntary transport of enslaved Africans and the great industrial expansion of the 20th century, are framed against the background of immigration.
3. The elemental structures of this narrative might include the following 'mythemes' (Lévi-Strauss, 1963, pp. 206-31): 1) poor, but 2) hard working European peasants 3) pulling themselves up by their bootstraps, 4) willingly giving up their counterproductive old-world views, values, and languages – if not their accents! – to 5) become prosperous, proud and loyal US citizens. These mythemes frame the various key issues in today's immigration debate, such as whether immigrants should be allowed access to welfare and social services and whether immigrant children should be given bi-lingual education.
4. In addition to attending to diachronic matters, a good case can be made that scholars of the new immigration have a great deal to learn from the recent experience of immigration in other post-industrial democracies such as France, Germany, and Japan. This, then, suggests a synchronic or comparative programme for research: just how is the new immigration to the United States both like and unlike immigration in other post-industrial democracies? Again, because of the mythico-historical place of immigration in the national imaginary, research on the new immigration continues to be filtered through the powerful lenses of 'American exceptionalism'.
5. Because Latin American immigrants, especially Mexicans, display a pattern of 'linguistic loyalty', retaining their home language after settling in the United States more than other new immigrants such as those from Asia (Estrada, 1997; Portes and Hao, 1997), and because there is now a massive Spanish-speaking media and business infra-structure in many large US cities, we can predict that the Spanish language – as well as new hybrid versions of 'Spanglish' – will continue to thrive in the USA in the next century.
6. There is evidence to suggest that these changes, when combined with economic stagnation – especially unemployment – generate unsettling psycho-cultural anxieties and anti-immigrant sentiment among more established

citizens. For example, public opinion data suggest that the US public today seems most anxious about immigration from Latin America – of which Mexico is the principal source (see Espenshade and Belanguer, 1998). Because Mexican immigration will continue to dominate patterns of immigration to the United States in the near future, it is important to develop a better understanding, and help contain, the nature of this anxiety.

7. Some scholars, such as George Borjas (1994), have suggested that what is new about immigration is that – relative to non-immigrant citizens – large numbers of immigrants today tend to be less educated and less skilled. This argument, unfortunately known as the 'declining quality argument', in essence claims that what is new is that since 1965 the USA has been 'importing poverty'. (For a critique of the 'declining quality' argument, see Myers, 1998).

8. Borrowing the delicious words of Luis Rafael Sánchez, many new immigrants today live neither here nor there but rather in 'la guagua aérea' – the air bus.

9. Since 1990, while the Latino population in the United States grew by more than 30 per cent, its buying power has grown by more than 65 per cent to about $350 billion in 1997. This is changing the way business is conducted in many parts of the country (see Steinhauer, 1997, p. 3).

10. Cornelius (1998), however, argues that over time Mexican immigrants in the United States are less likely to invest in capital improvements in their sending communities. In fact, he argues that a new feature of the Mexican experience in the USA is that as Mexican immigrants become increasingly rooted on the US side of 'the line', they mainly go back to their sending communities for rest and relaxation.

11. A great deal of energy has gone into assessing the economic consequences of immigration. The research findings on the economic consequences of immigration are far from conclusive. Indeed, they are often contradictory – some economists claiming that the new immigrants are a burden to taxpayers and an overall negative influence on the US economy (Huddle, 1995) and others suggesting that they continue to be an important asset (Simon, 1995).

12. Indeed, new data suggest that children of Mexican immigrants today are enrolling in large numbers in poor and racially segregated schools (see Suárez-Orozco, 1998, pp. 276-80).

13. In 1997, real wages in Mexico were 60 per cent of what they were in 1980 – although in some sectors of the economy (such as the automobile industry) real wages have increased.

14. Will the more 'pro-immigrant' Democrats get the lion's share of their votes? Or will the culturally conservative – but more hostile to immigration – Republicans reap the benefits?

15. It can be argued that in some ways the expressive appeal of citizenship has been decoupled from its instrumental aspects. In other words, people are taking on citizenship today almost entirely for instrumental purposes. Is it then the case that the current immigration-related legislation will 'cheapen' the concept of citizenship? (See Suárez-Orozco, 1998, pp. 404-12).

PART IV

CUBA

CHAPTER 12

CUBA'S ECONOMIC TRANSFORMATION AND CONFLICT WITH THE UNITED STATES

Juan Triana Cordovi

In contrast to other interpretations in which relations between Cuba and the United States are described in terms of a post-1959 'dispute', this chapter will refer to the relationship as a conflict. The intention is to establish clearly from the outset that this conflictual relationship is not confined to the post-1959 period, but that it has formed part of Cuban history since the mid-19th century, although it was not until 1959 that the conflict reached crisis point.

In trying to understand and explain the present characteristics of Cuban-US relations it is necessary first to appreciate them in their historical context, and second to bear in mind that it is impossible to isolate their different dimensions, and even more so to separate the economic from the political aspects. I subscribe to the opinion that 'the economic policy – with the economic blockade in the lead – represents a subordinate category of National Security, which plays a predominant role in the conflict between Cuba and the United States'.[1]

This chapter approaches relations between Cuba and the United States from a historical perspective, thus allowing for the conflict to be seen as transcending its present stage. At the same time it demonstrates that the economic measures, deployed by the United States from the very beginning to exercise pressure, have a special significance in this most recent stage. This is why a considerable part of this study is dedicated to explaining relations between the two countries prior to 1959 and as well as to a comprehensive explanation of the development strategy adopted by the Cuban Revolution in the 1960s.

The Relations of Economic Dependency in Historical Perspective

The main characteristic of relations between the two countries prior to 1959 was the high degree of Cuban dependency on the United States in all areas of national life. The origins of this dependency can be traced to United States geo-political aspirations and to the penetration of US capital into the Cuban sugar industry from the last quarter of the 19th century, becoming consolidated in the first quarter of the 20th century, on both the economic and political fronts. On the political front there was the Yankee intervention in the Spanish-Cuban wars of independence, the imposition of a military government of intervention for four years and US involvement in the design of the Cuban government and constitution from 1902, which allowed the USA to impose its plans and policies, including military intervention when deemed appropriate. On the economic front there was the predominance of United States capital in Cuban agriculture, achieved primarily through the purchase of existing sugar-mills (see Table 12.1).

Table 12.1:
US Investment in Cuba (1929-58)
($ million and percentage)

Sector	1929	%	1950	%	1958	%
Agriculture	575	62.6	263	40.0	265	26.5
Petroleum	9	1.0	20	3.0	90	9.0
Mining	-	-	15	2.3	180	18.0
Manufacturing	45	4.9	54	8.2	80	8.0
Public Services	215	23.4	271	41.2	344	34.4
Commerce	15	1.6	13	1.9	7	0.7
Others	60	6.5	13	1.9	7	0.7
Total	919	100.0	657	100.0	1001	100.0

Source: Department of Commerce of the United States, Washington, D.C., 1956. Cited in: López Segrera (1972).

Subsequently the economic dependency would change and acquire new characteristics. A series of trade agreements, under the guise of reciprocity, would contribute to guaranteeing a situation of almost absolute dominance of the US economy over the Cuban economy.[2] By 1958, 68.4 per cent of Cuba's foreign trade was conducted with the United States.[3] Although US investment in the sugar industry slowed down and was redirected towards other sectors, particularly the service sector and some branches of industry, US control over the sugar sector was reinforced by trade agreements which left Cuban sugar production dependent on the interests of the US government.[4] As sugar was the country's main export product, Cuban exports to the United States met almost 40 per cent of that market's demand and represented around 60 per cent of Cuba's total sugar sales. If in addition we consider that the largest sugar mills and a sizeable part of the most productive sugar producing land were owned by US companies, the extent and the nature of US control over Cuban sugar production can be appreciated (Table 12.2).

Table 12.2:
Ownership of Sugar-Mills (1957)

Owners	Number	Production in 250lb bags	%
United States (1)	40	20,938,188	42.45
Cuba	117	27,842,294	56.46
Spain	3	425,861	0.86
France	1	114,660	0.23
Total	161	49,321,003	100.00

(1) There was Cuban participation in several US sugar-mills.
Source: Ministerio de Azúcar (1958), p. 87.

However, Cuba's economic dependency on the United States was not only evident in the commercial sphere. This was merely an expression and confirmation of the more deeply-rooted ties of dependency that were supported by an almost absolute US presence in and predominance over the supply of technology, machinery and components, the control of the supply of fuel and its processing in the country, the production of electricity and of communication systems – sectors which saw preferential US investment from the 1930s.

The above allows us to understand better the nature of Cuban-US relations. In particular it helps to explain the US government's response to the programme of national liberation embarked on by Cuba in 1959 and the important role of economic reprisals as part of the non-military actions planned by the US administration from the very beginning to defeat the nascent Revolution.

Economic Blockade: Response to Development Aspirations

The structuring of the economic blockade against Cuba, rather than a precise exercise, was, and continues to be, an on-going process of measures and counter-measures that have generated a complicated set of legal requirements for the United States. Moreover, depending on the state of relations between the two countries, different moments have seen either heightened tensions or degrees of flexibility.

This process began in the summer of 1960 when, primarily in response to the Agrarian Reform Law, but also in response to other measures of a nationalist and popular nature by the revolutionary government, President Eisenhower decided to suspend technical assistance to Cuba and reduced the Cuban sugar quota by 700,000 tons.[5] This action reduced Cuban sugar exports to the United States to only five per cent of their original volume. The logical conclusion to the escalation of this process was the severing of diplomatic relations, announced by the US government in January 1961. The period from then until 1964 saw both parties engaging in an accelerated process of measures and counter-measures that without doubt contributed to the radicalisation of the Cuban Revolution. It is within this context that we have to consider the decision by the oil companies Texaco, ESSO and Shell to cut off oil supplies and cease their refining activities in Cuba, and the logical Cuban response of expropriating US properties, including the Cuban Electricity Company, the Cuban Telephone Company, ESSO, Texaco, Sinclair, as well as the sugar-mills owned by US companies in Cuba.[6] Thereafter the remaining US properties, including banks, would also be expropriated.[7] The US administration for its part banned all exports to Cuba, with the exception of foodstuffs, medicines and medical supplies.

On 7 February 1962 President Kennedy made the United States blockade against Cuba official in his presidential decree 3447 and on 14 May 1964 the issuing of general export licences for foodstuffs and medicines from the USA to Cuba ceased, leaving these products subject to specific licences. Thus, the USA eliminated any possibility of direct trade and made any activity in this area dependent on precise decisions by the administration.

Proclamation 3447 laid down the Regulations for the Control of Cuban Assets under the jurisdiction of the Office of Foreign Assets Control. These regulations determined the following:

- Severe restrictions on exporting US goods, technology or services to Cuba directly or via another country. This meant that the export of US goods or technical data, as well as of foreign goods produced with US technology, was banned.
- Cuban goods and services could not be imported into the United States, either directly or indirectly, even if they were substantially transformed.
- Only US citizens with close family ties in Cuba were authorised to travel there; government employees were not permitted to do so.
- Transactions involving transportation and shipments were prohibited, except under special circumstances.
- Cuban assets, both government and private, were frozen. Transfers of money to Cuba were no longer authorised, with the exception of the remittance of funds to relatives up to the sum of $300 per household per quarter.[8]

By means of specific licences certain transactions with Cuba were permitted such as payment in respect of:

- Services for passengers travelling to and from Cuba.
- Services afforded to aircraft for overflights or emergency landings.
- Imports of works of art by Cuban painters.
- Transactions related to the reception or transmission of certain communications, such as telephone services.[9]

Within a relatively short period of time Cuba had to confront its isolation from the US economy, being forced to integrate its economy with countries that were not only geographically distant but also had a fundamentally different economic culture. In addition, the country had to face a severe and rapid drain of its most highly qualified human resources.

The US blockade determined the need to restructure Cuban industry completely, to reorientate import and export markets and to create several months worth of storage capacity. It also made it impossible for Cuba to obtain new credits for its development needs. At the same time the blockade necessitated an accelerated process of training human resources, not only to substitute those that had emigrated, but also because of the differences between the new technologies and the ones existing in the country. Thus, the political decision to build socialism in Cuba was reinforced by the need rapidly to expand relations with the Soviet Union (USSR) and the socialist camp on pain of economic collapse.

In this way economic relations between Cuba and the United States practically came to a standstill in the 1960-75 period. From 1975, however, a relaxation of the blockade began, mainly motivated by the US administration's perception of the solidity of the Cuban Revolution, demonstrated not only by its ability to withstand the blockade, but also by the tendency towards rebuilding relations with the capitalist countries of Latin America, Europe and Asia[10] and at the same participating more fully in the Council for Mutual Economic Aid (COMECON) system. In 1975 the US administration modified the Regulations for the Control of Cuban Assets, authorising US subsidiaries in third countries to trade with Cuba, thereby giving rise to what has become known as 'indirect trade'. The basic conditions under which this trade was conducted are the following:

- Transactions are conducted by subsidiaries based in third countries, provided that the subsidiary holds independent legal status.
- Goods exported to Cuba must not be of a strategic nature.
- US technical data cannot be transferred.
- US parts and components cannot be exported to Cuba. Re-export is only authorised when these parts and components do not constitute more than 10 per cent of the final value of the equipment or product.
- Financing in dollars or in dollar accounts is not authorised.
- No individual US citizen can participate in transactions; thus, the subsidiaries should take decisions, consider the risks, and effect negotiations and financing independently.
- Subsidiaries should generally be independent from US companies in their management of transactions authorised by licence.
- The laws and policies of the country where the subsidiary is based should permit trade with Cuba.
- Exports to and imports from Cuba should be authorised.[11]

In the first ten years the performance of this trade was very variable, ranging between $80 million and $206 million.[12] However, the end of the 1980s and the beginning of the 1990s saw a tendency towards steady growth (see Table 12.3).[13]

Table 12.3:
Indirect US Trade with Cuba ($ million), 1988-92

Years	Value
1988	246 million
1989	332 million
1990	705 million
1991	718 million
1992	768 million

Source: Calculated by the author on the basis of interviews with Custom officials.

Along with the increase in absolute value, the relative importance that this trade came to have for Cuba should also be stressed. This was primarily due to the sudden drop in trade with the countries of eastern Europe, but also to the type of product Cuba was buying from these countries, mainly foodstuffs.[14]

The First Transformation of the Cuban Economy

After the triumph of the Revolution, Cuba began a far-reaching process of socio-economic transformation, which essentially changed previous economic relations and which had, and has, as its declared objective the building of socialism. In securing this objective, transformations in the economic sphere have played a particularly important role.

In this regard it is worth remembering that in 1961 the country's development efforts were directed at transforming Cuba into an industrialised country in the short-term,[15] starting with the development of heavy industry, the diversification of agriculture and a policy of increased import substitution. This strategy, which in some ways followed the development model promoted by the Economic Commission for Latin America (ECLA), differed fundamentally from it in the predominant role that it assigned to heavy industry from the beginning of the industrialisation effort. This was in contrast to ECLA's recommendation that it should be the final link in the chain of the industrialisation process.

In the Cuban case factors that were considered conducive to achieving the fundamental objective were: the availability of sufficient foreign reserves from export earnings and increasing foreign aid, the utilisation of idle industrial capacities, the possibility of a significant rise in productivity, an extensive increase in production through the incorporation of the large number of unemployed, as well as the existence of favourable conditions in the agricultural sector.[16]

New conceptual elements were added to the development strategy for the 1962-65 period which had as their main objective '(...) to repair the damages inflicted on our economy by imperialism during over half a century of domination'.[17] In essence, it was a matter of transforming Cuba into an agro-industrial nation within a short period of time. A series of goals were defined for what were considered the key sectors of the economy, that is the agricultural, the industrial and the external trade sectors.

It can basically be asserted that the strategy based on rapid industrialisation, agricultural diversification and import-substitution did not meet its intended objectives. This was due to a wide range of factors. Among them were those of an obviously political nature linked to the very survival of the Revolution – the intensification of the class struggle and the US blockade. Others included the inadequate training of human resources which prevented the adoption of a management structure, the lack of regulations regarding accounting statistics, an inadequate productive structure (high external dependency) and the coexistence of different systems of controlling economic activity (private enterprise in a significant part of the agricultural sector, a system of modified state budgetary control and a system of state budgetary control). These factors gave rise to serious problems for the coherent functioning of the economy as a whole. Thus, by 1964 it became necessary to devise a new strategy for the transformation of the Cuban economy.

The development strategy between 1964 and 1975 was based on agriculture and particularly on sugar production as the pivotal sector of the Cuban economy.

In this respect Fidel Castro argued that:

> Agriculture will be the basis of our economic development, and it will be the basis of our industrial development... With our sugar we have foreign currency, we have the necessary resources for the development of our industry...[18]

The most important element, although not the only one, was without doubt the change in international economic relations. Already in 1963 trade with the socialist bloc amounted to 75.8 per cent of the total, while trade with the USSR amounted to 40 per cent of this total. The signing in January 1964 of an agreement with the USSR for the sale of 24.1 million tons of sugar at 6.11 cents per pound over a period of six years guaranteed sufficient income to finance the development strategy.

The pivotal sector for the country's economic development was thus decided on, as a result of which a strategy was defined that was supported by the theory of 'uneven development' and also by other theories which promoted the 'Big Push'.[19] In other words, this 'Big Push' would be provided by the injection of resources into agriculture and the sugar industry. This would be disproportionate to resources for other sectors (for example light and chemical industry), but would allow – through the income from sugar exports – for the expansion of other sectors (for example metal-mechanics), that would expand the industrial base of the country.

It has to be admitted that uneven development in Cuba was not particularly successful. As José Luis Rodríguez stated: 'In general terms it could be said that the fundamental economic objectives of the development strategy between 1965 and 1970 were only partially achieved.'[20] The strategic relationship between development and political economy played a very important role in this partial achievement of the proposed objectives or goals.[21] It could indeed be asserted that there was a lack of consistency in the strategy planned and the economic policy practised, particularly regarding economic management.

Nevertheless, although the objectives or goals of the strategy were only partially achieved, Cuba made substantial advances, above all if we consider the magnitude of the tasks that faced the country. This is particularly evident with regard to the process of industrial restructuring that Cuba was forced to carry out in order to replace western with socialist technology. This entailed a work force not trained in the use of this technology having to 'learn by doing'. On the other hand, there was the additional factor of the confrontation with the United States on all fronts. Among the advances achieved, the following can be identified:

- An increase in agricultural land under cultivation.
- Mechanisation of the sugar harvest.
- Increased use of fertilisers in agriculture.
- An increase in the range of industrial output of vital importance for the development effort, such as steel, oxygen, pesticides and electrical energy.
- Improvements in education extended practically to the entire population,

raising the average level of schooling.
- A substantial improvement in public health, with declining mortality from infectious diseases and a reduction in the infant mortality rate to almost half of the 1959 level.
- An increase in the short- and long-term benefits in the area of social security.

Consistent with the social objectives of the Revolution, the real significance lay in the extensive coverage achieved by the system, more than in the large amounts of money invested.[22]

The economic difficulties of the 1960s and the favourable option for Cuba in its exchange with the socialist countries determined the entry of Cuba into COMECON in 1972 (it had been an observer since 1964) and the adoption of a model of economic organisation consistent with the one existing in the countries of this integrationist bloc. As a result a series of measures designed to prepare conditions for the subsequent introduction of the Economic Management and Planning System (SDPE – *Sistema de Dirección y Planificación de la Economía*) were adopted between 1970 and 1975. In 1972 a process of labour regulation was initiated and a new system of economic records was drawn up. In 1973 the 13th Congress of the Cuban Confederation of Labour (*CTC – Central de Trabajadores de Cuba*) restored the link between wages and labour inputs, and the commission charged with the task of setting up the SDPE project began its work.

The following year saw the disintegration, and subsequent evaluation, of the economic plan for 1975 and the restructuring of the Central Planning Board (*JUCEPLAN – Junta Central de Planificación*) and the ministries. The SDPE project was approved by the First Congress of the Cuban Communist Party in December 1975. Its implementation began in 1976 with the creation of the National Commission for the Establishment of the SDPE in January, followed by the setting-up of State Committees for Finance and Statistics and the restructuring of the National Bank of Cuba. In 1978 there was a return to the centralised state budget and a series of private enterprise activities were legalised. In April 1980 the Free Farmers Market was created and in September direct contracting of the workforce was introduced. In 1982 Decree-Law # 50 regulating foreign investment was passed. Moreover, the banking system was restructured, prices were revised and a large number of new companies were formed.

The introduction of the system brought about an accelerated growth of the Global Social Product (GSP) at an annual rate of 6.7 per cent (at constant 1981 prices) between 1975 and 1985.[23] However, this accelerated growth owed much to the marked rise in sugar prices and to the financing on favourable terms received from the USSR and in smaller proportion from the market economy countries. Despite this growth, serious problems were emerging: inadequate planning (obsolete methodology and procedures, inattention to financial balances, lack of comprehensiveness and consistency), generalisation of positive incentives, proliferation of bureaucracy, prices not in accord with supply and demand, weaknesses in regulatory practice and above all the incapacity to generate exports.

These met with other exogenous problems, such as an increase in the interest rate on Cuba's growing foreign debt, a fall in sugar prices and the effects of the international economic crisis of the early 1980s on an economy as vulnerable to external shocks as the Cuban one. Already in 1982 the country faced serious problems of liquidity, which forced it to renegotiate its foreign debt payments.

At the Third Congress of the Cuban Communist Party the economic and social priorities for the five-year period 1986-90 were approved. These sought to restore the country's payments capacity, the saving of available resources, the promotion of new exports and the substitution of imports from the market economies. In addition, it was established that the industrial sector should represent between 48 per cent and 50 per cent of GSP, that labour productivity should increase to three per cent annually and that subsidies to loss-making industries should be reduced.

From 1986 the implementation of the Process of Rectification of Errors (PRE) began. This represented a break with the thinking of the beginning of the decade. At the same time it became obvious that in 1986 there were numerous inconsistencies with the objectives for the five-year period 1986-90. This was effectively the beginning of a period of stagnation of economic growth. Exports fell in 1986 by 11 per cent (due to a decline in production of sugar, farming and livestock and mining) and imports fell by 5.5 per cent (see Table 12.4).

Table 12.4:
Cuba's External Trade[a] (1986-90)
(million pesos)

Years	Total Exports[b]	In FCC[c]	Percentage Change[d]	Total Imports[b]	In FCC[c]	Percentage Change[d]
1986	5321.5	879	(11.2)	7596.1	2658	(5.5)
1987	5401.0	968	1.5	7611.5	1790	0.2
1988	5518.3	1346	2.2	7579.8	2152	(0.4)
1989	5399.2	1066	(2.2)	8139.7	1221	7.4
1990	5415.0	1381	0.3	7416.6	3365	(8.9)

(a) *Includes trade conducted with Eastern Europe and the former Soviet Union in transferable roubles and exchanged for Cuban pesos, barter with other countries, and trade conducted in Free Convertible Currency (FCC) exchanged for pesos (P) at a rate of $1 =1P.*

(b) *In 1989 exports were broken down into: 73.2% sugar, 9.2% minerals and concentrates, 1.6% tobacco products, 2.4% fish and fish preparations, 3.9% agricultural and livestock products and 9.7% others. 10.4% of imports were consumer goods, 66.2% intermediate goods and 22.8% capital goods.*

(c) *FCC = Free Convertible Currency.*

(d) *Figures in brackets are negative.*

Sources: Rodríguez (1990) p. 291; Terrero (1994) No. 22, p. 31; Alegría et al. (1992).

In 1987, in spite of the measures taken, the economic crisis continued to consolidate, the impact of the external factors continued to be felt and the key economic indicators pointed to a rather critical situation. The sugarcane harvest of that year fell by 11 per cent compared to 1985, while GDP fell by 1.6 per cent (see Table 12.5).

Three fundamental programmes, which constituted the basis for the economic strategy, were drawn up in 1988. The first was a programme for the food industry designed to stimulate agricultural and livestock production, which had stagnated due to climatic and organisational factors. It was based on plans for large-scale production, the leading role of the state-owned enterprises, a decrease in the importing of foodstuffs, the development of livestock farming and of state marketing of produce. For the sugar sector, harvests of between 10 and 12 million tons of sugarcane were forecast for the beginning of the 1990s.

Table 12.5:
Cuba's Gross Domestic Product (1986-90)
(million pesos)

	1986	1987	1988	1989	1990	1986-90
GDP	18,480	18,177	19,048	19,335	18,735	n/a
Growth Rate (%)[b]	—	(1.6)	4.8	1.5	(3.1)	0.4[a]
GDP per capita (in constant pesos)	1,784	1,753	1,820	1,827	1,753	1,788
Growth rate[b]	—	(1.6)	3.7	0.4	(4.1)	(0.4)[a]

(a)   Corresponds to the period 1987-90.

(b)   Figures in brackets are negative.

Source: Terrero (1994), p. 34.

The second was a programme for the tourist industry aimed at exploiting the country's comparative advantage, reversing the many years of marginalisation of the sector, especially after its 1953-58 boom, addressing the pressing need for hard currency which was no longer being secured *via* the already established traditional sectors nor from non-socialist country financing. From 1987 this sector was given priority, firms with a different management style to the rest of the state sector appeared and a part of the productive and services apparatus was directed towards this activity.

Finally, the third was a programme for the development of biotechnology. This was planned for the longer term, given the special characteristics of this sector and the world monopoly exercised by US companies in this field. Taking advantage of the advances achieved in public health, considerable investments were made in the development of scientific research activities and technology, as well as in necessary and adequate infrastructure.

In the late 1980s the country saw little improvement in its economic situation, yet at the same time external events such as the radicalisation of reforms in eastern Europe and the continuation of the reform process in the former Soviet Union led to a gradual loss of markets. To summarise, Cuba's economic situation in 1990 was extraordinarily complex, with the key macroeconomic indicators for the five year period reflecting stagnation in production.

1990s: The Second Transformation of the Cuban Economy

The collapse of the socialist bloc and the subsequent disintegration of the USSR led the US administration once again to perceive the solution to the 'Cuban problem' in very similar terms to the early 1960s. The US administration began an escalation of actions which had as their main weapon the intensification of the blockade. This renewed policy design towards Cuba was in the initial stages based on the US perception that Cuba would be unable to survive the disappearance of the USSR because of its high dependency on that country.

The deterioration of economic relations with the USSR was effectively the external factor which had most impact on the triggering of the economic crisis (see also Chapter 13). The ties established between the two countries over a period of more than 30 years developed on the basis of considerable support and economic aid from the former USSR to Cuba. In summary, this aid was effected in three fundamental ways:

- Credits to cover the trade deficits.
- Development loans.
- Preferèntial prices.

In terms of bilateral trade, the Soviet market represented 59.9 per cent of Cuban exports and 68.0 per cent of imports in 1989, i.e. 64.5 per cent of all commercial transactions. This also meant that the USSR was absorbing 83.8 per cent[24] of the Cuban trade deficit, which between 1985 and 1990 exceeded $2,000 million.[25] Likewise, Cuban exports to the Soviet Union in 1989 were 85.2 per cent sugar, 5.4 per cent nickel, 2 per cent citrus fruit, 0.3 per cent tobacco and alcohol and 7.1 per cent other products.[26] Imports consisted mainly of oil (48 per cent), but also included machinery and equipment (17.3 per cent), manufactured goods and spare parts (9.8 per cent), foodstuffs (8.1 per cent) and other products (16.8 per cent).[27] The breadth of earlier relations determined that 83 per cent of Cuban foreign trade would be conducted using as a means of payment the convertible rouble, 8.7 per cent using direct barter and 8.3 per cent using free convertible currency (except US dollars).[28]

The US administration's perception of Cuban dependence on the USSR was not unfounded. Even though Cuba's socialist system did not collapse, the impact of the loss of the external sector of its economy was very significant. In macroeconomic terms the magnitude of the imbalances are without doubt closely linked to the loss of or change in the country's traditional external relations. Thus, after five years in which GDP growth stagnated (1986-90), the Cuban economy experienced a systematic decline, manifested by an accumulated fall in GDP of around 36 per cent from 1990 to 1993.

Cuba's economic situation in the second half of the 1980s severely restricted the initial capacity for manoeuvre needed by the economy in order to face the difficult processes that were unfolding from 1990. Among these restricting factors was the exhaustion of a growth model based on the extensive use of natural resources, together with the continuing deterioration of external conditions that had partly supported this growth model. Here we should note the continuing deterioration of relations with the socialist bloc, the fall in prices of the country's basic export products, and the implications of the moratorium on debt interest payments from 1986. These factors, among other effects, provoked a steep rise in the foreign debt in free convertible currency from \$3,621 million in 1985 to \$6,165 million in 1989.[29]

The sudden disappearance of a significant part of the country's external relations from 1990 had a strong influence on the magnitude and the depth of the crisis – in 1989 55 per cent of GSP directly depended on the external exchange of goods[30] – and consequently on the macroeconomic imbalances that characterised the performance of the economy in those years.[31]

At the beginning of the 1990s the conflict between Cuba and the United States intensified in all spheres, particularly through the strengthening of the blockade. The two most widely discussed and well-known policy instruments have been the so-called Cuban Democracy Act (Torricelli Act), passed in 1992, and the Helms-Burton Act signed into law by President Clinton in 1996. Although there are significant differences between the two, both express an essentially interventionist policy by the US government. At the same time they go against the general trend in economic relations between the USA and the rest of Latin America in the 1990s. In fact, between 1990 and 1995 Latin America partially regained its importance for US foreign trade, particularly as the destination for its exports and also for US capital flows. To a certain extent this responds to: 'changes in the economy and in the perceptions that make Latin America once again profitable and functional with regard to the requirements of United States reproduction'.[32]

The Torricelli Act was the initial instrument deployed by the United States to reinforce Cuba's external isolation and to provoke the downfall of Cuban socialism. This law added new sanctions to the already existing ones. These included: a ban on trade with Cuba by US subsidiaries in third countries, banning vessels that entered Cuban ports from loading or unloading in US ports for 180 days; restrictions on consignments to Cuba; pressure from the US president on third countries to restrict their aid to, and trade with, Cuba.[33]

It is difficult to establish the precise cost for Cuba of the Torricelli Act, since a large number of direct and indirect costs derived from its application would have to be added to the loss of a significant volume of Cuba's foreign trade. Nevertheless, the law's main objective was not accomplished, it did not succeed in destroying the Cuban regime. Indeed, by 1994 the Cuban economy showed signs of recovery reaching a 0.7 per cent growth in GDP. This, if not in quantitative terms, was significant qualitatively. Among other things it marked the arrest of the fall in GDP, achieved moreover in extraordinarily complex conditions.

In 1996 President Clinton made relations with Cuba even more complex by signing into law the Cuban Liberty and Solidarity Act, better known as the Helms-Burton Act. Although this is not the central objective of this study, it seems pertinent to point out that this law radically changed the rules of formulating and implementing policy with regard to Cuba.[34]

The law contains four Titles:

Title I. Strengthening of international sanctions against the Castro government.

Title II. Assistance for a free and independent Cuba

Title III. Protection of US nationals' property rights

Title IV. Exclusion of certain foreigners.

Although the entire body of the law is a flagrant attack on international law, as can be well appreciated, the first and second titles are specifically aimed at Cuba and are a palpable expression of US geopolitical and colonialist aspirations towards Cuba.

Some aspects of interest with regard to Title I, whose basic objective is to achieve the destruction of the Cuban Revolution, should be pointed out:

- It attempts to give the conflict between Cuba and the United States an international character, explicitly in the demand that the US government should bring pressure to bear on other governments engaging in transactions with Cuba to adjust their relations to fit in with the aims of the Helms-Burton Law, as well as on the United Nations in order to gain support for the law from this quarter.
- Sanctions on the internal 'violators' of the law are reinforced via the administrative route.
- All previous regulations with regard to the blockade are given legal status.
- The president is obliged to present Congress with a report on Cuba's relations with other countries.
- The authorisation of Congress to assist groups opposed to the Revolution is made explicit.
- The law explicitly authorises government departments to carry out espionage (intelligence) activities against Cuba.

With regard to Title II, which would come into effect once the Cuban Revolution had been overthrown, the following aspects are of interest:

- The US president will be the one to determine when there is a democratic government in Cuba (section 201)
- Only after this presidential decision will steps be taken to lift the 'embargo'.
- It is the Helms-Burton Law that establishes the criteria of what should be considered a democratic government in Cuba.
- Economic relations, and in fact the economy of the country, will be organised by a US-Cuban Council, made up of representatives from the United States and US private enterprise.
- Even after the Revolution has been overthrown, the lifting of the blockade will be preceded by a period of transition (the duration of which is not specified).

- The definition of what is considered a democratic government (section 206) is linked to the ability of said government to demonstrate progress in the return of confiscated properties. It in fact acknowledges the 'satisfactory solution' to the legal claims to be the main precondition for the lifting of the blockade.
- The concept of legal claims is extended to Cubans who have been granted US citizenship after 1959.

Title III, together with Title IV, is one of the most well-known, because of its international implications. It is nevertheless worth pointing out the following:

- United States courts are granted the right to decide in lawsuits brought by US nationals against third parties trafficking in confiscated US properties.
- It legalises a kind of international blackmail by establishing the presidential prerogative of 'waiver'.

As is well known, Title IV completes the international blackmail by establishing the possibility of exclusion from the United States of foreign nationals for 'the crime of trafficking' in US properties. The passing of the Helms-Burton Law was without doubt an indication of the extent to which extreme right-wing Cuban exile factions were able to influence the Clinton administration. It also demonstrated the president's willingness to sacrifice US interests in order to secure his re-election. The negative effects on relations between the USA, Cuba and Latin America of the passing of this law have been pointed out on several occasions and are well known.

In the first place, because by strengthening the blockade and by granting Congress the power of decision-making with regard to the application of this law, possibilities of resolving the conflict were effectively eliminated and, at the same time, it was extended to third countries. Other Latin American countries, with whom Cuba had increased its economic relations in recent times, would therefore be affected.[35]

Thus, Cuban-Latin American relations suffered a further complication, which undoubtedly formed part of the law's objectives of economically strangling Cuba. Yet, at the same time it cast a shadow on the process of restructuring of relations between the United States and the region, even more than in the economic sphere, in terms of Latin American aspirations to independence and sovereignty. Hence the unanimous resistance by the countries of the region to accept such a law and their repeated public objection to it. Moreover, the Latin American countries' reading of this law as setting a strong precedent for future relations with the United States also needs to be taken into consideration.[36]

On the other hand, the restructuring of US-Latin American relations falls within the context of the current globalisation process, which, as is commonly acknowledged, is characterised by tendencies towards liberalisation and elimination of obstacles to economic relations in general. It would, therefore, appear that this law is not compatible with the basis on which the United States was realigning its relations with the region. On the contrary, the law appears to be compatible with 'other tendencies of seeking leadership, hegemony and pressures to ensure a standardisation of conduct and supranational control over politics and economics',[37] values that are implicit in the political culture of the United States. Cuba could be the test case the United States needs to prove its ability to impose its new form of making politics in a globalised world on internal sectors and 'allies' alike.

Although the immediate objective of passing this law was the destruction of Cuban socialism, its scope is far greater and amounts to the modern expression of the long-established geopolitical aspirations of 20th century US political thinking. Thus, in the US perception that the Cuban economy will not be able to withstand such pressure, the strengthening of the blockade represents the most efficient means of bringing about the destruction of Cuban socialism through economic strangulation.

In contrast to what had occurred in previous years, when Cuba could rely on stability and guarantees for its development plans, given its integration into the socialist bloc, the effects of the blockade, increased by the Helms-Burton Law, now have an important influence, not only in terms of the magnitude of the recovery efforts, but also in terms of the means and the time needed to achieve this recovery.

With regard to the magnitude of the efforts it is worth highlighting the cost of the blockade for Cuba (see Table 12.6):

Table 12.6:
Economic Effects on Cuba of the US Blockade

Income Not Received for Exports and Services	million US$
Sugar	5,618.1
Tobacco	252.5
Fishing	35.0
Rayon Products	31.3
Tourism	14,464.9
Aviation	1,237.0
Communications	3,834.0
Total*	**25,472.8**
Losses Due to Geographic Relocation of Trade	
Increase in transport costs	6,162.5
Loss of produce due to storage conditions	5,200.2
Extraordinary expenditure on port installations and warehouses as well as handling and distribution costs	2,896.3
Increase in prices and costs of buying from other markets	525.0
Increase in costs of marketing exports to other markets	270.1
Total	**15,054.1**

Table 12.6: (cont.)
Economic Effects on Cuba of the US Blockade

Reported Effects on Production and Services	million US$
Sugar	279.0
Nickel	190.2
Industrial gases	8.8
Fertilisers	50.6
Rayon	12.1
Electricity	122.0
Rail and road transport	101.2
Fishing	74.4
Petroleum derivatives	16.0
Aviation	34.8
Communications	18.3
Expected fall in equipment	1,600.0
Reconditioning of factories and workshops	257.3
Technological blockade	6,170.0
Total	**8,934.7**
Effects on the Population	
Replacement of electrical appliances	374.0
Services to the population	1,110.9
Total	**1,484.9**
Effects on Sport and Culture	**61.4**
Monetary and Financial Effects	
No access to dollars and impact of exchange rate variations on foreign trade and foreign debt	2,603.8
Frozen accounts in US banks	109.1
Obstacles to securing financing	464.4
Impossibility of renegotiating foreign debt	3,302.7
Total	**6,480.0**
Incitement to Emigration and 'Brain Drain'	**2,070.7**
Total Effects of US Blockade	**59,558.6**

* Only those exports and incomes that could not be relocated to other markets are included.

Source: Instituto Nacional de Investigaciones Económicas, 1996.

These figures demonstrate the effort that will have to be made in order to overcome the intensification of the blockade in the future. However, they only show part of the problem; there are further intangibles that are difficult to quantify. Certainly no other country in the region has had to undertake a far-reaching process of transformation of its economy with the external restrictions that the blockade, and subsequently the Helms-Burton Law, have imposed on the Cuban economy. Nor have any of them had to suffer the disadvantage of being considered an enemy of the United States in their economic negotiations.

However, in 1994, and in spite of the Torricelli Law, the Cuban economy showed the first signs of recovery, with a halt in the fall of GDP and a slight growth of 0.7 per cent, which has been consolidated in subsequent years. This has been the result, among other things, of a process of economic transformation that had as its first priority the survival of the country and thereafter of achieving the macroeconomic balances which would allow the Cuban economy to be adjusted to global tendencies and to the present restrictions (see also Chapter 13).

Bearing in mind the difficulty of the Helms-Burton Law being repealed in the short or even the medium term either by the USA itself or as a result of pressure from the international community, reasoning leads to think that only Cuba's internal capacity, both on the political and the economic front, can guarantee that this law does not achieve its objectives.

One of the most commonly reiterated fallacies by those defending the law and even by the US administration, has been that the Helms-Burton Law, the same as the Torricelli Law in its time, is a factor in promoting internal changes in the Cuban economy. An examination of other countries demonstrates the need for those countries undergoing internal changes to enjoy certain conditions of stability on the domestic political front and in their external relations, as well as sufficient room to manoeuvre economically in order to achieve success. Therefore, in the eyes of many analysts, the US pressures, rather than contributing to an acceleration of the processes of change taking place in Cuba, actually delay them.

The battle against the Helms-Burton Law will be decided in Cuba. If the policy designs for future transformations and their execution are capable of demonstrating that, despite the external limitations, the economy can continue the process of recovery initiated in 1994, then arguments in favour of this law will lose their support.

Conclusions

The conflict between Cuba and the United States is not limited to the years following the triumph of the Revolution, although the conflict reached its critical point in 1959. Without doubt this is one of the most important factors in the socio-political and economic dynamic of Cuba. With regard to this, and especially after the promulgation of the Helms-Burton Law, some of the old clichés that have always formed part of the discussion of the Cuban-US conflict take on new dimensions.

The first is the one that cites the origin of the conflict as the expropriations carried out by Cuba after 1959 and the solution of it through compensations. Certainly in the body of the most recent anti-Cuban law the favoured US solution to this issue becomes the key to the beginning of the lifting of the blockade, but always preceded by the destruction of socialism in Cuba.

Much has been written about the compensation issue, but it is worth remembering some of the most salient aspects. The characteristics of the nationalisations carried out by Cuba were as follows:

- They were not discriminatory, they affected both Cubans and foreigners alike.
- They were for public and not private benefit.
- All provided appropriate compensation to those affected.
- They were applied by means of regulations at a constitutional level, through legal procedures, of forced expropriations for the purpose of public benefit and national interest.

The liabilities owed by Cuba to the United States as compensation run to $1,799 million which, when the $200 million claimed by the US government are included, makes a total of almost $2,000 million. With an annual interest rate of 6 per cent, the total claimed by the United States from Cuba would amount to $5,600 million in 1996.[38] In order to understand the lack of economic rationality of the blockade, rather than comparing this figure to the cost of the blockade to Cuba, it would make more sense to compare it to the cost of lost trade opportunities for US companies (see Table 12.7). This shows that the cost of potential trade by US companies with Cuba, on the basis that these could capture around 60 per cent of Cuban trade, is far in excess of what the US government claims in compensation. The facts, therefore, irresistibly refute the most widely used pretext for upholding the blockade – that is, the question of compensations.

Table 12.7:
Cost of the Blockade on Cuba for US Companies
(in Cuban pesos)

Product	Losses Incurred by US Companies in 1985	Losses Incurred by US Companies over 25 Years
Chemicals	86,450,000	2,264,660,000
Herbicides and pesticides	61,258,850	415,789,000
Grain	100,000,000	2,452,588,000
Rice	37,063,000	562,784,000
Iron and steel	12,000,000	1,625,002,000
Medicines and medical equipment	180,000,000	n/a
Textiles	88,212,000	1,121,236,000
Transport	335,096,000	3,004,994,000

Source: Jones and Rich (1998).

All the above reinforces once more the arguments set out at the beginning of this chapter regarding the nature and roots of the conflict between the United States and Cuba as a process of clear geopolitical aspirations by the USA towards Cuba, in which the Helms-Burton Law is the last weapon in the armoury of non-military aggressions by the United States to eliminate not Cuban socialism, but Cuban national independence.

Notes

1. See Batista Odio (1996).
2. Under the terms of these agreements, Cuba received guarantees for 73 per cent of its sugar exports and granted 81.6 per cent of US industrial and agricultural products duty-free right of entry into the country.
3. 65 per cent of all exports and 74 per cent of all imports respectively were destined for and originated from the United States. See Castro and Fernández (1992).
4. The US Sugar Act of 1948 conferred on the US government the prerogative of setting export quotas from different countries.
5. See Castro and Fernández (1992), p. 3.
6. Resolutions 1, 2 and 3 of Law 851 of the Revolutionary Government.
7. Law 890 of the Revolutionary Government.
8. See Castro and Fernández (1992).
9. See Castro and Fernández (1992).
10. In 1970 Cuban trade with capitalist countries was around $680 million; five years later it had risen to $3,000 million. See Rich (1990).
11. See Castro and Fernández (1992).
12. Office of Foreign Assets Control (1991).
13. These figures have not been officially confirmed.
14. While Cuban exports concentrated mainly on sugar (and for a short period between 1981-84 on naphtha), imports of grains and wheat were very important, reaching 71 per cent of the total in 1990.
15. See Rodríguez (1990).
16. *Ibid.*
17. *Ibid.*, p. 84.
18. Quoted in Rodríguez (1990), p. 16.
19. The theory of uneven development was developed by the Swedish economist Ragnar Nurkse in the mid-1950s and together with Rosenstein-Rodan's theory of the Big Push formed part of the 1950s boom in development theories.
20. Rodríguez (1990), p. 124.
21. See Bekarevich (1982).
22. See Rodríguez (1990) p. 128.
23. Calculations based on the Comité Estatal de Estadística (1988), p. 99. The GSP is not the same as the GDP, which has been calculated officially in Cuba only since 1989 (see Chapter 13). For a comparison of GDP and GSP, see Mesa-Lago (1998).
24. Author's calculations based on Cuban-USSR trade figures.
25. Author's calculations based on Cuban foreign trade figures cited in Rodríguez (1990), p. 291 and in Terrero (1994), p. 31.
26. See Mesa-Lago (1993), p. 138.
27. *Ibid.*
28. Interview with Tania García, Head of International Relations of the National

Bank of Cuba, 12 July 1990.

29. See Rodríguez (1990).

30. See Marquetti Nodarse and Pérez Villanueva (1995).

31. The disintegration of the socialist bloc meant the loss of 67 per cent of exports and 72 per cent of imports, the reduction in the rate of gross fixed capital formation from 25 per cent to 7 per cent of GDP and a decline in consumption by 30 per cent. See CONAS (1995).

32. See Romero Goméz (1997).

33. See *Cuadernos de Nuestra América*, 1992.

34. See Morales (1997).

35. European countries are also affected. See Chapter 3.

36. It should be remembered that in June 1996 the Organisation of American States (OAS) agreed to investigate the Act in order to establish whether it represented a violation of international law. In August of the same year the OAS's Judicial Commission ruled that it did indeed represent a violation.

37. See Morales (1997).

38. See Batista Odio (1996).

CHAPTER 13

THE CUBAN EXTERNAL SECTOR IN THE 1990s

Jorge F. Pérez-López

In the 1990s, Cuba has faced its worst economic crisis of the century. According to official figures, between 1989 and 1993 the island's Gross Domestic Product (GDP) contracted by one-third, exports by 79 per cent and imports by 75 per cent. The budget deficit nearly tripled, as did also monetary balances in the hands of the population. Population consumption levels dropped sharply, with even public services such as education and public health suffering cut backs. During the summer of 1993, probably the time period when the crisis was most acute, electricity shortages and blackouts were commonplace, a large number of plants had shut down or curtailed hours of operation because of shortages of power and raw materials, and the public transportation system had virtually collapsed (Pérez-López, 1997). Very modest positive economic growth during 1994-98 has arrested the economic deterioration experienced over the early 1990s, but has not resulted in a significant improvement in the standard of living of the population.

The events that triggered the island's economic crisis of the 1990s were undoubtedly the shifts in trade and economic relations with the former socialist countries, shifts that began in 1989 as those countries abandoned central planning and began a transition to market economies. In the second half of the 1980s, the former Soviet Union and the socialist countries of eastern Europe purchased 85 per cent of Cuba's exports, provided a like share of the nation's imports, and were the main sources of development financing. The disappearance of socialist regimes in these countries, and their demands that trade relations be conducted using convertible currencies and following normal commercial practices, meant that Cuba lost the very favourable economic treatment to which it had become accustomed and on which the economy depended. Carmelo Mesa-Lago has estimated that the former Soviet Union alone extended economic assistance to Cuba amounting to more than $65 billion during the period 1960-90, with about two-thirds of such assistance provided during the 1980s; approximately 40 per cent of the assistance took the form of repayable loans (e.g. credits to finance trade deficits and development credits) and about 60 per cent was in the form of nonrepayable price subsidies (Mesa-Lago, 1993).

The aim of this chapter is to analyse the performance of Cuba's external sector during the 1990s and policies adopted by the Cuban government to stimulate it. It should be noted at the outset that there is very little official information on the performance of the Cuban economy during this period.[1] The analysis that follows is based primarily on aggregate balance of payments (BOP) statistics for the period 1989-96 (Table 13.1) purportedly originating from the Oficina Nacional de

Estadísticas and the Banco Nacional de Cuba (BNC) contained in a recent report by the Economic Commission for Latin America and the Caribbean (CEPAL, 1997),[2] supplemented with data in reports by the Banco Nacional de Cuba (Banco Nacional, 1995 and 1996) and other sources.

Current Account

The current account records transactions between residents and foreigners such as two-way flows of merchandise and services and transfers. A surplus in the current account generally denotes that a country is gaining net claims on the rest of the world, and may be interpreted as an outgoing foreign investment. Conversely, current account deficits are associated with insufficient domestic savings relative to investment and the net inflow of foreign capital. Neither the level of the current account nor its direction (credit or deficit) are important in and of themselves. Developing countries generally show a tendency to experience current account deficits financed by inflows of foreign savings (in the form of foreign investment and loans). However, persistent and escalating current account deficits may indicate structural problems in the external sector.

   Data in Table 13.1 show that Cuba's current account was in a deficit position throughout the period 1989-96. The deficit was very large during 1989-91, a period when the Soviet Union was still financing the bulk of Cuba's trade deficit and offering other forms of assistance. With the disappearance of special economic relations with the Soviet Union, beginning in 1992 Cuba was forced to limit imports to what it could finance through exports and the current account deficit fell to $242 million in 1994; in 1995-96, the current account deficit was about twice as high as in 1994.

Table 13.1:
Cuban Balance of Payments, 1989-96
(million US dollars)

	1989	1990	1991	1992	1993	1994	1995	1996*
Current account balance	-3001	-2545	-1454	-420	-388	-242	-515	-520
Trade balance	-2615	-2076	-1138	-215	-382	-211	-500	-1082
Exports of goods and services	5993	5940	3563	2522	1992	2197	2687	3380
Goods	5392	5415	2980	1779	1137	1315	1479	1967
Services	601	525	583	743	855	882	1208	1413
Imports of goods and services	8608	8017	4702	2737	2373	2408	3187	4462
Goods	8124	7417	4233	2315	2037	2111	2772	3695
Services	484	600	469	422	336	297	415	767
Current transfers (net)	-48	-13	18	43	255	310	532	1112
Factor services	-338	-456	-334	-248	-262	-340	-547	-550
Capital account balance	4122	2621	1421	419	404	240	435	510
Global balance	1121	76	-33	-1	16	-2	-80	-10

Note: Reported in US dollars, at the official rate of 1 peso=1 US dollar.

* *Estimate*

Source: CEPAL (1997, Table A-15), based on official statistics of the Oficina Nacional de Estadísticas, the Banco Nacional de Cuba and unofficial statistics.

Merchandise Trade

Cuban merchandise exports in 1993 amounted to slightly over $1.1 billion, 79 per cent lower than the $5.4 billion recorded in 1989 (Table 13.2). Over the same period, merchandise imports fell from $8.1 billion to just over $2.0 billion, or by 75 per cent. In 1994, exports recovered slightly, increasing by about 16 per cent to about $1.3 billion, while imports grew by 4 per cent to about $2.1 billion. In 1995 and 1996, exports increased again to nearly $1.5 and $2.0 billion respectively, but imports grew at a much faster rate, rising by 31 per cent in 1995 and 33 per cent in 1996 to nearly $2.8 and $3.7 billion respectively.

Prior to the changes in international economic relations that occurred in the 1990s, Cuba routinely ran a very large merchandise trade deficit, financed mainly by bilateral credits from the Soviet Union. The disappearance of the Soviet Union as a source of trade financing meant that Cuba had to reduce its imports drastically in order to bring them closer to exports. Thus, without financing from the former Soviet Union, the trade deficit fell sharply in 1992, to $536 million, compared to over $2.7 billion in 1989, but grew thereafter to $900 million in 1993, nearly $800 million in 1994, $1.3 billion in 1995 and $1.7 billion in 1996. The 1996 merchandise trade deficit was 222 per cent higher than in 1992.

Table 13.2:
Cuban Foreign Merchandise Trade, 1989-96
(million US dollars)

Year	Exports	Imports	Turnover	Balance
1989	5392	8124	13516	-2732
1990	5415	7417	12832	-2002
1991	2980	4233	7213	1253
1992	1779	2315	4094	-536
1993	1137	2037	3174	-900
1994	1315	2111	3426	-796
1995	1479	2772	4251	-1293
1996*	1967	3695	5662	-1728

Note: Reported in US dollars, at the official rate of 1 peso=1 US dollar.
* Estimate.
Source: Same as for Table 13.1.

Cuba has begun to make structural changes to adjust to the new international trading environment, decentralising some of its foreign trade activities. Prior to the 1990s, foreign trade was a state monopoly, grounded on Article 18 of the Socialist Constitution of 1976. Cuban foreign trade institutions mirrored those of the Soviet Union and eastern European socialist nations: export trade was conducted by specialised enterprises of the Ministry of Foreign Trade (Ministerio de Comercio Exterior), while import trade was primarily the responsibility of the State Committee on Technical-Material Supply (Comité Estatal de Abastecimiento Técnico-Material).[3] Currently, organisations that produce goods and services are also permitted to import and export, with many working on the basis of convertible-currency self-financing schemes.

Disaggregated merchandise trade statistics – either by country of destination/origin or by commodity – are not available from official sources. Using statistics published by partner countries, the US Central Intelligence Agency (1997) has constructed Cuban merchandise trade accounts by country and commodity for the period 1985-96. These estimates are the basis for the discussion that follows.

Merchandise trade by country: Table 13.3 shows Cuba's top ten destinations of merchandise exports and sources of merchandise imports in 1996. Russia topped the list of destinations of Cuban exports and occupied the same position with regard to sources of imports. With the exception of Canada, China and Japan, the remaining six top destinations of Cuban exports in 1996 were western European nations: Netherlands, Spain, France, Italy, the United Kingdom and Germany. As a group, the top ten destinations accounted for 75.4 per cent of Cuba's total exports in 1996; for previous years, this group of 10 countries accounted for between 64 and 73 per cent of exports.

Table 13.3:
Top Ten Destinations of Cuban Merchandise Exports and Sources of Cuban Merchandise Imports, 1996
(million US dollars)

	1991	1992	1993	1994	1995	1996
Top 10 Destinations of Merchandise Exports						
Russia	NA	632	436	301	225	523
Canada	133	212	132	142	234	294
Netherlands	118	131	89	101	172	230
China	202	183	74	121	214	138
Spain	91	85	65	78	96	131
Japan	142	115	51	63	89	67
France	61	44	39	44	57	48
Italy	48	51	33	50	54	38
United Kingdom	32	23	13	16	13	30
Germany	19	21	14	25	31	22
Top 10 as a % of total exports	NA	71.8	71.4	64.2	72.9	75.4
Top 10 Sources of Merchandise Imports						
Spain	285	199	191	289	396	465
Russia	NA	NA	NA	249	237	465
Mexico	107	120	189	271	355	318
Canada	114	100	107	84	200	197
France	63	90	127	133	148	197
Argentina	99	63	72	48	65	125
Italy	163	104	64	63	81	114
China	224	200	177	147	146	101
Germany	123	59	40	41	70	70
Netherlands	36	42	55	50	71	54
Top 10 as a % of total imports	NA	NA	NA	66.9	63.1	65.7

Source: Central Intelligence Agency (1997).

Spain and Russia shipped the same value of merchandise to Cuba in 1996. Rounding up the list of top ten suppliers to Cuba in 1996 were Canada, Mexico and Argentina in the Americas, China, and four western European countries: France, Italy, Germany and Netherlands. The top ten Cuban suppliers in 1996 accounted for 65.7 per cent of imports in that year, 63.1 per cent in 1995 and 66.9 per cent in 1994.

Merchandise trade by commodity: Table 13.4 shows estimates of Cuban exports and imports by broad commodity groups. With regard to merchandise exports, several trends are worth noting:

- First, fuel exports, which were a significant source of exports in the mid-1980s, disappeared altogether by the end of the decade; this is not surprising since these were actually sales by Cuba of Soviet oil in the world market in order to obtain hard currency.[4]
- Second, sugar and associated products remained as the most significant hard currency earner. Even in the 1990s, when Soviet price subsidies no longer existed, sugar and associated products accounted for over 50 per cent of the value of Cuban merchandise exports in every year.[5]
- Third, after slumping in the early 1990s, nickel exports recovered in 1995-96, contributing about one-fifth of total export revenue in those years.
- Fourth, exports of medical products – a proxy for exports of products of the biotechnology industry – performed erratically. Starting from a very low level in the mid-1980s, exports of medical products peaked at $130 million in 1990, fell to $20 million by 1993, recovered in 1994 to $110 million, and fell again in the next two years.
- And fifth, exports of fruits – an indicator of the performance of the food production programme Cuba has been pursuing since the late 1980s – also behaved erratically in the 1990s, failing to reach the levels recorded in the mid-1980s and falling from $100 million in 1990 to about half that amount during 1991-96.

Throughout the 1990s, fuels continued to be the most significant import category, accounting for 33-35 per cent of the total value of merchandise imports. The Cuban leadership slashed imports of machinery, semi-finished goods, raw materials and consumer goods in order to finance imports of fuels and foods: in 1993, imports of machinery amounted to 13 per cent of their level in 1989, raw materials to 15 per cent, consumer goods to 22 per cent and semi-finished goods to 26 per cent. In 1995-96, imports in all four of these categories rose, contributing to the doubling of the increase in the trade deficit that occurred between 1994 and 1996.

Services Trade

Cuba ran a deficit in services trade in 1989-91 (Table 13.1), but recorded surpluses in every year beginning in 1992; during 1993-95, the surpluses were quite sizeable, averaging around $250 million. There is no additional information on specific traded services, but presumably the favourable balance in the services export

Table 13.4:
Composition of Cuban Merchandise Trade, 1985-96
(million US dollars)

	1985	1986	1987	1988	1989	1990	1991	1992	1993	1994	1995	1996
Exports	6531	6439	5402	5518	5392	4910	3565	2085	1325	1465	1625	2015
Sugar, molasses and honey	4873	4698	4020	4124	3959	3690	2670	1300	820	785	855	1095
Fuels	677	326	365	197	221	52	25	0	0	0	0	0
Nickel	323	365	317	440	485	400	260	235	170	190	345	450
Fish	129	149	141	146	127	125	115	120	90	110	115	125
Tobacco	100	94	91	98	85	95	100	95	75	80	90	90
Medical products	11	12	11	8	55	130	50	50	20	110	40	85
Fruit	157	182	163	171	139	150	100	50	50	80	45	50
Other	262	342	556	335	320	268	245	235	100	110	135	120
Imports	8758	9191	7584	7579	8124	6745	3690	2235	1990	2055	2805	3205
Fuels	2871	3038	2600	2569	2598	1950	1240	835	750	750	835	1060
Food	1067	961	794	816	1011	840	720	450	490	430	560	610
Machinery	2023	2183	1752	1780	1922	1790	615	350	235	240	405	510
Semifinished goods	1078	1116	821	816	838	700	425	195	180	220	385	410
Chemical products	447	525	447	434	530	390	270	170	150	180	280	230
Consumer goods	281	325	245	234	277	225	90	50	50	80	130	160
Transport equipment	614	645	601	629	609	590	170	125	80	110	100	120
Raw materials	353	371	302	281	307	240	140	40	35	25	85	90
Other	23	27	22	19	33	20	20	20	20	20	25	15
Trade deficit	2227	2752	2182	2061	2732	1835	125	150	665	590	1180	1190

Source: Central Intelligence Agency (1997 and earlier issues).

account reflects the performance of the international tourism industry. As is discussed below, foreign investment has played an important role in the development of this industry.

Revenue generated by tourism rose by 467 per cent between 1990 and 1996; it first exceeded the $1 billion mark in 1995 and reached nearly $1.4 billion in 1996. Thus, tourism surpassed nickel to become the second largest source of revenue in 1991 and overtook sugar exports in 1994. These figures regarding revenue generated by tourism refer to gross income and include the value of imported goods and services consumed by visitors; the foreign exchange cost of capital investment; payments that leave Cuba in the form of profits, interest payments, royalties, management fees, payments to foreign travel agents and so on; the cost of advertising and promoting travel to Cuba; and the overseas cost of training service personnel (Espino, 1994, pp. 158-9). Unlike other nations, Cuba also reports aviation receipts from its airlines and airport fees as part of gross tourism revenues (Simon, 1995, p. 30). A better measure of tourism's contribution to the BOP would be net receipts, i.e., gross receipts minus the associated hard-currency imports and other expenditures. For the Cuban tourism industry, net receipts are a fraction of gross income: in the range of 30-38 per cent, according to Espino[6] and about 33 per cent according to another expert (Simon, 1995, p. 30). Reports on the performance of the Cuban tourism industry often do not distinguish between gross and net receipts, with Cuban officials tending to report only gross receipts, which are, of course, larger.

Transfers
The Banco Nacional de Cuba reports identify transfers as 'the most dynamic element of the balance of payments, mainly due to the income from donations and remittances' (Banco Nacional, 1995, p. 4) and 'an important source in generating hard currency for the nation' (Banco Nacional, 1996, p. 23). What are these 'transfers'? Where do they originate? What motivates them? What is the Cuban government's policy regarding transfers?

In the BOP methodology, unrequited transfers are defined as 'transactions stemming from the non-commercial considerations, such as family ties or legal obligations, that induce a producer or owner of real resources and financial items to part with them without any return in those same forms' (IMF, 1977, p. 71). That is, they represent flows of resources from one economy to another for which there is no *quid pro quo*. Unrequited transfers could be of an official nature (e.g. foreign grants or aid in kind for which no repayment is required) or of a private nature (e.g. remittances from persons who have migrated to relatives or friends who have remained at home).

According to data in Table 13.1, net transfers were negative in 1989-90, meaning that resources actually flowed out of the Cuban economy in the form of transfers in those two years. They turned positive beginning in 1991, however, and boomed thereafter, rising from $18 million in 1991 to over $1.1 billion in 1996. Transfers were Cuba's most significant source of hard currency in 1996, exceeding gross revenues from sugar or nickel and *net* revenues from tourism. The quadrupling of transfers between 1993 and 1996 reflects in part a shift in government policy to attract remittances from abroad.

Cuban BOP statistics do not distinguish between official and private transfers. According to CEPAL (1997, p. 172), transfers received by Cuba are predominantly private and take the form of cash remittances from residents of the United States to persons in Cuba. CEPAL estimates that private transfers amounted to $600 million in 1995[7] and $800 million in 1996. These estimates are in line with those of Díaz-Briquets (1995), who estimated remittances in the range of $300 to $400 million annually in the early 1990s.

For nearly three decades, the Cuban government had no overt policy on remittances. Although it was well known that the Cuban expatriate community regularly sent monetary and in-kind (i.e., goods) remittances to relatives and friends in the island through different channels, this was not recognised in official statistics or in statements by the leadership. In fact, Article 282 of the Penal Code of 1979 made illegal the export, import, possession or use of foreign currency, or the purchase of goods using foreign currency. Moreover, Cuban citizens who received cash remittances from abroad were required to exchange them into pesos through the Banco Nacional at the very unfavourable official exchange rate (Díaz-Briquets and Pérez-López, 1997, pp. 424-5).

Faced with a dire foreign sector situation, in mid-1993 the Cuban government began to take action to stimulate hard currency remittances to Cuban citizens from family and friends living abroad, mostly in the United States. President Castro for the first time recognised the importance of remittances in July 1993, when he stated: 'We ... had been very strict regarding all this matter of transfer of money, although it was not prohibited and it was carried out in a normal fashion in specific amounts through the banks. This is a source of foreign exchange' (Castro, 1993, p. 6). Specific government actions to spur remittances included:

- In the summer of 1993, Cuba decriminalised the holding and use of hard currency (mostly US dollars) by Cuban citizens.[8]
- Shortly after, the government created special stores at which Cuban citizens holding hard currencies could shop – obtaining items that were not available to Cubans holding pesos – and liberalised travel to the island by relatives and friends of Cuban citizens.
- In December 1994, Cuba announced the creation of a new currency, the 'convertible peso,' that would gradually replace the US dollar and other foreign currencies within the island. The convertible peso, whose value was set at par with the US dollar, could also be used in hard currency stores.
- In September 1995, the Cuban National Bank for the first time began to accept deposits from the population denominated in hard currency, offering to pay interest on such savings.
- In mid-October 1995, foreign currency exchange houses (Casas de Cambio, CADECA) were created at which Cuban citizens could exchange hard currencies in exchange for pesos at rates close to those prevailing in the black market (Rohter, 1995; *El Nuevo Herald*, 28 November 1995, p. 1B).

Cuba is making use of the latest technology to make it easier for individuals to send remittances to family and friends in the island. The official World Wide Web page of the Government of Cuba, www.cubaweb.cu, prominently advertises 'Quick Cash', a service provided by a Canadian firm Careebe Consolidated Management and a Cuban entity American International Service, S.A., whereby remittances can be sent to Cuba by charging the amount on-line to either a VISA or MasterCharge credit card. The service claims delivery within 1 to 5 working days at a banking institution in Cuba; nearly 130 outlets (primarily offices of the Banco Popular de Ahorro) located in all 14 provinces and in the Isla de Juventud can receive the transfers and make them available to recipients. The advertisement states that the transfers comply with all Cuban laws and, to conform with United States laws, must be made in Canadian dollars (although the sender may pay for the transfers in US dollars).

It should be noted that since the 1960s, the United States has regulated remittances by its citizens and residents to Cuba. The Cuban Assets Control Regulations authorised family remittances for the support of close relatives in Cuba not to exceed $300 per quarter. In addition, a one-time remittance to one payee of up to $500 to allow a close relative to emigrate from Cuba was also authorised. In response to the outflow of migrants departing in rafts and small boats (the so-called *balseros*) during the summer of 1994, the United States imposed several punitive measures in August 1994, among them revoking the general authorisation to send family remittances except to facilitate lawful emigration. In February 1996, in the aftermath of the shoot-down by the Cuban government of two aircraft operated by 'Brothers to the Rescue', the United States took the further measure of halting all charter flights between the United States and Cuba, the only form of direct air transportation between the two countries and the preferred way for US citizens and residents to travel to the island carrying remittances (Díaz-Briquets and Pérez-López, 1997, pp. 429-31). On 20 March 1998, the US administration reauthorised family remittances of up to $300 per quarter and resumed licensing direct humanitarian charter flights (US Department of State, 1998). Thus, the four-fold increase in the inflow of remittances into Cuba over the period 1993-96 occurred despite the limits placed by the United States government on remittances ($300 per quarter), and the strengthening of those limitations during 1994-96 that resulted in banning them altogether.

Capital Account

Cuba has released publicly so little information on its capital account that analysis is tantamount to a guessing game. The BOP statistics provided by the Cuban government to CEPAL (Table 13.1) group together all elements of the capital account into a single datum. However, BOP statistics in Cuban National Bank reports (Table 13.5) are somewhat more revealing in this regard since they break the capital account into long- and short-term debt and investment; but they are only available for three years, 1993-95.

Debt

Cuba suspended service on its hard currency debt effective on 1 July 1986. While this action had a favourable impact on the BOP – since outflows associated with debt service payments were eliminated – it seriously impaired Cuba's ability to turn to foreign markets to obtain new credits. As a result, since the mid-1980s, Cuba has had to rely primarily on short-term debt at very high interest rates (CEPAL, 1997, p. 156). According to BOP data in Table 13.5, Cuba had inflows of long-term loans of $64 million in 1993, $254 million in 1994 and $20 million in 1995, while short-term loans were $238 million in 1993, outflows were $555 million in 1994 and loans were $473 million in 1995.

Table 13.5
Cuban Balance of Payments, 1993-5
(million pesos)

	1993	1994	1995*
Current account balance	-371.6	-260.2	-418.2
Exports of goods and services	1990.3	2552.8	2956.8
Exports	1136.6	1381.4	1528.5
Nonfactor services	831.6	1160.4	1418.9
Factor services	22.1	11.0	9.4
Imports of goods and services	2624.8	3283.2	4021.2
Imports	1984.0	2352.8	2865.4
Nonfactor services	354.9	496.6	621.6
Factor services	285.9	433.8	534.2
Current transfers (net)	262.9	470.2	646.2
Capital account balance	356.1	262.4	496.7
Long-term capital (net)	118.4	817.4	24.2
Direct investment	54.0	563.4	4.7
Others	64.4	254.0	19.5
Other capital (net)	237.7	-555.0	472.5
Variation in reserves	15.5	-2.2	-78.5

* Preliminary

Source: Banco Nacional de Cuba (1995, p. 20 and 1996, p. 22).

Table 13.6 shows statistics on Cuban hard currency debt in 1993-95. Outstanding debt grew from $8.8 billion in 1993 to $9.1 billion in 1994 and $10.5 billion in 1995. The fact that the outstanding debt grew annually does not mean that Cuba actually obtained fresh loans: the year-to-year value of this debt is affected by several factors, among them the accumulation of unpaid interest and relative changes in the value of currencies in which the debt was contracted.

In addition to this hard currency debt, Cuba is also liable for debt in 'soft currencies' incurred with the former Soviet Union and the socialist countries of eastern Europe. There are no official Cuban statistics on the value of this debt or its composition. According to Soviet and eastern European sources, Cuba's debt to the Soviet Union on 1 November 1989 amounted to 15.49 billion transferable roubles or 18.1 per cent of total debt, making Cuba the largest debtor country to the Soviet Union. Cuba reportedly also had an outstanding debt of 1 billion roubles with Czechoslovakia (now Czech Republic and Slovakia), Bulgaria and Hungary, and a debt of 2 billion GDR marks with East Germany in 1989 (Mesa-Lago, 1993, pp. 151-2).

Table 13.6:
Cuban Foreign Debt in Convertible Currency, 1993-95
(million US dollars)

	1993	1994	1995
Total debt	8785	9083	10504
Official bilateral	4067	3992	4550
Intergovernmental loans	40	44	47
Credits for development aid	151	164	181
Export credits with government guarantee	3855	3784	4321
Official multilateral	438	503	601
Suppliers	1867	2058	2403
Financial institutions	2406	2501	2919
Bank loans and deposits	2156	2254	2602
Medium and long-term bilateral and consortium loans	1027	1135	1222
Short-term deposits	1130	1119	1380
Credits for current imports	249	248	317
Other credits	27	29	31

Source: Banco Nacional de Cuba (1995, p. 25 and 1996, p. 24).

Mesa-Lago (1993, p. 152) has estimated Cuba's overall debt to the Soviet Union and eastern Europe in 1989 at $27 to $30 billion at the then official rouble-dollar exchange rate.[9] Since the value of the rouble *vis-à-vis* the US dollar has fallen sharply in the 1990s, so has the value of the Cuban debt in US dollar terms. There is no information available on the currency in which the Cuban debt to the former Soviet Union and eastern Europe is to be valued or repaid.

Investment

BOP statistics (Table 13.5) report that direct investment in the island amounted to $54 million in 1993, $564 million in 1994 and under $5 million in 1995. These statistics are significant for at least two reasons: 1) they are the first official statistics on actual investment flows reported by the Cuban government; and 2) they suggest lower investment flows than has been reported by Cuban officials and in Cuban investment promotion literature.

The foreign investment decision is a complex one, with investors having to consider a variety of factors, economic and political. In the case of investment in Cuba, investors face significant economic and political obstacles. Among the economic obstacles are the poor condition of the economy and infrastructure and the lack of institutions to support foreign investment; a positive economic factor might be the above-average quality of human resources in Cuba. The numerous political obstacles include the statist outlook of the Cuban government, the discriminatory treatment accorded foreign investors, and uncertainty associated with the reliability of Cuban government assurances regarding the sanctity of investments, the likelihood of changes in economic policy, the risk of sanctions by the United States and the possibility of expropriation by a future Cuban government (Pérez-López, 1996/97).

Cuba first passed legislation allowing foreign investment in the island in 1982. This initiative generated very little interest among investors until the 1990s, when Cuba began an aggressive campaign to attract foreign capital. In 1992, Cuba's National Assembly passed several amendments to the 1976 Constitution clarifying the concept of private property and providing a legal basis for transferring state property to joint ventures established with foreign partners.[10]

One of the areas in which Cuba has been particularly active in seeking foreign investment has been mining. A new mining law (Ley No. 76, 1995), aimed at facilitating foreign investment in exploration and production of oil and minerals, was passed by the National Assembly in December 1994 and became effective in January 1995. In September 1995, the National Assembly adopted a new foreign investment law that codified the *de facto* rules under which joint ventures had been operating and introduced some innovations to the legal framework for foreign investment (Ley No. 77, 1995). For example, pursuant to the new law, 100 per cent foreign ownership of investments would be permitted, up from the 49 per cent generally allowed by the earlier statute. Similarly, the new law simplified the screening of foreign investment practised by Cuba and explicitly allowed foreign investments in real estate.

Complementing the September 1995 foreign investment law, in June 1996 the Council of State passed legislation creating export processing zones (*zonas francas y parques industriales*) (Decreto-Ley No. 165, 1996). Regulations establishing an official registry of export processing zone operators and investors and issuing special customs regulations applicable to foreign investments locating in the zones were issued in October 1996 (Ministerio para la Inversión Extranjera, 1996, and Aduana General de la República, 1996).

In response to the perception by foreign investors that the financial sector was not sufficiently developed and there were not sufficient financial institutions to support their activities, in the 1990s Cuba has taken a number of steps to allow more choice.[11] In 1994, Cuba granted a licence to ING Bank of Holland to operate in the island, the first foreign bank to be so permitted since 1960. In 1995, similar licences were issued to the Société Générale de France and to Banco Sabadell from Spain. Other foreign banks have also been allowed to establish representative offices in Cuba.

In order to expand the number of financial services available to foreign investors and semi-autonomous enterprises, the BNC created the New Banking Group (Grupo Nueva Banca, S.A., GNB), a holding company for a network of new financial institutions which include an International Bank of Commerce (Banco Internacional de Comercio, S.A., BICSA), the export-import bank National Financier (Financiera Nacional, S.A., FINSA), the already-mentioned CADECA foreign exchange houses and an Investment Bank (Banco de Inversiones, S.A.).

Long-expected legislation to reform the basis of the banking system was finally passed by the Council of State in May 1997. Decree-Law 172 established the Cuban Central Bank (Banco Central de Cuba, BCC) as an autonomous and independent entity and assigned to it the traditional central banking functions. The Banco Nacional de Cuba, which had performed central and commercial banking functions since 1960, remained in existence, but its role was relegated to commercial banking. Decree-Law 173, passed at the same time, set out the legal framework for registration and operation of commercial banks and financial institutions under the supervision of the BCC.[12]

Cuban officials have justified the secrecy with which they treat investment data on the basic of concerns about possible action by the United States government against prospective or actual investors. The rationale behind the policy of 'minimum reporting', as articulated by Vice-President Carlos Lage, is 'the pressure to which everyone who comes to invest in Cuba is subjected by the United States'. [13] While this may be so, it is also possible that the lack of transparency in reporting foreign investment information may be a deliberate effort by Cuban officials to influence the investment climate by giving the impression that larger investments have occurred, or are under negotiation, than is actually the case.

Flows of foreign investment reported by Cuban officials appear too optimistic in the light of other information and the BOP data mentioned above. For example, in October 1991, Julio García Oliveras, chairman of the Cuban Chamber of Commerce, had been cited as stating that negotiations were ongoing with investors representing investments of $1.2 billion (Business International Corporation, 1992, p. 24). Vice-President Carlos Lage stated in November 1994 that by the end of 1994, joint ventures would have provided Cuba with $1.5 billion in investments. [14] By the end of 1995, according to official sources, foreign investment had reached more than $2.1 billion.[15] There are reasons to believe that the estimates of foreign investment provided by official sources overstate actual equity capital flows into the island: (1) multi-year disbursements may be involved; (2) some investments may be contingent on performance; (3) some 'investments' may represent assets rather than fresh investments; (4) some of the investments may be management

Table 13.7:
Foreign Investment in Cuba, December 1997
(million US dollars)

Country	Announced	Committed / Delivered	Committed / Delivered as a % of Announced
Australia	500.0	0.0	0.0
Austria	0.5	0.1	20.0
Brazil	150.0	20.0	13.3
Canada	1341.0	150.0	11.2
Chile	69.0	30.0	43.5
China	10.0	5.0	50.0
Dominican Republic	5.0	1.0	20.0
France	15.0	10.0	66.7
Germany	10.0	2.0	20.0
Greece	2.0	0.5	25.0
Honduras	7.0	1.0	14.3
Israel	22.0	7.0	31.8
Italy	397.0	387.0	97.5
Jamaica	2.0	1.0	50.0
Japan	2.0	0.5	25.0
Mexico	1806.0	450.0	24.9
Netherlands	300.0	40.0	13.3
Panama	2.0	0.5	25.0
Russia	25.0	2.0	8.0
South Africa	400.0	5.0	1.3
Spain	350.0	80.0	22.9
Sweden	10.0	1.0	10.0
United Kingdom	75.0	50.0	66.7
Uruguay	0.5	0.3	60.0
Venezuela	50.0	3.0	6.0
Total	5551.0	1246.9	22.5

Note: The above figures 'represent amounts of announced, committed, and delivered investments since 1990 by private sector companies and government-controlled companies from various countries to enterprises within the Republic of Cuba as of December 1997. Information, which may or may not be in the public domain, compiled through the media, other public sources, individual discussions with company representatives, non-Republic of Cuba government officials, and Republic of Cuba-based enterprise managers and government officials.'

Source: US-Cuba Trade and Economic Council, www.cubatrade.org.

Table 13.8:
Foreign Joint Ventures in Cuba, by Country of Origin, 1988-95

	1988	1990	1991	1992	1993	1994	1995	Total
Spain	1		3	9	10	14	10	47
Mexico		2		3	3	4	1	13
Canada				2	8	16		26
Italy				1	5	4	7	17
France		1		3	5	2	2	13
Netherlands				1	2	3	3	9
Tax havens		1	3	10	5	12		31
Rest of Latin America			2	3	11	9	4	29
Rest of the World			1	1	11	10	4	27
Total	1	2	11	33	60	74	31	212

Source: CONAS (1995), p. 18.

contracts, production partnership agreements (particularly in mining and oil exploration) or debt-equity swaps, where funds invested are minimal; and (5) others may actually be supplier contracts rather than equity investments (Pérez-López, 1995, and 1996/97; Werlau, 1996 and 1997). At best, the figures reported by Cuban government officials might represent *intentions* of foreign investors, but they significantly overstate – by a factor of three or even higher – actual capital that has flowed into the island.

The US-Cuba Trade and Economic Council (USTEC), an organisation with collaborative relations with agencies of the Cuban government,[16] has compiled statistics on foreign investment in Cuba from a variety of sources, including discussions with individual company representatives and government officials in Cuba and abroad. The latest such compilation (Table 13.7), covering the period from 1990 through December 1997, lends credence to the cleavage between investment intentions and realisations: thus, according to USTEC, while investments amounting to nearly $5.6 billion had been 'announced', the volume 'committed/delivered' was a more modest $1.2 billion, or 22.5 per cent of the announced amount.

Table 13.8 shows the number of foreign joint ventures established in Cuba in each of the years 1988-95. Only one joint venture was established in 1988 and two in 1990. Foreign investment activity picked up in 1992-94, with 33 joint ventures established in 1992, 60 in 1993 and 74 in 1994; it slowed in 1995, when only 31 joint ventures were created.

In all, Cuban government statistics indicate that 212 joint ventures with foreign investors had been established through the end of 1995; Spanish investors were responsible for the largest number of joint ventures (47 or 22 per cent) followed by Canada (26 or 12 per cent), Italy (17 or 8 per cent) and France and Mexico (13 or 6 per cent each). The largest concentration of joint ventures was in the industrial sector (56 or 26 per cent), followed by tourism (34 or 16 per cent), mining (28 or 13 per cent) and the oil sector (25 or 12 per cent).

In the aftermath of the tragic 24 February 1996 incident, in which Cuban military planes shot down two civilian planes piloted by Cuban-Americans, the United States adopted the Cuban Liberty and Solidarity Act (the so-called Helms-Burton Act). Title III of the Act gives US citizens who hold valid claims a right of action in US courts against those who knowingly 'traffic' in their confiscated properties. Title IV allows the exclusion of traffickers and their immediate families from the United States. Under the terms of the Helms-Burton Act, the US State Department reportedly issued letters in late 1996 warning companies that they were suspected of trafficking in confiscated property.[17]

Canada, Mexico and the European Union (see Chapter 3) have vigorously protested the enactment of Helms-Burton, claiming that it impinges on their sovereignty and the Act's extraterritorial reach is inconsistent with international obligations of the World Trade Organisation (WTO) and the North American Free Trade Agreement (NAFTA). Cuban official reaction to the legislation has been mixed:

- Vice-Minister of Tourism Eduardo Rodríguez de la Vega told a visiting group of Catalonian tourism writers and journalists in late June 1996 that 'surprisingly, the Helms-Burton law benefits the marketing and ranking of Cuban tourism because it stirs interest in the island in places where it was not known before'.[18]

- At about the same time, Minister of Foreign Investment and Economic Cooperation Ferradaz described the reaction of foreign investors to the enactment of Helms-Burton as follows: 'The 230 investors from 50 countries present in Cuba knew beforehand what could happen. I do not doubt that some partners will be frightened off and will delay their plans. Some have announced this even though we have not yet received official notification. We do not reproach the victims of an unjust law but rather those who have promulgated this law. The vast majority of companies have opted to stay and are seeking, with us and their countries of origin, legal formulas to defend themselves and thus reduce the risk.'[19]

- On the other hand, Vice-President Lage told journalists in Havana in July 1996 that the Helms-Burton Law had 'negative effects' on the Cuban economy: 'The effects [of the Helms-Burton Law] are negative not because of the practical application of the law itself, but because of its objective of intimidation and the concerns that it raises with a significant number of entrepreneurs' (Alfonso, 1996).

- At its December 1996 session, Cuba's Asamblea Nacional approved an 'antidote' to Helms-Burton, which declares the US legislation 'null, invalid and without merit', gives Cuban citizens the right to claim compensation from the United States for damages incurred as a result of US actions (including the embargo and military actions conducted from US territory) and proclaims measures to protect foreign companies investing or trading with Cuba, including maintaining such operations in secret (Tamayo, 1997).

According to Minister of Foreign Investment and Economic Cooperation Ferradaz, by the end of 1996 260 joint ventures with foreign capital had been established in the island – an increase of 48 joint ventures or 23 per cent over the 212 at the end of 1995 – in 34 sectors of the economy. Slightly over 50 per cent of all investments originated from member countries of the European Union. During the first half of 1997, according to Minister Ferradaz, more joint venture deals were consummated than during a like period in 1996 and 140 new projects were under active consideration. Minister Ferradaz also stated that the impact of the Helms-Burton legislation on foreign investment in Cuba was 'difficult to estimate', noting that some foreign investors had 'become fearful [of Helms-Burton] and called off their projects'.[20]

Conclusions

The economic crisis that has enveloped Cuba during the 1990s has affected every aspect of Cuban society. The standard of living of the Cuban population has dropped significantly and even their access to public services has been curtailed. The bottom of the crisis seems to have been reached in 1994. The modest growth recorded since then has made a very small contribution to the average Cuban's standard of living, but has stabilised the domestic political situation.

The economic crisis of the 1990s was most clearly manifested in the external sector. Faced with a sudden loss of financing and aid from the Soviet Union and the socialist countries, Cuba was forced to adjust import levels to relate them to what could be financed through exports. This meant drastic, across-the-board cutbacks in imports, sharp reductions in economic activity, unemployed workers, and an inability to provide basic services (such as transportation) to the population. The initial response from the Cuban leadership was 'special period' austerity. Economic reforms implemented during the summer of 1993 and subsequently have been quite successful at macro stabilisation, but less so at promoting economic growth. This is not surprising since the Cuban government has been reluctant to make meaningful changes (for example, by undertaking enterprise reform, privatisation, creation of factor markets) for fear of losing political control. Some of the policy initiatives taken in the 1990s have had a salutary effect on the external sector, particularly those that have stimulated tourism, foreign investment and remittances from abroad.

Structurally, the Cuban external sector accounts in the 1990s differ significantly from the 1980s. Exports of services (tourism) and remittances play a much more significant role than in earlier periods. The absence of economic assistance from the Soviet Union and the arrears in the hard currency debt mean that foreign investment has become one of the keys to Cuba's effort to attract resources from abroad. Cuba has very little access to foreign loans, and those that are available are short term and carry extremely high interest rates. In this context, it is puzzling that Cuba has not made renegotiation of its hard currency debt a higher priority. In fact, Cuban Central Bank President Francisco Soberón told journalists in October 1997 that, although Cuba is maintaining a dialogue with creditors, it 'does not feel pressured' to enter into a multilateral agreement that would potentially restore its access to international capital markets (*El Nuevo Herald*, 26 October 1997). Very little is known about Cuba's debt with the former Soviet Union – taken over by Russia – and eastern European countries and what arrangements, if any, are being made to determine its current dollar value and terms of repayment.

After falling below the $1 billion per annum level in 1992-94, merchandise trade deficits began to rise again in 1995-96 as Cuba increased imports – particularly of raw materials, semi-manufactured products and machinery, which had been severely cut back in earlier years and virtually shut down significant portions of the industrial sector – in the expectation that exports would also rise. Meanwhile, sluggish agricultural production has forced higher levels of food imports and the disappointing performance of the sugar sector has thwarted the expected recovery of exports.

Economic growth in 1997 was 2.5 per cent, about half of the 5 per cent rate of growth predicted at the beginning of the year. The 1998 growth rate is estimated to have been equally disappointing, following a very poor sugar harvest of 3.2 million tons. In this scenario, the external sector is likely to perform as it has in the most recent two or three years, providing foreign exchange to allow the economy to continue to operate at very low levels of capacity and efficiency.

Notes

1. The most recent comprehensive statistical yearbook that has been published is for 1989 (Comité Estatal, 1991). For a review of Cuba's external sector during the 1970s and 1980s see Pérez-López (1990).
2. Although the BOP statistics in Table 13.1 are given in terms of US dollars, the conversion from pesos has been made at the official rate of 1 peso=1 US dollar; therefore, the figures refer equally to pesos or US dollars. See CEPAL (1997, pp. 624-5 and Table A1).
3. The State Committee on Technical-Material Supply was abolished in April 1994 as part of a reorganisation of central government administration.
4. On the oil reexports issue, see Pérez-López (1987).
5. For a detailed discussion of Cuban-Soviet sugar trade and Soviet sugar price subsidies, see Pérez-López (1991).
6. Espino (1994, p. 159), based on studies conducted by the Ministry of Tourism.
7. BOP statistics (Table 13.1) show net transfers of $532 million in 1995; this means that sizeable outgoing transfers must have occurred in this year to offset the estimated $600 million in private transfers.
8. Decreto-Ley No. 140 (1993) and 'Informa Banco Nacional de Cuba sobre uso de las monedas libremente convertibles', *Trabajadores*, 15 August 1993.
9. His calculations used two alternative exchange rates: 1 rouble=1.58 US dollars and 1 rouble=1.78 US dollars.
10. On changes to the 1982 foreign investment law in the area of property rights, see Pérez-López (1984), pp. 193-4.
11. On the Cuban financial sector, see Companys (1997).
12. 'Central Bank of Cuba established', *Granma International Electronic Edition*, no. 25 (1997).
13. 'Carlos Lage comments on Economy', Havana Tele Rebelde and Cuba Vision (7 November 1992), as reproduced in FBIS-LAT-92-219 (12 November 1992).
14. 'Carlos Lage Addresses Conference 21 November', Havana Tele Rebelde Network (23 November 1994), as reproduced in FBIS-LAT-94-229-S (29 November 1994).
15. 'Support for Economic Changes', Havana Radio Havana Cuba (12 July 1995), as reproduced in FBIS-LAT-95-137 (18 July 1995).
16. The objective of USTEC, an organisation created in the United States in 1994, is to 'provide an efficient and sustainable educational structure in which the United States business community may access accurate, consistent and timely information and analysis on matters and issues of interest regarding United States-Republic of Cuba commercial, economic, and political relations'. See

more information at www.cubatrade.org.

17. Marquis (1997). The companies include Canada's Sherritt, Israel's Group BM and a Panamanian company selling automobiles in Cuba. Mexico's Grupo Domos and CEMEX reportedly withdrew from Cuba before being formally warned.
18. 'Helms-Burton Law Said to Benefit Tourist Trade', Havana Prensa Latina (24 June 1996), as reproduced in FBIS-LAT-96-126 (18 June 1996), p. 4.
19. 'Foreign Investment Minister on Helms-Burton Law', *El País* (Madrid), 15 June 1996, as reproduced in FBIS-LAT-96-119 (19 June 1996).
20. 'Hay empresas de 40 países en la isla, dice Ministro', *El Nuevo Herald* (17 October 1997).

CHAPTER 14

THE POLITICS OF THE CUBAN DIASPORA IN THE UNITED STATES*

Maxine Molyneux

'The exile's grief for the Cuba that had been lost was an all but inescapable part of the ambient noise of Cuban Miami. For all its glittering appurtenances, its prosperity, and, at times, its self-satisfaction, there was a level on which no pleasure, no level of attainment, nor any material accumulation could make up for what had been taken away from these exiles by the triumph of Fidel Castro.'

(Rieff, 1994, p. 64).

Political theorists from Madison to Dahl have long warned of the risks to democratic government represented by factions, the dangers of bias in the formulation of policy, and the risk to the national interest if such bias distorts policy. The concerns of these theorists were primarily with domestic policy, but they apply equally to international relations: they draw attention to the extent to which domestic lobbies, constituencies and pressure groups succeed in gaining a decisive influence on the development of foreign policy. The Cuban exiles would seem to be a *prima facie* case of a lobby group successfully influencing US foreign policy. They distorted policy after 1959, and in the post-Cold War era US policy towards Cuba has become both anachronistic and inconsistent.[1]

The purpose of this chapter, based on research in Miami and on an extensive secondary literature, is to look not at Cuban-US relations in general, or at overall prospects for political change inside Cuba, but at the exile community and its place in the context of those issues. It will examine five aspects of the Cuban-American community: its origins and composition; its orientation to US politics; its attitudes to the Cuban government; indications of change in attitude in the 1990s; and the current thinking of some of the main exile groupings with regard to the longer term future of the island.

The Cuban Diaspora

Few diasporas in the world have had a history as contentious, and a political role as significant, as that of the Cuban-Americans in the USA. For close on forty years this community has been to all appearances committed to the overthrow of the

Cuban government, and has used its influence, directly on the island, and indirectly via political leverage in Washington, to pursue that end. The most dramatic episodes in this relationship were undoubtedly in the first three years after the Revolution. In a context of successive acts of sabotage carried out with varying degrees of US assistance, this period saw the failed invasion at the Bay of Pigs in April 1961, and, even more dramatically, the Cuba missile crisis of October 1962. As recently released research on that crisis has shown, it was the fear of another invasion by exiles, this time more effectively backed by the USA, which, as much as any considerations of the nuclear arms race, led to the deployment of Soviet missiles on Cuba in the summer of 1962. Without exaggeration, therefore, it could be said that the conflict between the Cuban government and its exiles has been one of the most acute in US-Latin American relations in this century and was the central factor in the crisis that, more than any other in the Cold War, brought the world to the edge of destruction.

Events thereafter were not so dramatic, but the passage of time did not lead to any significant diminution of exile hostility to the island. Acts of sabotage by Cuban exiles, through such groups as Alpha 66 and Omega 7, continued through the 1960s. In October 1976 a Cuban aeroplane was blown up near Barbados. In 1979 pressure from Cuban exiles was a factor in the Soviet-US dispute over a Soviet 'combat brigade' in Cuba, one of the harbingers of the deterioration in relations between Moscow and Washington at that time. In 1996 Cuba, faced with new pressures from exiles, shot down two planes of the exile group Brothers to the Rescue which it claimed entered its territorial space, thus ensuring the passage in Congress of the Cuban Liberty and Democratic Solidarity Act, otherwise known as the Helms-Burton Law. If these crises have helped to place Cuba in conflict with the USA, they have also made it a factor in the broader course of world politics. In the Cold War Cuba was a major irritation in US-Soviet, Latin American and African relations and it has now, through the provisions of the Helms-Burton Law, become one in relations between Washington and its European and other trading partners (see Chapter 3). Cuba and the exile community are therefore an enduring factor in US-Latin American relations. Equally they may, directly and also via the impact on Washington, be a factor in the future of Cuba itself.

There are therefore few cases of relations between homeland and diaspora that are more antagonistic and complex than that of Cuba with its exiles. For almost forty years there has existed a mutual and intransigent hostility from representatives of the two sides, which has been ferocious in its denunciatory rhetoric. Contrasts with other ethnic communities from former revolutionary states are striking: neither the Chinese in Taiwan nor the exiled Vietnamese have been so enduringly irreconcilable to their communist regimes, and both, after decades of hostility, have shown themselves willing to take a leading role as investors in the homeland. More analogous to the Cuban exiles would be those from eastern European countries – what in the Cold War were termed 'captive nations' – who played a role in ensuring hard line policies *vis-à-vis* their countries of origin. There are parallels too with the Protestants of Northern Ireland, the Jewish diaspora in the USA and the Afrikaaners in South Africa, in their role as veto groups, blocking policy initiatives aimed at ending political deadlock.

The collapse of the Soviet bloc and the end of the Cold War might have been expected to inaugurate a new chapter in the relations between Cuba and its diaspora, one more amenable to dialogue if not reconciliation. However, in the first few years there was little change, and in 1992 there occurred a marked deterioration in relations with the passage of the Cuba Democracy Act (or Torricelli Law), to be followed by the Helms-Burton Law of 1996, both energetically promoted by the Cuban-American lobby.

The Cuban-American Community: Formation and Integration

The more than one million people in the USA of Cuban origin make up around 5 per cent of the total Hispanic population.[2] Most of these (750,999) were born in Cuba, and most (65 per cent) are residents of Florida, principally located in the Miami metropolitan area (Dade County), which, on account of its proximity to the island, has been a recipient of Cuban migrants since the 19th century.[3] The Cuban diaspora is more geographically concentrated than that of other Latin American countries, and became more so in the decades following the Revolution.[4] The percentage of those of Cuban origin in the USA who lived in the metropolitan area of Miami comprised 23.6 per cent of the total in 1960, 38.8 per cent in 1970, 50.5 per cent in 1980 and 54 per cent in 1990. In 1959 some 20,000 Cubans were resident in Miami; over the next twenty years they were joined by a further half a million. In 1990 there were approximately 517,000 Cubans living in Miami.[5]

As with most exile communities Cuban Americans are divided along class and generational lines, divisions which are to some extent reflected in the successive waves of migration from Cuba since 1959. Each of these brought different sorts of migrants to the USA, such that it is possible to identify four broad categories among the more recent immigrant population.[6] The 'historic' and largest first wave came in the years following the Revolution: between 1959-62, 215,000 migrants arrived; between 1962-65 a further 74,000 Cubans left the island for the USA.[7] As a result of an agreement between Castro and the USA, between 1965 and 1973 the first airlift programmes (the 'Freedom Flights') began, marking a peak in the number of Cuban departures. More than 340,000 migrants, around a third of the total influx, arrived in the USA in this period. Castro's ending of the flights in 1973 reduced the flow to a trickle; only some 13 per cent of the total arrived during the 1970s, and about 20 per cent during the 1980s.

The first wave of *émigrés* differed from subsequent arrivals in that it contained a sizeable proportion of professionals and business people, as well as the military and administrative personnel associated with the previous regime. Its overall educational level was relatively high and surpassed the median for most immigrant communities. It was from this first wave that the strongest opposition to the revolutionary regime came, but it also contained many less hostile elements, including a handful of writers and musicians who left after the hardening of cultural policy in Cuba in the 1960s. As the most privileged of the generations of exiles both in terms of wealth and as beneficiaries of the US government's generous assimilationist policies, it was able to create in Miami a material prosperity that it contrasted unfavourably with conditions on the island.

The second wave of *émigrés* was that of 1980 when 129,000 Cubans left in the crisis of Mariel, 125,000 of them entering the USA. These Cubans were poorer and some were darker than their predecessors (an estimated 40 per cent, or 50,000, were blacks or mulattos)[8] and some were sent as 'undesirables' by the Cuban government, including a proportion of mentally disabled and some 26,000 with criminal records.[9] Fears were voiced in the established exile community that 'Mariel destroyed the image of Cubans in the USA', and that the cohesiveness of the exile community was itself threatened. One high ranking official explained: 'Tensions got worse in Miami after Mariel. Even within the Cuban community we did not see eye to eye. When the whole thing started, I was proud to see how we (Cubans) all worked together – the support among families and neighbours; but when we realised what Castro had done, what he had sent us, it all fell apart' (Croucher, 1997, p. 57). At the same time a latent racism surfaced in community attitudes. One Cuban American city official stated that 'The Marielitos are mostly black and mulattos of a colour that I never saw or believed existed in Cuba. They don't have social networks, they roam the streets desperate to return to Cuba. There will be 200 more plane kidnappings (i.e. hijackings)' (Portes and Stepick, 1993, p. 21).

This change in the composition of the migrants coincided with a shift in US attitudes to Cuban immigration: the so-called *marielitos* were less welcome arrivals than their predecessors, and President Carter (1977-81) passed a Refugee Act which eliminated preferential treatment of people from communist states including Cuba. The Act also placed an unprecedented ceiling of 1,000 on the number of refugees admitted from Cuba. The positive, even heroic, image of the Cuban exile dimmed as Dade County grappled with the problems of absorbing the new arrivals. Governor Clinton of Arkansas had his first encounter with the less acceptable side of the Cuban diaspora when a group of them rioted outside an army fort in his state. It is at this time that, in a general reaction against the influx of Spanish speakers, an 'English Only' movement started in the USA; one of the first towns it organised successfully in was Miami. Without the generous re-settlement programmes of the first phase, the *marielitos* assimilated less rapidly and were soon blamed for rising crime rates in Miami, increasing social tensions and deteriorating race relations. Immigration in general was seen by the early 1980s as a major factor in the McDuffie riots, which erupted only weeks after the Mariel Cubans arrived, representing the accumulated frustrations of black residents in the city.[10] Yet in time this wave of migrants proved to be similar in its occupational profile to its predecessors, and the majority were absorbed without much difficulty into Cuban exile society.[11]

The next wave of immigrants came a decade and a half later during the third post-Castro emigration crisis: it consisted of around 33,000 *balseros* or rafters, who left Cuba after 1990, when the country was plunged into economic crisis following the collapse of its former allies in the Soviet Union and eastern Europe (see Chapter 12). Given the arduous conditions associated with the crossing of the Miami straits, 86 per cent of the rafters were young people, less than 40 years of age, and only 20 per cent were women.[12] The first wave of *balseros* left in 1991, a year in which the US Coast Guards picked up 2,203 Cuban rafters attempting to cross the Florida straights, but the majority (around 31,500) left in a large scale exodus between 7

August and 14 September 1994, causing a major crisis in US-Cuban relations. In order to head off a situation of uncontrolled out-migration from Cuba, Clinton signed the US-Cuban Agreement of 9 September 1994 which agreed to admit 21,700 *balseros* who were being held at Guantánamo, the US naval base in Cuba. However, the *balsero* crisis showed that the USA was unwilling to accept Cuban migrants as refugees; future rafters would be returned as illegal aliens.

Finally, there are the recently arrived legal migrants. From 1965 to 1973 Cubans were able to leave in an airlift, the annual average running at 44,000. Later this was regularised with successful applicants able to leave in accordance with quotas agreed to first by President Carter and then by President Reagan (1981-89). In the 1980s the Cuban lobby was able to gain approval for the immigration to the USA of Cubans who had succeeded in reaching third countries. The numbers of legal entrants were greatly expanded at the height of the *balsero* crisis: in the US-Cuban Agreement President Clinton signed up to an annual minimum of 20,000 legal exiles (excluding immediate kin of US citizens), which has been observed in the last few years. In 1995, 17,937 Cubans were admitted, and in 1996, 26,466. Given that the scheme was organised through a visa lottery system (instituted by the US Interests Section in Havana), this migrant population was socially and regionally diverse, but the majority was drawn from Havana. It is often said that their reasons for leaving, if not solely economic, were to a considerable extent influenced by the difficulties of life on the island. More immigrants than refugees, these *émigrés* include skilled workers and professionals: as one beneficiary of the scheme, a doctor who had arrived in Miami in 1996, said: 'the Revolution gave me the opportunity to become a doctor, but could not give me the means to make a decent life for my family'. The thwarting of professional aspirations and the desire to use their skills to forge a better life abroad does not make these people a natural constituency for the militant anti-communism of the extremists. Cuba certainly claims these as economic rather than political refugees, and as with the *balseros* there is a degree of official sympathy for their fate, in sharp contrast to the rhetoric directed at the *gusanos* ('worms'), a term generally applied to first generation exiles.

The Miami exiles are therefore not as socially homogeneous as they might appear. Different waves of immigration have influenced the socio-demographic character of the community, which is highly stratified by differences of class, gender, colour and generation. Moreover, despite its economic successes, the diaspora contains a significant number of poorer Cubans.[13] While these comprise some of the more recent, less assimilated arrivals, there are also those among the earlier generations of migrants who remain on the edges of the Cuban-American success story. These factors are relevant, as we shall see, to the orientation of the community towards Cuba itself.

Cuban-Americans and US Politics
The Cuban diaspora in Miami has certain distinctive characteristics which help to explain both its remarkable success as a political lobby group and its hard-line politics. First, as noted above, there is the fact of spatial concentration: not only do the majority of Cuban-Americans live in Gran Miami, but so too do the majority of

all Cuban-born citizens of the USA i.e. those who maintain the sharpest memories of what they left behind and, if they left early enough, are likely to bear the greatest grievances at having been forced into involuntary exile. This concentration of exiles in Miami, as well as the close proximity of the island they departed from, have been determining factors in the shaping of the Cuban-American diaspora, giving it an unusually high degree of cohesion, and a concentration of political weight, greater than that of most other diasporic communities.[14]

Cuban-Americans are also on average more assimilated, and more economically successful,[15] than most other immigrant groups.[16] No other large non-English speaking exile community in the USA exhibited such rapid upward mobility, a trajectory which caused them to be known as 'the Golden Exiles'. They also contrast with other Latinos in being more right-wing – more Cuban-Americans vote Republican than other Latinos and even those who do not tend to support a hard-line policy on Cuba.[17] They are characterised by a relatively high degree of communal solidarity and interdependency, an effect not only of a shared experience of exile, but of the dynamic character of the ethnic enclave economy they helped to create in Miami (Portes and Stepick, 1993).

Cuban-Americans are an exemplary case of 'long distance citizenship' (Anderson, 1992): this means that although exile communities may be citizens of their host country they maintain a strong identification with their homeland and consider that they have the right to intervene in its affairs. In the case of the Cuban-Americans the character of that intervention has been associated historically with the goal of ending the Castro regime, one in which it received substantial support from a succession of US governments. The means of attaining the goal included support for a violent overthrow culminating in the failed 1961 invasion, and numerous attempts at destabilisation. Since the 1980s, however, other more indirect means have been pursued, although the goal remains one of ridding the island of the Castro regime. The form of that activity has been given in large measure by the US context: in contrast to most other exile communities, there was little sign in Miami by the 1980s of the political parties and leaders that had been active in Cuba prior to 1959 and which lost out in 1959, or earlier, under President Batista.

Thus, despite a relatively high degree of assimilation and identification with the USA, the Cuban-American community retained both an undiminished sense of its *Cubanidad* and abiding interest in the politics of the island. This was even at the expense of local, more immediate needs. It is a joke among Cuban-Americans themselves that Florida is the only state with its own foreign policy, one that has imposed a heavy cost on local administration and public services. Following its introduction by Alex Penelas in 1992, both Florida and Dade County adopted their own versions of the Cuban Democracy Act, forbidding the state and county from doing business with firms that deal with Cuba. A supporter of the resolution, Fernando Rojas, of the largest exile organisation, the Cuban American National Foundation, in supporting this move said: 'There is no reason why Dade County's taxpayers, many of whom are victims of Castro's tyranny, should benefit companies that insist on trading with Castro and providing him with the resources to violate the human rights of the Cuban people.'[18]

If the Cuban diaspora has a distinctive political character, this is in part a product of its historic relationship with the USA. The Cuban exile community warmly embraced the USA as the enemy of the enemy, and it was in turn treated as a privileged immigrant group, one which had suffered at the hands of a communist dictatorship. For Cubans the USA was the first destination of political asylum and their status as refugees entitled them to certain kinds of federal support, but also lent a potent human dimension to the Cold War, the victims of which now resided within the very borders of the USA. In one dramatic and emotional chapter, the Eisenhower and Kennedy administrations organised a Cuban Children's Program under which over 14,000 Cuban children were sent by their parents to the USA.

The assimilation programme set up in the 1960s for the first generation of exiles was explicitly designed to create a solid base for US anti-Cuban propaganda and policies. In this it largely succeeded. The *comunidad*'s leitmotif was an abiding and militant anti-communism channelled through an unrelenting hatred of Castro. Cuban exiles were used by various administrations as spokespersons for the authentic anti-Castro resistance, and in the 1960s it was from the exiles that the troops of the counter-revolution were drawn, men who fought in the Bay of Pigs invasion and participated in the various initiatives directed at the overthrow of the Cuban government. Given the community's *raison d'être*, it is hardly surprising that when Cuban exiles have entered political office they have more often than not done so as the advocates of hard-line policies on Cuba, positioning themselves as representatives of a community forced into exile and impatient for redress.[19]

Cuban-Americans have been strikingly successful in gaining political influence. In 1972 the first Cuban exile was appointed to the Miami City Commission. By 1988 'Hispanics', the majority of whom were Cuban,[20] constituted 24 per cent of all registered voters in Dade County and the 'Hispanic bloc' has proved effective in Congressional elections. In the 1990s they have elected two Republican congressmen for Florida – Ileana Ros-Lehtinen (with 98 per cent of the Hispanic vote), Lincoln Diaz-Balart, and a third, Robert Menendez, from New Jersey. Cuban-born, but US-educated, Alex Penelas was elected in 1996 to the post of executive mayor of Dade County, one of the most important positions in the state.[21] Cuban-Americans have also secured positions of influence within the local government structures of Miami, and in the state legislature.

What this has meant is, in effect, a solid constituency that directly, through its elected representatives, and indirectly, through its influence in Washington, has been able to lobby for a continued hard-line US policy towards Cuba. Thus, Cuban-Americans mobilised in support of the establishment of Radio and TV Martí, the Torricelli Law of 1992, which tightened the embargo, and the Helms-Burton Law of 1996. In 1993, when newly-elected President Clinton sought to appoint a more conciliatory Cuban-American, Mario Baez, as Assistant Secretary of State for Inter-American Affairs, the exile lobby ensured that he was blocked in Congress.[22] They also campaigned against any broadening of the dialogue between Washington and Havana, during negotiations on the *balsero* crisis in 1994. In October, 125,000 marched through Little Havana in Miami to show their support for hard-line policies and demonstrate their opposition to negotiations with the Cuban government.

The pattern of this relation to US politics has evolved over time. In the first two decades of exile, activists tended to work either in autonomous groups, or in collaboration with the Central Intelligence Agency (CIA). By 1981, however, in a reflection both of the maturing of the community and of the political opening provided by the election of President Reagan, perspectives shifted to embrace domestic politics. The twenty years since the first arrivals had seen two linked changes in exile attitudes. The hope of returning to the island was gradually extinguished as a result of their greater integration in the society of adoption, and the realisation that Castro's regime was not about to fall. The majority of Cubans now sought to acquire citizenship and became an active and committed voting constituency. These trends supported the establishment in 1981 of what became the most important exile lobbying organisation, the Cuban American National Foundation (CANF). The relation between Cuban-Americans and power at the centre was consolidated during the Republican presidencies of Reagan and Bush: Cuban-Americans have tended to suspect Democrats ever since Kennedy betrayed them at the Bay of Pigs in 1961. But they have been careful to keep lines open to Democrats as well and have, as a result, continued to be influential in the Clinton years. In 1992, when Clinton was running against the incumbent Bush for the presidency, he, like Reagan before him, was invited to Little Havana, the Cuban district of Miami, and, before his rival George Bush was able to, gave his support to the Torricelli Bill (though, in the end, he did not win the majority of the Cuban vote).

The Politics of Exile Organisations: the Cuban American National Foundation

There exist hundreds of exile organisations in Miami, with others or affiliated organisations in places like New York with significant concentrations of Cuban exiles. The most influential exile organisations are those of the right, notably the Cuban American National Foundation (CANF), established by exiles of the first, 'historic' generation. It had wealthy patrons, notably its long-serving leader and president, the late Jorge Mas Canosa, one of the ten richest 'Hispanics' in the USA (with business interests *inter alia* in telecommunications).[23] CANF gained political influence both locally and nationally over the course of the 1980s partly as a consequence of the assimilation of Cuban-Americans into US politics under sympathetic administrations.

The character of CANF's political stance was given by its militant opposition to communism in general, and to the Cuban regime in particular, which it charged with 'barbarism and tyranny', and sought to discredit at every opportunity both in the USA and in Cuba through its control of Radio and TV Martí.[24] Its advocacy of hard-line policies to isolate Cuba was taken as *the* exile line on Cuban/US relations, and CANF itself brooked no dissent either within the exile community or beyond, whether from its own members, government officials in Washington or from critics in the press. The *Miami Herald* and its publisher, David Lawrence, were the targets of a hate campaign in 1992 for running a series of editorials questioning the logic of the Torricelli Bill.[25] Mas Canosa's well-known intransigence and intolerance extended into the organisation itself leading to rifts with numerous influential individuals: Raúl Masvidal (left the Foundation in 1987); Frank Calzón (former CANF Executive

Director; left to join Freedom House), and Ernesto Betancourt (Director of Radio Martí) among them. Rivalry among different exile organisations resulted in the collapse of an initiative in 1994 to create a coalition organisation in Unidad Cubana.[26] CANF members have been accused of terrorising dissenters, of bombing exhibitions showing the work of islanders, and of threatening harm to those they considered to be promoting dialogue and conciliationist strategies *vis-à-vis* Cuba.[27] It wields its control through its numerous radio channels in Florida, its press outlets, and recently established website, as well as through an extensive network of patronage.[28] CANF supports scholarship and research programmes through a $2 million 'Endowment for Cuban American Studies', and various forms of assistance have been extended to arriving immigrants through the Cuban Exodus Relief Fund that claims to have helped in the resettlement of more than 7,000 exiles. Another programme, Mission Martí, trains hundreds of volunteers in the 'reconstruction of Cuba after Castro' (CANF, undated, p. 2). Its considerable resources enable it to mount sizeable well-orchestrated campaign events which bring thousands into the streets.[29] This extensive presence, and a membership which it claims at 50,000, has sustained it as the major influence within the *comunidad*. Its offices in Miami and in Washington, where it conducts effective lobbying, are complemented by others in New York, New Jersey and Puerto Rico. CANF has been able to secure a certain amount of Congressional influence through its extensive campaign contributions; in 1992 through the Free Cuba Political Action Committee, more than $200,000 went into lobbying efforts for sympathetic Congressmen, $26,750 of which went to Torricelli.[30] In more recent years it has been active in Latin America and Europe[31] – east and west – where it has been campaigning against any softening of attitudes towards Cuba and in support of the Torricelli and Helms Burton legislation, which it helped to draft and promote.

In the 1990s CANF has had to alter its rhetoric, if only because in the post-Cold War era it can no longer identify itself as the bulwark against communist influence in the USA. It continues its campaign for human rights on the island and gives support to dissident groups. But it now advocates the goal of a peaceful transition to democracy and a market economy in Cuba via free elections. It has even produced a transition document (product of its 'Blue Ribbon Commission'), which bears a remarkable resemblance to that produced by Clinton. Needless to say, while Clinton's was denounced ('We are not for sale!' as the banner headline in *Granma* proclaimed), CANF's proposals have met with little response from the island. To many US liberals, CANF's objectives seem reasonable enough, but the means by which the organisation seeks to achieve them are questionable. The essence of its hard line stance is opposition to any negotiations with the Castro regime, a refusal to consider lifting the embargo, and continuing, indeed increasing, support for policies which put pressure on the island. CANF strategy stops short of publicly and actively supporting destabilisation in the island, but there is little doubting that destabilisation leading to the downfall of the Castro regime is what some of its leaders and many of its members are hoping for.

But is the Foundation representative of Cuban-American opinion in Miami? The answer is a qualified affirmative. One index of the support it enjoys was the response to the funeral of Jorge Mas Canosa in September 1997 that brought 40,000 Cuban-

Americans out in attendance, with live broadcasts throughout, and an entire issue of the *Miami Herald* dedicated to a celebration of his life. The numerous opinion surveys carried out in Miami confirm that the majority of the diaspora supports the continuation of the mix of hard-line policies towards the island, including the embargo. The most recent survey of 1997, the *1995 FIU Cuba Poll*, part of a repeated investigation carried out since 1991 by Florida International University, shows that as many as three-quarters of respondents favoured continuation of the embargo and thought that Helms Burton was a 'good measure to promote change on the island' (Grenier, Gladwin and McClaughlin, 1995). More surprising was that 63 per cent of respondents supported US military action to overthrow Castro, and 71.3 per cent supported exile military action to the same end (FIU, 1997). Such responses indicate that CANF retains considerable support for its hard-line policies within the community, and, this, together with its effective organisational and campaigning capacity, ensures that little real progress is made towards improving official relations between island and diaspora.

Changing Circumstances, Unchanging Attitudes?

Yet, despite the successes that the Cuban-American lobby had chalked up by the mid-nineties with respect to US policy towards the island, there are reasons to think that the influence of the hard-liners within CANF and outside it may be on the wane. More optimistic readings of the polls indicate that, although there is clear and continuing support for hard-line policies, there is also support for negotiation to achieve specific ends. One survey of 1996 showed that 65 per cent were in favour of negotiations to exclude medicine from the embargo while 82 per cent favoured negotiations to improve human rights; 43 per cent favoured negotiations to allow unrestricted visits of Cuban-Americans to the island and 24 per cent favoured negotiations to facilitate free trade with Cuba. Significantly, almost half of those surveyed (46 per cent) supported the call of the Catholic Church in Cuba for 'national dialogue.'[32] By 1997 this figure had risen slightly to 48 per cent, and the visit of the Pope in January 1998 may have strengthened this view. Also apparent is a trend since the 1990s towards a greater realism in attitudes towards Castro's capacity to survive the crisis brought about by the fall of his former allies. Only 10.6 per cent now expected rapid political change in Cuba compared with the 77 per cent who expected the regime to fall within a year in 1991 – the moment when exile hopes of a collapse of the communist system in Cuba were at their highest. In the summer of 1997, talk in the exile community and across the political spectrum was of having to accept that change would not come in Cuba until Castro retired or died. 'And that', said one veteran of the Bay of Pigs, 'could take another ten years.'[33]

It is evident from the varied responses cited above that such surveys simplify quite complex and possibly contradictory attitudes. But they also reflect the existence of important divisions within the community on issues of policy, and indicate that certain attitudinal changes have taken place that could have significance for future diaspora-island relations. As far as divisions are concerned, the most important of these are of generation and class, themselves variables which, as noted above, are closely related in Miami.

These divisions should not be exaggerated; ties within the community function reasonably well and, despite the arrival of poorer immigrants, poverty levels are comparatively low. The Cuban diaspora has less poverty than any other migrant community in the USA with the exception of the Chinese. This has to do in some measure with the effectiveness of community assistance that supports high if uneven levels of integration. Such tension as exists within the community is to a considerable extent generational, as between the historical *émigrés* and the recent arrivals, and between those born in Cuba and the second generation born in Miami. With respect to the tension between generations of immigrants, those who arrived in Miami after the first wave, and especially those who arrived since Mariel, maintained strong links with the island, sending remittances to kin and visiting in large numbers when US and Cuban policy allowed. In December 1978 Castro announced that Cuban-Americans were allowed to return for one week to visit their families. Some 100,000 visitors to the island took advantage of this before the agreement was rescinded in 1980, spending an estimated $100 million. That these diaspora-island ties continue to be meaningful is evidenced in the size of the remittances received in Cuba in the 1990s. Data suggest that as much as $800 million was reaching Cuba from exiles by 1996 (see Chapter 12). An improvement in the telephone system (resulting from Torricelli Track II) led to a rise in communication between the two communities. This indicates that the ties between the island and the diaspora not only continue, but may even have strengthened in the period since 1990 as a result of the harsher conditions faced by relatives in Cuba. As noted earlier, the issue of family visits to the island is one which divides the exile community: 56 per cent approved visits, 44 per cent opposed. Most significant, however, is that among Cubans who arrived during this decade 93 per cent approved of visits. The severing of financial and regular charter flight links in 1996, following active lobbying by the exile right, was therefore not universally welcomed.[34]

Although opposed to the political situation on the island, a substantial proportion of the exile community do not wish to see a brutal deterioration in the conditions in Cuba and fear the consequences of a violent termination of Castro's rule. They favour change, but in the form of a negotiated, peaceful transition. The Catholic Church has undoubtedly played an increasing role in fostering these attitudes in recent years. It is significant in this respect that substantial numbers of Cuban-Americans have been involved in various forms of humanitarian aid through church organisations, as well as in the *municipios en el exilio*,[35] and in associations such as the Coalición Cubano Americano which works for the rights of separated families, with an agenda motivated by hope of reconciliation. It is a reasonable assumption that those with close ties to family on the island would tend to favour dialogue, still a dirty word among the hard-liners.[36] If, as seems evident from the polls, there exists a sizeable portion of exile opinion which favours some form of dialogue, it remained a view which was difficult to express: according to the 1997 survey mentioned earlier, 70 per cent of respondents complained that in Miami not all points of view were heard on the matter of how to deal with Cuba. This supports the repeated claims of human rights organisation as to the felt lack of freedom of expression in the Miami exile community, something which is only now beginning to change (*Americas Watch*, 1992).

Generational divisions have considerable significance in another sense. The children of Cuban exiles, numbering some 300,000, have reached maturity and many of these, while they are far from being pro-Castro, nonetheless wish to establish some distance from the hard-line politics of their elders. As one woman from the *generación histórica* put it: 'a los jóvenes les falta la rabia. No les importa lo que pasó en el pasado'.[37] It is of course not just that young people lack rage, but they also exhibit some indifference to the political passions of the past. They, like the more recent waves of migrants, have made the transition from exiles to 'ethnics', and can claim, even more than their parents, the dual identity ascribed to the 'Hyphenated-Americans'. They are a 'post-exile generation'.[38] On all indicators, exile children show high levels of conformity with US cultural norms, yet maintain some sense of their *cubanidad*.[39] As Gustavo Pérez Firmat (1994, p. 5) has written, US born, Miami-raised children retain and re-invent their Cubanness, *and* their Cuba: for exile children Cuba is 'an endearing fiction. Cuba is for them as ethereal as the smell of their grandfather's cigars...' Cuban-American novelists, such as Cristina García, capture exactly this imaginary and entirely benign *nostalgie de place.*[40] As Rumbaut has noted 'To claim Cuba, nostalgically as a place of origin, is significantly different to claiming it as a destiny' (Rumbaut 1996, p. 6). It is not surprising that these generational differences are reflected most clearly in the realm of cultural politics: it has largely been young people, supported by artists, singers and writers, who were among the first to explore issues of culture and identity in a non-tendentious way. Already in the 1970s they were producing magazines such as *Nueva Generación, Cuba Va!, Joven Cuba, Krisis* and *Areito*. In the 1990s too it is often young people who have opposed Florida's policies of cultural isolation *vis-à-vis* Cuba: they have favoured the exchange of musicians and artists, something which the Miami conservatives, many of them parents of the younger generation, vigorously opposed.[41]

The community is not then, as homogeneous, culturally or politically, as it is often portrayed, and while far from exhibiting the fluid hybridity which some theorists have seen as characteristic of US Latino identity, some modest pluralisation of political attitudes is evident if as yet only with regard to a limited set of issues.

Perspectives on the Cuban 'Transition'

The changes in the political orientation of the Cuban-American community have to be seen in three contexts: the end of the Cold War and its consequences, the shifting character of politics in Washington, and the evolution of the community itself. This concluding section will briefly survey the policies of some of the main Cuban-American political organisations with regard to the future of the island.

The political culture of the Cuban diaspora exhibits features both of continuity and discontinuity, and while intolerance and intransigence remain abiding features there has opened up a space in exile politics for greater debate which has allowed more moderate positions to be articulated. There has always existed within the exile community a diverse if small body of opinion in favour of dialogue with the island, and there was a time in the late 1970s when the Carter administration sought to open negotiations with the Castro government. In 1975, amidst much opposition in Miami, and publicity in Cuba, a party of *dialogueros* representing a broad spectrum of opinion went on a visit to Cuba to request greater contact and discussion between 'los de aquí and los de allá'. Contacts continued at various times, and in autumn 1978 Castro agreed to negotiations with exile representatives, and with representatives of the US government. This led to the release of 3,600 political prisoners, and the agreement allowing exiles to visit relatives in Cuba.[42] These visits occasioned much turmoil on both sides of the Florida Straits and an exchange of population, both temporary and permanent: 100,000 exiles returned to visit Cuba in 1979-80, followed by the eruption of Mariel which delivered 129,000 Cubans to the USA. If Mariel was a warning to Cuba of the destabilising consequences of greater contact with the exile community, the $100 million which the visitors had spent on their brief sojourn was welcomed. For its part the issue of visits and of the usefulness of dialogue bitterly divided the exile community, and continued to do so over the following decade. However, what changed through the 1990s was the broader cultural and political context, and if public attitudes in Miami were still out of step with international opinion with regard to Cuba, there were clear signs that some shift was taking place.

One index of this shift was in the character of Miami's civil society. Cultural events, open meetings and conferences which were impossible only a few years back, could take place without exciting more than controversy.[43] Newspapers and radio in Miami could allow a variety of views on Cuban issues, including views critical of US policy towards Cuba, without fear of reprisal. It was not uncommon to hear exiles of various political persuasions arguing that these policies had been counter-productive in helping Castro consolidate his position, by permitting him to play the nationalist card while justifying the repression of internal opposition. Such views must also be seen in the context of US public opinion, where The *Washington Post*, the *Herald Tribune*, the *Wall Street Journal* and the *New York Times*, among others, editorialised in the mid-90s against Helms-Burton and the embargo, on the grounds that such policy was inappropriate in the post-Cold War era and was inconsistent with US treatment of China and latterly Iran.

Within the exile community itself, it became increasingly evident that the policies of the US government, supported and fortified by hard-line Cuban-Americans, did not enjoy unconditional or even tacit support. As illustrated by the polls, the ending of visits to the island (except in cases of humanitarian emergency or in exceptional circumstances such as the visit of the Pope), and the 1994 prohibition against sending remittances (lifted in 1998), were seen by many as causes of unnecessary suffering, in the context of economic recession and acute scarcity that Cuba was experiencing.[44]

Beyond the humanitarian concerns, there was a growing awareness of the need to think through the consequences of diaspora politics. This was evident in the preoccupation with transition scenarios which became a focus of the Cuban-American scholarly literature[45] and political discussion in the community in the 1990s. Numerous symposia on themes such as 'Post-Castro Cuba', and 'Dealing with the Transition', were held in Miami, while radio programmes called 'Transition' went on the air. A variety of possible transitions have been entertained, including Spanish, Russian, Chinese, Chilean, Brazilian and Romanian versions, but the threat of a violent outcome leading to civil war, mass emigration and a destabilisation of the Caribbean is not ruled out. Exile organisations have had to move beyond a generic opposition to Castro, to position themselves more precisely in relation to the future of the island. In so doing they have had to confront the possible consequences and dangers of hard-line policies. More generally, in these less adventurist times, extreme politics towards Cuba have lost some of their force.

One of the lessons of transitions from authoritarian rule drawn from elsewhere is that institutional stability can be crucial in assuring a favourable outcome. So too, in the case of Cuba, a growing body of exile opinion is prepared to take a longer view of the process that is already under way in Cuba, placing on hold aspirations of any rapid move towards institutional democracy. Some Cuban exiles believe that Washington has already made that accommodation. As one recently arrived exile, a former expert in international relations, expressed it, the USA could do worse than have a stable neighbour, one which did not threaten US interests, and did not participate in the drugs trade. This, he said, 'Clinton could easily tolerate a few years more'.[46]

New CANF? The Cuban American National Foundation Mark II

If considerations other than vengeance have begun to weigh with some hard-liners, this shift has been reflected within CANF itself. The Foundation has been undergoing a gradual evolution and partial accommodation with the realities of the Cuban situation, encouraged in part by international pressure for dialogue which gained momentum after the passing of the Torricelli Bill. In 1994, following the lead given by Felipe Gonzales, Spain hosted a meeting at which Roberto Robaina, Cuba's foreign minister, met with three leaders of opposition exile groups, while Mas Canosa represented CANF. A long-time opponent of dialogue, CANF found itself participating in several such meetings, and has come round to the view that some kind of presence at the table is necessary, even if *rapprochement* is still off limits. The organisation is not of one mind on this, and Mas Canosa, no conciliationist himself, was criticised by some of his colleagues for joining the *dialogueros* on the grounds that, whatever is said at these meetings, the very fact of participation appears to legitimise the Castro regime.

CANF's policy on Cuba's eventual transition remains one of keeping up the pressure on the regime in the expectation that it will eventually crack. But it lends formal support to a process of peaceful transition and has sought to soften its public image in recent years. It may be significant that in its transition document CANF has even felt it necessary to reassure the Cuban people that it harbours no revanchist proclivities as far as claims to individual homes are concerned: 'no pretendemos sacar a nadie de su casa'. Moreover, its formal support of a peaceful transition extends to accepting what Helms-Burton rules out, namely that it might tolerate Castro in power if he were elected on the basis of free elections. In the debate televised between Cuban minister Ricardo Alarcón and Jorge Mas Canosa in September 1996, the latter was asked whether, if Cuba held elections and the Cuban people voted for Castro, he would be willing to deal with Castro: he responded in the affirmative.

Nonetheless, despite this apparently moderate stance, CANF speaks with different tongues and still claimed the loyalty of a more hard-line, even extremist constituency.[47] Organisation spokesmen were divided in their public response to the bombing campaign which hit Cuba in 1997: while some denounced it, others were quoted as having welcomed it as an 'escalada de la resistencia en la isla'. The Cuban government announced on 11 September 1997 that it had irrefutable evidence that CANF had financed the attacks against tourist areas which took place that year, but it remained unclear what level of support, if any, the terrorist groups had from the organisation. More substance was given to Cuban claims of the foundation's destabilisation efforts by the indictments of CANF leaders in 1998 for involvement in the 'assassination plot' directed against Castro in Puerto Rico the previous year. If the aim of these actions was to tempt the US and Cuban authorities into open confrontation, they failed. As Domínguez has argued,[48] they were able, much to the annoyance of the hard-liners, to continue their practical collaboration over issues of migration, customs and FBI investigations (Domínguez, 1997).

A key strand of CANF strategy has been to continue to call for human rights to be observed and to support dissidents on the island.[49] There are those who argue that while the issue of human rights should be central in any process of negotiation, the fact that CANF is so prominently associated with it and with dissident groups has been used to discredit the very movements they support. CANF members informally expressed the view that Castro would eventually fall as a result of the will of his own people, although they lament the absence of widespread manifestation of dissent. Puerto Rican CANF representatives have in particular lent support to various campaigns on the island which they see as 'promoting democracy' and some have openly called for an uprising on the island.[50] CANF's continuing efforts in support of the embargo and for isolationist policies is open to the interpretation, for all the talk of peaceful transition, that this is the most effective means of prosecuting this goal.

Yet the death of Jorge Mas Canosa has been accompanied by expressions of hope that it might enable a shift in the politics of 'la Comunidad' towards a more reasonable accommodation with the island's ruling party in its declining years, and even with its ageing leader.[51] Following the Pope's visit in January 1998, CANF hard-liners found themselves at odds with their usual Cuban-American supporters in Congress over proposals to lift the embargo on food and medicines to Cuba.[52] Some CANF members are known to share the view that 'ahora que el mundo ha cambiado se puede tratar con comunistas' – now that the world has changed one can talk to communists. Moreover, there exists in the milieu that CANF inhabits, and more broadly within the business community, a less ideological and more pragmatic group among the element who were formerly the most hostile to the Castro regime.

There are also those in CANF itself who acknowledge that open confrontation with the Cuban leadership failed to yield the hoped for result, and may not be the way forward now. Against all expectations, the Cuban leadership has shown itself capable of weathering the economic crisis, and if hard-line exile lobbies are forced to forego their political aspirations, they still have some hope of realising their economic ones. It is not surprising that new groups of exile businessmen, impatient with the hard-liners, but not in sympathy with more moderate forces, nonetheless argue for dialogue in order to secure conditions for business in the future. This coincides with the efforts of some US-based business groups to oppose sanctions and to resume trade with states that have been blacklisted for one reason or another. As early as 1991 and 1992 conferences were held in Miami to discuss the business opportunities that were expected to open up on the island. Some Cuban-Americans were among the Fortune 500 visit to Cuba in February 1997 and there is anecdotal evidence that Cuban exile money is already being invested in small businesses in anticipation of things to come. This is a critical aspect of Cuba's future: State Department estimates put the potential investment power of the exile community at $10 billion, and the Atlantic Council has projected that under favourable circumstances the Cuban exile community could deliver up to $1billion per year. While this may exaggerate the likely sums available, there is a Cuban-American business constituency interested in investment, but the longer it is blocked by political factors, the more it stands to lose out to other interests, and the more delayed will be Cuba's economic recovery. Helms-Burton has come to be seen as hurting those who promoted it.

The Moderate Centre and Centre-Left

If CANF remains the voice in the exile community with the greatest weight, it is no longer a monolithic voice, or the one that everyone wants to listen to. In the course of the 1990s, organisations with more moderate policies have gained some recognition within the broader political community. This has been possible because of changes within the diaspora itself, but also because of growing international pressure, spurred by opposition to Helms-Burton, to engage a broader set of political positions in debates on the future of the island.[53]   Among those who have achieved some international recognition for their activities and presence in a number of 'dialogue meetings' on both sides of the Atlantic are the Comité Cubano por la Democracia (CCD), and *Cambio Cubano*.[54]   These organisations have participated, along with CANF, in meetings between exile groups and the Cuban government, such as those which took place in Madrid in 1994 and 1997.[55]

The CCD, founded in 1993, represents a centre-left coalition largely made up of professionals, which includes prominent Cuban-American academics such as Alejandro Portes and Marifel Pérez-Stable.[56]   Its president until 1997,[57] Alfredo Duran, represents a trajectory that some other moderate exiles have followed: a former ex-militant of the right, and veteran of the Bay of Pigs, he helped to found the CCD as a counterweight to the 'hegemony of the CANF' over Cuban-American politics. CCD's main work is dedicated to lobbying in Washington, where it has an office. It enjoys various means of diffusing its ideas, including a publication, *Cuban Affairs*, and a daily radio programme entitled *Transición* where news and calls from listeners are discussed. The CCD has two principal goals: the first is that of 'opening a political space' in Miami and in Congress, to allow for the introduction of more moderate Cuban-American views; the second is the repeal of the Helms-Burton Law (along with Torricelli), and the end of the embargo, the latter considered to be immoral because, in Duran's words, it 'undermines the sovereignty of our nation'. Duran testified to this effect in June 1995 at the hearings held by the Senate Foreign Relations Committee on Helms Burton. CCD actively campaigned for the lifting of the embargo on food and medicine, and in support of the Cuban Women and Children Humanitarian Relief Act of 1997. In an interview in August 1997 Duran stated that 'Cuba must resolve its own problems by herself, since international powers have failed'.[58]

CCD is a strong supporter of dialogue, and opposes the culture of 'vengeance and violence' which so long dominated diaspora politics. Duran has himself participated in various meetings with representatives from the island and met with Roberto Robaina, (the nearest approximation to an official Cuban *dialoguero*) both in Spain and in Cuba. Above all, CCD supports moves towards the normalisation of relations with Cuba, although Duran has emphasised that Castro also has a responsibility to promote the conditions favouring dialogue if it is to have a chance of 'maintaining some of the gains of the Revolution'. Moreover, unless moderate Cuban-Americans can show that dialogue works, and that Cuba is a serious participant, their position is not one that will hold much weight.

Although the CCD represents minority views, Duran believes that support for more moderate policies is growing, helped by the climate of greater political tolerance in Miami that allows open meetings on difficult issues such as the embargo for the first time. Like others, he believes that 'the extremists are losing credibility. Perhaps they can see at last that their approach has delivered nothing in almost four decades'.

An important dimension of the work of CCD has been within the cultural field. María Cristina Herrera, a member of CCD, is particularly active in this area. Her own organisation, the Cuban National Institute, originated in a meeting held in 1969. It has long promoted cultural exchanges and church efforts in support of greater discussion within the community and between exiles and islanders. A continuing priority of the Institute in the 1990s has been to promote cultural exchanges which aim to foster a sense of Cuban identity across the political divide.[59] The work of the church has been given special recognition in this regard: the Archbishop of Havana, Cardinal Jaime Ortega, was given an award by CCD for his efforts to promote Cuban national reconciliation.[60] This kind of work within the civil society of the diaspora has helped to challenge some of the sclerotic tendencies which characterise its political society and there is a basis of support for it within the Miami community, although cultural policy is an issue on which opinion remains divided. Even on the matter of the Pope's visit to Cuba, the community distinguished itself by endless wrangling and fractious dissent over travel arrangements to the island. Cultural censorship, as it is called, is also a hotly contested issue: the 1997 FIU poll shows that, while 53.2 per cent opposed banning the music of island-based performers from local radio stations (and 54.8 per cent disapproved of the cancellation of Andy Montanez's appearance at the Calle Ocho festival), 45 per cent approved of such prohibitions, a substantial number but a minority nonetheless. Viewed positively, this does indicate a substantial body of opinion in favour of cultural exchange. Another positive sign has been the reaction to Cuban artists and writers who have emigrated to Miami. In the past they would have been shunned for remaining in Cuba 'so long' (as happened with Reynaldo Arenas and Carlos Alfonso in the 1980s), but recent arrivals have been welcomed (for example, painter José Bedía and musician Albita Rodríguez).[61]

Evidence of changing diaspora attitudes provides organisations such as CCD with qualified grounds for optimism. There is also a growing consensus against the embargo in some sectors, especially with regard to medicine and visits to the island coupled with positive shifts in US attitudes. A seminar in Madrid at the end of August 1997, which Duran attended, was significant in being one of the few public meetings of Cuban exiles that called for an end to the embargo of food and medicinal products. The attendance of a US Congressman signified for Duran that the US government 'are at last ready to listen to a different view to that of the radical right'. His view was validated in April 1998 by the passing of legislation permitting the resumption of visits by relatives and re-legalising the sending of remittances.

CCD's favoured transition scenario, like that of other moderate groups, is gradualist, an evolution towards regime change and eventual democracy resulting from normalisation and the end of US isolationist policies. In the meantime efforts should continue to secure the incorporation of Cuba 'into the discussion' and to promote dialogue among the various parties (CCD, 1996).

Cambio Cubano

Another presence in the international exile meetings representing moderate views is *Cambio Cubano*, established in 1992. Its founder, Eloy Gutiérrez Menoyo, has a distinctive background among exile politics as a former hero of the Cuban Revolution, who later turned against Castro. His plan was discovered and he was jailed for 22 years, to be released in 1986. Menoyo's views are similar in certain respects to those of the CCD, with regard to the need for dialogue and the positive signs of change within the Cuban-American diaspora. Also, like CCD, *Cambio Cubano* supports an end to isolationism and to the politics of confrontation. In a series of open letters to Clinton, Gutiérrez Menoyo has called for the end of the embargo and appealed to Clinton's humanity (and pride) to resolve the gridlock in the Cuban situation.

However, what is distinctive about Gutiérrez Menoyo's strategy is that it rests on some variant of a pacted or negotiated transition, whereby Cuba would offer a limited slate in national elections. Gutiérrez Menoyo met with Castro on a visit to Cuba in 1995 where he proposed that he be allowed to form a party to stand in the event of such an election. He has formally requested Castro's permission for *Cambio Cubano* to operate in Cuba, to have what he calls a 'legal space' to work for the eventual establishment of a political party. In return, Gutiérrez Menoyo would pledge not to campaign for the overthrow of the regime or to undermine the electoral process. Gutiérrez Menoyo's vision is thus of a negotiated transition which would inaugurate a process of controlled democratisation. While Castro has apparently promised to consider this offer, there has so far been little evidence of progress.

In contrast to CCD's efforts within the diaspora, Gutiérrez Menoyo's gaze is directed at a political future in Cuba itself, and it is difficult to find many in Miami who take his project seriously. Hard-liners dismiss his strategy as a pact with the devil. But he does have support from some Congressmen, some liberal lobbyists (such as Wayne Smith) and from abroad (he receives money from a Swedish trade union). He is a regular participant in dialogue meetings, and an active campaigner for the end of the embargo.

Gutiérrez Menoyo, like Duran, is optimistic in relation to the evolution of diaspora politics, but his emphasis is upon the 'factor biológico' – a phrase also beloved of islanders who use it to refer to their own ageing leaders. The most intransigent exiles are found among older Cubans, a population which is ageing and many of whom are at the end of their lives. According to the results of his consultation of the mortuary archives, dozens of elderly Cuban-Americans die each month; Gutiérrez Menoyo has calculated that some 40 per cent of the 'real old guard' died in 1997 alone. 'En un par de años... Clinton no va tener ese problema generacional.' If the biological factor enters into the politics of the diaspora as much as it does on the island, there is reason indeed to expect the shift in its political culture to continue.

Conclusions

US policy towards Cuba has borne the marks of Cuban-American involvement, but it cannot be ascribed solely to the political efficacy of the exile community. On the one hand, as long as the Cold War lasted, Washington had its own strategic and ideological reasons for being opposed to Cuba, and, even with that conflict gone, influential sections of the political elite in the USA retained an abiding resentment towards Havana. On the other hand, as with Israel and Ireland, attitudes in US politics are espoused much more widely than by the community ethnically linked to the country in question – polls show that almost two thirds of the US public favour the trade embargo on Cuba. What the exile lobby has been able to do is to ensure that this broader support for the embargo and related issues is maintained and that, in the absence of any remotely comparable lobby on the other side, their interests have prevailed. In the passing of the Torricelli and the Helms-Burton Laws, they were undoubtedly assisted by favourable opportunity contexts: the US presidential elections of 1992 and Havana's shooting down of the exile planes in 1996.[62] But they were not able to prevent the US-Cuban immigration agreement of 1994 nor the 1995 agreement to repatriate rafters. By 1998 they were losing the battle against the sending of medicine and permitting of remittances to the island, and they were unable to make much of a mark on international opinion: in April 1998, despite intense lobbying, the UN Commission on Human Rights voted against a US backed resolution critical of Cuban human rights policies. In May, Clinton's meeting with the European Union resulted in a watering down of US sanctions against investment in the island (see Chapter 3). International opinion remains opposed to Helms Burton and there is less support for sanctions than ever. At home, the exiles may retain support in Congress, but they have lost some influence in the White House.[63] Secretary of State Madeleine Albright's meeting with 15 Cuban-American political leaders in spring 1998 was with moderates, most of whom were critical of the embargo.

The role of the exiles in the future of Cuba is uncertain. On the one hand, it is possible to imagine a diminution in the influence of the more hard-line views, along with a broader role for the moderate opposition. But, as noted at the beginning, this depends on the strategy of the USA, and on how the policies of the Cuban regime evolve. On an optimistic scenario, greater dialogue and co-operation could help to ease both relations between Miami and Havana, and the situation inside Cuba itself. Such a strategy involves time and patience: any precipitate collapse of the Castro government could cause destabilisation on the island, and encourage more extremist elements in Miami to intervene. For a peaceful change of regime some institutional continuity is probably necessary. Such a process requires the good will of the Cuban government, but also the support of the US government and the exile community, or at least significant sectors of it. The positive fallout from the Pope's visit, evident in statements by US bishops and by a new anti-embargo lobby, may provide such support; but until now moderate organisations have lacked effective weight in the community. The major room for change lies at the moment with the US government itself; but faced with a still largely intransigent exile community, policies written into law, an obstructive Congress, and with weak political will in Washington itself, the prospects for this appear slim. This leaves the initiative where it has been for the past forty years, with the islanders themselves. What influence the exiles will have on them, or on the future of the island, remains an open question.

Notes

*   This research could not have been done without the hospitality of the North-South Center in Miami, and the generous assistance of Max Castro and Ambler Moss while I was there. Thanks are also due to Jean Stubbs and Saul Landau, as well as to those in Miami and Europe who gave me their time in interviews.
1.   Gillian Gunn Clissold puts this argument in Gunn (1997).
2.   The 1990 census recorded that almost 1.1 million Cubans were in the USA.
3.   A sizeable Cuban migration to the USA occurred during the 19th century as a result of the Independence Wars, and again in the 1930s when many Cubans fled to escape the effects of the revolution against President Machado.
4.   Nicaragua may be the exception here. After the Sandinistas came to power in 1979, Dade County became a primary recipient of Nicaraguan exiles, some 150,000 having arrived by 1990.
5.   Studies of Cuban immigration include: Boswell and Curtiss (1983 and 1991), Castro (1997a), Cobas and Duany (1997), Croucher (1997), Flores and Yúdice (1990),Grenier and Stepick (1992), Masud-Piloto (1996), Pérez (1986 and 1990), Portes and Bach (1985), Portes and Stepick (1993), Portes and Rumbaut (1996), Pedraza-Bailey (1985). For a Cuban view, see Bolio (1991).
6.   These categories can be further sub-divided resulting in six or seven waves. See Boswell and Curtis (1983), Portes and Bach (1985), and Pérez (1986).
7.   Figures on migration given in different sources may appear inconsistent, a result of different methods of compilation, and of the fact that a proportion of migrants from Cuba went to other countries before their arrival in the United States.

8. These are Dixon's figures; others are more conservative.
9. 'Castro flushed his toilets on us.' This comment, attributed to Miami Mayor, Maurice Ferré, has become common currency among first generation Miami exiles to describe the effects of Mariel. Boswell and Curtiss (1991, p. 53) note that most of those with criminal records were petty offenders, while some 5,000 were estimated to be 'hard core criminals'. For the issue of Cuban immigrant criminality, see Aguirre (1994).
10. A Dade County Citizens' Committee report published in 1980 stated: 'As many blacks see it, the recent influx of Cuban refugees into the Miami area has exacerbated the jobs problem'. See Croucher (1997) for a discussion of how inter-ethnic tension in Miami was created and expressed. The quotation is from p. 74.
11. Portes and Bach (1985).
12. See Castro (1995), Kapcia (1995) and Mesa-Lago (1995) for a full analysis. While no data on the racial composition of the *balseros* were collected at the time of this study, Mesa-Lago suggests that the majority were white.
13. Unemployment and poverty rates within the Cuban-American community in Miami are comparable with the US national average, at 5.8 per cent and 15.2 per cent respectively.
14. 87 per cent of all Cuban-Americans live in four states: Florida, 65 per cent, New Jersey, 8 per cent, New York 7 per cent, California 7 per cent. 56 per cent live in Miami alone (Cuba On-Line, Characteristics of the Cuban American Population, 1997; www.shopmiami.com.cubaol).
15. In 1993 Cuban-Americans had by far the highest family incomes among Hispanics, and the lowest percentage (excepting whites) in poverty at 19.9 per cent, as compared to 33.1 per cent for blacks, 31.8 per cent for Mexicans, 38.7 per cent for Puerto Ricans, 27.4 per cent for other Hispanics, and 25.4 per cent for Central and South Americans. The percentage for the white population stood at 10 per cent. From Castro (1997a); see also Cobas and Duany (1997) on the economic success of Cuban immigrants.
16. They also have fewer children than other Hispanics, and a very low birthrate overall, mirroring the demographic trend on the island itself.
17. Pérez (1992).
18. *Miami Herald* 1992, cited in Croucher (1997).
19. For discussions of the elements of exile ideology, see Pérez (1992), García (1996), and Castro (1997a).
20. Cuban numerical supremacy was declining relatively over time; the percentage of Dade County's Latinos who were of Cuban origin had declined from 83 per cent in 1970 to 66 per cent in 1990. Nicaraguans became Dade's second largest Latino group by 1990 (Boswell and Curtiss, 1991, quoted in Croucher, 1997). Many Nicaraguans saw themselves as the natural allies of the Cuban exiles and collaborated actively with their anti-Castro activities.
21. Castro (1997a) lists the influential Cuban-Americans in 1997: 'el alcalde y el administrador del area metropolitana, el superintendente de las escuelas públicas, dos congresistas federales, el rector de la universidad estatal, el

presidente del community college, el jefe de la policía metropolitana, y los alcaldes de tres de los municipios principales (Miami, Hialeah, y Coral Gables) son de origen Cubano. El número de Cubanoamericanos que ocupan cargos de legisladores estatales, concejales municipales, y magistrados se ha multiplicado en los últimos díez años.'

22. This was presaged in 1992 by the defeat of Magda Davis who stood against Ileana Ros-Lehtinen on a more progressive ticket that opposed the Torricelli Bill, and with support from moderate and liberal Cuban-American organisations and non-Cuban Democrats. She lost the election to Ros-Lehtinen 69 per cent - 31 per cent.

23. To join the board of CANF, candidates had to put up a minimum of $10,000 and be prepared to put personal funds into political campaigns.

24. The mobilisation of patriotic sentiments was also a key aspect of CANF rhetoric, something which repays separate analysis.

25. Mas Canosa accused the *Herald* of taking the same positions as the Cuban government on Torricelli, and ran advertisements on Dade County buses saying 'I don't believe in the Herald'. Lawrence and two of his editors received death threats within days of the campaign and the paper's vending machines were jammed and defiled.

26. Unidad Cubana sought to unify some 80 exile organisations.

27. It is alleged that CANF members were involved in an incident in 1994 when two molotov cocktails were thrown at a Cuban exile magazine which supported dialogue and included the embargo among the issues to be discussed.

28. In a surprise move in 1997, shortly before his death, Mas Canosa dropped a long-running legal suit against Wayne Smith for slander, something that was taken as evidence of mellowing on the part of the CANF President. However, in November 1998 CANF was again suing Smith (and others) over allegations of its involvement in 'terrorism' (See Noguera, 1998b).

29. In 1993, when Mexico threatened to expel rafters, CANF organised daily demonstrations outside the Mexican Embassy, a boycott of Mexican products, and a vigorous lobby campaign which soon achieved a Mexican capitulation. The rafters were flown to Miami where they were welcomed as heroes, and the seven who had died at sea were given a televised funeral with over 25,000 in attendance (Moreno, 1994).

30. Booth, 1992. Castro (1997a) states that between 1982 and 1995, Public Action Committees are reported to have given $758,696 to congressional candidates, while individual members were said to have given even more.

31. It has been particularly active in Spain where Mas Canosa was able to develop close relations with the Aznar government. He also had extensive financial interests in Spain.

32. See Castro (1997a).

33. Author's interview, Miami, 1997.

34. These links were restored in 1998. The change of heart by the Clinton administration, despite opposition from CANF, may have had something to do

with the visit of the Pope to Cuba in January 1998.

35. Exile Municipalities, voluntary organisations set up after 1962 to assist new arrivals who came from their home township. The *municipios* were named after those in Cuba, and 114 were officially recognised in Miami in the early 1980s. See Boswell and Curtiss (1991), García (1996).

36. Pérez (1992) is surely right to see kin ties as a major influence on diaspora politics.

38. 'Young people don't have (our) rage. What happened in the past doesn't matter to them' (author's interview).

38. This is Ruben Rumbaut's term (Rumbaut, 1996).

39. See Pérez (1992) and Rumbaut (1996) on inter-generational tensions and shifts.

40. García (1992). See de la Campa (1994) for a thoughtful autobiographical essay, a discussion of Cuban exile writing and reflections on the younger generation's identity.

41. Ruben Rumbaut's research on Cuban-American youth showed a tendency for those born on the island to identify themselves as 'American' (meaning the USA), while a majority of those born in the USA identified themselves as Cuban. This repeats a pattern found among other immigrant communities. See Rumbaut (1996), pp. 5-6.

42. In the event only about two thirds of these were allowed into the USA.

44. Some public meetings could still be heated and acrimonious, with CANF representatives disrupting gatherings organised by conciliationists, who were denounced as 'mouthpieces for Havana' (Nogueras, 1998a).

45. The publication of reports such as Kuntz 1994 and the ensuing debate undoubtedly contributed to this.

45. Miguel Angel Centeno has a detailed discussion of Cuba's possible transition scenarios in Centeno and Font (1997).

46. Author's interview, August 1997.

48. The disclosure in the summer 1998 of Luis Posada Corriler that he was involved in terrorist plots against the island at CANF's instigation were vigorously denied by the organisation. (They were later retracted by Posada.)

48. See Domínguez (1997).

49. The fact that this is such a prominent feature of CANF activities has served to undermine the credibility of dissident activity on the island and has played into the hands of the hard-liners in Cuba.

50. One initiative is support for the 'national Cuban movement' which has organised a survey asking in somewhat *simpliste* terms 'do you want democracy or Marxist Leninism in Cuba?' By late 1997, 4,000 responses had allegedly been gathered and the aim was to collect 10,000.

51. The successor to Mas Canosa as CANF President is Francisco 'Pepe' Hernandez, who was denounced by *Trabajadores*, a Cuban newspaper, for masterminding the bombing campaign on the island and who has been implicated in an alleged plot to kill Castro.

52. CANF has opposed the Dodd-Torres bill which was supported by Clinton and

aimed to lift the embargo on food and medicine. Instead it proposed a scheme of humanitarian aid which many saw as unworkable.

53. It is reported that recently declassified State Department records detailed early plans to weaken more moderate opposition leaders such as Manolo Ray and Felipe Pazos who were considered too soft on communism and insufficiently pro-American. Operation 40 called for assassinating the moderates after their return to the island following an invasion.

54. The other organisations with a more moderate stance that have made some headway are Carlos Alberto Montaner's Cuban Democratic Platform, the late Enrique Baloyra's Cuban Social Democratic Coordination and the Christian Democrats. Like the organisations discussed here, they enjoy some elite support but have little response among the grass roots. A small pro-Castro left has organised itself since the mid 1970s through the Antonio Maceo Brigade, but enjoys even less support among the exile community.

55. The CCD was represented by Alfredo Duran and *Cambio Cubano* by its founder, Tomás Eloy Gutiérrez. CANF also participated and was represented by Jorge Mas Canosa.

56. Both of these were on the Board of Directors of CCD, along with María Cristina Herrera, Jorge Du-Breuil, Mauricio Font, and Rolando Castaneda. CCD has brought together people with very different political trajectories.

57. Eliseo Pérez-Stable took over the presidency in 1997.

58. All quotations from here on are, unless otherwise stated, from interviews conducted with the author in Miami during August 1997.

59. Author's interview with María Cristina Herrera, 1997.

60. Most exile church activity is still unsympathetic to the regime in Havana. See Tweed (1997) for an ethnographic account of exile religion in Miami.

61. An important cultural exchange was the meeting of Cuban poets, exiles and islanders that took place in 1994. The results of the meeting were published in Vázquez Díaz (1994).

62. See Domínguez (1997) and Castro (1997a) for variants on this view.

63. Portes (1998) sees signs of a backlash against the right-wing Cuban lobby, which along with the death of Mas Canosa, the Pope's visit and the indictment of members of the CANF leadership for terrorism may considerably weaken its influence.

CHAPTER 15

CONCLUSIONS

Victor Bulmer-Thomas and James Dunkerley

The chapters in this volume have presented a variety of styles and analytical perspectives. This is to be expected from authors drawn not only from different academic disciplines, but also from distinct national cultures and political systems. It is our hope that such a plural approach has given the present study a breadth not usually to be found in books written by a single author. However, all our contributors share a number of values and positions. Perhaps most prominent amongst these is the conviction that the profound asymmetry of power and resource between the United States of America and the rest of the continent does not have to take its current form of a thoroughly inequitable relationship. Indeed, all the chapters of this book show – albeit in differing degrees of explicitness – that the prevailing structure of relations both needs to be altered and can be transformed to the palpable advantage of all concerned. It is not necessary to make recourse to a highly moralised discourse nor to draw on a utopian prospectus to see this. A few comments about these less tangible aspects of the relationship in the past and present are, though, required before we move to the new agenda for the future.

Rupture and Continuity in US-Latin American Relations

We may place the decisive establishment of the asymmetry in continental power at the Spanish-American War of 1898, the centenary of which falls as this text goes to press. Prior to that moment the considerable differences of culture, religion and political practice (as opposed to constitutional ambition) existed within a notably less imbalanced relationship, which was so loose in terms of both commercial and institutional links that it did not amount to a system. With the notable exception of the Mexican-American War of 1847, the US governments of that earlier era desisted from translating the rhetoric of the Monroe Doctrine or Manifest Destiny into practical action. Moreover, as demonstrated by the continued presence of Great Britain and the occasional incursion of other European powers, principally during and immediately after the US Civil War, the inter-American relations of the nineteenth century incorporated a European element that was important to all sections of the continent. In terms of Latin America these trans-continental ties diminished in all but cultural terms from 1914 onwards, and after 1945 they were reduced to an almost marginal status. For the next forty years US hegemony in the Americas was based on an open and confident calculation of 'national interest' drawn from anti-communism and the logic of the global Cold War. Europe, of course, was divided and partitioned by that same Cold War, with its capitalist states anxious not to irritate their dominant ideological ally in its own hemisphere and, as a rule, reconciled to policies seen as exaggerated in their 'realism' or aggressively narrow formulation of the US interest and its implementation abroad.

The USSR, by contrast, stumbled upon an extra-continental role almost by accident in Cuba, and this has had an immeasurably greater impact on world politics than could have been conceived in 1959-60, notwithstanding Cuba's 'exceptional' status over the previous century (see Chapter 1). The eventual sponsor of the Cuban Revolution has itself disappeared into history whilst the regime headed by Fidel Castro and pledged to the maintenance of core Marxist-Leninist orthodoxies for 40 years continues to survive. It has not, however, flourished and it remains the source of considerable complications in US domestic political life (through the Cuban-American diaspora concentrated in Florida and New Jersey) as well as for US foreign relations (through the Helms-Burton law). Additionally, the existence of that Cuban government has kept alive a vestigial anti-communist impetus within the public opinion and political elite of the USA. This highlights the degree to which the Cold War remains a recent phenomenon, bequeathing ideological and institutional legacies that have yet to be flushed out of the system and the mindset of the hemispheric elite. Almost all of the present political actors in North, Central and South America were brought up under the aegis of the Cold War, which was unhappy and fearful but also stable and reassuring. Many of the interpretations addressed here by Jorge Domínguez (see Chapter 2) and generally known as 'neo-realist' are associated with this outlook and methodology.

Nevertheless, the fall of the Berlin Wall in 1989 did have critically important consequences for both Latin America and the USA. In the first place, it both confirmed and encouraged the transition from dictatorial forms of government in the south since these had almost always been founded on an anti-communist culture. This helped to demilitarise (to a certain degree) Washington's relations with its Latin sister-republics. It also somewhat broadened the ideological spectrum of the governments with which the USA had now to deal, increasing demands on diplomatic practice and skills both in the region and back in Washington. However, the shifts in the world economy which began with the 'debt crisis' that opened in the Americas in the 1980s and which were forcefully advanced at the end of that decade by the collapse of communism in Europe meant that, whatever their ideological ambition and rhetorical practice, most Latin American governments in the 1990s were perforce cleaving to policies of capitalist orthodoxy promoted by the USA.

'Globalisation', then, was far from simply coincidental with the end of the Cold War and the bi-polar form of superpower relations; it was and is intimately connected with that political transformation. We must recognise that the termination of a world of images and reflexes founded upon the existence of an anti-capitalist project has greatly increased the confidence of the managers of liberal economies. Two effects of this are plainly visible: the poor of Latin America received minimal material benefit (beyond the curtailing of inflation) to accompany the disappearance of Cold War politics, and the Latin American political elite found its ideological repertoire sharply constrained as ties with the USA tightened. A decade after the fall of the Soviet system it is hardly surprising that many Latin Americans look to a revival of Europe as an external actor in their affairs on both economic and political fronts.

There are many laudable and potentially rewarding aspects to the expectation that the 'Old World' might act as an intrinsically benign influence, help to diversify hemispheric contacts, and offset direct US influence. However, one also encounters a number of contradictions and misconceptions. From a European perspective probably the most evident of these is the extent to which Americans – Anglo and Latin alike – are inclined to construe 'Europe' as a unitary actor and coherent international interlocutor. Perhaps the fact of a colonial past and the much-vaunted institutional convergence in western Europe during recent decades has helped to draw a veil over the stresses and divisions caused by this as well as over the socio-political diversity of the continent. Many of the attendant complications are evident in Laurence Whitehead's chapter, which highlights the complexity and limits of bi- and multilateral relations with the European Union (EU) as well as those with its member-states. The extraordinary experience of the detention of General Pinochet in London in October 1998 illustrates the matter in acute form, touching on the erratic legal accords between Spain and the United Kingdom (in both bi- and multi-lateral forms), the division of powers and independence of the courts in both states, the military and political alliances and conflicts of the previous governments of both countries with Chile, the prospects for arms sales, the links between domestic political pacts in Chile and the claims to sovereignty sustained by Santiago abroad, the concern of Washington not to revisit its role in the coup of 1973, and, finally, the unfolding of a new agenda for the international prosecution of criminal cases concerned with genocide or the widespread violation of human rights on a consistent and enforceable basis. The fact that Paris had earlier refused Pinochet a visa whilst London issued one, and that both Fidel Castro and Carlos Saúl Menem argued publicly for the release of the ex-dictator, underlines the political complexity of the emerging inter-continental dimension.

A further, occasional illusion encouraged by the revival of the 'European card' after so long is that it might, somehow, relieve Latin American states of the burden of developing a serious and autonomous strategy of their own for dealing with the USA. The chapter by Eduardo Gamarra highlights this as a problem in the case of Bolivia, but it is applicable to several smaller countries in South America and almost all of those in Central America and the Caribbean. This issue embraces elements of both equity and efficiency. Clearly, so long as La Paz (or Asunción or Tegucigalpa) continues to appoint ambassadors on purely political, prebendalist or family grounds, the conduct of diplomacy cannot be expected to go beyond the confines of ceremony and passive response to State Department initiatives. Countries that staff their embassies with relatives of the ruling party are not being run by governments that take foreign policy seriously, and one cannot be surprised if they are treated accordingly by their US counterparts. On the other hand, a state that cannot afford to pay and service a full professional diplomatic effort will of necessity take short-cuts, especially if this does not figure high on the domestic political agenda. In the Bolivian case discussed by Gamarra the response of the present government of General Banzer has been to combine a traditional, clientelist conduct of diplomacy with a platform on the drug issue which is so exaggerated in its offers to Washington that it is both unrealisable and the source of new, unnecessary conflict at home. This is in the medium-term interest of almost nobody – neither of the two governments concerned nor most of the institutional and social actors willingly or otherwise caught up in this complicated issue.

Some states, such as Mexico, Brazil, Chile and Argentina, have qualitatively superior strategies and institutions through which to realise them in the medium- and long-term, but that is not yet the general pattern in Latin America. The consequence has been to diminish the confidence and ambition of its populace as well as to exaggerate that of US political leaders and diplomatic employees, who can only sensibly be expected to react to the culture and behaviour around them. The matter is, of course, not restricted to the field of diplomatic practice. It has also to do with some of the fundamental preconceptions underlying inter-American relations, and too often these have been depicted in terms of simplistic dichotomies – either of the Cold War type or that of a culturalist determinism – which encourage narrow, unilateralist and zero-sum manoeuvres. As we have seen, there have existed for some time institutions capable of upholding a wider, fluid and multilateral set of interactions. The rhetoric for this has existed for longer still. But the culture, trust and political prerequisites are still insufficiently developed on both sides, not just in Anglo-America. In this respect, though, the fact that 'globalisation' has accompanied the conversion of the USA into the world's solitary superpower is welcome because it has encouraged the dispersion of certain flows of power and has helped to fragment some activities in a manner potentially conducive to the reduction of the asymmetries in the Americas, at least with respect to state-to-state relations.

The financial crisis that hit Latin America in mid-1998, having haemorraged out from its origins in south-east Asia over the previous year, makes it difficult to spot this consequence of the deepening internationalisation of capital, labour and commodities of all kinds. But it is a fact that such a process has reduced the direct control of most individual national governments over economic performance even while their political fortunes remain as tightly linked to it as before (or even more so). At the same time, the strategies of private corporations have become more telling, and insofar as many are of North American or European origin, their role as international actors with shared regional associations yet without a determinate 'national interest' to formulate and implement is increasingly important. The point is not that governments are losing their political authority – still less their necessary claims on sovereignty – but rather that the realms of economic efficiency and political legitimacy that were once treated as linked but separate and primarily within the confines of national borders are now widely taken as being inseparable and trans-national in character.

The US Perspective

The chapters by Marcelo Suárez Orozco and Maxine Molyneux in this book show eloquently just how far this is the case with respect to the movement of human beings into the USA itself, which now possesses a Latino population as large as many fully Latin American countries; in addition, of course, the USA possesses some of the largest conurbations of the continent populated by Latin people. Once again, the interaction between the 'domestic' and the 'foreign' spheres is so tight that on occasions these seem to lose their meaning and become misleading. At the very least, it will become increasingly necessary for holders of federal office in the USA to take very seriously, and sometimes as a top priority, the views of immigrants from Latin America and their US-born offspring. At state, city and county level the distinction between those of Latino background and identity who are living formally as citizens and those who are not, as well as between both these groups and those who consider themselves as somehow more authentically members of domestic civil society, may well continue to be the source of prejudice, conflict and manipulation of the type witnessed in California under Proposition 187. Undoubtedly, the large and growing number of people involved, the state of the regional economy, the fiscal pressures, and the consequences for law and order will not lessen in the short-term. If they continue to be confronted in a narrow and exclusivist conception of what constitutes 'the national interest', they will assuredly grow rapidly both 'at home' and outside the borders of the USA.

Behind these stark alternatives, though, there lies a real dilemma, which is readily lost in any construction of hemispheric relations as one simply between neo-imperialist arrogance and passive victimhood, with the US federal government on the one hand, and a mix of supine elite lackeys and impotent poor folk on the other. In itself such a vision contains important elements necessary to an understanding of the inter-American structure of power; and these elements have been valid for a century or more, requiring emphatic change in the modern world. US politicians and public servants do, for sure, need to display (and often to acquire in the first place) a much more sincere and profound respect for Latin American societies and states, and they should learn to approach them on a much more equitable basis precisely within the asymmetry that so patently exists and will persist. This is as much a moral or ethical requirement as it is a prerequisite for efficacious diplomacy and healthier intercourse. National sovereignty of the smaller countries is not merely a convenient fiction inherited from the past; it withholds a plethora of powers, rights and responsibilities critical for the maintenance of the law of nations as well as the improvement of the human condition. The extent to which condescension currently obtains is generally unacceptable and often retrograde for the purposes of implementing avowed US policy, let alone formulating fresh approaches for the future.

Nevertheless, it is implausible to expect matters to improve solely through 'a change of heart' or better behaviour by US politicians and public servants. One must look beyond the elite and diplomats for an explanation of the past pattern and for indicators for future behaviour. After all, if the democratic claims at the heart of the US political tradition have a scintilla of authenticity, the government in Washington must to some degree be reflecting the opinion and disposition of a significant sector of its citizenry.

Many of the claims that the USA is 'exceptional' as a nation-state have proved to be exaggerated, and some have been hijacked for less than worthy political ends. All the same, the country is surely one that may be described in its own parlance as an 'outlier'. Its revolutionary permutation of British bourgeois liberties, embracing of classical republicanism, parallel slave and free states and modern Civil War, high levels of immigration, expansion through an internal frontier to the West, and industrialisation on the basis of adult white male suffrage were all in place – along with the more trumpeted Anglo-Saxon puritan tradition – before the war of 1898 and the 'American Century' that is now closing. Yet they combine to provide us with clues to the manner in which foreign policy, and particularly that towards Latin America, has been played out in the modern era by a society of exceptionally heterogeneous ethnic origin, religious conviction and cultural disposition. Perhaps most important of all is the celebration of a republican morality, which over the years has transmuted from a critique of monarchism, through an argument for expansionism, into a complement for anti-communism, and which now idles uneasily without either an ideological counterpoint or a ready geographical locus through which to find a comfortable expression.

This discourse of high principle has, however, never been exclusively at the service of foreign policy activism and interventionism. It has always coexisted with another current – that of isolationism, which sometimes takes the form of championing a kind of apartheid with the rest of the world, sometimes masks pure pragmatism, and sometimes gels in a much more positive conviction that it is wrong to intervene in the affairs of others, even on the declared grounds of altruism. These two currents have not, of course, been the sole property of, respectively, conservative and 'progressive' opinion. Although there has been a tendency to identify a strong conservative tendency towards interventionism, one should not discount the attractions of isolationism to that sector of society, as the arguments of John C. Calhoun and Ross Perot demonstrate. Nor, indeed, have those seeking to change domestic US society in an avowedly progressive fashion – Woodrow Wilson, Lyndon Johnson, Bill Clinton – forborne from interventionism abroad.

The pattern is still less closely tied to party political tradition. Although in recent years the Republican administration of Ronald Reagan (1981-89) has been fiercely and justifiably criticised for its aggressive role in Central America, that of George Bush (1989-95) was – notwithstanding the invasion of Panama – far more modulated and enjoyed a much better relationship with Congress than has Clinton (1993-). Indeed, it is probable that had a Republican president ever been presented with legislation like the Helms-Burton bill, he or she would have succeeded in vetoing it (on the grounds of its incursion into presidential powers rather than its extra-territoriality). Again, a feature of the US system rooted deep in history – the division of powers established by the founding fathers – is directly germane to an understanding of current affairs.

This fitful exchange between interventionism and isolationism, high principle at the service of modern republican morality (or a money-making democracy) and short-cuts on behalf of capitalist rationality will not disappear as 'globalisation' proceeds, the rest of the world acquires more 'American' characteristics, and the USA itself becomes less exceptional in many ways. If for no other reason, the USA will continue to be exceptional because it is the world's only superpower. Equally, as Elizabeth Joyce's chapter shows with respect to the logic of 'certification', US politics continue to possess an unusually high theatrical and gesticulatory quality in which inherited mannerisms sometimes outweigh cool calculation of interest. It is, however, our optimistic belief that the present circumstances are conducive to a modulation and collaborative tempering of exaggerated 'realism' or 'liberalism'. That said at a quite high level of abstraction and cultural generalisation, let us now turn briefly to the more specific issues and short-run considerations addressed in the previous chapters.

The Scope of the New Agenda

It must be recognised that, with the possible exception of Mexico (see below), Latin America is not today a priority for the USA. There is a strong feeling in Washington that relations with the region are relatively healthy – perhaps, indeed, as good as they have ever been – and they are not, for this reason, in need of further promotion or attention. At least until the onset of the economic crisis of 1998, it was the absence of friction that permitted the USA to give priority to other regions – Europe, Japan, Russia, China and the Middle East. The handover of the Panama Canal to local control and the withdrawal of troops was proceeding with a smoothness that would have been unimaginable in the Cold War epoch; foreign investment in Cuba has not been targeted with the rigour allowed for under the Helms-Burton Law; trade diversion in Mercosur – temporarily an issue in 1996 – has been virtually ignored, and the raising of tariffs in 1997 was not subjected to open challenge. Washington has not seriously set itself against the Latin American desire to deepen ties with the EU, nor has it sought to spoil the series of annual Ibero-American meetings of heads of state held since 1990 or the first EU-Latin American summit in 1999.

Mexico is a rather different case. Bounded together by geography, Mexico and the USA share one of the longest, most complex and most symbolic frontiers in the world. Nowhere else does the rich First World face the poor Third World so starkly. Yet that frontier is no Berlin Wall, and it is not only legal goods that pass from one side to the other. The flow of migrants and drugs make Mexico's relationship with the United States special. Certainly, it is not just the US government that fears the consequences of social and political upheaval in Mexico – the central reason why Washington is able to treat Mexico differently not only from the rest of Latin America but also from the rest of the world. This was true during the 1980s debt crisis, and it was even more apparent during Mexico's financial crisis after the collapse of the peso in December 1994.

The most visible evidence of US exceptionalism towards Mexico is the North American Free Trade Agreement (NAFTA). A bold and ambitious project, NAFTA can in theory be extended to other countries through the accession clause or it might even be replaced in 2005 by the Free Trade Area of the Americas (FTAA). However, at present NAFTA is deeply unpopular in the USA – a victim of the way in which it was marketed in 1993, opposition to Mexican immigration, and the 1995 rescue package – and this is unlikely to change in the short-term. NAFTA, then, is here to stay (see Chapter 5) but it has reinforced Mexican exceptionalism in the minds of the US policy-making elite and reduced the chances that other parts of Latin America might receive similar treatment. Indeed, with Puerto Rico undertaking a new attempt at statehood, one can expect renewed efforts from US politicians to dampen expectations elsewhere in the region.

The current reluctance of the hegemon to exploit its privilege to maximum effect is met with mixed feelings in the rest of the hemisphere. Washington's general reluctance to wield the big stick is, of course, welcomed in Latin America, but most republics have a long list of needs that can only be satisfied by greater US involvement in their affairs. The small states of the Caribbean seek NAFTA parity, but to little effect; indeed, such is the negative connotation of the word 'NAFTA' that the latest attempt to secure congressional parity has dropped any reference to it at all. At the same time, a number of Andean countries, notably Colombia, call for much greater understanding and cooperation on the drug issue; Southern Cone states are pressing for an end to non-tariff barriers and for greater market access; and Brazil wants US support for its claim to a permanent seat on the UN Security Council.

The US government has not been unsympathetic in its public response to these requests, but, as we have stressed, there is still a considerable imbalance between what it wants from the region and what the region wants of the USA. Much of the US agenda was met by the Washington Consensus, by means of which all the administrations since President Reagan's have found themselves in the agreeable position of pushing on an already opened door. Since Latin America already meets much of the agenda that Washington has laid out on a global scale, minor differences, such as Argentine intellectual property laws, have been tackled on an *ad hoc* basis, which provides flexibility but also discourages general review, particularly of region-wide issues. Whether this will continue to be the case depends to a very large degree on whether the economic problems welling up in 1998 become deeper and wider, requiring more than short-term bail-outs. In all events, the speed with which contagion shifted from the Asian Tigers to China and Russia and on to Latin America underlines the danger of reposing on formal agreement and expectations of residual stability.

Multilateralism versus Unilateralism

The identification of a general satisfaction in Washington with the state of hemispheric affairs may initially seem to sit uneasily with the new preference for summitry. Starting with the Miami summit of December 1994, when the FTAA concept was formally launched, the 34 countries of the Americas – all of them except Cuba – have been meeting regularly at ministerial and vice-ministerial level to discuss a wide range of trade and non-trade issues. The negotiations for the FTAA were formally initiated at the summit in Santiago in April 1998. Yet the pomp and circumstance of summitry often masks its limitations. In over four years of such high-level meetings little or nothing practical has been achieved, and the non-trade agenda at the Santiago summit – education, democracy and human rights, the eradication of poverty, the rights of women and indigenous peoples – suggests that little new is expected on the commercial front, where President Clinton's failure to acquire fast-track authority to negotiate would seem to have crippled all but long-term prospects.

On the other hand, the summitry experience does confront the US government with a clear choice between unilateralism and multilateralism. Washington has been historically reluctant to submit to multilateral authority and has shown a marked preference for unilateralism. No serious student of Latin America can fail to notice the numerous occasions in this century in which Latin American republics have been subjected to unilateral action without even a figleaf of support from the international community (the chapters here by Domínguez, Coatsworth and Dunkerley make this point in different ways). In more recent years, though, US administrations have adopted a multilateral approach on a number of important issues. Some of these are trade-related and are effectively forced on the USA by its commitments under the World Trade Organisation (WTO) or NAFTA. Others, such as the invasion of Haiti, have had the support of the international community expressed through the UN Security Council.

The present government of the United States shows every sign of being authentically torn between multilateralism and unilateralism. On Cuba it maintains an aggressive unilateralism, although this has been sharply reinforced since 1996 by congressional involvement. On drugs Washington as a whole has hitherto shown little sympathy for multilateralism, the process of annual certification being maintained despite universal condemnation from Latin America. Even if this mechanism is dropped or radically revised, one would still wish to see further indications of a different approach. Similarly, measures to control migration have been adopted with little or no concern for their impact in the south. On these issues, then, there is very little evidence to suggest a serious commitment to multilateral collaboration.

Nevertheless, there does exist a multilateral strand to US diplomacy in the region, and the Summits of the Americas are helping to build it into a trend. Hemispheric security is addressed through military cooperation across a range of activities, and the USA has worked efficiently and smoothly with Argentina, Brazil and Chile to resolve the border dispute between Peru and Ecuador. The Organisation of American States (OAS), for most of its fifty years little more than a tool for US unilateralism, has been playing a discernibly more independent role in the monitoring of elections. The Economic Commission for Latin America and the Caribbean (ECLAC), of which the USA is a member, has had some success in repairing its tattered reputation following the demise of import-substituting industrialisation (ISI). The USA has been content to allow the international financial agencies – the Inter-American Development Bank (IDB), the International Monetary Fund (IMF) and the World Bank – a greater role in economic supervision in the region; although many will remain sceptical as to the extent of genuine multilateralism involved because of the dominant US position within each of these organisations.

What, then, is still critically lacking is an institutional commitment to multilateralism. While members of the European Union have decreasing scope for unilateral activity, the United States has kept its options as open as possible. Where the issues are perceived as relatively unimportant – or at least not of strategic concern – the US government suspends its suspicions of the multilateral approach. In other fields, the familiar rhetoric of sovereignty and national security and interest is wheeled out to mask a refusal to collaborate on any terms other than Washington's own. It is at the very least an uncomfortable state of affairs for the other states of the hemisphere: multilateralism when it is unimportant and unilateralism in other cases. However, complaint alone is insufficient, and the most likely framework for encouraging progress through institutionalisation would seem to be through the Summit of the Americas, where Washington might be more willing to accept an agenda not entirely of its own construction.

Trade and Investment

With respect to trade and investment, US-Latin American relations in recent years have been dominated by discussion over the future FTAA. The regular meetings of working groups have defined the agenda and established a huge pool of knowledge about the different systems in place in the 34 states. The points of conflict are now better understood. At the ministerial level some progress has been made in marking out the route towards hemispheric integration: negotiation can be by country (the NAFTA preference) or by block (the MERCOSUR choice); implementation depends on consensus; nothing is to be agreed unless everything is agreed, although an 'early harvest' may be permitted where its fruits are uncontroversial.

The Santiago summit formally launched the negotiations and these duly began in Miami in November 1998, but progress beyond Santiago will be much more difficult. The absence of fast-track is one obstacle, but there are many others. Merging a myriad bilateral arrangements and a handful of multilateral ones into a single FTAA is immensely complicated. MERCOSUR, as an (imperfect) customs union will survive, but NAFTA would have to perish – there cannot be a free trade agreement (FTA) within a FTAA. If the NAFTA treaty devoted 200 pages to rules of origin, the FTAA will require several volumes on this topic alone. The agricultural sector must be included by common consent, but most of the countries of the Americas – not just the USA – are no more enthusiastic about agricultural trade liberalisation than their European counterparts. A level playing field for public procurement goes far beyond what most politicians in Latin America consider acceptable.

If the United States, and to a lesser extent Brazil, throw the full weight of their formidable diplomatic arsenal behind the FTAA, it could still be achieved despite the obstacles listed above. However, neither country has yet shown much disposition to do so. Brazil has other priorities as it seeks to consolidate its regional position through an extension of MERCOSUR to all South American republics. The Clinton administration took three years from the Miami summit to ask Congress for fast-track negotiating authority, only to withdraw the request when it became clear that the President's own party would not back it (it was defeated in September 1998 when the Republicans in Congress forced a vote). Brazil and the USA do not even share a common vision of the route towards the FTAA, disagreeing on almost all issues of substance.

Brazil's reluctance to give priority to the FTAA is understandable. Adjusting to trade liberalisation has not been easy and many weak points remain, as the financial crisis faced by Brazil at the end of 1998 showed; this is not the moment, argue many in Brazil, to permit a much greater challenge from US firms in the domestic Brazilian market. US reluctance is also rational. Trade (albeit skewed towards Mexico) and investment are developing healthily without the FTAA. The USA has kept its market share of a fast-growing market for imports despite the re-emergence of regional integration schemes, and enjoys an undisputed dominance of Mexican trade. The USA has been much quicker than other countries to exploit the new opportunities for foreign investment and the financial press in recent weeks has highlighted the travails of European firms seeking to match the power and prestige of US conglomerates in financial services. On the principle that 'if it ain't broke, don't fix it', the US administration has no particular reason to take political risks in the pursuit of hemispheric integration.

And risks there would be. NAFTA has gone from a political asset to a political liability in a very short time, making it difficult to sell the concept of a FTAA to a sceptical US public. It was already clear that the US economy cannot maintain the extraordinary dynamism of recent years, and a more moderate rate of growth in the future will raise the spectre of job losses attributable to hemispheric integration. Even if the gains outweigh the losses, it remains the case – as with NAFTA – that losers are more vocal than gainers and often more electorally concentrated. And NAFTA is more than trade in US perceptions; Mexico's association in the public mind with illegal migration, drugs, corruption and instability makes an extension of NAFTA through the FTAA a risky option for any US president. Perhaps there are parallels here with the European debate on extending the EU to include Turkey.

Democracy

Democracy, in the Cold War, was considered a luxury to which the United States needed to pay little attention. What mattered at root was a country's willingness to support the USA in the global struggle against communism. Governments in Latin

America of whatever stripe, from kleptocracies in the Caribbean Basin to military dictators in the Southern Cone, were tolerated as long as they abided by this simple rule. Those that flaunted it were implacably opposed. On occasions the victims of this hostility, as in Sandinista Nicaragua, were authoritarian regimes, but more often than not, as in Chile under Allende, they were democratic governments.

Such a clear-cut state of affairs ended along with the Cold War. US administrations now pay more than lip-service to democracy and US intervention since the end of the Cold War – in Panama (1989) and Haiti (1993) – have removed dictators. Indeed, where a democratic regime has been under threat – as in Venezuela after 1990, Guatemala in 1992 and Paraguay in 1996 – a US government has been quick to show its displeasure and has been content to join forces with others in doing so. It is now hard to imagine any dictator coming to power through a military coup in Latin America and surviving for more than a few months. On the other hand, this is not the only route to an authoritarian regime, and manipulation of constitutions by civilians (often with extensive popular support), such as Alberto Fujimori in Peru, has both concentrated political power and transgressed fundamental protocols of liberal democracy. More of this could occur and might well, as in the Peruvian case, be tolerated by Washington.

The new US approach to political form has been tested to the limit in Mexico, where ballot-rigging survived the Cold War and the electoral playing-field was until recently anything but level. However, with discreet prodding from the US government the Mexican authorities have now adopted a system of electoral rules that allows Mexico to be classified as an electoral democracy on all but the harshest of tests. It remains an imperfect democracy on a wider definition and even in electoral terms the willingness of the ruling party to sacrifice the greatest prize has yet to be fully tested, but there can be no doubting that elections in Mexico now take place under very different circumstances to those of a few years ago.

However, there is no room for complacency. As John Coatsworth's chapter makes plain, the US definition of democracy is an absolutely minimalist one, and reduces essentially to the holding of periodic contested elections. This allows the US government to declare Costa Rica and Paraguay both to be democracies, although it is obvious to most serious observers that the differences in political practice in these two countries are more important than the similarities. Equally, because the promotion of a democratic culture in Latin America is a relatively low priority, US actions in other areas take little or no account of the impact of other measures on the democratic process. It is something of a miracle that Colombian democracy survived the US campaign from 1994 to 1998 to remove President Samper from office because of the alleged involvement of narco-dollars in his election campaign; its survival owes no thanks to the Clinton administration or its envoys in Colombia. Bolivian democracy has also suffered from the US priority given to drug-trafficking in that country, while the authoritarian elites who dominate governments in Central America (including Panama) have become extremely skilled at addressing the major US priorities in the region in exchange for a blind eye to some of their less democratic practices.

Cuba

From the start of the 19th century, the United States has nurtured an interest in Cuba out of all proportion to its size and wealth. While all countries pay particular attention to their neighbours, the US concern with Cuba in the last 200 years has been remarkable. During the Cold War this was more understandable, although the Soviet Union never paid quite the same attention to Turkey. What is more surprising is that the end of the Cold War appears not to have brought any diminution of interest in the affairs of the Caribbean island. Altogether impoverished, Cuba is in no position to threaten any country – least of all the United States – and yet it is subject to criteria that the USA does not apply in the same way anywhere else.

The impression of Cuba's special status for the United States is reinforced by the passage of both the Torricelli law in 1992 and the Helms-Burton law in 1996. The latter in particular uses a language and set of assumptions that sit oddly with US policies towards the rest of Latin America. This time the blueprint for democracy is detailed and prescriptive, unlike the vague declarations considered sufficient in the case of other countries. Only in the case of Cuba does Congress have the right to approve, if not determine, US policy. All efforts to promote a multilateral approach by US allies inside and outside the Americas are spurned in favour of an aggressive unilateralism reminiscent of President Theodore Roosevelt almost 100 years ago.

It is tempting to assume that this strange state of affairs is due to the overwhelming influence of the Cuban-American lobby in the United States and, in particular, the role played by the Cuban American National Foundation (CANF). The latter, after all, was largely responsible for the wording of the Helms-Burton law and has been very successful in promoting the image of a single voice in the exile community. Yet US concerns with Castro's Cuba predate the formation of CANF, and US policy has not always reflected CANF interests – most notably in 1994 when Cuban *émigrés* lost the automatic right to asylum they had previously enjoyed. Thus, the influence of CANF should not be exaggerated; the death of its founder, Jorge Mas Canosa, and the failure to find an equally charismatic successor are matters of considerable consequence, but they should not yet be taken as marking the start of a new era in the politics of exile, still less a change in US policy towards Cuba. That policy may well change, but it will not primarily be due to the decline in influence of CANF.

Here it is worth reiterating our earlier point that US policy towards Cuba is subject to a great deal of inertia. The high profile Cuba acquired after the revolution has left a legacy of hostility and mistrust that cannot easily be changed. And there is no great incentive to bring about a change of direction. Cuba may no longer be a threat to US interests, but the costs to the USA of maintaining the *status quo* remain remarkably slight. There will be benefits, particularly for US capital, from a more normal relationship, but there are also heavy political costs. No US President, not even one from the Republican Party, can afford to be seen as 'soft' on Fidel Castro and there may even be some advantages from his continued presence; the flow of migrants is controlled, there is (almost?) no onward transit of drugs and no need to renegotiate the Guantanamo naval base.

Drugs and Migration

Even before the end of the Cold War drugs and migration had come to represent for the United States two of the most important issues in its relations with Latin America. With the fall of the Berlin Wall, however, these two issues have rapidly filled the void created by the collapse of communism. The importance of migration wanes as one goes further south, but drugs is a crucial issue in US relations with many Latin American countries.

As with multilateralism, the United States is ambivalent towards (legal) migration, now running at nearly one million per year (much of it from Latin America). As with other developed countries running a service-based economy, migrants in the USA play an important function in reducing the segmentation of the labour market and applying downward pressure to wage rates. Yet legal migration from Latin America in the USA is not limited to unskilled workers; skilled migrants in high-tech activities are also important. Indeed, without both types of migrants it is hard to imagine the US economy functioning as well as it has done in the last ten years.

Thus, legal migration is here to stay, but illegal migration, running at from 200,000 to 400,000 per year (mainly from Latin America), is another matter. This has become deeply unpopular, as the campaign over Proposition 187 in California has shown. Even if efforts to prevent it are largely ineffectual, it can always be argued that illegal migration would be even higher in the absence of such measures. Washington has to confront the sober and compelling evidence that the flow of illegal migration from Latin America may accelerate in response to both economic and cultural changes in the region.

If the flow is not seen to be reduced, the US government will almost certainly be tempted to adopt more radical measures to keep potential migrants at home. NAFTA, after all, was adopted in part to create opportunities for Mexicans to stay at home. Had NAFTA been a political success in the USA, it might have led to other measures of a similar nature. However, it is not seen in those terms within the US polity, and history does not suggest that such measures will work. Operation Bootstrap may have given Puerto Rico an income per head that is the envy of the region, but it also did little to moderate migration to the USA. Migration therefore appears as a problem without solution for the foreseeable future, as it is in Europe and increasingly in Japan. On the other hand, Suárez-Orozco's chapter provides us with hints as to how, if it were to be taken in a regional context and seen through an optic that expands and modifies the traditional culture and ideology of Anglo-America, it could be approached in a positive light, taken as a contribution to US society, and at the same time be palliated at its origins.

The prospects for an early improvement in US relations with Latin America over the drugs issue are remote. The certification process may have been modulated in 1998 to assuage Latin American sensibilities, but there was no doubting the unilateral – and unfair – nature of the process. As long as there is a US demand, there will be a Latin American supply, since the countries of the region (including, of course, the Caribbean) are so much better placed than those elsewhere to satisfy that demand. A shift in consumption patterns in the USA towards synthetic drugs or, less probably, a fall in demand could make a difference, but there seems little likelihood of either change.

As in Europe, the nature of the debate within the USA – this is not a dialogue with Latin America – may shift towards decriminalisation and legalisation. At present the prospect is remote, but one should never underestimate the capacity of the agenda to shift rapidly and unpredictably in the USA. This is an issue where each generation has very different views and the coming to power in the next 20 years of a new wave of politicians many of whom will have first-hand experience of drug consumption could make a difference, although the most realistic forecast is that drugs will continue to plague relations between the United States and Latin America for many years to come.

The European Union

The closer ties between Latin America and the USA since the end of the Cold War have certainly encouraged republics to diversify their trade and investment links. The European Union, with its vast internal market and substantial outward flow of investment, has been the obvious candidate. Mexico – since the launch of NAFTA ever more closely integrated into North America – is a case in point. From President de la Madrid (1982-88) onwards, there has been a desire for closer ties to the European Union to offset the dominant position of the USA.

The European Union (EU) has been pleased to respond. Once nervous of entering into the US 'backyard', the EU now favours a diversification of its own external links to compensate for the inward-looking bias of the single market. There is also a missionary zeal to do so where the prospective partners are members of a regional integration scheme, for which the EU feels, with some justification, that it is the world's market leader. Its 'third generation' agreements with Latin American countries have been well received and its bold foray into Central America in the mid-1980s has been widely praised as a responsible and humanitarian gesture.

Both partners therefore favour the creation of closer links through fourth generation accords involving free trade agreements (based on reciprocal concessions), technology transfer and joint ventures. The agreement between Mexico and the EU is the furthest advanced, with negotiations on the free trade pact starting in November 1998, but the EU-Latin America summit in June 1999 should provide an opportunity to make progress with MERCOSUR and Chile as well.

On the surface, then, matters seem remarkably well-starred, but – as with the FTAA – many obstacles remain. The European agenda for the next few years is intense and difficult: the single currency in 1999; the need to reduce unemployment without the use of monetary and exchange rate policy at the national level; enlargement to the east at the start of the new millennium; a renewal or replacement for the Lomé Convention linking the EU to over 70 African, Caribbean and Pacific states. Fitting Latin America into this hectic agenda will not be easy.

New trade agreements, in any case, require trade concessions. The WTO launches a new round of trade liberalisation for agriculture in 1999 and the EU must brace itself for that. If the EU was convinced the FTAA would go ahead, there is no doubt that the fourth generation of agreements would stand a better chance. There is no urgency, however, until 'fast-track' is approved. Thus, Latin American republics should not assume that the EU will soon be playing a much larger part in hemispheric affairs. For better or for worse, the USA will remain the hegemonic power in the region, with Europe able to offer only token resistance to US unilateralism and unable to offer a real alternative to US multilateralism. The good will expressed on both sides of the Atlantic will remain, but the EU is not a simple alternative to the USA for Latin American states. In external relations it is the relationship with the USA that will continue to weigh most heavily for Latin America, and that relationship will continue to be shaped by an asymmetry in power and resource. The negotiation and management of such asymmetry is not, however, irredeemably doomed as a rhetorical, inequitable and patronising enterprise. However, the countries of the Americas will need to show their skills in this area and it is our sincere hope that this book will make that task easier.

BIBLIOGRAPHY

Acevedo, Domingo E. and Grossman, Claudio (1996) 'The Organization of American States and the Protection of Democracy', in Tom Farer (ed.), *Beyond Sovereignty: Collectively Defending Democracy in the Americas* (Baltimore and London: Johns Hopkins University Press)

Adams, John Quincy (1913) *Writings of John Quincy Adams*, vol. VII (New York: Macmillan)

Aduana General de la República (1996) 'Resolución no. 34/96 – Sobre el Régimen Especial Aduanero en las Zonas Francas y Parques Industriales' (18 October), www.tips.cu

Aguilar, A. (1994) 'Is there an alternative? The political constraints on NAFTA', in V. Bulmer-Thomas, N. Craske and M. Serrano (eds.), *Mexico and the North American Free Trade Agreement: Who Will Benefit?* (Basingstoke: Macmillan), pp. 119-30

Aguirre, B.E. (1994) 'Cuban mass migration and the social construction of deviants', *Bulletin of Latin American Research*, vol. 13, no. 2 (May), pp. 155-84

Ainslie, Ricardo (1998) 'Cultural Mourning, Immigration, and Engagement: Vignettes from the Mexican Experience', in Marcelo M. Suárez-Orozco (ed.), *Crossings: Mexican Immigration in Interdisciplinary Perspectives* (Cambridge, MA: DRCLAS/Harvard University Press), pp. 285-300

Albert, Bill (1988) *South America and the First World War: The Impact of the War on Brazil, Argentina, Peru and Chile* (Cambridge: Cambridge University Press)

Albright, Madeleine K., Secretary of State (1997) *Welcoming Remarks to the Council of the Americas*, Washington, D.C., 28 April

Alegría, Reynaldo R., Cué, Félix and Vélez, Gustavo (1992) *Normalización de relaciones entre Cuba y los Estados Unidos. Retos y oportunidades para Puerto Rico* (San Juan, PR: Oficina del Gobernador, Consejo de Desarrollo Estratégico para Puerto Rico)

Alexeev, Aleksandr (1984) 'Cuba después del triunfo de la revolución (I)', *América Latina* (October), pp. 56-67

Alfonso, Pablo (1996) 'Lage: Ley tiene "efectos negativos" en Cuba,' *El Nuevo Herald*, 24 July

Americas Watch (1992) 'Dangerous Dialogue: Attacks on Freedom of Expression in Miami's Cuban Exile Community', *Americas Watch* (New York), vol. 4, no. 7

Andelman, D.A. (1994) 'The Drug Money Maze', *Foreign Affairs*, July/August, pp. 95-108

Anderson, B. (1992) 'The New World Disorder', *New Left Review*, no. 193 (May/June), pp. 3-13

Andreas, Peter (1998) 'The U.S. Immigration Control Offensive: Constructing an Image of Order on the Southwest Border', in Marcelo M. Suárez-Orozco (ed.),

Crossings: Mexican Immigration in Interdisciplinary Perspectives (Cambridge, MA: DRCLAS/Harvard University Press), pp. 343-56

Anstey, Roger (1980), 'The Pattern of British Abolitionism in the Eighteenth and Nineteenth Centuries', in C. Bolt and S. Drescher (eds.), *Anti-Slavery, Religion and Reform* (Folkestone: Dawson)

Bagley, B.M. (1995) 'After San Antonio', in B.M. Bagley and W.O. Walker III (eds.), *Drug Trafficking in the Americas* (Miami: North-South Center Press, University of Miami)

Bagley, B.M. and J.G. Tokatlian (1991) *Droga y dogma: La narcodiplomacia entre Estados Unidos y América Latina en la década de los ochenta y su proyección para los noventa*, Documentos Ocasionales C.E.I., no. 23, September-October

Baldwin, Deborah (1990) *Protestants and the Mexican Revolution: Missionaries, Ministers, and Social Change* (Urbana, Ill.: University of Illinois Press)

Banco Nacional de Cuba (1995) *Informe económico 1994* (Havana: Banco Nacional de Cuba)

Banco Nacional de Cuba (1996) *Economic Report 1995* (Havana: Banco Nacional de Cuba)

Barrios Morón, Raúl (1989) *Bolivia y Estados Unidos: Democracia, Derechos Humanos y Narcotráfico* (La Paz: FLACSO, HISBOL)

Basch, L., Schiller, N.G. et al (1995) *Nations Unbound: Transnational Projects, Postcolonial Predicaments and Deterritorialized Nation-States* (Basel: Gordon and Breach Science Publishers)

Batista Odio, Carlos (1996) 'La política económica de Estados Unidos contra Cuba. Bloqueo y compensaciones', Centro de Estudios de los Estados Unidos, Universidad de la Habana

Baumann, Renato and Carvalho, Alexandre (1997) *Simulação dos efeitos comerciais da ALCA para o Brasil* (Brasília: CEPAL)

Bean, F., de la Garza, R. et al (eds.) (1997) *At the Crossroads: Mexico and U.S. Immigration Policy* (Lanham, Maryland: Rowman & Littlefield Publishers)

Bekarevich, A.D. (1982) *El Gran Octubre y la Revolución Cubana* (Havana, 1982)

Bemis, Samuel Flagg (1943) *The Latin American Policy of the United States* (New York: Harcourt, Brace & Co.)

Bergquist, Charles (1996) *Labor and the Course of American Democracy. US History in Latin American Perspective* (London: Verso)

Bernal, Richard L. (1997) *Trade Blocs: A Regionally Specific Phenomenon or a Global Trend?* (Washington, D.C.: National Policy Association)

Berríos, Rubén (1989) 'The USSR and the Andean Countries: Economic and Political Dimensions', in Eusebio Mujal-León (ed.), *The USSR and Latin America: A Developing Relationship* (Boston: Unwin Hyman)

Bertram, E., Blachman, M., Sharpe, K. and Andreas, P. (1996) *Drug War Politics: The Price of Denial* (Berkeley: University of California Press)

Bhagwati, J., Greenaway, D. and Panagariya, A. (1998) 'Trading Preferentially: Theory and Practice,' *Economic Journal*, vol. 108, no. 449, July

Binational Study on Migration (1997) *Binational Study: Migration Between Mexico and the United States* (Washington, D.C.: prepublication copy)

Blasier, Cole (1978) *The Hovering Giant* (Pittsburgh: University of Pittsburgh Press)

Blasier, Cole (1985) *The Hovering Giant: U.S. Responses to Revolutionary Change in Latin America, 1910-1985*, rev. edn. (Pittsburgh: University of Pittsburgh Press)

Blasier, Cole (1987) *The Giant's Rival: The USSR and Latin America* , rev. edn. (Pittsburgh: University of Pittsburgh Press)

Bolivia, República de (1997) '¡Por la Dignidad! Estrategia Boliviana de la lucha contra el narcotráfico, 1998-2002' (La Paz: República de Bolivia)

Booth, Cathy (1992) 'The Man who would oust Castro', *Time*, October 26

Borjas, G. (1994) *Tired, Poor, on Welfare. Arguing Immigration* (New York: Simon and Schuster)

Boswell, T.D. and Curtis, J.R. (1983) *The Cuban-American Experience: Culture, Images and Perspectives* (Totowa, NJ: Rowman and Allanheld)

Boswell, T.D. and Curtis, J.R. (1991) 'The Hispanization of Metropolitan Miami', in Thomas Boswell (ed.), *South Florida: The Winds of Change* (Miami: T. Boswell for the Association of American Geographers)

Buchanan, James (1911) *The Writings of James Buchanan*, ed. J.B. Moore, vol. VIII (Philadelphia: J.B. Lippincott)

Bulmer-Thomas, V. (1994) *The Economic History of Latin America since Independence* (Cambridge: Cambridge University Press)

Bulmer-Thomas, V. (1997) 'Regional Integration in Latin America since 1985: Open Regionalism and Globalisation', in El-Agraa, A. (ed.), *Economic Integration Worldwide* (Basingstoke: Macmillan)

Bulmer-Thomas, V. (1998), 'The Central American Common Market: From Closed to Open Regionalism', *World Development*, vol. 26, no. 2

Bulmer-Thomas, V., Craske, N. and Serrano, M. (1994) *Mexico and the North American Free Trade Agreement: Who Will Benefit?* (Basingstoke: Macmillan)

Bureau of the Census (1996) *Population Projections of the United States by Age, Sex, Race, and Hispanic Origin: 1995 to 2050* (Washington, D.C.: Government Printing Office)

Business International Corporation (1992) *Developing Business Strategies for Cuba* (New York: Business International Corporation)

CANF (undated) *Blue Ribbon Commission on the Economic Reconstruction of Cuba* (Miami: Cuban American National Foundation)

Cárdenas, Enrique (1987) *La industrialización mexicana durante la Gran Depresión* (Mexico: El Colegio de México)

Carmagnani, Marcelo (1994) *Estado y mercado: la economía pública del liberalismo mexicano, 1850-1911* (Mexico: El Colegio de México and Fondo de Cultura Económica)

Carothers, Thomas (1991) *In the Name of Democracy: U.S. Policy toward Latin America in the Reagan Years* (Berkeley: University of California Press)

Carter, Thomas P. and Segura, Roberto D. (1979) *Mexican Americans in School: A Decade of Change* (New York: College Entrance Examination Board)

Castro, Fidel (1993) 'Castro Gives Speech at Moncada Barracks Anniversary', *FBIS-LAT-93-142* (27 July)

Castro, Max (1992) 'The Politics of Language in Miami', in Guillermo Grenier and Alex Stepick (eds.), *Miami Now!* (Gainsville, Fla.: University Press of Florida)

Castro, Max (1995) 'Cuba: The Continuing Crisis', Paper no. 13: *The North-South Agenda*, April, University of Miami

Castro, Max (1997a) 'Transition and the Ideology of Exile', in Miguel Angel Centeno and M. Font (eds.), *Toward a New Cuba? Legacies of a Revolution* (Boulder and London: Lynne Rienner)

Castro, Max (1997b) 'Sondeando a los cubanos', *El Nuevo Herald*, 29 June

Castro, Soraya and Fernández, Luis R. (1992) 'Comercio directo y compensaciones, el patrón de negociación en las relaciones EE:UU-Cuba', Centro de Estudios de los Estados Unidos, Universidad de la Habana

Caulfield, Norman E. (1987) 'The Industrial Workers of the World and Mexican Labor, 1905-1925', unpub. Ph.D. diss., University of Houston

Centeno, Miguel Angel and Font, Maurice (eds.) (1997) *Toward a New Cuba? Legacies of a Revolution* (Boulder and London: Lynne Rienner, 1997)

Central Intelligence Agency (1997) *Cuba: Handbook of Trade Statistics, 1997.* APLA 97-10006 (Washington, D.C.: Central Intelligence Agency, November)

CEPAL/BID (1998) *La Integración Centroamericana y la Institucionalidad Regional* (Mexico City)

Cerdas Cruz, Rodolfo (1986) 'Nicaragua: One Step Forward, Two Steps Back', in Guiseppe Di Palma and Laurence Whitehead (eds.), *The Central American Impasse* (New York: St. Martin's Press)

Cerdas Cruz, Rodolfo (1989) 'New Directions in Soviet Policy towards Latin America', *Journal of Latin American Studies*, vol. 21, part 1 (February)

Cerdas Cruz, Rodolfo (1996) 'Condicionalidad y democracia en Centroamérica. La promoción de la democracia desde el exterior', *Cuadernos de FLACSO*, no. 89 (San José)

Cerdas Cruz, Rodolfo (1996) *Informe político sobre las elecciones de la República Dominicana de 1996. Análisis y perspectivas*, mimeo, IIDH/CAPEL, San José

Chávez, Leo (1992) *Shadowed Lives: Undocumented Immigrants in American Society* (Fort Worth, TX: Harcourt Brace)

Chen, Jorge (1996) 'Las relaciones entre México y Europa hoy', *Revista Mexicana de Política Exterior*, vol. 49, pp. 149-58

Christian Freres (ed.) (1998) *La Co-operación de las Sociedades Civiles de la Unión Europea con América Latina* (AIETI, Madrid)

Clark, Ian (1989) *The Hierarchy of States. Reform and Resistance in the International Order* (Cambridge: Cambridge University Press)

Coatsworth, John H. (1985) 'El Estado y el sector externo en México, 1810-1910', *Secuencia: Revista Americana de Ciencias Sociales,* vol. 2, pp. 40-54

Coatsworth, John H. (1988) 'Patterns of Rural Rebellion in Latin America: Mexico in Comparative Perspective', in Friedrich Katz (ed.), *Riot, Rebellion, and Revolution: Rural Social Conflict in Mexico* (Princeton: Princeton University Press), pp. 21-62

Cobas, Jose A. and Duany, J. (1997) *Cubans in Puerto Rico: Ethnic Economy and Cultural Identity* (Gainsville, Fla.: University Press of Florida)

Coffey, Peter and Corrêa de Lage, Luis (1988) (eds), *The EEC and Brazil* (London: Frances Pinter)

Comisión de Análisis (1997) 'Informe de la Comisión de Análisis y Recomendaciones sobre las Relaciones entre Colombia y Estados Unidos', *Análisis Político* (IEPRI, Universidad Nacional, Bogotá), July

Comisión Económica para América Latina y el Caribe (CEPAL) (1997) *La economía cubana: Reformas estructurales y desempleo en los noventa* (Mexico: Fondo de Cultura Económica)

Comité Estatal de Estadísticas (1991) *Anuario estadístico de Cuba 1989* (Havana)

Commission of the European Communities (1995) 'European Community Support for Regional Economic Integration Efforts among Developing Countries', Communication from the Commission to the Council and the European Parliament, Brussels, 16 June, mimeo

Companys, Yosem E. (1997) 'Institution-Building: Financial Sector Reform in Cuba', *Cuba in Transition – Volume 7* (Washington: Association for the Study of the Cuban Economy)

Congressional Research Service (1988) *International Narcotics Control and Foreign Assistance Certification: Requirements, Procedures, Timetables and Guidelines*, Report prepared for the use of the Committee on Foreign Relations, US Senate, Washington, D.C., March

Congressional Research Service (1996) *International Drug Trade and the U.S. Certification Process: A Critical Review*, Proceedings of a Seminar held by the CRS, 1 March 1996. Report prepared for the Caucus on International Narcotics Control of the US Senate, Washington, D.C., September

Consultores Asociados, S.A. (CONAS) (1995) *Cuba: Inversiones y Negocios, 1995-1996* (Havana: CONAS)

Contributions (1993) Konrad-Adenauer-Stiftung, A.C., no. 3 (Buenos Aires)

Cornelius, Wayne (1998) 'The Structural Embeddedness of Demand for Mexican Immigrant Labor: New Evidence from California', in Marcelo M. Suárez-Orozco (ed.), *Crossings: Mexican Immigration in Interdisciplinary Perspectives* (Cambridge, MA: DRCLAS/Harvard University Press), pp. 115-44

Council on Foreign Relations, Task Force Report (1997) *Rethinking International Drug Control: New Directions for U.S. Policy* (New York: Government Printing Office)

Croucher, Sheila L. (1997) *Imagining Miami: Ethnic Politics in a Postmodern World* (Charlottesville: University Press of Virginia)

Cuban Committee for Democracy (CCD) (c. 1996), *Toward a Peaceful Transition to Democracy in Cuba* (Washington and Miami: CCD)

Davidow, Jeffrey, Assistant Secretary for Inter-American Affairs (1997) *Testimony before the Trade Subcommittee of the House Ways and Means Committee* (Washington, D.C., 22 July)

Davidow, Jeffrey, Assistant Secretary for Inter-American Affairs (1997) 'U.S. Foreign Policy Toward Latin America and the Caribbean in the Clinton Administration's Second Term.' Address before the Council of the Americas, Washington, D.C., 28 April

Davidow, Jeffrey, Assistant Secretary for Inter-American Affairs (1996) 'U.S. Policy Toward Latin America and the Caribbean. Building Upon A Solid Foundation'. Remarks by Assistant Secretary of State Jeffrey Davidow to the Miami Conference on the Caribbean and Latin America, Miami, Florida, 9 December

Davidow, Jeffrey, Assistant Secretary of State for Inter-American Affairs (1997) *Testimony before the House Ways and Means Committee*, Washington, D.C., 22 July

Davis, Nathaniel (1985) *The Last Two Years of Salvador Allende* (Ithaca: Cornell University Press)

de la Campa, R. (1994) 'The Latino diaspora in the United States: sojourns from a Cuban past', *Public Culture*, vol. 6, no. 2 (Winter), pp. 293-318

de la Torre, A. and Kelly, M.R. (1992) 'Regional Trade Arrangements', *Occasional Paper 93* (Washington, D.C.: International Monetary Fund)

de Paiva Abreu, M. (1997) 'O Brasil e a Alca: interesses e alternativas', in J. dos Reis Velloso (ed.), *Brasil: Desafios de um País em Transformação* (Rio de Janeiro: José Olympio)

Deconde, Alexander (1992) *Ethnicity, Race and American Foreign Policy. A History* (Boston)

Decreto-Ley no. 140 (1993) *Gaceta Oficial* 13 August 13

Decreto-Ley no. 165 (1996) Ley sobre Zonas Francas y Parques Industriales: www.prensa-latina.org., 3 June

Desch, Michael C. (1993) *When the Third World Matters; Latin America and United States Grand Strategy* (Baltimore: Johns Hopkins University Press)

Desch, Michael C. (1998) 'Why Latin America May Miss the Cold War: The United States and the Future of Inter-American Security Relations', in Jorge I. Domínguez (ed.), *International Security and Democracy: Latin America and the Caribbean in the Post-Cold War Era* (Pittsburgh: University of Pittsburgh Press)

Devlin, R. and Garay, L.J. (1996) 'From Miami to Cartagena: nine lessons and nine challenges of the FTAA', *Working Papers Series 211* (Washington, D.C.: Inter-American Development Bank)

DeVos, G. (1992) *Social Cohesion and Alienation: Minorities in the United States and Japan* (Boulder: Westview Press)

Diamond, Larry (1996) 'Democracy in Latin America. Degrees, Illusions, and Directions for Consolidation', in Tom Farer (ed.), *Beyond Sovereignty. Collectively Defending Democracy in the Americas* (Baltimore and London: Johns Hopkins University Press)

Díaz-Briquets, Sergio (1995) 'Emigrant Remittances in the Cuban Economy: Their Significance During and After the Castro Regime', *Cuba in Transition – Volume 5* (Washington: Association for the Study of the Cuban Economy)

Díaz-Briquets, Sergio and Pérez-López, Jorge (1997) 'Refugee Remittances: Conceptual Issues and the Cuban and Nicaraguan Experiences,' *International Migration Review*, no. 31 (Summer)

Dominguez, J. (1997) 'US-Cuban Relations: From the Cold War to the Colder War', *Journal of Interamerican Studies and World Affairs*, vol. 39, no. 3, pp. 49-75

Domínguez, Jorge I (1989) *To Make a World Safe for Revolution: Cuba's Foreign Policy* (Cambridge, MA: Harvard University Press)

Drake, Paul (1991), 'From Good Men to Good Neighbor, 1912-1932', in A. Lowenthal (ed.), *Exporting Democracy. The United States and Latin America* (Baltimore: Johns Hopkins University Press)

Dunkerley, James (1984) *Rebellion in the Veins* (London: Verso)

Durand, Jorge (1998) 'Migration and Integration: Intermarriages among Mexicans and Non-Mexicans in the United States', in Marcelo M. Suárez-Orozco (ed.), *Crossings: Mexican Immigration in Interdisciplinary Perspectives* (Cambridge, MA: DRCLAS/Harvard University Press) pp. 209-21

Dussel Peters, Enrique (1997) *La Economía de la Polarización: Teoría y Evolución del Cambio Estructural de las Manufacturas Mexicanas (1988-1996)* (Mexico: UNAM-Editorial Jus)

Dussel, Enrique P. (1998) 'Recent Structural Changes in Mexico's Economy: A Preliminary Analysis of Some Sources of Mexican Migration to the United States', in Marcelo M. Suárez-Orozco (ed.), *Crossings: Mexican Immigration in Interdisciplinary Perspectives* (Cambridge, MA: DRCLAS/Harvard University Press), pp. 55-74

Eck, D.L. (1996) 'Neighboring Faiths', *Harvard Magazine*, no. 99

Edmonston, B. and Passel, J. (eds.) (1994) *Immigration and Ethnicity: The Integration of America's Newest Arrivals* (Washington, D.C., The Urban Institute)

Ellsworth C.S. (1940), 'The American Churches and the Mexican War', *American Historical Review*, XLV

Emerson, Ralph Waldo (1969) *The Journals and Miscellaneous Notebooks of Ralph Waldo Emerson*, vol. VII (Cambridge, MA: Harvard University Press)

Espenshade, Thomas and Belanger, M. (1998) 'Immigration and Public Opinion', in Marcelo M. Suárez-Orozco (ed.), *Crossings: Mexican Immigration in Interdisciplinary Perspectives* (Cambridge, MA: DRCLAS/Harvard University Press), pp. 79-105

Espinal, Rosario (1998) 'Elecciones en la década de los 90s', in Rodolfo Cerdas Cruz, Juan Rial and Daniel Zovatto (eds.), *Elecciones y Democracia en América Latina 1992-1996: urnas y desencanto político* (San José: IIDH/CAPEL)

Espino, María Dolores (1994) 'Tourism in Cuba: A Development Strategy for the 1990s?' in Jorge Pérez-López (ed.), *Cuba at a Crossroads* (Gainesville, Fla.: University Press of Florida)

Estrada, Leo (1997) 'Demographics and the New Immigration', Paper presented to the Spencer Foundation Conference on Immigration and Education, University of California, Los Angeles, 8 October

Ethier, W.J. (1998) 'The New Regionalism', *Economic Journal*, vol. 108, no. 449, July

Euro-Latin American Forum (1995*) Open Integration: The European Union and Mercosul and the International System* (Lisbon: IEEI)

Fauriol, Georges (ed.) (1995) *Haitian Frustrations: Dilemmas for U.S. Policy* (Washington, D.C.: Center for Strategic and International Studies)

Fernández, R. (1997) 'Returns to Regionalism: An Evaluation of Non-traditional Gains from RTAs', *CEPR Discussion Paper 1634*

Fernández, R. and Portes, J. (1998), 'Return to Regionalism: An Analysis of Non-traditional Gains from Regional Trade Agreements', *World Bank Economic Review*, vol. 12, no. 2, May

FitzGerald, E.V.K. (1994) 'The impact of NAFTA on the Latin American economies', in V. Bulmer-Thomas, N. Craske and M. Serrano (eds.), *Mexico and the North American Free Trade Agreement: Who Will Benefit?* (Basingstoke: Macmillan), pp. 133-48

FitzGerald, E.V.K. (1997) 'International Capital Markets and Open-Economy Macroeconomics', *Oxford Development Studies,* vol. 24, no. 1, pp. 79-92

FitzGerald, E.V.K. (forthcoming) 'Short-term capital flows, the real economy and income distribution in developing countries', in S. Griffith-Jones, M. Montes and A. Nasution (eds.), *Managing Capital Flows in Developing Countries* (Oxford: Oxford University Press)

FitzGerald, E.V.K. and Grabbe, H. (1997) 'Integración financiera: la experiencia europea y sus lecciones para América Latina', *Integración y Comercio*, vol. 1, no. 2, pp. 85-124

FitzGerald, E.V.K. with Cubero, R. and Lemann, A. (1998) *The Development Implications of the Multilateral Agreement on Investment* (London: Department for International Development)

Fortín, Carlos (1975) 'Principled Pragmatism in the Face of External Pressure: The Foreign Policy of the Allende Government', in R. Hellman and H. J. Rosenbaum (eds.), *Latin America: The Search for a New International Role* (New York: Sage Publications)

Forum Euro-Latino-Americano (1997) *Além do Comércio: Ampliar as Relaçoes Europa-Mercosu*e (Lisbon: IEEI)

Gamarra, Eduardo (1991) 'The Administration of Justice in Bolivia: An Institutional Analysis' (Miami: Florida International University, Center for the Administration of Justice)

Gamarra, Eduardo (1998) 'Las relaciones entre Estados Unidos y Bolivia durante el gobierno de Gonzalo Sánchez de Lozada', in Andrés Franco (ed.), *Estados Unidos y los países andinos, 1993-1997: poder y desintegración* (Bogotá: Pontificia Universidad Javeriana)

Gamarra, Eduardo A. (1987) 'Political Stability, Democratization, and the Bolivian National Congress', unpubl. PhD dissertation, University of Pittsburgh

Gamarra, Eduardo A. (1994a) *Entre la Droga y la Democracia* (La Paz: ILDIS)

Gamarra, Eduardo A. (1994b) 'Market-Oriented Reforms and Democratization in Bolivia', in Joan Nelson (ed.), *A Precarious Balance: Democracy and*

Economic Reforms in Latin America (Washington, D.C.: International Center for Economic Growth and Overseas Development Council), pp. 21-94

Gamarra, Eduardo A. (1997a) 'Transnational Criminal Organizations in Bolivia', paper prepared for Tom Farer and Michael Shifter's Inter-American Dialogue Project on Transnational Crime

Gamarra, Eduardo A. (1997b) 'Fighting Drugs in Bolivia: United States and Bolivian Perceptions at Odds', in Madeline Barbara Leons and Harry Sanabria (eds.), *Coca, Cocaine and the Bolivian Reality* (Albany: State University of New York Press)

Gamarra, Eduardo A. (1997b) 'Militarization, the War on Drugs, and the Prospects for Bolivian Democracy', paper presented at the XVI Congress of the Latin American Studies Association

Ganoe, W.A. (1964) *The History of the United States Army* (New York: no publ. details)

Garcia M.C. (1992) *Dreaming in Cuban: a Novel* (New York: Ballantine Books)

Garcia M.C. (1996) 'Los exiliados Cubanos y los Cubanoamericanos', in L.A. de la Cuesta and M.C. Herrera (eds.), *Razón y Pasión: Veinticinco años de Estudios Cubanos* (Miami: Instituto de Estudios Cubanos). Also *Havana USA: Cuban Exiles and Cuban Americans in South Florida, 1959-1994* (Berkeley: University of California Press)

Gautenbeim, J.W. (ed.) (1950) *The Evolution of our Latin American Policy. A Documentary Record* (New York)

Gleijeses, Piero (1992) 'The Limits of Sympathy: The United States and the Independence of Spanish America', *Journal of Latin America Studies*, vol. 24, part 3, pp. 481-505

Gómez, Aurora (1998) 'The Evolution of Prices and Real Wages in Mexico from the Porfiriato to the Revolution', in John H. Coatsworth and Alan M. Taylor (eds.), *Latin America and the World Economy Since 1800* (Cambridge, MA: Harvard University Press), chap. 13

González Baker, Susan, Bean, Frank D. et al (1998) 'U.S. Immigration Policies and Trends: The Growing Importance of Migration from Mexico', in Marcelo M. Suárez-Orozco (ed.), *Crossings: Mexican Immigration in Interdisciplinary Perspectives* (Cambridge, MA: DRCLAS/Harvard University Press), pp. 79-105

Grenier, G.G., Gladwin, H. and McLaughen, D. (1995) *The 1995 FIU Cuba Poll* (Miami: Florida International University, Institute for Public Opinion Research)

Grenier, Guillermo J. and Stepick, Alex (eds.) (1992) *Miami Now! Immigration, Ethnicity, and Social Change* (Gainesville: University Press of Florida)

Grieb, Kenneth (1977) *The Latin American Policy of Warren G. Harding* (Fort Worth)

Grieco, Joseph (1995) 'The Maastricht Treaty, Economic and Monetary Union, and the Neorealist Research Program', *Review of International Studies*, vol. 21, no. 1

Griffith, Ivelaw Lloyd (1997) 'EU Drug Policy in the Andes: International Cooperation and the Politics of Illicit Cocaine Supply', unpublished DPhil thesis, Oxford University

Griffith-Jones, S. (forthcoming) 'The Mexican Peso Crisis', in S. Griffith-Jones, M. Montes and A. Nasution (eds.), *Managing Capital Flows in Developing Countries* (Oxford: Oxford University Press)

Gruben, W.C. and Welch, J. (1994) 'Is NAFTA more than a free trade agreement? A view from the United States', in V. Bulmer-Thomas, N. Craske and M. Serrano (eds.), *Mexico and the North American Free Trade Agreement: Who Will Benefit?* (Basingstoke: Macmillan), pp. 177-202

Gunn, Clissold G (1997) 'Cuba-US relations and the process of Transition: Possible Consequences of Covert Agendas', in M.A. Centeno and M. Font (eds.), *Toward a New Cuba? Legacies of a Revolution* (Boulder and London: Lynne Rienner), pp. 73-90

Gutiérrez, David (1998) 'Ethnic Mexicans and the Transformation of "American" Social Space: Reflections on Recent History', in Marcelo M. Suárez-Orozco (ed.), *Crossings: Mexican Immigration in Interdisciplinary Perspectives* (Cambridge, MA: DRCLAS/Harvard University Press), pp. 79-105

Haber, Steve and Rozo, Armando (forthcoming) 'Political Instability and Economic Performance: Evidence from Revolutionary Mexico', *World Politics*

Higham, J. (1955) *Strangers in the Land: Patterns of American Nativism, 1860-1925* (New Brunswick and London: Rutgers University Press)

Hing, B.O. (1993) *Making and Remaking Asian America Through Immigration Policy* (Stanford: Stanford University Press)

Hirst, Monica (1992) 'MERCOSUR and the New Circumstances for its Integration', *CEPAL Review*, no. 46

Hoffmann, Stanley (1994) 'La quimera del orden mundial', *Estudios Internacionales, Revista del IRIPAZ*, año 5, no. 10 (Guatemala, July-December), p. 43 onwards, translated from *The New York Review of Books*, 9 April, 1992

Hull, Cordell (1948) *The Memoirs of Cordell Hull*, II Vols (London: Hodder & Stoughton)

Human Rights Watch (1994) 'Dangerous Dialogue Revisited', *Human Rights Watch*, vol. 14 (Nov.)

Hurrell, Andrew (1996) 'The Case of MERCOSUR', paper presented at LSE workshop on regionalism, London, 4 July

IDB (1998) 'Integration and trade in the Americas: a preliminary estimate of 1997 trade' (Washington, D.C.: Interamerican Development Bank)

IMF (1977) *Balance of Payments Manual*, Fourth Edition (Washington, D.C.: International Monetary Fund)

IMF (1997), *Direction of Trade Statistics Yearbook* (Washington, D.C.: International Monetary Fund)

IMF (1998) *World Economic Outlook, May 1998* (Washington, D.C.: International Monetary Fund)

Immigration and Naturalization Service (1998) *Statistical Yearbook* (Washington, D.C.: Government Printing Office)

Instituto Nacional de Investigaciones Económicas (1996) '*Afectaciones a la economía cubana ocasionado por el bloqueo económico a Cuba por los EE.UU.*', Havana, December

International Counternarcotics Strategy Report (INCSR) (1998) 1998 Report, Office of International Narcotics and Law Enforcement Matters, 28 February

IRELA (1997a) *La Unión Europea y México: Una Nueva Relación Política y Económica* (Madrid: IRELA)

IRELA (1997b) *Closer European Union Links with Eastern Europe: Implications for Latin America* (Madrid: IRELA)

IRELA (1998) *The European Union and the Rio Group: The Biregional Agenda* (Madrid: IRELA)

Jefferson, Thomas (1955) *Notes on the State of Virginia*, ed. W. Peden (Chapel Hill: University of North Carolina Press)

Johnson, R.A. (1971) *The Administration of United States Foreign Policy* (Austin: University of Texas Press)

Jones, Kirby and Rich, Donna (1998) *Opportunities for US-Cuban Trade* (Baltimore: Johns Hopkins University Press)

Joyce, Elizabeth (1997) 'EU Drug Policy in the Andes: International Cooperation and the Politics of Illicit Cocaine Supply', unplubl. DPhil thesis, University of Oxford

Kapcia, A. (1995) *Political Change in Cuba: Before and After the Exodus*, Institute of Latin American Studies Occasional Paper no. 9 (London: Institute of Latin American Studies)

Katz, Friedrich (1978) 'Innen- und aussenpolitische Ursachen des mexikanischen Revolutionsverlaufs', *Jahrbuch für Geschichte von Staat, Wirtschaft, und Gesellschaft Lateinamerikas*, vol. 15, pp. 95-101

Katz, Friedrich (1981) *The Secret War in Mexico: Europe, The United States, and the Mexican Revolution* (Chicago: University of Chicago Press)

Katz, Friedrich (1998) *The Life and Times of Pancho Villa* (Stanford: Stanford University Press)

Kaufman Purcell, Susan and Simm, Françoise (eds.), (1995) *Europe and Latin America in the World Economy* (Boulder: Lynne Rienner)

Kennedy, Paul (1989) *The Rise and Fall of Great Powers* (London: Fontana)

Keohane, Robert (1983) 'Theory of World Politics: Structural Realism and Beyond', in Ada W. Finifter (ed.), *Political Science: The State of the Discipline* (Washington, D.C.: American Political Science Association)

Klein, Herbert (1982) *Bolivia: The Evolution of a Multiethnic Society* (Oxford: Oxford University Press)

Knight, Alan (1987) *U.S.-Mexican Relations, 1910-1940: An Interpretation*, Monograph Series no. 28 (La Jolla, California: Center for U.S.-Mexican Studies, University of California, San Diego)

Krasner, Stephen D. (1978) *Defending the National Interest: Raw Materials Investments and U.S. Foreign Policy* (Princeton: Princeton University Press)

Krasner, Stephen. D. (1983) *International Regimes* (Ithaca: Cornell University Press)

Kuntz, D. (1994) 'The politics of suffering: the impact of the U.S. embargo on the health of the Cuban people', *International Journal of Health Services*, vol. 24, no. 1, pp. 161-79

LaFeber, Walter (1963*) The New Empire. An Interpretation of American Expansionism, 1860-1898* (Ithaca: Cornell University Press)

LaFeber, Walter (1993a) *The Cambridge History of American Foreign Relations.* Vol. 2: *The American Search for Opportunity, 1865-1913* (Cambridge: Cambridge University Press)

LaFeber, Walter (1993b) *Inevitable Revolutions. The United States and Central America*, 2nd. ed. (New York and London: Norton)

Laurent, Pierre-Henri and Maresceau, Marc (eds.) (1998) *The State of the European Union*, vol. 4: Deepening and Widening (Boulder: Lynne Rienner)

Leiva, Patricio (ed.) (1997) *América Latina y la Unión Europea: Construyendo el Siglo XXI* (Santiago, Chile: Ediciones CELARE)

LeoGrande, William M. (1990) 'From Reagan to Bush: The Transition in U.S. Policy towards Central America', *Journal of Latin American Studies*, vol. 22, part 3 (October)

Lerner, R. (1998) 'The Drug Trade in Peru', in E. Joyce and C. Malamud (eds.), *Latin America and the Multinational Drug Trade* (Basingstoke: Macmillan Press and New York: St. Martin's Press)

Levine, Michael (1993) *The Big White Lie: The CIA and the Cocaine/Crack Epidemic* (New York: Thunder's Mouth Press)

Lévi-Strauss, C. (1963) *Structural Anthropology* (New York: Basic Books)

Levitt, P. (1997) 'Future Allegiances: The Social and Political Implications of Transnationalism', Paper presented to the David Rockefeller Center for Latin American Studies, Harvard University

Ley no. 76 (1995) Ley de Minas, *Gaceta Oficial*, 23 January

Ley no. 77 (1995) Ley de Inversión Extranjera, *Gaceta Oficial*, 6 September

López Segrera, Francisco (1972) *Cuba: capitalismo dependiente y subdesarrollo (1510-1958)* (Havana: Ediciones Casa de las Américas)

Lowenthal, Abraham F (1972) *The Dominican Intervention* (Cambridge, MA: Harvard University Press)

Lowenthal, Abraham F. (ed.) (1991) *Exporting Democracy. The United States and Latin America* (Baltimore and London: Johns Hopkins University Press)

Lustig, N., Bosworth, B.P. and Lawrence, R.Z. (eds.) (1992) *North American Free Trade: assessing the impact* (Washington, D.C.: Brookings Institution)

Mabry, D.J. (1995) The U.S. Military and the War on Drugs, in B.M. Bagley and W.O. Walker III (eds.), *Drug Trafficking in the Americas* (Miami: North-South Center Press, University of Miami)

MacDonald, S.B. (1989). *Mountain High, White Avalanche: Cocaine Power in the Andean States and Panama* (Washington, D.C.: CSIS, The Washington Papers, Praeger)

Mahler, S. (1997) 'Immigration and Gender in Transnational Perspective', Paper presented to the Harvard Graduate School of Education

Maingot, Anthony P. (1996) 'Haití: Sovereign Consent versus State-Centric Sovereignty', in Tom Farer (ed.), *Beyond Sovereignty. Collectively Defending Democracy in the Americas* (Baltimore and London: Johns Hopkins University Press)

Maingot, Anthony P. (1998) 'Haití Paradójico. Su sistema político y su cultura política', in Rodolfo Cerdas Cruz, Juan Rial and Daniel Zovatto (eds.), *Elecciones y Democracia en América Latina 1992-1996: urnas y desencanto político* (San José: IIDH/CAPEL)

Malamud Goti, J. (1992) *Smoke and Mirrors: The Paradox of the Drug Wars* (Boulder and Oxford: Westview Press)

Malloy, James M. (1970) *Bolivia: The Uncompleted Revolution* (Pittsburgh: University of Pittsburgh Press)

Malloy, James M. and Gamarra, Eduardo (1988) *Revolution and Reaction: Bolivia 1964-1985* (New Brunswick: Transaction Publishers)

Mann, Michael (1993) *The Sources of Social Power*, vol. II (Cambridge: Cambridge University Press)

Maravall, José María (1993) 'Politics and Policy: Economic Reforms in Southern Europe', in Luiz Carlos Bresser Pereira, José María Maravall and Adam Przeworski (eds.), *Economic Reforms in New Democracies: A Social Democratic Approach* (Cambridge: Cambridge University Press, 1993), pp. 77-131

Mariátegui, José Carlos (1988) *Temas de Nuestra América* (Lima: Biblioteca Amanta)

Marquetti Nodarse, H. and Pérez Villanueva, O. (1995) 'Cambios en el Comercio Exterior Cubano', *Panorama Económico Latinoamericano* (Havana, February)

Marquis, Christopher (1997) 'Two Firms Face Helms-Burton Sanctions', *The Miami Herald*, 22 January

Martí, José (1975) *Inside the Monster. Writings on the United States and American Imperialism* (New York: Monthly Review Press)

Martin, Philip L. (1994) 'The United States: Benign Neglect toward Immigration', in Wayne Cornelius, Philip L. Martin and James F. Hollifield (eds.), *Controlling Immigration: A Global Perspective* (Stanford, CA: Stanford University Press), pp. 83-99

Martz, John D. (ed.) (1994) *United States Policy in Latin America: A Decade of Crisis and Challenge* (Lincoln, Neb. and London: University of Nebraska Press)

Masud-Piloto, Felix R. (1996) *From Welcomed Exiles to Illegal Immigrants: Cuban Migration to the US 1959-1995* (Boston and London: Rowman and Littlefield)

Matthiesen, T. (1997) 'Drug Trafficking, international pressure and domestic influence: Colombian-US relations, 1986-1994', mimeo, New School for Social Research, New York

May, Ernest (1975) *The Making of the Monroe Doctrine* (Cambridge, MA: Harvard University Press)

Merk, Frederick (1963) *Manifest Destiny and Mission in American History* (New York: Knopf)

Merk, Frederick (1966) *The Monroe Doctrine and American Expansionism, 1843-1849* (New York: Knopf)

Mesa-Lago, Carmelo (1993) 'The Economic Effects on Cuba of the Downfall of Socialism in the USSR and Eastern Eupe,' in C. Mesa-Lago (ed.), *Cuba After the Cold War* (Pittsburgh: University of Pittsburgh Press)

Mesa-Lago, Carmelo (1993) *Cuba after the Cold War* (Pittsburgh: University of Pittsburgh Press)

Mesa-Lago, Carmelo (1995) *Cuba's Raft Exodus of 1994: Causes, Settlements, Effects, and Future*, North-South Agenda Papers, no. 12 (Coral Gables: North-South Center, University of Miami, April)

Mesa-Lago, Carmelo (1998) 'Assessing Economic and Social Performance in the Cuban Transition of the 1990s', *World Development*, vol. 26, no. 5, pp. 857-76

Mesa-Lago, Carmelo, and Gil, Fernando (1989) 'Soviet Economic Relations with Cuba,' in Eusebio Mujal-León (ed.), *The USSR and Latin America: A Developing Relationship* (Boston: Unwin Hyman, Inc.)

Meyer, Lorenzo (1991) 'Mexico: The Exception and the Rule', in Abraham F. Lowenthal (ed.), *Exporting Democracy: The United States and Latin America* (Baltimore: Johns Hopkins University Press)

Ministerio de Azúcar (1958) *Anuario Azucarero de Cuba* (Havana: Ministerio de Azúcar)

Ministerio para la Inversión Extranjera y la Colaboración Económica (1996) 'Resolución No. 66/96 – Sobre el Registro Oficial de Concesionarios y Operadores de Zona Franca', 24 October, www.tips.cu

Morales, Estéban (1997) '*Cuba frente a la Ley Helms-Burton en el contexto de la llamada globalización*', Centro de Estudios de los Estados Unidos, Universidad de la Habana

Moreno, Dario (1994) 'Cuban-Americans and the United States Cuban Policy', mimeo, Miami, Florida International University

Morse, Richard (1973), 'Independence in a Patrimonial State', in J. Tulchin (ed.), *Problems in Latin American History. The Modern Period* (New York)

Munro, Dana G. (1964*) Intervention and Dollar Diplomacy in the Caribbean, 1900-1921 (*Princeton: Princeton University Press)

Muravchik, Joshua (1996) 'Affording Foreign Policy. The Problem Is Not Wallet, But Will', *Foreign Affairs*, vol. 75, no. 2, March/April

Myers, Dowell (1998) 'Dimensions of Economic Adaptations by Mexican-Origin Men', in Marcelo M. Suárez-Orozco (ed.), *Crossings: Mexican Immigration in Interdisciplinary Perspectives* (Cambridge, MA: DRCLAS/Harvard University Press), pp. 159-89

National Narcotics Intelligence Consumers Committee (NNICC), *The Supply of Illicit Drugs to the United States*, several issues

National Research Council (1997) *The New Americans: Economic, Demographic, and Fiscal Effects of Immigration* (Washington, D.C., National Academy Press)

Nelson, Joan M. and Eglinton, Stephanie J.(1992) *Encouraging Democracy. What Role for Conditioned Aid?* (Washington, D.C.: Overseas Development Council)

Nelson, Joan M. and Eglinton, Stephanie J. (1996) 'The International Donor Community: Conditioned Aid and the Promotion and Defence of Democracy', in Tom Farer (ed.), *Beyond Sovereignty. Collectively Defending Democracy in the Americas* (Baltimore and London: Johns Hopkins University Press)

Nogueras, Olance (1998a) 'Candentes Debates en Conferencia sobre Cuba', *El Nuevo Herald*, 1 November

Nogueras, Olance (1998b) 'Refutan demanda presentada por FNCA', *El Nuevo Herald*, 2 November

Nolt, James H. and Maxfield, Sylvia (1990) 'Protectionism and the Internationalization of Capital: U.S. Sponsorship of Import Substitution Industrialization in the Philippines, Turkey, and Argentina', *International Studies Quarterly*, vol. 34, no. 1, pp. 49-82

O'Donnell, Guillermo, Schmitter, Philippe C. and Whitehead, Laurence (eds.), (1986) *Transitions From Authoritarian Rule: vol. III Comparative Perspectives* (Baltimore and London: Johns Hopkins University Press)

Office of Foreign Assets Control, US Department of the Treasury (1991) (Special Report) *An Analysis of Licensed Trade with Cuba by Foreign Subsidiaries of U.S. Companies* (Washington, D.C., July)

Office of Inspector General (1991) 'Report of Audit: Drug Control Activities in Bolivia' (Washington, D.C.: Department of State)

Office of National Drug Control Policy (ONDCP) (1995, 1997) *What America's Users Spend on Illegal Drugs*, Report prepared by Abt Associates Inc

Office of National Drug Control Policy (ONDCP) (1996) *The National Drug Control Strategy, 1996* (Washington, D.C.: Office of National Drug Control Policy)

Ogbu, John U. (1997) 'Racial Stratification in the United States: Why Inequality Persists', in A.H. Halsey, H. Lauder, P. Brown and A.S. Wells (eds.), *Education, Culture, Economy, and Society* (Oxford: Oxford University Press), pp. 765-78

Oman, Charles (1994) *Globalisation and Regionalisation: The Challenge for Developing Countries* (Paris: OECD)

Omestad, Thomas (1996/7) 'Foreign Policy and Campaign '96', *Foreign Policy*, no. 105 (Winter), pp. 38-51

Opción Cero (1994) (La Paz: SEAMOS Serie Drogas: El Debate Boliviano no. 11)

Orfield, G. (1995) 'Latino Immigrants in Education: Recent Trends', Harvard Graduate School of Education

Pastor, Robert A (1987) *Condemned to Repetition: The United States and Nicaragua* (Princeton: Princeton University Press)

Pedraza-Bailey, Silvia (1985) *Political and Economic Migrants in America: Cubans and Mexicans* (Austin: University of Texas Press)

Pérez Firmat, Gustavo (1994) *Life on the Hyphen: The Cuban-American Way* (Austin: University of Texas Press).

Pérez, Lisandro (1986) 'Immigrant Economic Adjustment and Family Organisation: The Cuban Success Story Re-examined', *International Migration Review*, vol. 20, no. 1 (Spring)

Pérez, Lisandro (1992) 'Cuban Miami', in Guillermo Grenier and Alex Stepick (eds.), *Miami Now!* (Gainsville, Fla.: University Press of Florida), pp. 83-108

Pérez, Lisandro (ed.) (1990) 'Cuban Americans in Miami', *Cuban Studies* (Miami), vol. 20

Pérez-López, Jorge F. (1987) 'Cuba's Oil Reexports: Significance and Prospects', *The Energy Journal*, no. 8

Pérez-López, Jorge F. (1990) 'Cuba's Foreign Economic Relationships', in Georges Fauriol and Eva Loser (eds.), *Cuba: The International Dimension* (New Brunswick: Transaction Publishers)

Pérez-López, Jorge F. (1991) *The Economics of Cuban Sugar* (Pittsburgh: University of Pittsburgh Press)

Pérez-López, Jorge F. (1994) 'Islands of Capitalism in an Ocean of Socialism: Joint Ventures in Cuba's Development Strategy,' in Jorge Pérez-López (ed.), *Cuba at a Crossroads* (Gainesville, Fla.: University Press of Florida)

Pérez-López, Jorge F. (1995) *Odd Couples: Joint Ventures Between Foreign Capitalists and Cuban Socialists*, North-South Agenda Paper no. 16 (Coral Gables: North-South Center, University of Miami)

Pérez-López, Jorge F. (1996/97) 'Foreign Investment in Socialist Cuba: Significance and Prospects,' *Studies in Comparative International Development*, vol. 31, no. 4 (Winter)

Pérez-López, Jorge F. (1997) 'The Cuban Economy in the Age of Hemispheric Integration', *Journal of Inter-American Studies and World Affairs*, vol. 39, no. 3 (Fall)

Perkins, Dexter (1927) *The Monroe Doctrine, 1823-1826* (Cambridge, Mass.: Harvard University Press)

Perkins, Dexter (1963) *A History of the Monroe Doctrine* (Boston: Little, Brown)

Perl, R.F. (1995) 'US-Andean Drug Policy', in B.M. Bagley and W.O. Walker III (eds.), *Drug Trafficking in the Americas* (Miami: North-South Center Press, University of Miami)

Pessar, P.R. (1995) *A Visa for a Dream* (Boston: Allyn and Bacon)

Piening, Christopher (1997) *Global Europe: The European Union in World Affairs* (Boulder and London: Lynne Rienner)

Pierson, W.W. (1920) 'Alberdi's View on the Monroe Doctrine', *Hispanic American Historical Review*, vol. 3

Portes, A and Bach, R. (1985) *Latin Journey: Cuban and Mexican Immigration in the US* (Berkeley: University of California Press)

Portes, A. (1996) 'Children of immigrants: segmented assimilation and its determinants', *The Economic Sociology of Immigration: Essays on Networks, Ethnicity, and Entrepreneurship* (New York: Russell Sage Foundation)

Portes, A. (1998) 'Morning in Miami: A New Era for Cuban-American Politics', *The American Prospect* (May-June)

Portes, A. and Hao, L. (1997) 'English First or English Only? Annandale-on-the-Hudson, NY', Paper presented to the 'Second Generation' Conference, The Jerome Levy Economics Institute of Bard College

Portes, A. and Rumbaut, R. (1996) *Immigrant America,* 2nd edn. (Berkeley and Los Angeles: University of California Press)

Portes, A. and Stepick, A. (1993) *City on the Edge: The Transformation of Miami Immigrants* (Berkeley: University of California Press)

Quirk, Robert E (1962) *An Affair of Honor: Woodrow Wilson and the Occupation of Vera Cruz* (New York: McGraw-Hill)

Radcliffe, Sarah and Westwood, Sallie (eds.) (1996) *Remaking the Nation: Place, Identity and Politics in Latin America* (London: Routledge)

Redmond, John and Rosenthal, Glenda G. (eds.) (1997*) The Expanding European Union: Past, Present, and Future* (Boulder and London: Lynne Riener)

Reuter, P. (1998) 'Foreign demand for Latin American drugs: the USA and Europe', in E. Joyce and C. Malamud (eds.), *Latin America and the Multinational Drug Trade* (Basingstoke: Macmillan and New York: St. Martin's Press)

Reynolds, C.W. and C. Tello (eds.) (1983) *US-Mexico Relations: Economic and Social Aspects* (Stanford CA: Stanford University Press) [previously published as *Las relaciones México-Estados Unidos* (Mexico DF: Fondo de Cultura Económica)]

Rhodes, Carolyn (ed.) (1998) *The European Union in The World Community* (Boulder: Lynne Rienner)

Rich, Donna (1990) 'U.S. and Cuba: Trading Partners?' *Cuba Update*, vol. XI, no. 1-2, April, pp. 33-66

Richard, Carl J. (1994) *The Founders and the Classics. Greece, Rome and the American Enlightenment* (Cambridge, Mass.: Harvard University Press)

Richardson, J.D. (ed.) (1898) *A Compilation of the Messages and Papers of the Presidents* (Washington, D.C.: U.S. Government Printing Office)

Rieff, D. (1994) *The Exile: Cuba in the Heart of Miami* (London: Vintage Books)

Rodó, José Enrique (1988) *Ariel* (Austin: University of Texas Press)

Rodríguez, J.L. (1990) *Estrategia del Desarrollo Económico en Cuba* (Havana: Editorial Ciencias Sociales)

Rohter, Larry (1995) 'Cuba Allowing Citizens to Buy and Sell Foreign Currencies,' *The New York Times*, 9 November, p. 3A

Romero Gómez, Antonio (1997) 'Estados Unidos: Relaciones económicas con América Latina', unpublished PhD thesis, Centro de Investigación de la Economía Internacional, Universidad de la Habana

Ronfeldt, David (1983) *Geopolitics, Security, and U.S. Strategy in the Caribbean Basin*, R-2997-AF/RC (Santa Monica: Rand Corporation).

Roosevelt, Theodore (1967) *The Writings of Theodore Roosevelt*, ed. W.H. Harbaugh (Indianapolis: Bobbs Merrill)

Ros, J. (1994) 'Mexico and NAFTA: economic effects and the bargaining process', in V. Bulmer-Thomas, N. Craske and M. Serrano (eds.), *Mexico and the North*

American Free Trade Agreement: Who Will Benefit? (Basingstoke: Macmillan), pp. 11-28

Rostow, W.W. (1960) *The Stages of Economic Growth* (London and Cambridge: Cambridge University Press)

Roy, Joaquin (ed.) (1992) 'The Identity of the New Europe and the San José Process', in *The Reconstruction of Central America: The Role of the European Community* (Coral Gables: North-South Center, University of Miami), pp. 139-54

Ruggie, John (1996) *Winning the Peace : America and World Order in the New Era* (New York and Chichester: Columbia University Press)

Rugman, A and M. Gestrin (1995), 'The NAFTA investment provisions as a model for a multilateral investment agreement', in *Market Access Issues after the Uruguay Round* (Paris: OECD)

Rumbaut, R. (1996) 'Severed Identities: The National Self and the Post-Exile Generation in Cuban-American Miami', *Cuban Affairs/Asuntos Cubanos* (Summer/Fall)

Rumbaut, R. (1997) 'Achievement and Ambition Among Children of Immigrants in Southern California', Paper presented to the Jerome Levy Economics Institute of Bard College

Sanahuja, José Antonio (1997) 'México y la Unión Europea, ¿Hacia un nuevo modelo de relación?' (Madrid: Instituto Complutense de Estudios Internacionales, Documentos de Trabajo DT:1/1997)

Schettino, M. (1994) *El Tratado de Libre Comercio: ¿qué es y cómo nos afecta?* (Mexico: Grupo Editorial Iberoamérica)

Schiff, Maurice and Winters, L. Alan (1997) *Regional Integration as Diplomacy*, World Bank Policy Research Paper no. 1801 (Washington, D.C.: World Bank)

Schoonover, Thomas (1978) *Dollars over Dominion. The Triumph of Liberalism in Mexican United States Relations, 1861-1867* (Baton Rouge and London: Louisiana State University Press)

Schoonover, Thomas (1991) *The United States and Central America, 1860-1911* (Durham, N. Carolina: Duke University Press)

Schoultz, Lars (1987) *National Security and United States Policy toward Latin America* (Princeton: Princeton University Press)

Schoultz, Lars (1998) *Beneath the United States* (Cambridge, MA: Harvard University Press)

Schulz, Donald E. (1997) *Between a Rock and a Hard Place: The United States, Mexico, and the Agony of National Security* (Carlisle Barracks, Pa.: U.S. Army War College, Strategic Studies Institute, SSI Special Report)

SELA (1998) 'Reflections on the European Union-Latin American and Caribbean Summit (1999)', mimeo (Caracas, May)

Sheinin, David (1991) *Argentina and the United States at the Sixth Pan-American Conference (Havana 1928)*, Research Paper No. 25, Institute of Latin American Studies (London: Institute of Latin American Studies)

Simon, Françoise L. (1995) 'Tourism Development and Transition Economies: The Cuba Case', *Columbia Journal of World Business*, vol. 30, no. 1 (Spring)

Simon, J. (1995) *Immigration: The Demographic and Economic Facts* (Washington, D.C.: The Cato Institute and the National Immigration Forum)

Slater, David (1997) 'Spatialities of Power and Post-modern Ethics – Rethinking Geographical Encounters', *Environmental Planning*, vol. 15

Smidt, Steffen (1996) 'The Maastricht Treaty, the Lomé Convention and the Future of EU Aid', paper presented at Overseas Development Institute meeting, London, 15 March

Smith, Hazel (1995) *European Union, Foreign Policy, and Central America* (Basingstoke: Macmillan)

Smith, Peter (ed.) (1993) *The Challenge of Integration: Europe and the Americas* (New Brunswick and London: Transaction Publishers)

Smith, Peter H. (1996) *Talons of the Eagle. Dynamics of U.S.-Latin American Relations* (New York and Oxford: Oxford University Press)

Smith, Robert Freeman (1972) *The United States and Revolutionary Nationalism in Mexico, 1916-1932* (Chicago: University of Chicago Press)

Steiner, R. (1997) 'Colombia: a long-standing tradition of formal democracy, violence and drugs', mimeo, America's Society, New York, December

Steiner, R. (1998) 'Colombia's Income from the Drug Trade', *World Development*, vol. 26, no. 6 (June)

Steinhauer, J. (1997) 'A Minority Market with Major Sales', *The New York Times*, 2 July

Stuart, G.H. (1949) *The Department of State: A History of its Organization, Procedure and Personnel* (New York: Macmillan)

Suárez-Orozco, M. (1989) *Central American Refugees and U.S. High Schools: A Psychosocial Study of Motivation and Achievement* (Stanford: Stanford University Press)

Suárez-Orozco, M. (ed.) (1998) *Crossings: Mexican Immigration in Interdisciplinary Perspectives* (Cambridge, MA: DRCLAS/Harvard University Press)

Suárez-Orozco, M., Roos, P. and Suárez-Orozco, Carola E. (1998) 'Cultural, Educational and Legal Perspectives on Immigration: Implications for School Reform', in J. Heubert (ed.), *New Perspectives on School Reform* (New Haven, Conn.: Yale University Press)

Subcommittee on Terrorism, Narcotics, and International Operations of the Committee on Foreign Relations (1987) 'Drugs, Law Enforcement and Foreign Policy: Money Laundering' (Washington, D.C.: U.S. Senate, 23 July)

Sucre Guzmán, José (1995) *Las relaciones boliviano-estadounidenses: saliendo del ultimatum* (La Paz: UDAPEX)

Tamayo, Juan O. (1997) '"Antídoto" contra la Ley Helms intenta socavar presión de Estados Unidos', *El Nuevo Herald*, 2 January

Tennery, Thomas (1970) *The Mexican War Diary of Thomas D. Tennery* (Norman: University of Oklahoma Press)

Terrero, A. (1994) 'Tendencias en un ajuste', *Bohemia*, La Habana, 28 Oct

Thoreau, Henry David (1996) *Thoreau. Political Writings*, ed. Nancy Rosenblum (Cambridge: Cambridge University Press)

Thoumi, F. (1995) *Political Economy and Illegal Drugs in Colombia* (Boulder & London: Lynne Rienner)

Tokatlian, J.G. (1995) 'Drug Summitry: A Colombian Perspective', in B.M. Bagley and W.O. Walker III (eds.), *Drug Trafficking in the Americas* (Coral Gables: North-South Center Press, University of Miami)

Tokatlian, J.G. (1996) 'Diplomacia coercitiva, narcotráfico y crisis: ¿el deterioro irreversible de las relaciones entre Estados Unidos y Colombia?' in F. Leal (ed.), *Tras las huellas de la crisis política* (Bogotá: Tercer Mundo Editores-Fescol-IEPRI)

Tokatlian, J.G. and A.M. Botero (1990) 'La política exterior de Colombia hacia Estados Unidos, 1978-1990', in C.G. Arrieta, L.J. Orjuela, E. Sarmiento and J.G. Tokatlian (eds.), *Narcotráfico en Colombia* (Bogotá: Tercer Mundo Editores-Ediciones Uniandes)

Topik, Steven (1987) *The Political Economy of the Brazilian State, 1889-1930* (Austin: University of Texas Press)

Torrico, Gonzalo (1993) *Un desafío para el siglo XXI* (La Paz: Los Amigos del Libro)

Tower Commission Report (1987) (New York: Bantam Books)

Trigueros, I. (1994) 'The Mexican financial system and NAFTA', in V. Bulmer-Thomas, N. Craske and M. Serrano (eds.), *Mexico and the North American Free Trade Agreement: Who Will Benefit?* (Basingstoke: Macmillan), pp. 43-57

Trueba, H.T. (1996) 'Latinos in the United States: The Emerging Majority in Our Schools and Society', *Harvard Graduate School of Education* (Cambridge, MA: Harvard University Press)

Tsoukalis, Loukas (1993) *The New European Economy: The Politics and Economics of Integration* 2nd edn. (Oxford: Oxford University Press)

Tweed, Thomas (1997) *Our Lady of the Exile: Diasporic Religion at a Cuban Catholic Shrine in Miami* (London and Oxford: Oxford University Press)

UNCTAD (1997) *World Investment Report 1997* (Geneva: United Nations Conference on Trade, Aid and Development)

UNIDO (1997) *Industrial Development Global Report 1997* (New York: Oxford University Press for the United Nations Industrial Development Organisation)

US Congress (1995) 'Extradition Treaty with Bolivia: Message from the President of the United States' (104th Congress 1st Session, 10 October)

US Department of Justice, Drug Enforcement Administration, *Illegal Drug Price/Purity Report*, several issues

US Department of Justice, *From the Source to the Street*, several issues

US Department of State (1998) 'Remittances to Cuba', Fact Sheet released by the Office of Cuban Affairs, Bureau of Inter-American Affairs (20 March)

US Department of State, Bureau of International Narcotics and Law Enforcement Affairs (several issues) *International Narcotics Control Strategy Report* (Washington, D.C.: US Government Printing Office)

US House of Representatives, Subcommittee on Inter-American Affairs (1975) 'United States and Chile during the Allende Years, 1970-1973', *Hearings* (Washington, D.C.: US Government Printing Office)

US House of Representatives (1996) 'A War on Drugs Really Should be Declared', House of Representatives, 16 May, page H5264

US Senate, Committee on Foreign Relations (1995) *The Drug Trade in Mexico and Implications for U.S.-Mexican Relations*, 104th Congress, 1st session, 8 August, Washington, D.C.: US Government Printing Office)

USAID, *Congressional Presentation, FY 1996*

USAID, *FY 1998 Development Assistance Request. Bolivia*

USAID, *FY 1998 Development Assistance Request. Brazil*

USAID, *FY 1998 Development Assistance Request. Dominican Republic*

USAID, *FY 1998 Development Assistance Request. Ecuador*

USAID, *FY 1998 Development Assistance Request. El Salvador*

USAID, *FY 1998 Development Assistance Request. Guatemala*

USAID, *FY 1998 Development Assistance Request. Haiti*

USAID, *FY 1998 Development Assistance Request. Latin America and the Caribbean*

USAID, *FY 1998 Development Assistance Request. Panama*

USAID, *FY 1998 Development Assistance Request. Paraguay*

USAID, *USAID Loans and Grants to Latin America and the Caribbean. From 1952 to 1996*

USITC (1993) *Potential Impact on the US Economy and Selected Industries of the North American Free-Trade Agreement* (Washington, D.C.: United States International Trade Commission)

Vaky, Viron P. and Muñoz, Heraldo (1993) *The Future of the Organization of American States* (New York: The Twentieth Century Fund Press)

Valenzuela, Arturo (1997) 'Paraguay: The Coup That Didn't Happen', *Journal of Democracy*, vol. 8, no. 1 (January), pp. 43-55

Van Klaveren, Alberto (1990) 'The Impact of Globalisation on Chile', paper presented at Canning House, London, 29 October

Varas, Augusto (1991) 'De la coerción a la asociación. ¿Hacia un nuevo paradigma de cooperación hemisférica?', *Estudios Internacionales, Revista del IRIPAZ*, año 2, no. 3 (Guatemala, January-June), p. 23 et seq.

Vázquez Díaz, R. (1994) *Bipolaridad de la Cultura Cubana* (Stockholm: Olaf Palme International Centre)

Véliz, Claudio (1980) *The Centralist Tradition in Latin America* (Princeton: Princeton University Press)

Waldinger, R. (1997) 'Social Capital or Social Closure? Immigrant Networks in the Labor Market', Paper presented to the Conference on Immigration and the Socio-Cultural Remaking of the North American Space, David Rockefeller Center for Latin American Studies, Harvard University

Waldinger, R. and M. Bozorgmehr (1996) *Ethnic Los Angeles* (New York: Russell Sage Foundation)

Walter, W. (1995) 'The Bush Administration's Andean Drug Policy in Historical Perspective', in B.M. Bagley and W. Walker III (eds.), *Drug Trafficking in the Americas* (Miami: North-South Center Press)

Waltz, Kenneth (1979) *Theory of International Politics* (Reading, Mass.: Addison Wesley)

Watson, Alexander F. (1996) 'Mutual Interest and Cooperation in Latin America', Remarks by Assistant Secretary of State for Inter-American Affairs to the Latin American Association of Japan, Marsuya Salon, Tokyo, Japan, 21 February 21

Weed, Thurlow (1884) *Life of Thurlow Weed*, Vol. II (Cambridge, Mass.: Houghton Mifflin)

Weigley, Russell F. (1984) *History of the United States Army* (Bloomington: Indiana University Press)

Weinberg, Albert K. (1968) *Manifest Destiny* (Chicago: Quadrangle)

Weintraub, S. (1997) 'Evaluación del TCLAN', *Integración y Comercio*, vol. 1, no. 2, pp. 3-34

Welch, Robert E., Jr. (1985) *Response to Revolution: The United States and the Cuban Revolution* (Chapel Hill: University of North Carolina Press)

Werlau, María C. (1996) 'Foreign Investment in Cuba: The Limits of Commercial Engagement', *Cuba in Transition – Volume 6* (Washington: Association for the Study of the Cuban Economy)

Werlau, María C. (1997) 'Update on Foreign Investment in Cuba: 1996-97,' *Cuba in Transition – Volume 7* (Washington, D.C.: Association for the Study of the Cuban Economy)

White House (1995) *A National Security Strategy of Engagement and Enlargement* (Washington, D.C.: U.S. Government Printing Office)

Whitehead, Laurence (1991) 'The Imposition of Democracy', in Abraham F. Lowenthal (ed.), *Exporting Democracy. The United States and Latin America* (Baltimore and London: Johns Hopkins University Press)

Whitehead, Laurence (ed.) (1996) *The International Dimensions of Democratization: Europe and the Americas* (Oxford: Oxford University Press)

Whynes, D.K. (1991) Illicit Drug Production and Supply-side Drugs Policy in Asia and South America, *Development and Change*, vol. 22, no. 3, pp. 475-96

Winters, A. (1990), 'The Road to Uruguay', *Economic Journal*, vol. 100, no. 403

Womack, John Jr. (1978) 'The Mexican Economy during the Revolution, 1910-1922: Historiography and Analysis', *Marxist Perspectives*, vol. 1, no. 4, pp. 80-123

Wonnacott, R. (1994) 'Canada's Role in NAFTA: To what degree has it been defensive?', in Bulmer-Thomas, V., Craske, N. and Serrano, M. (eds.), *Mexico and the North American Free Trade Agreement: Who Will Benefit?* (Basingstoke: Macmillan)

World Bank (1997) *Private Capital Flows to Developing Countries: the Road to Financial Integration* (New York: Oxford University Press)

WTO (1997) *World Trade Report 1997* (Geneva: World Trade Organisation)

Wyplosz, C. (1997) 'EMU: Why and How it Might Happen', *Journal of Economic Perspectives*, vol. 11, no. 4, Fall

Zormelo, Douglas (1995) *Regional Integration in Latin America: Is MERCOSUR a New Approach?*, ODI Working Paper no. 84 (London: Overseas Development Institute)

INDEX